ROY ORBISON
BLACK & WHITE NIGHT

AUTHENTIC TRANSCRIPTIONS WITH NOTES AND TABLATURE

Page	Title
3	Foreword
4	ONLY THE LONELY (KNOW THE WAY I FEEL)
9	DREAM BABY (HOW LONG MUST I DREAM)
24	BLUE BAYOU
40	THE COMEDIANS
51	OOBY-DOOBY
72	LEAH
79	RUNNING SCARED
86	UP TOWN
98	IN DREAMS
104	CRYING
112	CANDY MAN
123	GO, GO, GO
149	MEAN WOMAN BLUES
164	(ALL I CAN DO IS) DREAM YOU
175	CLAUDETTE
187	IT'S OVER
192	OH, PRETTY WOMAN
208	Guitar Notation Legend

Music transcriptions by Pete Billmann, Addi Booth, Paul Pappas and David Stocker

ISBN 978-1-4234-9991-6

7777 W. BLUEMOUND RD. P.O. BOX 13819 MILWAUKEE, WI 53213

For all works contained herein:
Unauthorized copying, arranging, adapting, recording, Internet posting, public performance,
or other distribution of the printed music in this publication is an infringement of copyright.
Infringers are liable under the law.

Visit Hal Leonard Online at
www.halleonard.com

FOREWORD

While I was in studio recording Roy Orbison's *In Dreams Greatest Hits* album, I was asked to perform with the TCB Band on the *Black and White Night*. In my opinion this was one of the greatest moments in music history. Every time I watch the video from that night, I see something new and different. It takes me right back to that time. I knew after the show that night that music magic had been created. It was one of the highlights of my career.

The stage was filled with some of the most talented music professionals of all time paired with the most incredible singer/songwriter of all time, Roy Orbison. Elvis Presley once told me how much he loved Roy's voice, so to be there among the greats was a big honor for me. The talent picked for this show could not have been more perfect. All that performed at that show were true friends of Roy's and respected his talent and that came through in the music. The chemistry between the singers, musicians, and Roy was electrifying.

The enthusiasm of the "All-Star" audience was so overwhelming. They were on their feet most of the four and half hours of filming. These were our peers and impressing them to that degree made the night that much more exciting. We fed off of their energy. T-Bone Burnett was ahead of his time in production of this video. He is a music genius.

A magic moment in the show for me was swapping licks during "Oh, Pretty Woman" with Bruce Springsteen. Roy was right there in the mix and I felt like we were all connected. The combination of artists, set list, producers, audience participation, and everything else that went into this show made it such a success.

I have a huge respect for all the musicians and singers on this show and I was privileged to have been a part of it. I loved Roy, not only as a great entertainer, but also as a great man.

James Burton
2011

Only the Lonely
(Know the Way I Feel)

Words and Music by Roy Orbison and Joe Melson

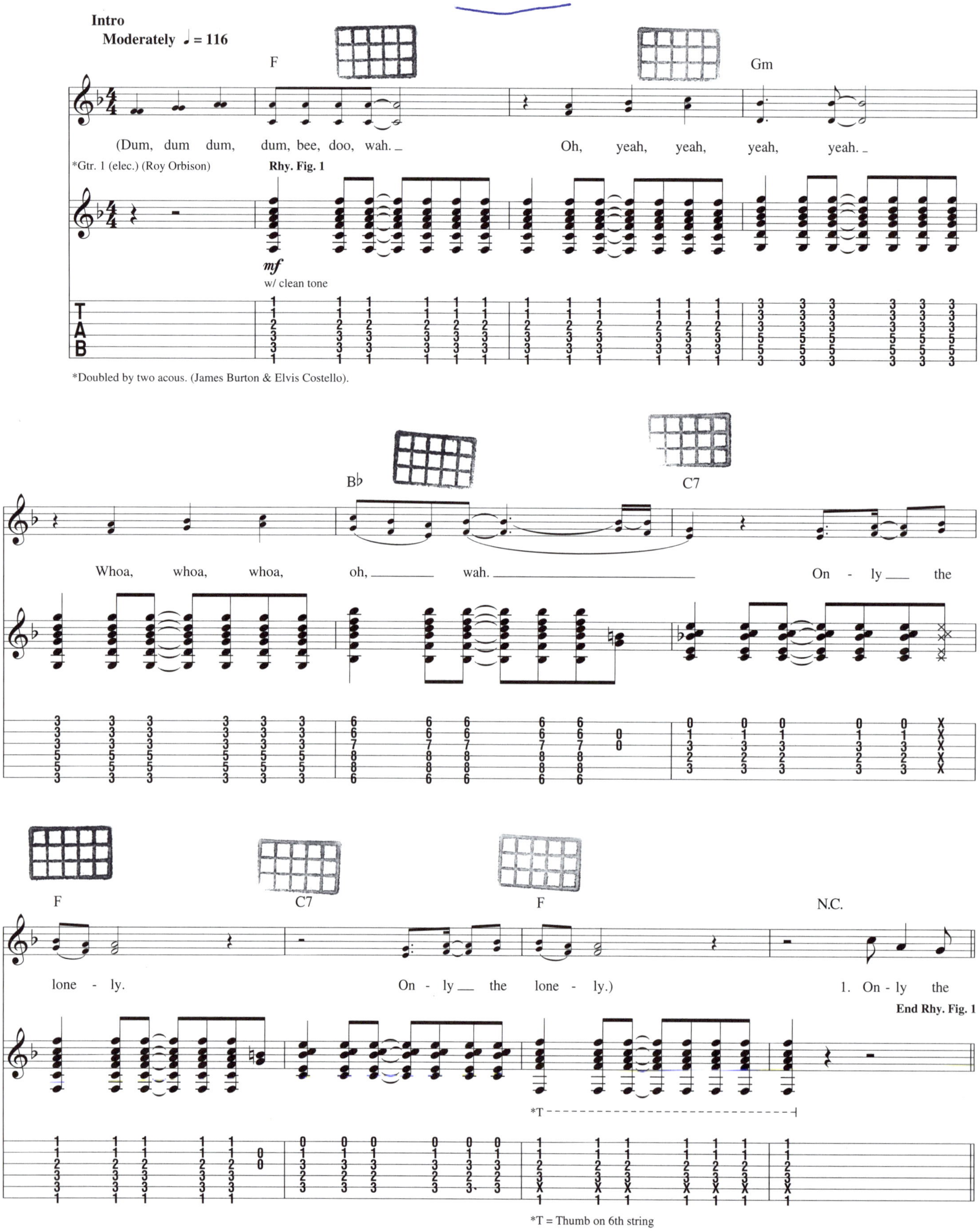

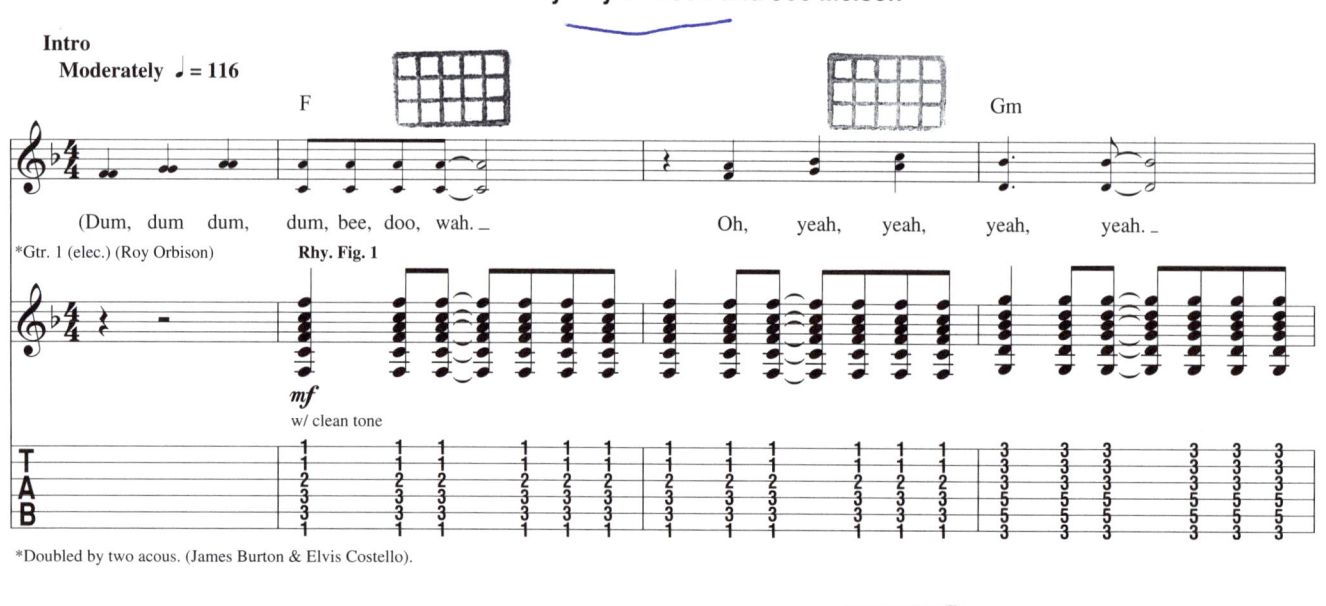

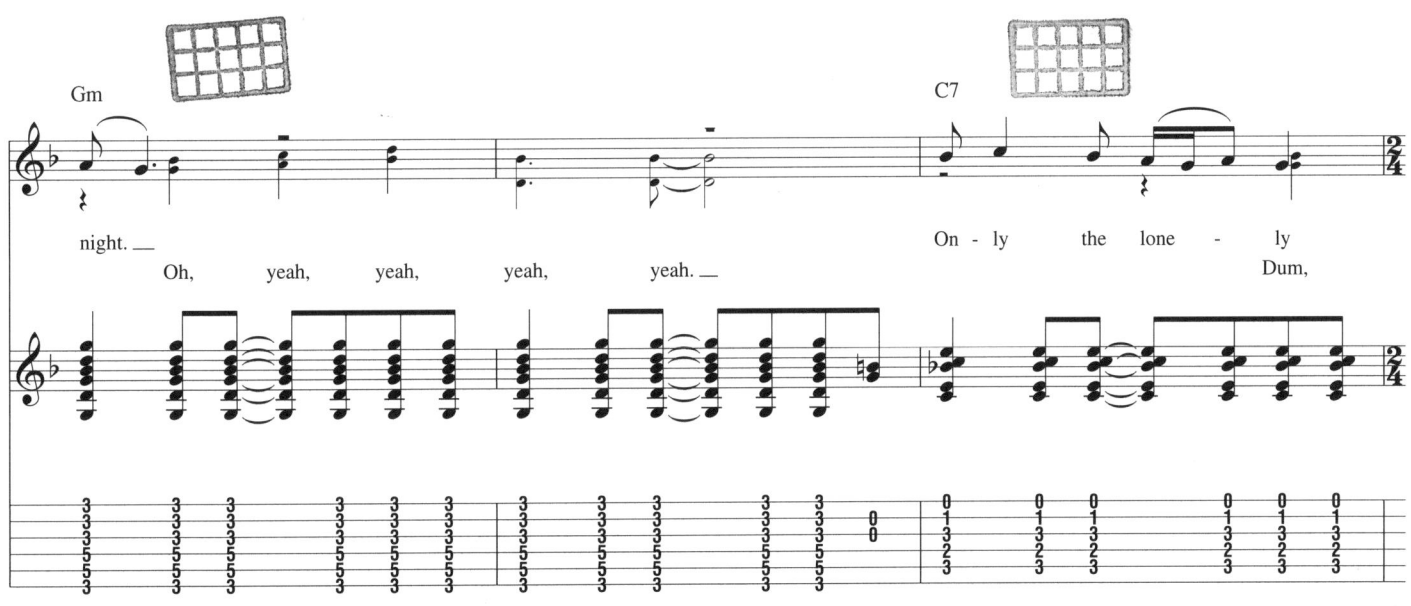

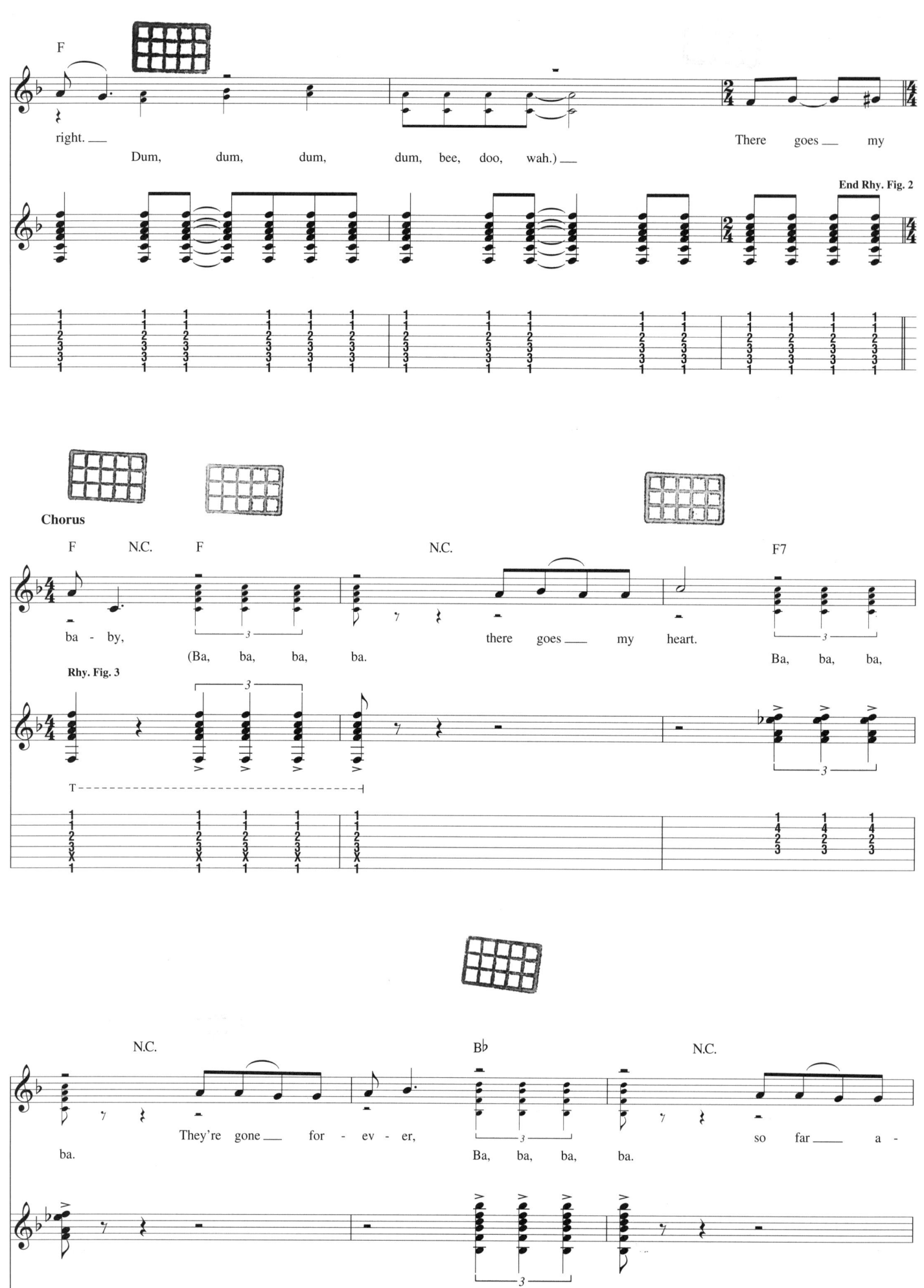

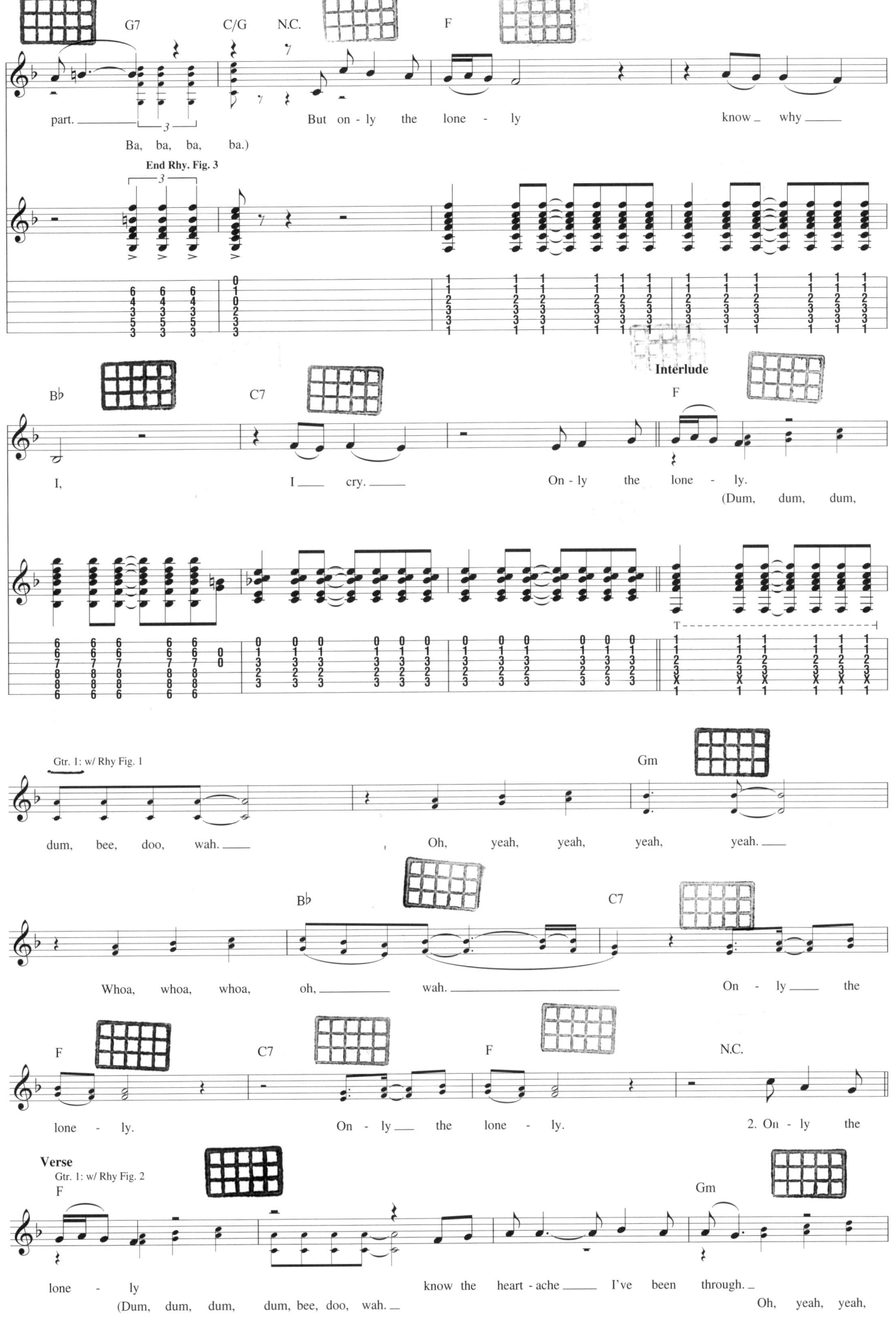

Dream Baby
(How Long Must I Dream)

Words and Music by Cindy Walker

F
T 3211

Intro
Moderately fast ♩ = 152

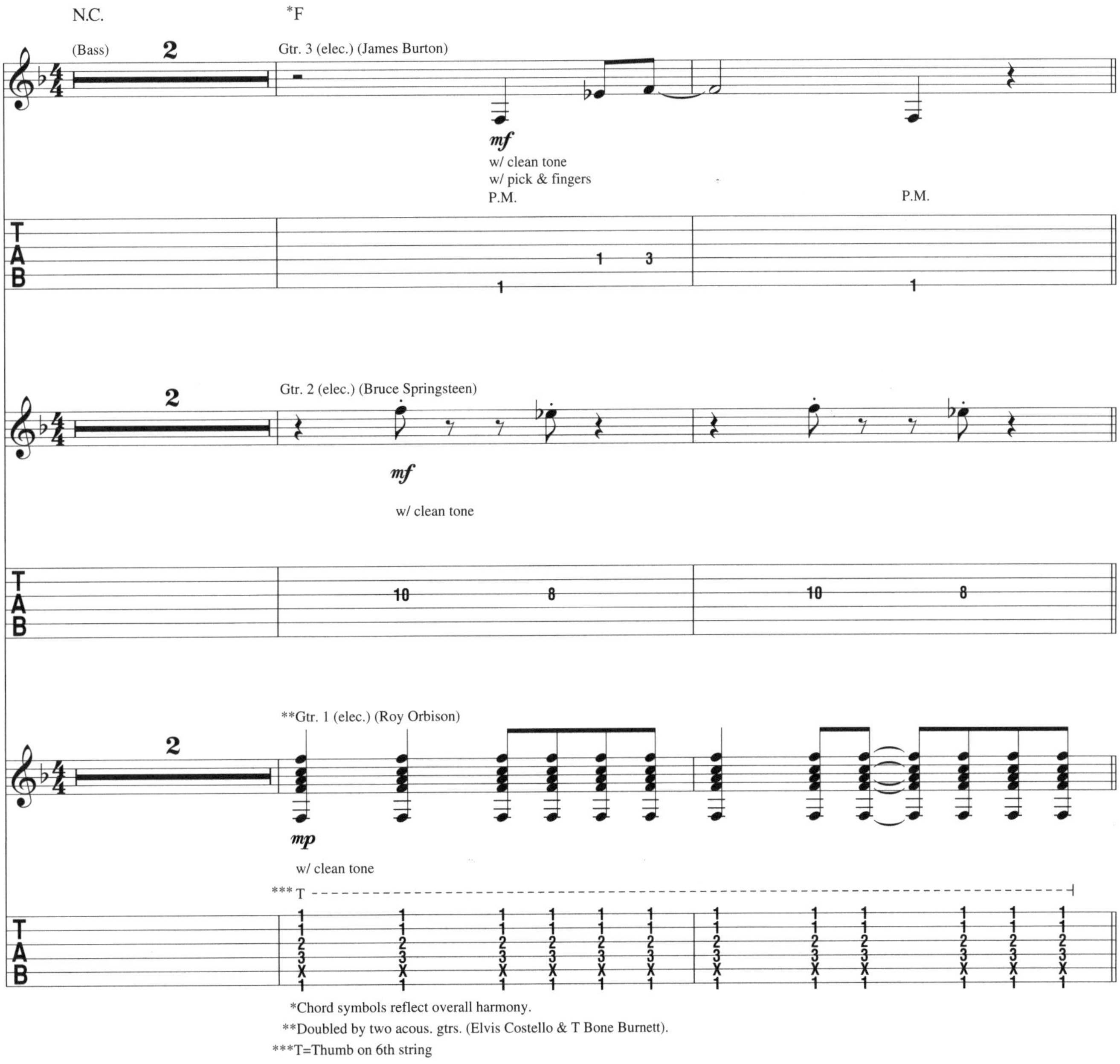

*Chord symbols reflect overall harmony.
**Doubled by two acous. gtrs. (Elvis Costello & T Bone Burnett).
***T=Thumb on 6th string

© 1962 (Renewed 1990) TEMI COMBINE INC.
All Rights Controlled by COMBINE MUSIC CORP. and Administered by EMI BLACKWOOD MUSIC INC.
All Rights Reserved   International Copyright Secured   Used by Permission

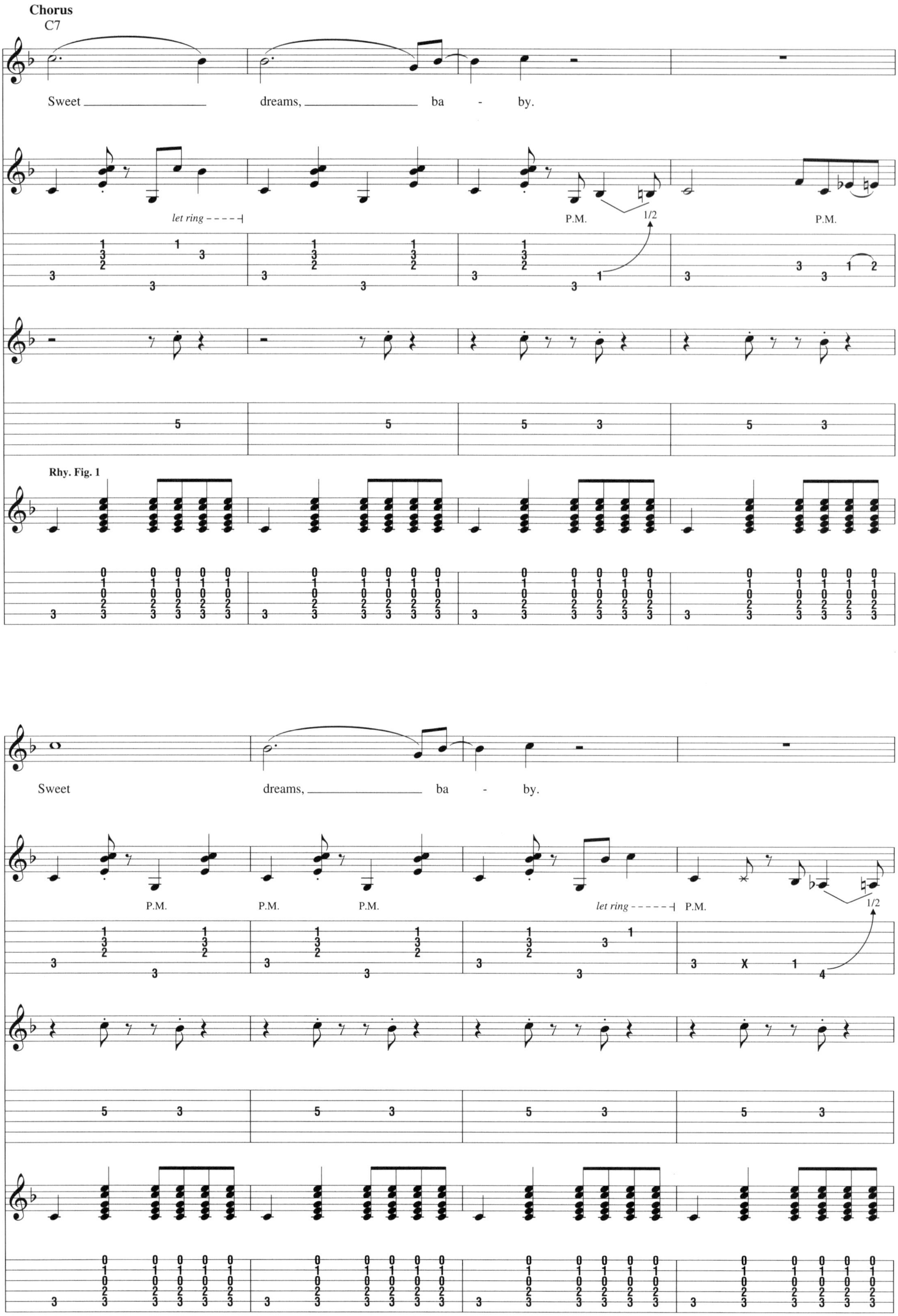
Chorus
C7
Sweet dreams, ba - by.
let ring
P.M.
1/2
Rhy. Fig. 1
Sweet dreams, ba - by.
P.M.
let ring
1/2

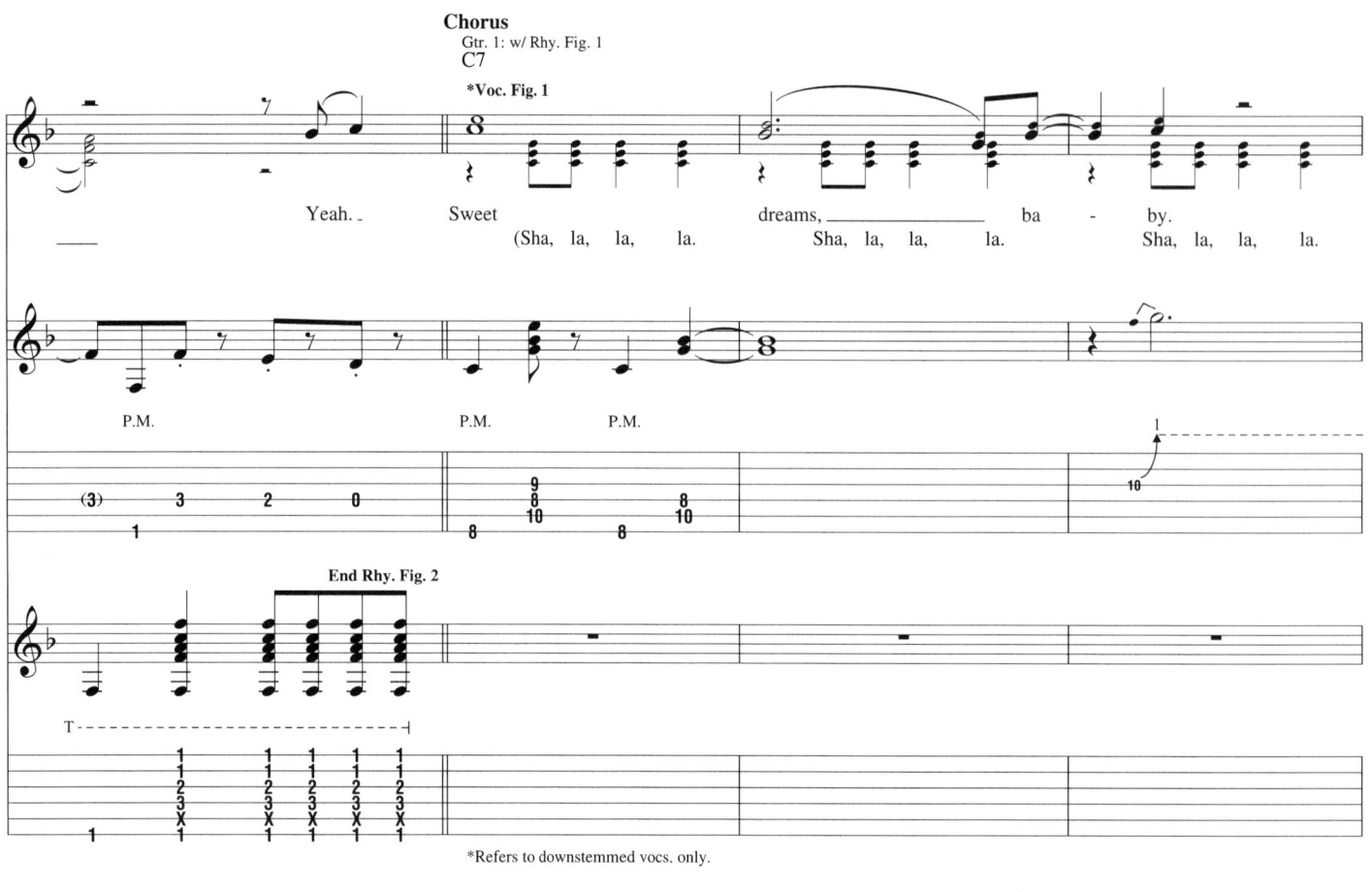

14

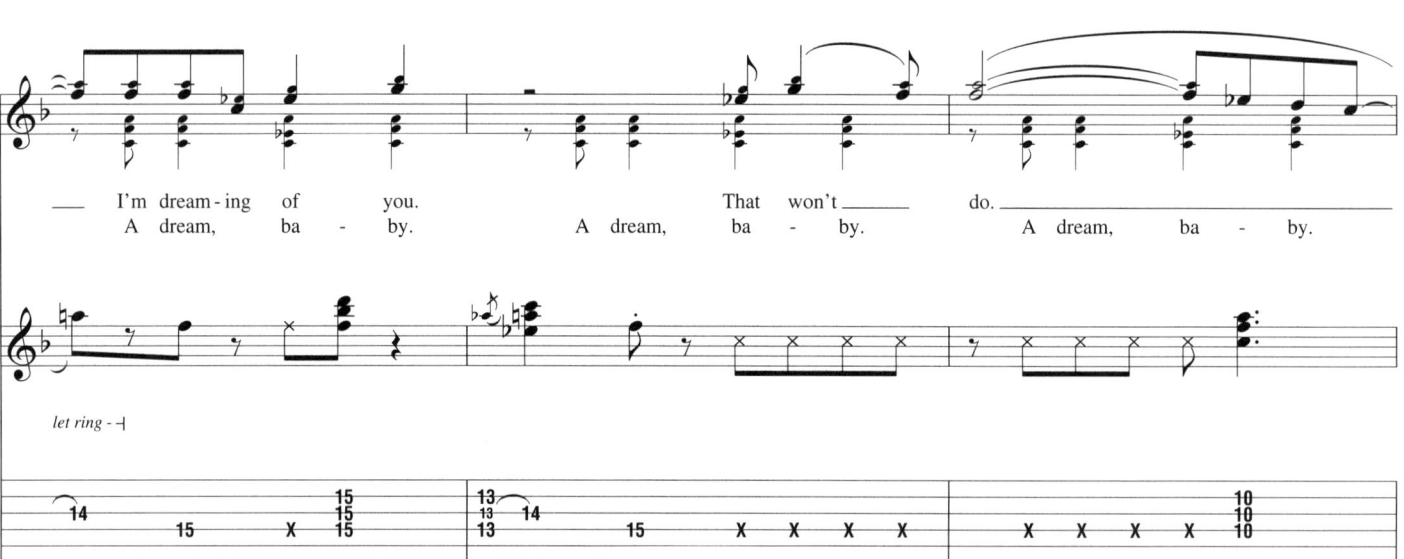

18

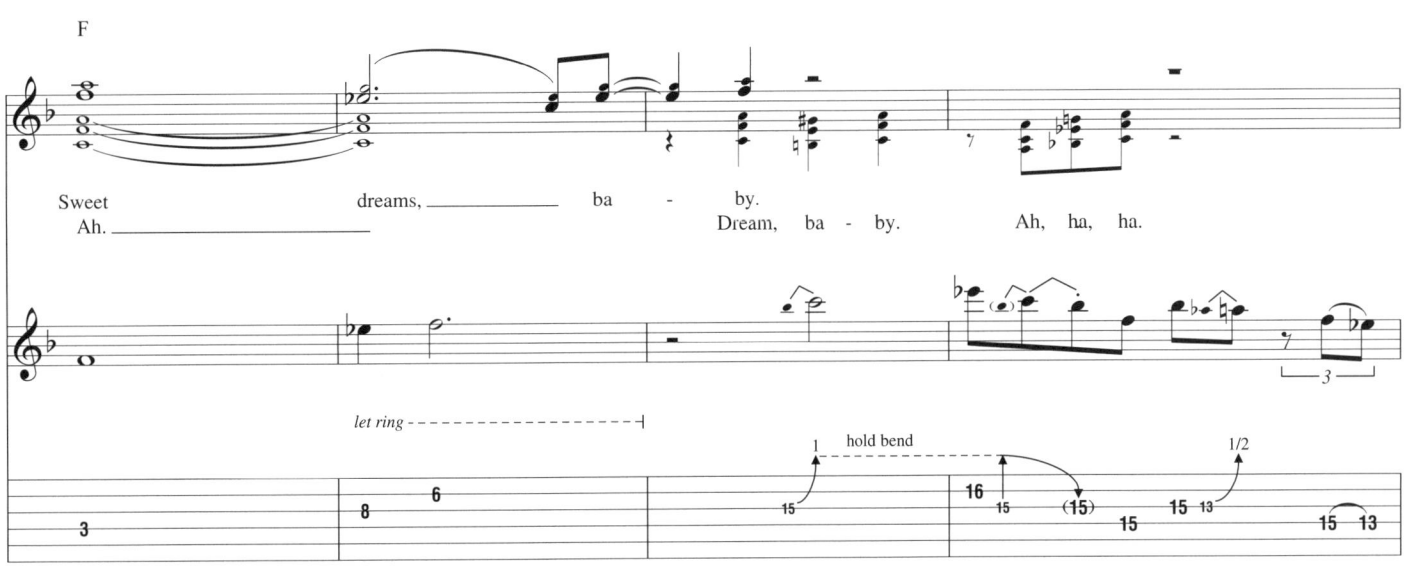

Outro-Chorus

Bkgd. Voc.: w/ Voc. Fig. 1 (2 times)
*Gtr. 1: w/ Rhy. Fig. 1 (1st 8 meas., 2 times)
Gtr. 2 tacet

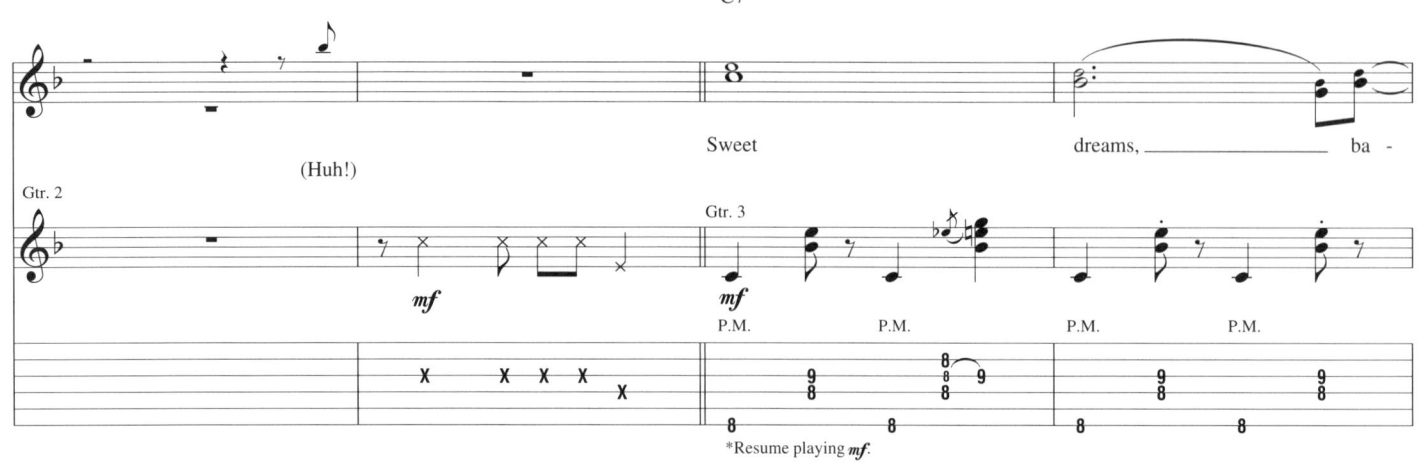

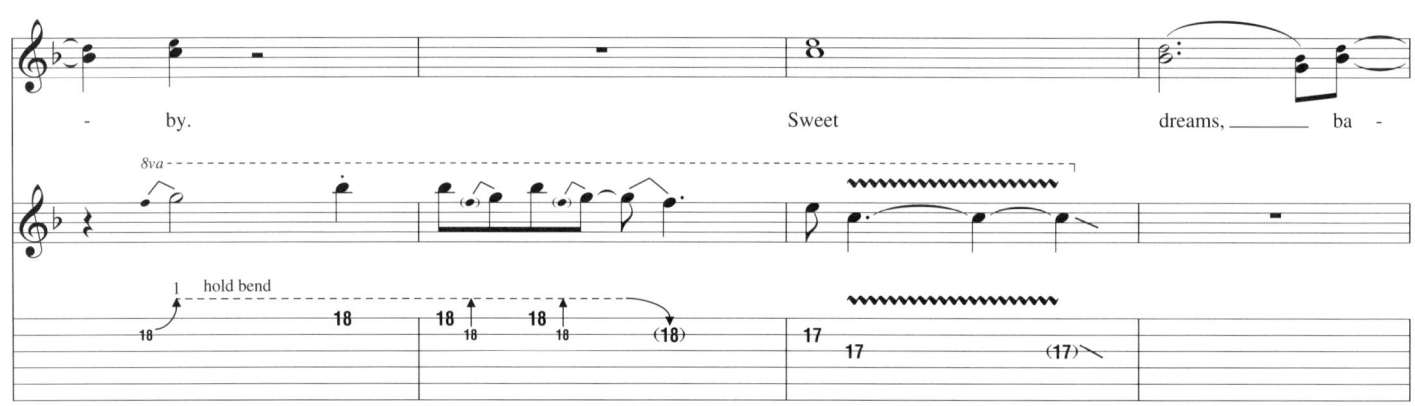

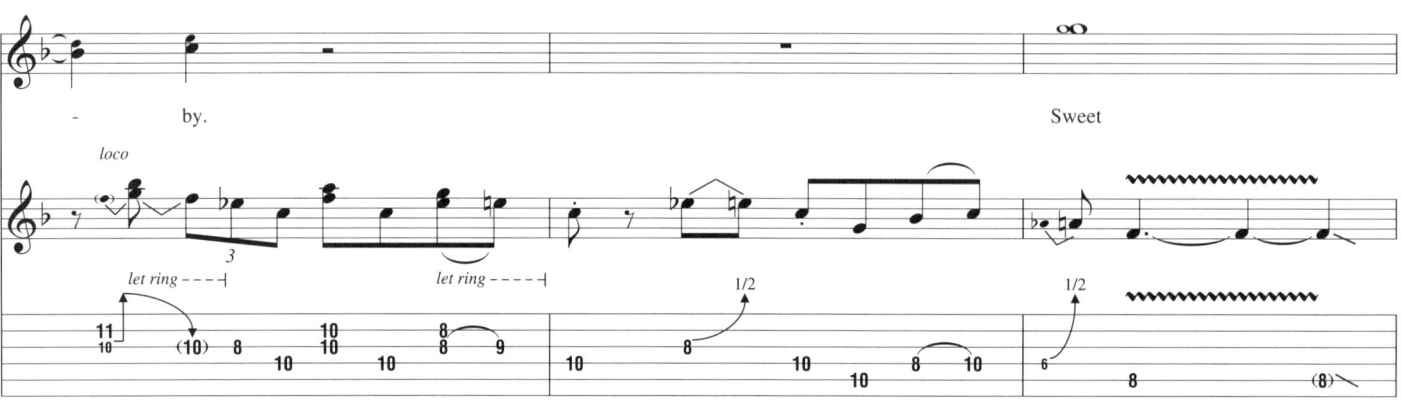

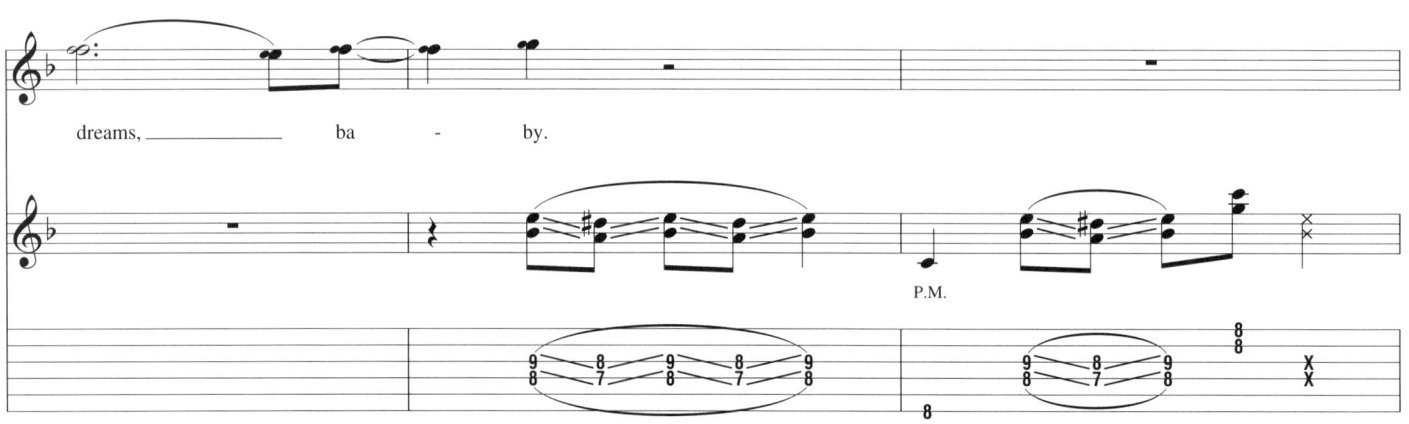

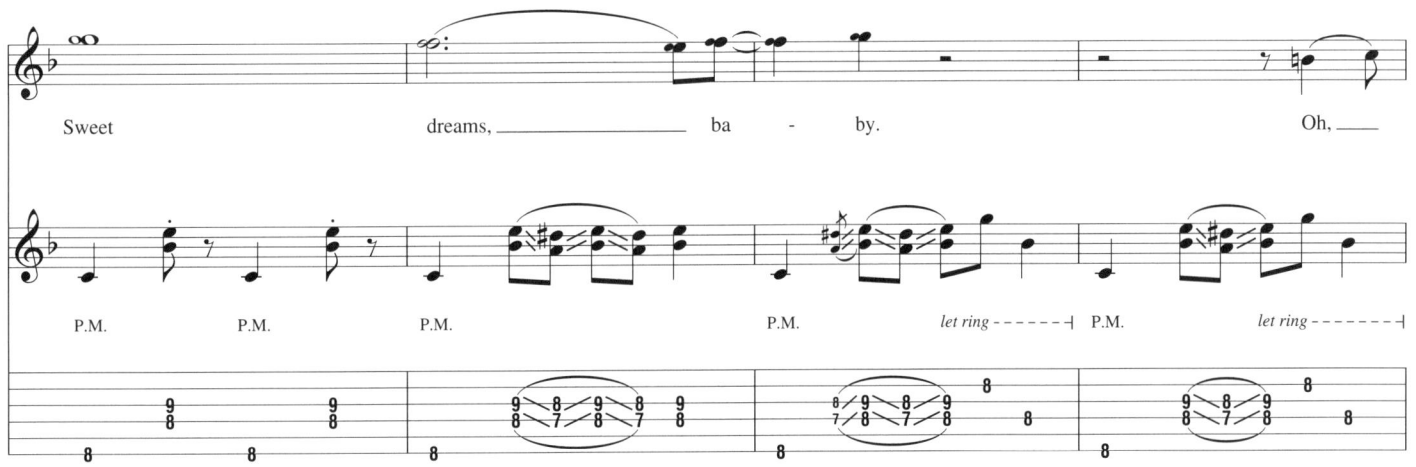

Free time

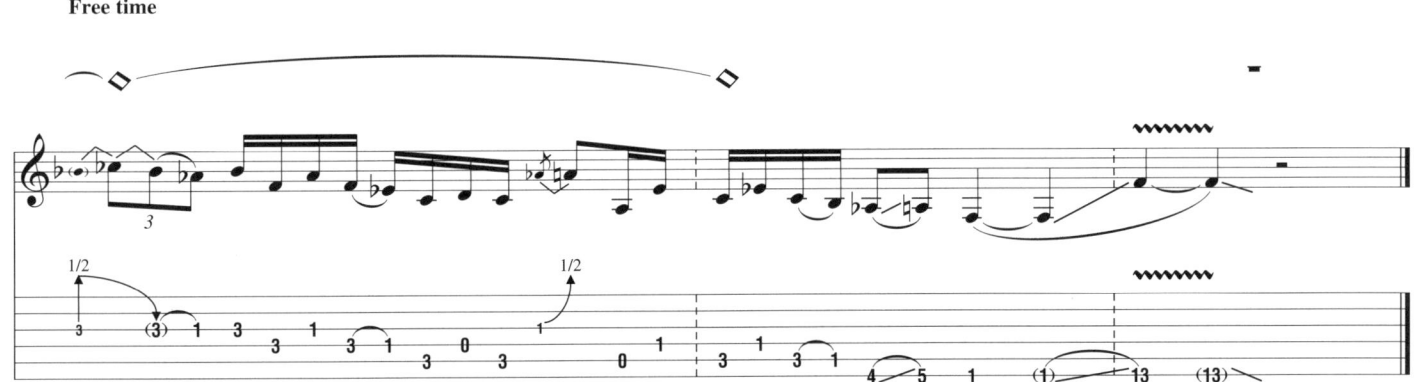

23

Blue Bayou

Words and Music by Roy Orbison and Joe Melson

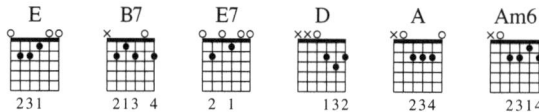

Intro
Moderately ♩ = 93

Verse

1. I feel so bad, I got a

*Chord symbols reflect overall harmony.
**Vol. swell
***Vol. swell
†Gtr. 3 (elec.) w/ clean tone (Roy Orbison);
Gtr. 4 (acous.) (Elvis Costello).
Composite arrangement

Copyright © 1961 (Renewed 1989) BARBARA ORBISON MUSIC COMPANY, ORBI-LEE MUSIC, R-KEY DARKUS MUSIC and SONY/ATV MUSIC PUBLISHING LLC
All Rights on behalf of BARBARA ORBISON MUSIC COMPANY, ORBI-LEE MUSIC and R-KEY DARKUS MUSIC Administered by EVERGREEN COPYRIGHTS
All Rights on behalf of SONY/ATV MUSIC PUBLISHING LLC Administered by SONY/ATV MUSIC PUBLISHING LLC, 8 Music Square West, Nashville, TN 37203
All Rights Reserved   Used by Permission

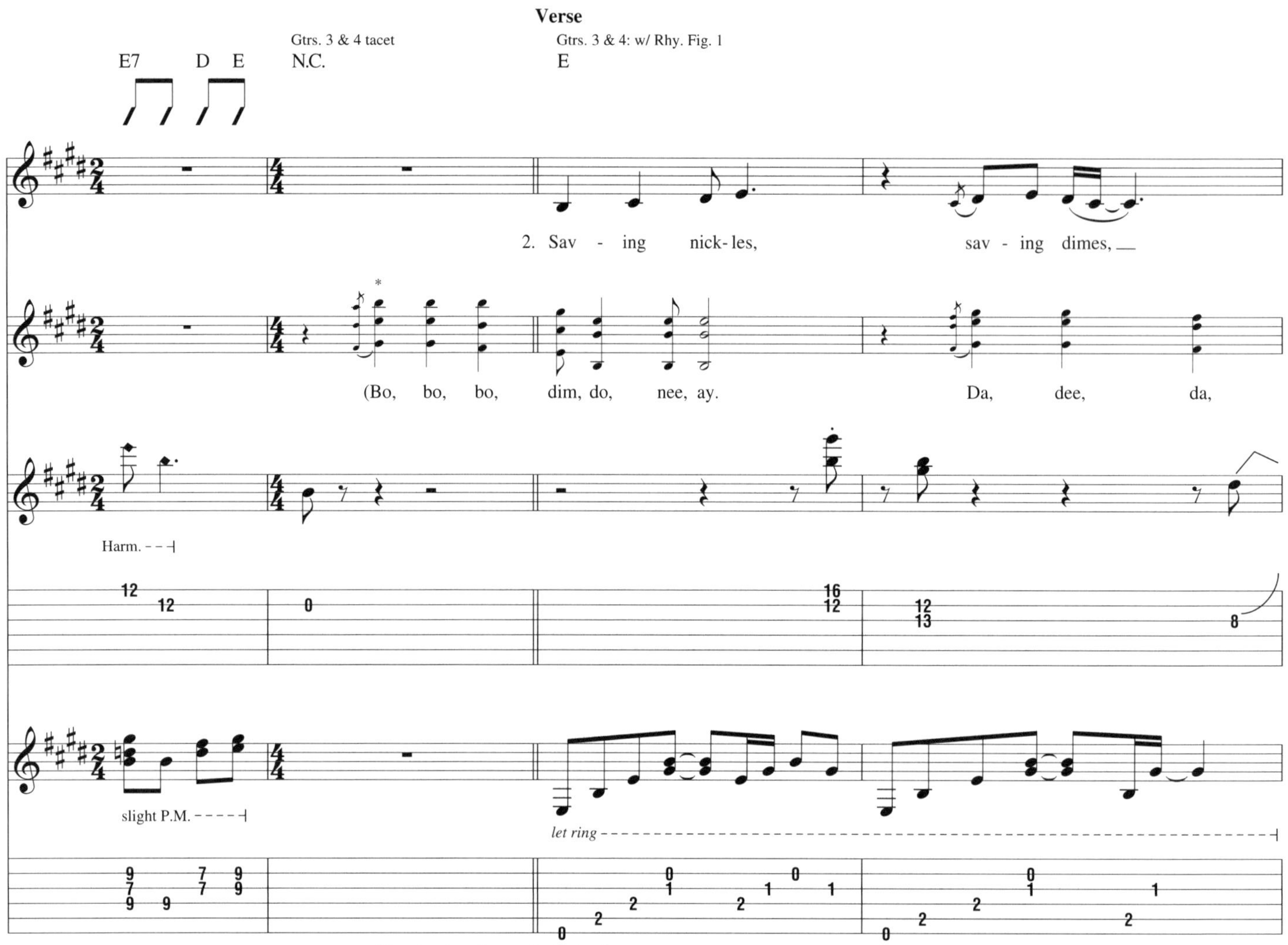

*Two female and one male bkgd. voice.
All voices sound one octave lower than written.

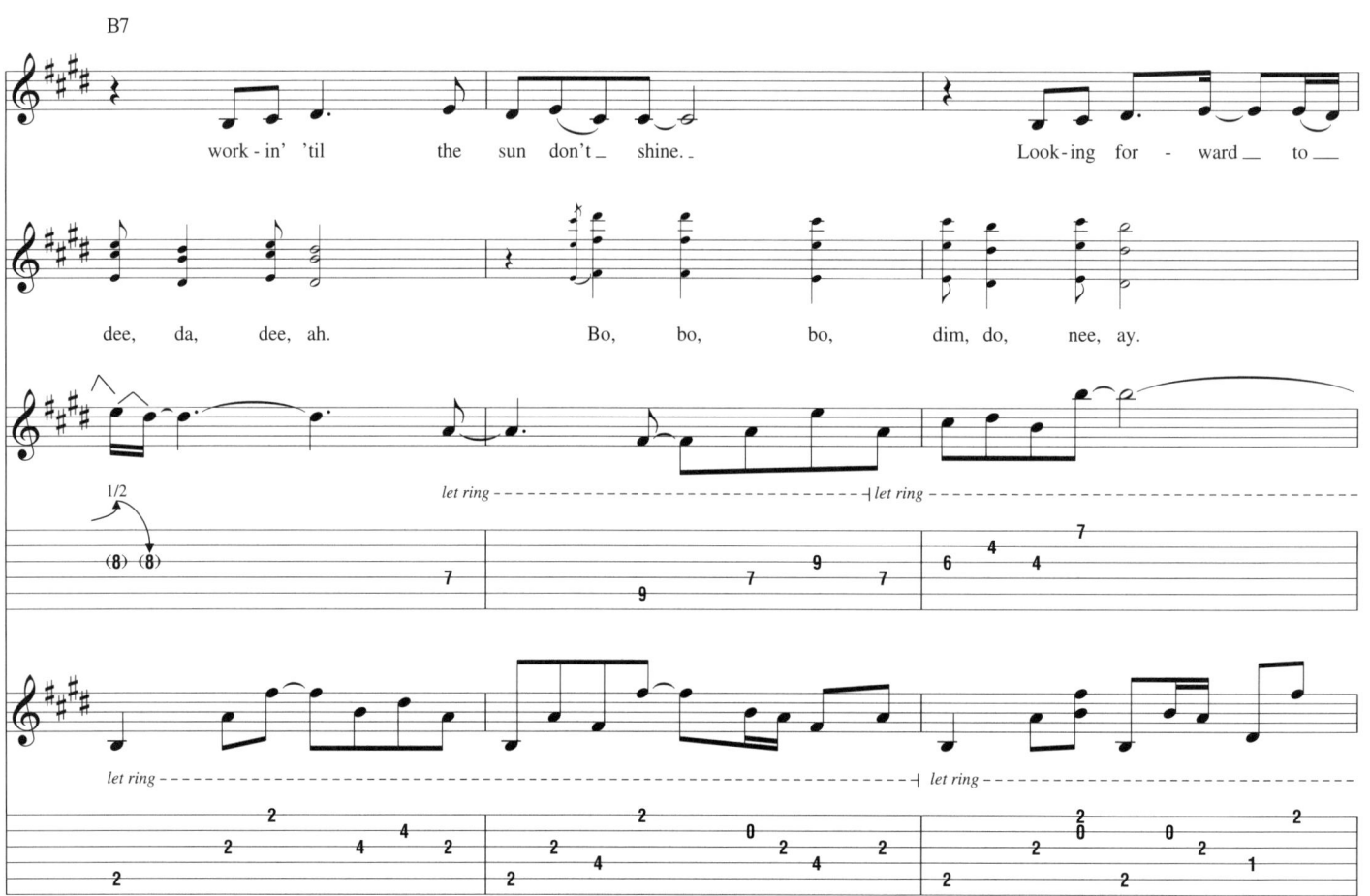

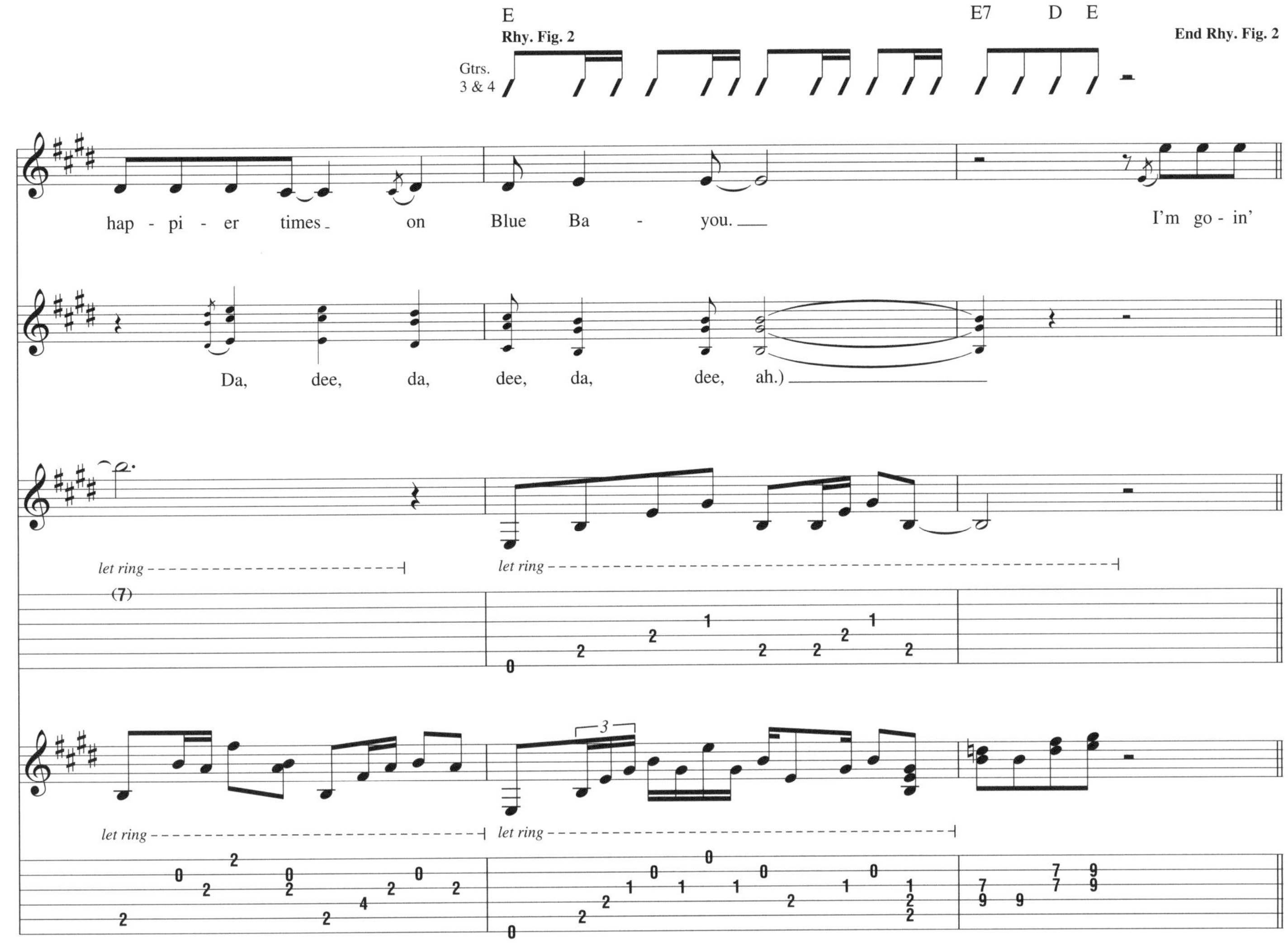
E
Rhy. Fig. 2
Gtrs. 3 & 4
E7 D E
End Rhy. Fig. 2
hap - pi - er times on Blue Ba - you.
I'm go - in'
Da, dee, da, dee, da, dee, ah.)
let ring
let ring
let ring
let ring

Chorus

Gtrs. 3 & 4: w/ Rhy. Fig. 1
E
back some day, come what may, to Blue
P.M.
P.M.
let ring

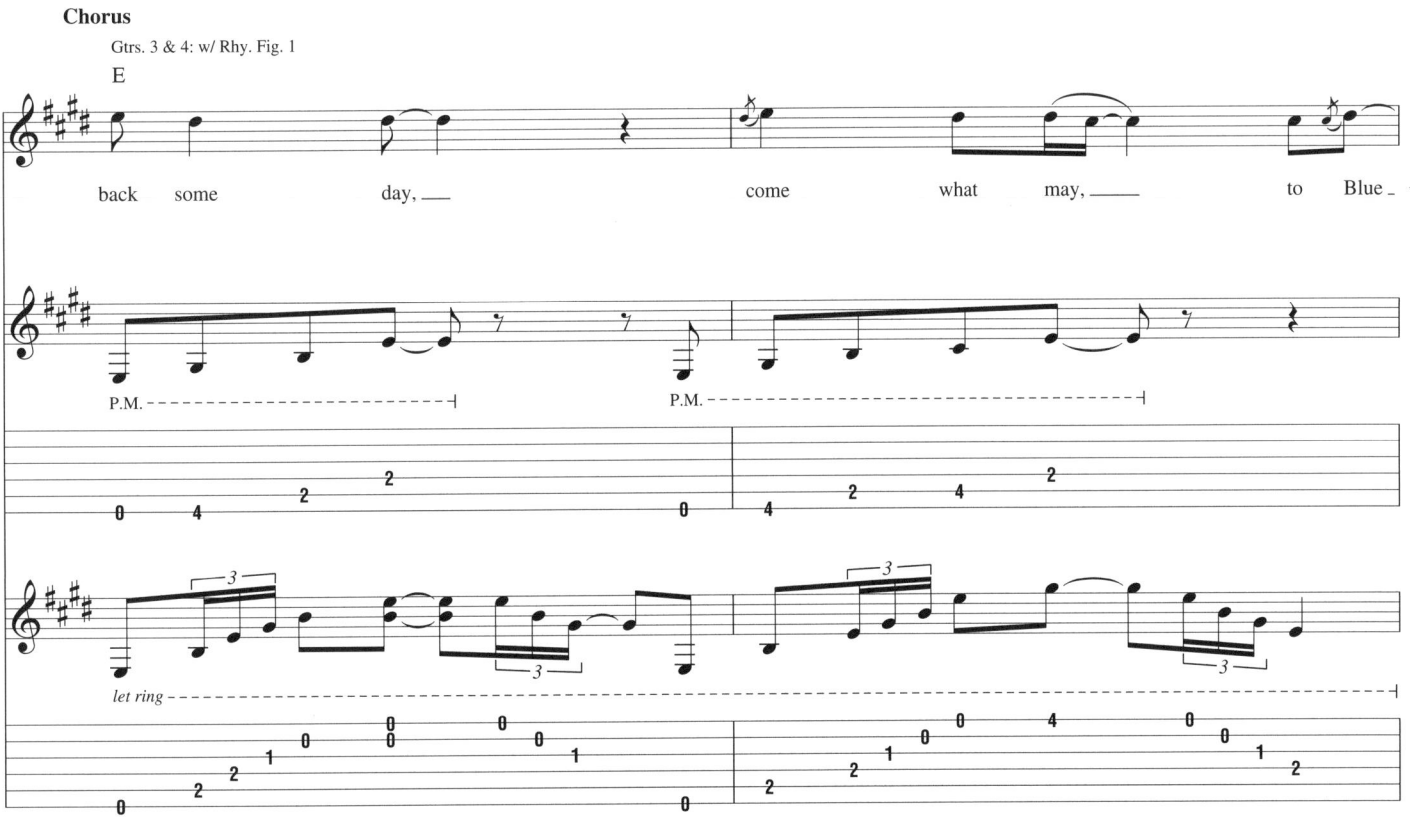

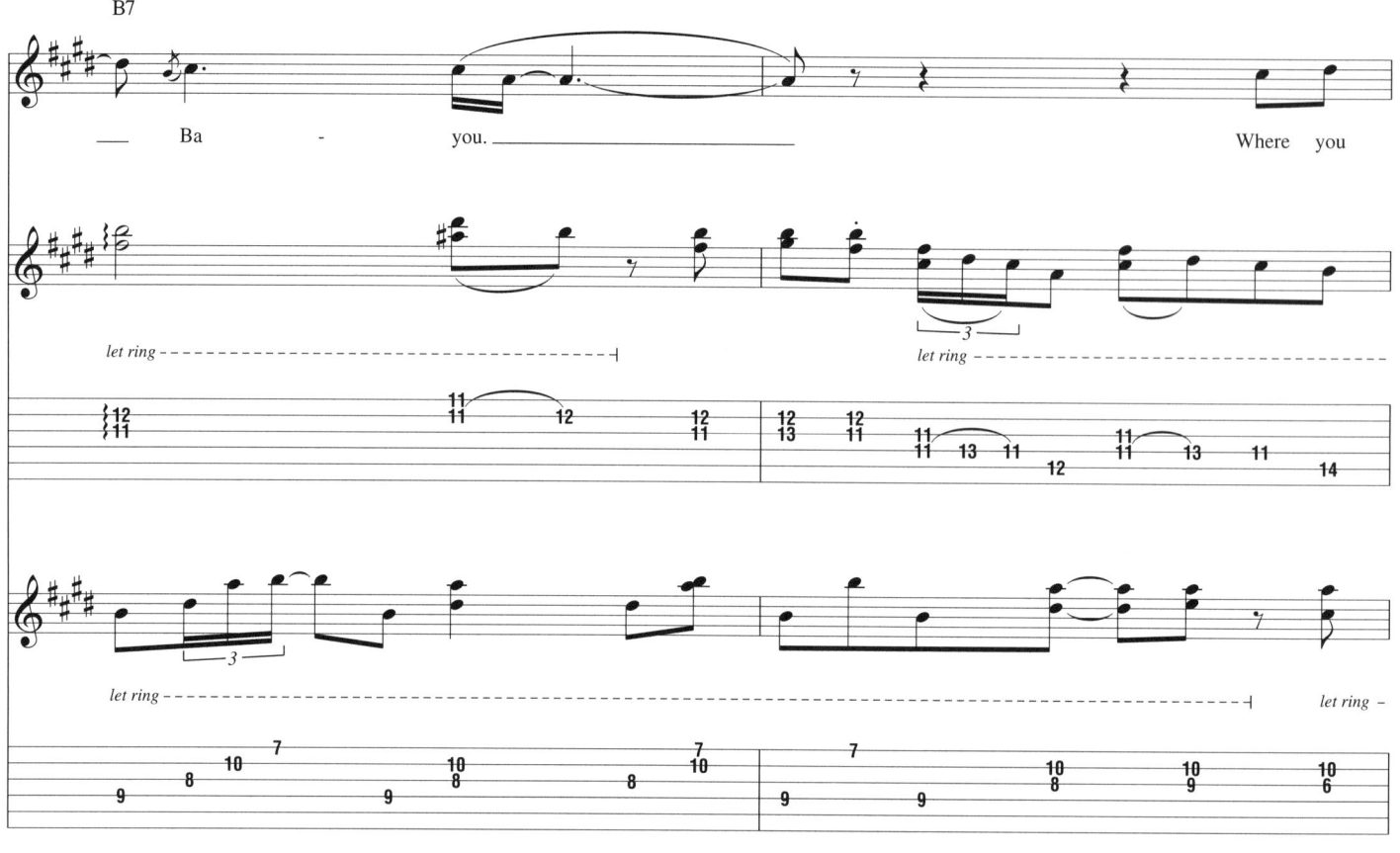

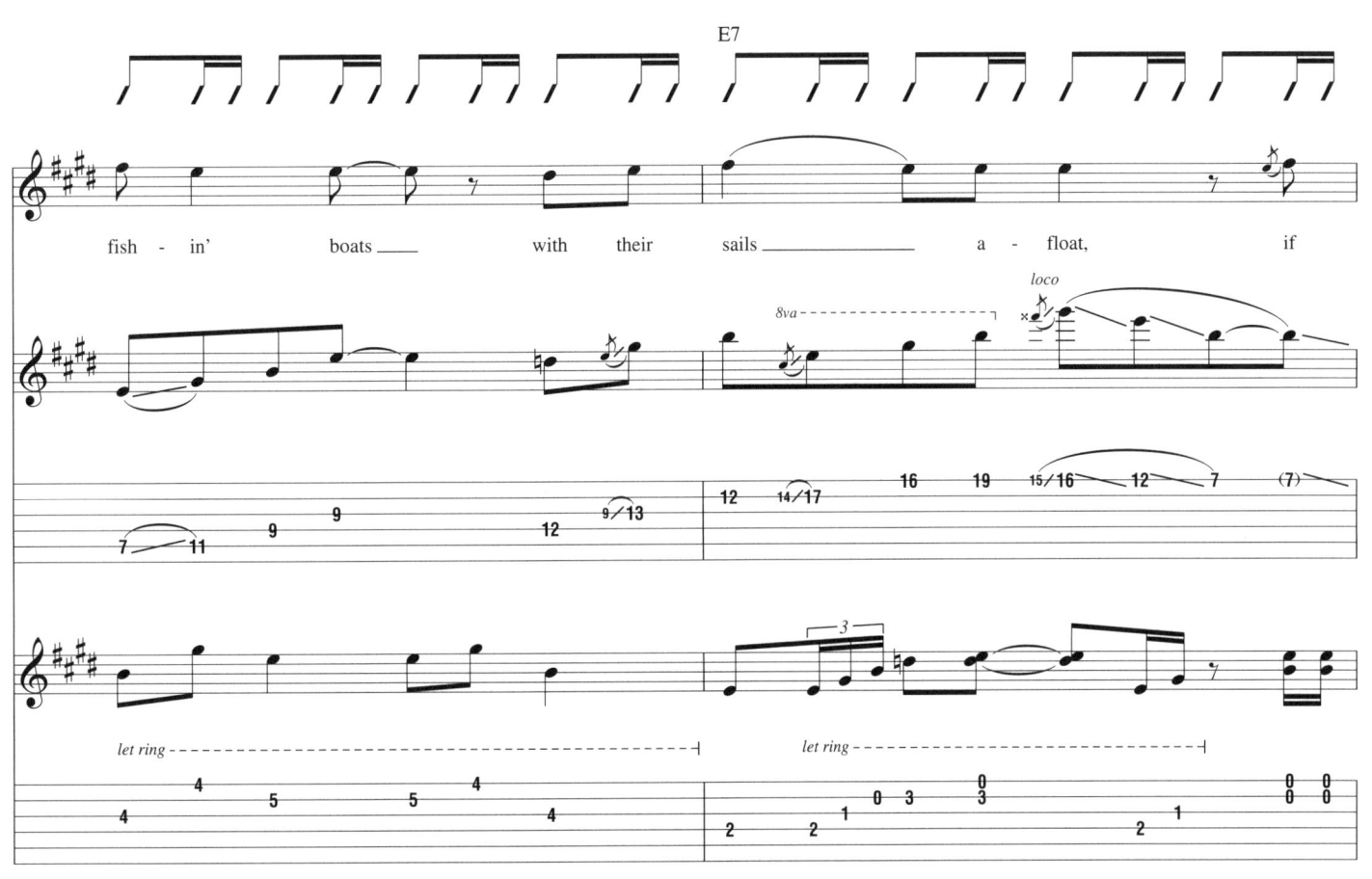

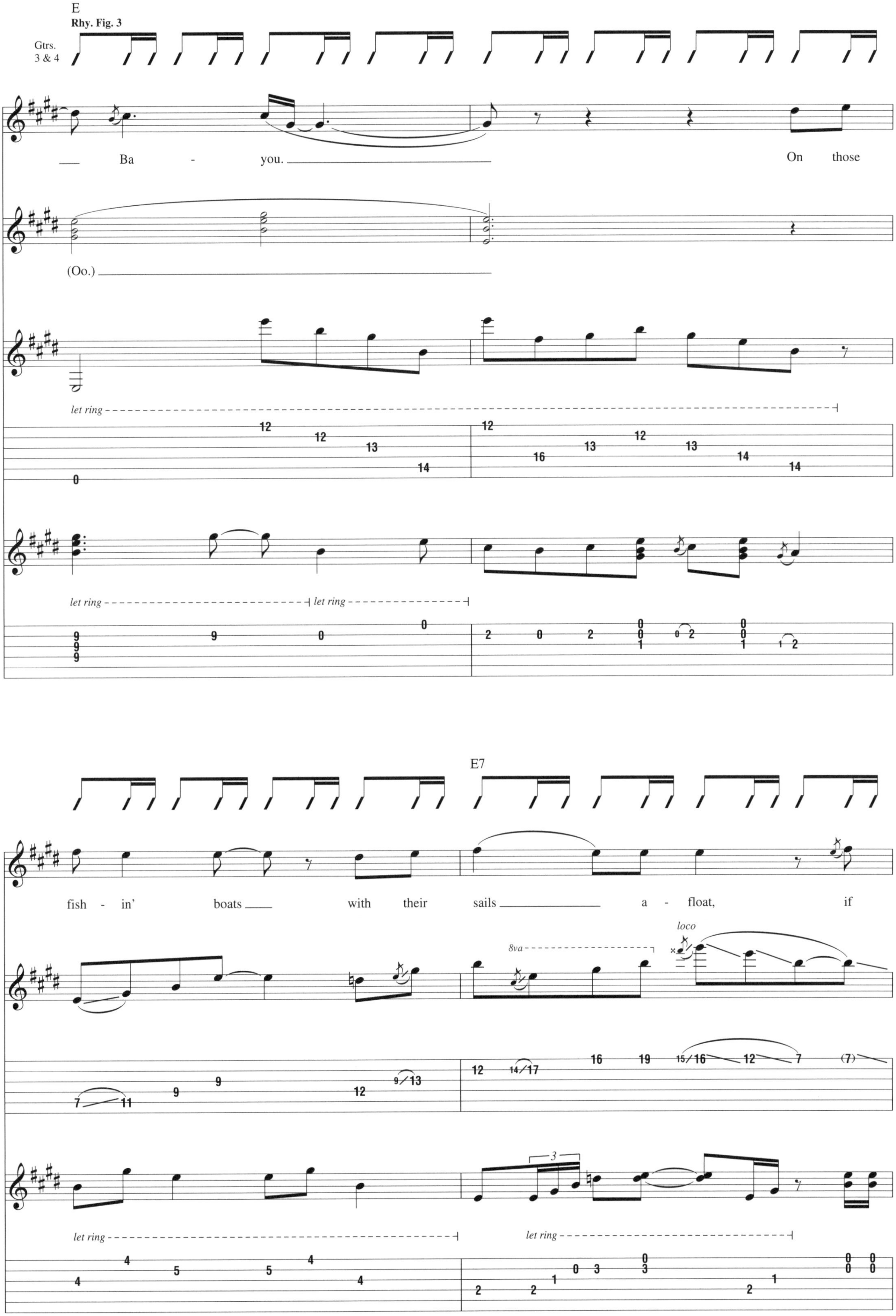
E
Rhy. Fig. 3
Gtrs. 3 & 4
Ba - you.
On those
(Oo.)
let ring
let ring
let ring
E7
fish - in' boats with their sails a - float, if
8va
loco
let ring
let ring

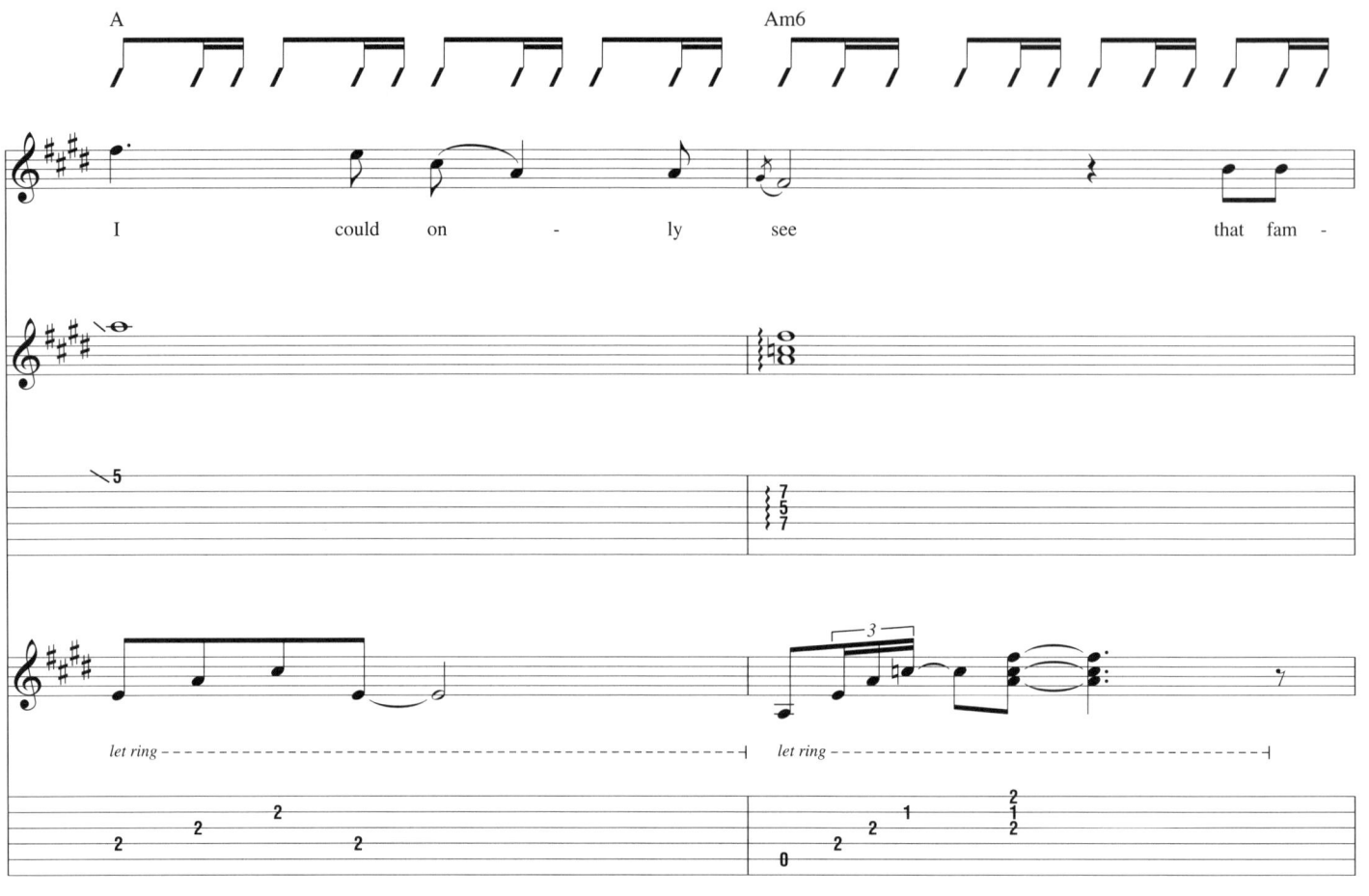

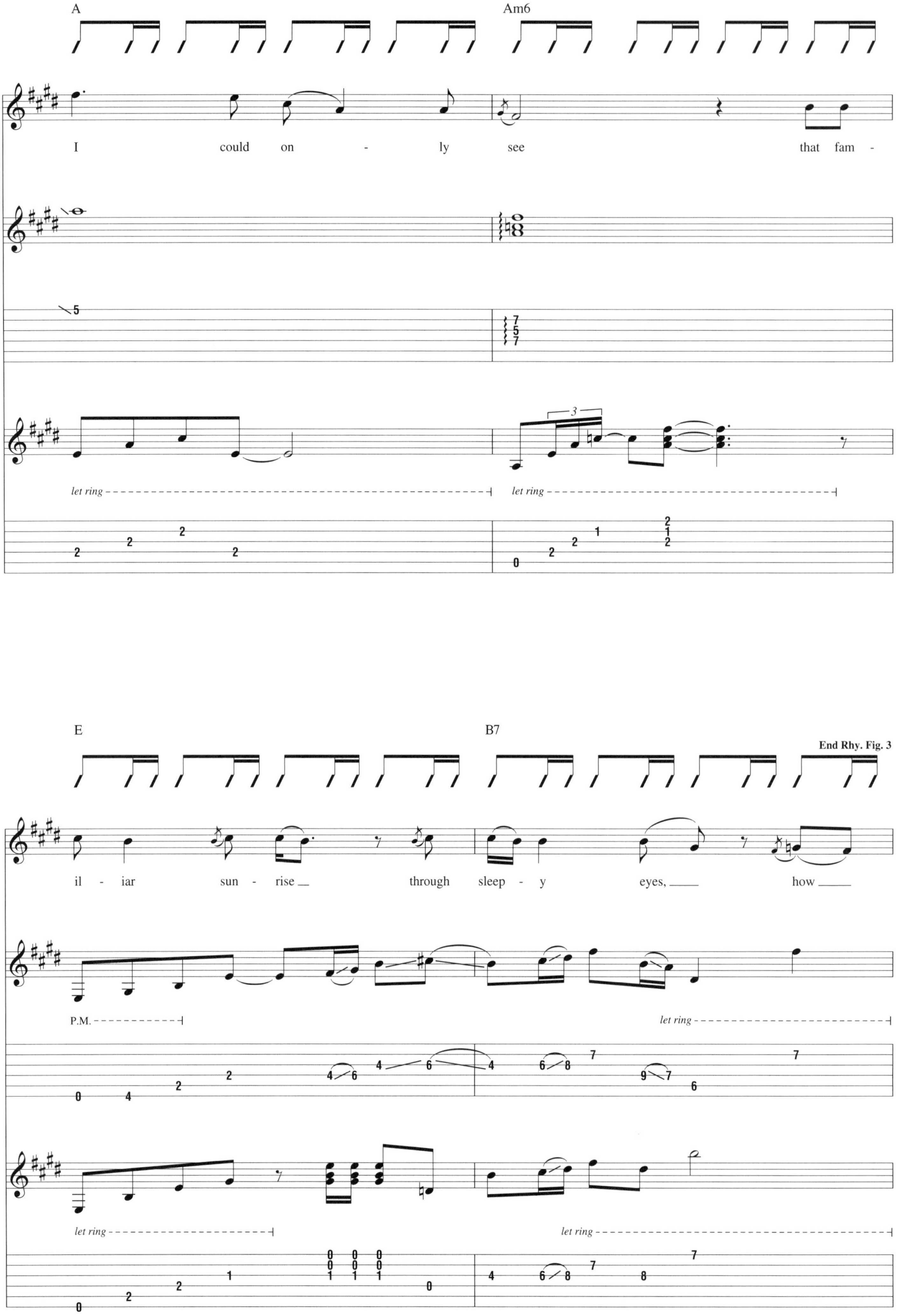
A
Am6
I could on - ly see that fam -
let ring
let ring
E
B7
End Rhy. Fig. 3
il - iar sun - rise through sleep - y eyes, how
P.M.
let ring
let ring
let ring

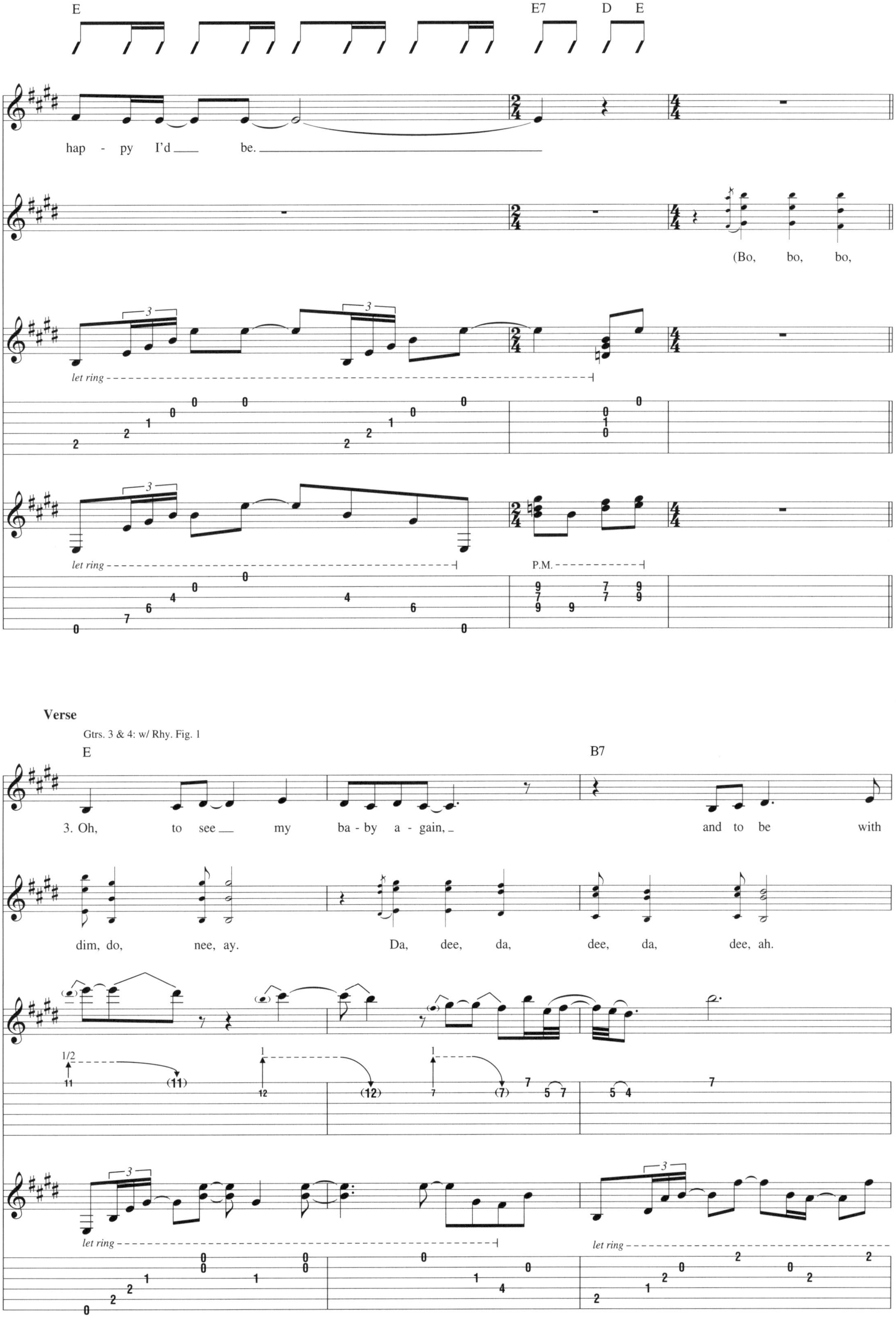
E
E7
D
E
hap - py I'd be.
(Bo, bo, bo,
let ring
let ring
P.M.
Verse
Gtrs. 3 & 4: w/ Rhy. Fig. 1
E
B7
3. Oh, to see my ba - by a - gain, and to be with
dim, do, nee, ay. Da, dee, da, dee, da, dee, ah.
1/2
1
1
let ring
let ring

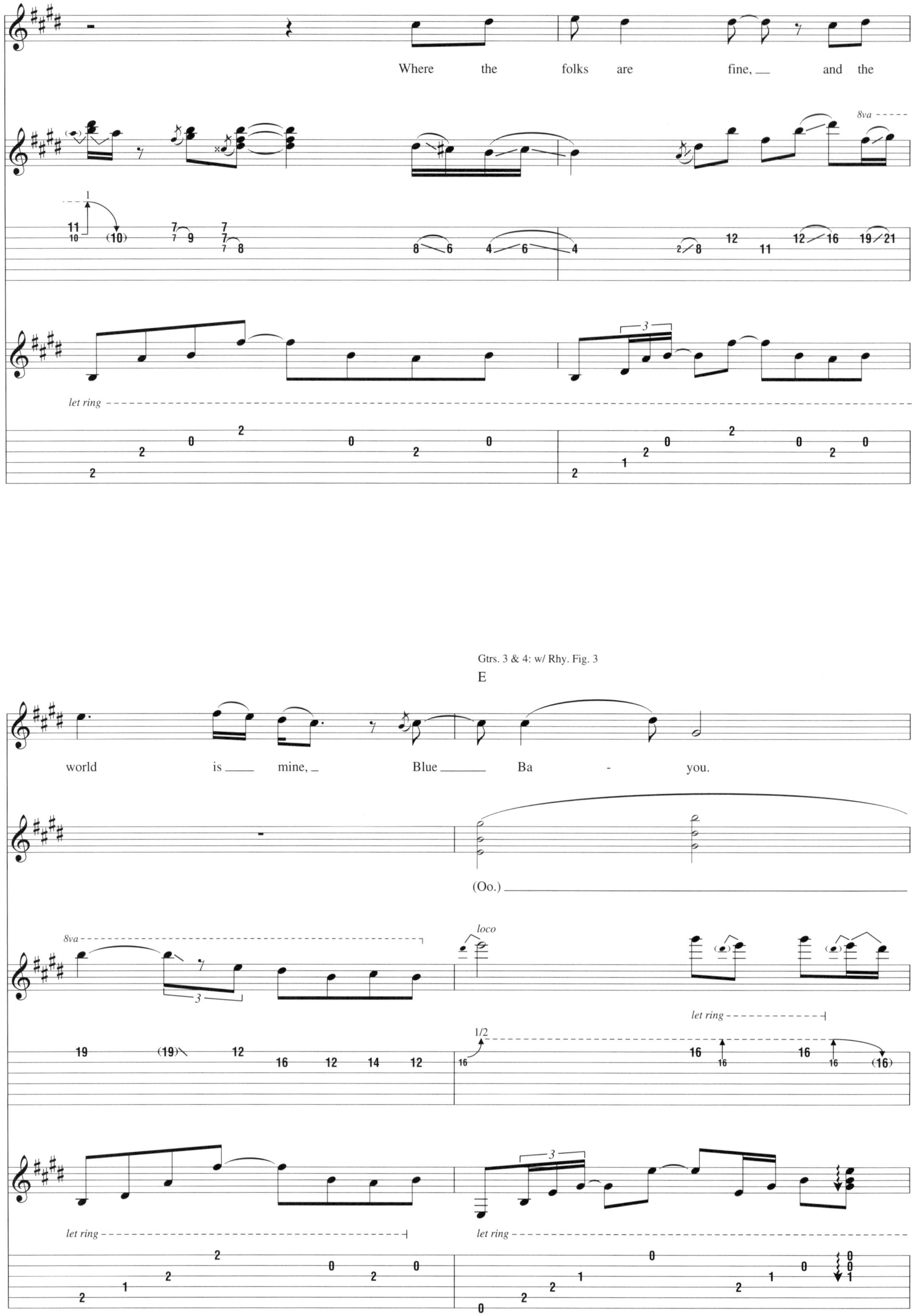
Where the folks are fine, and the
8va
let ring
Gtrs. 3 & 4: w/ Rhy. Fig. 3
E
world is mine, Blue Ba - you.
(Oo.)
8va
loco
let ring
1/2
let ring
let ring

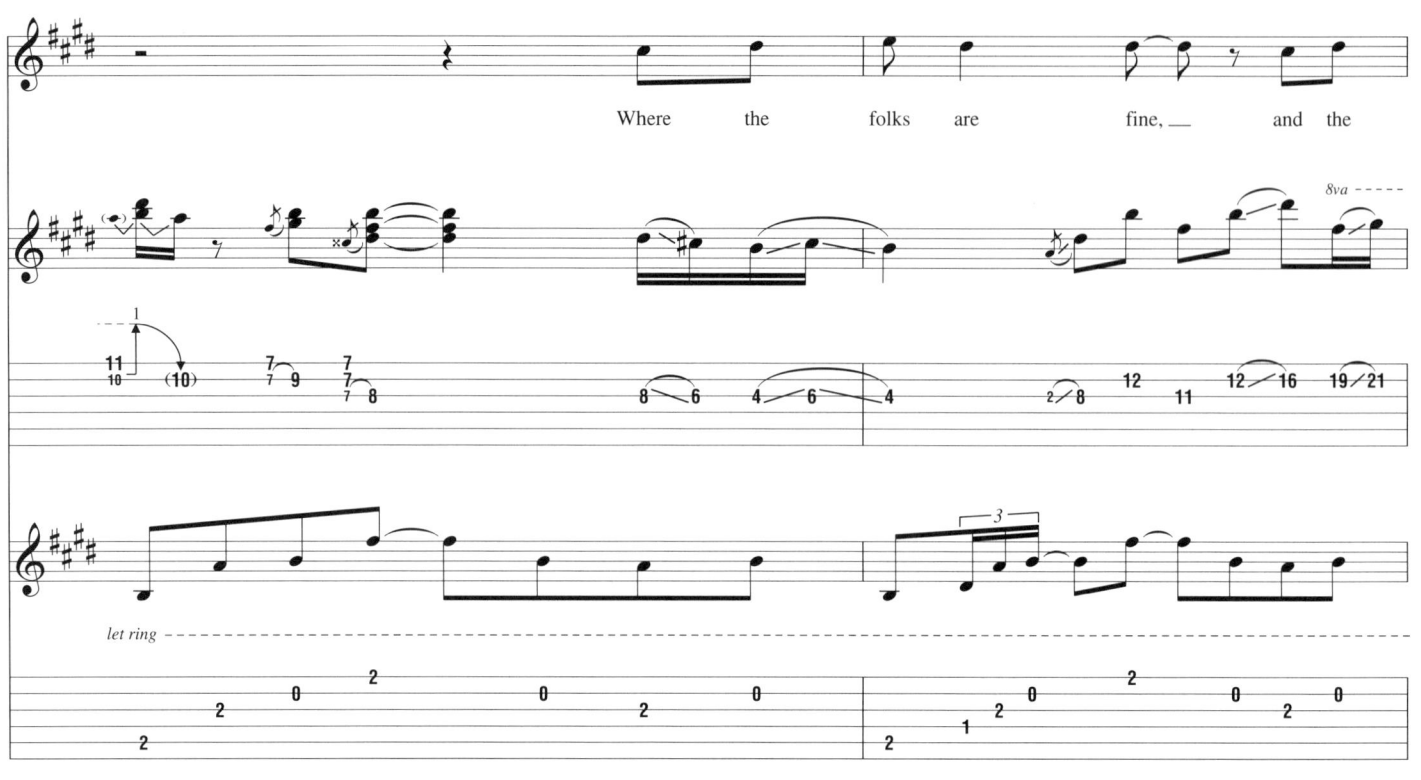

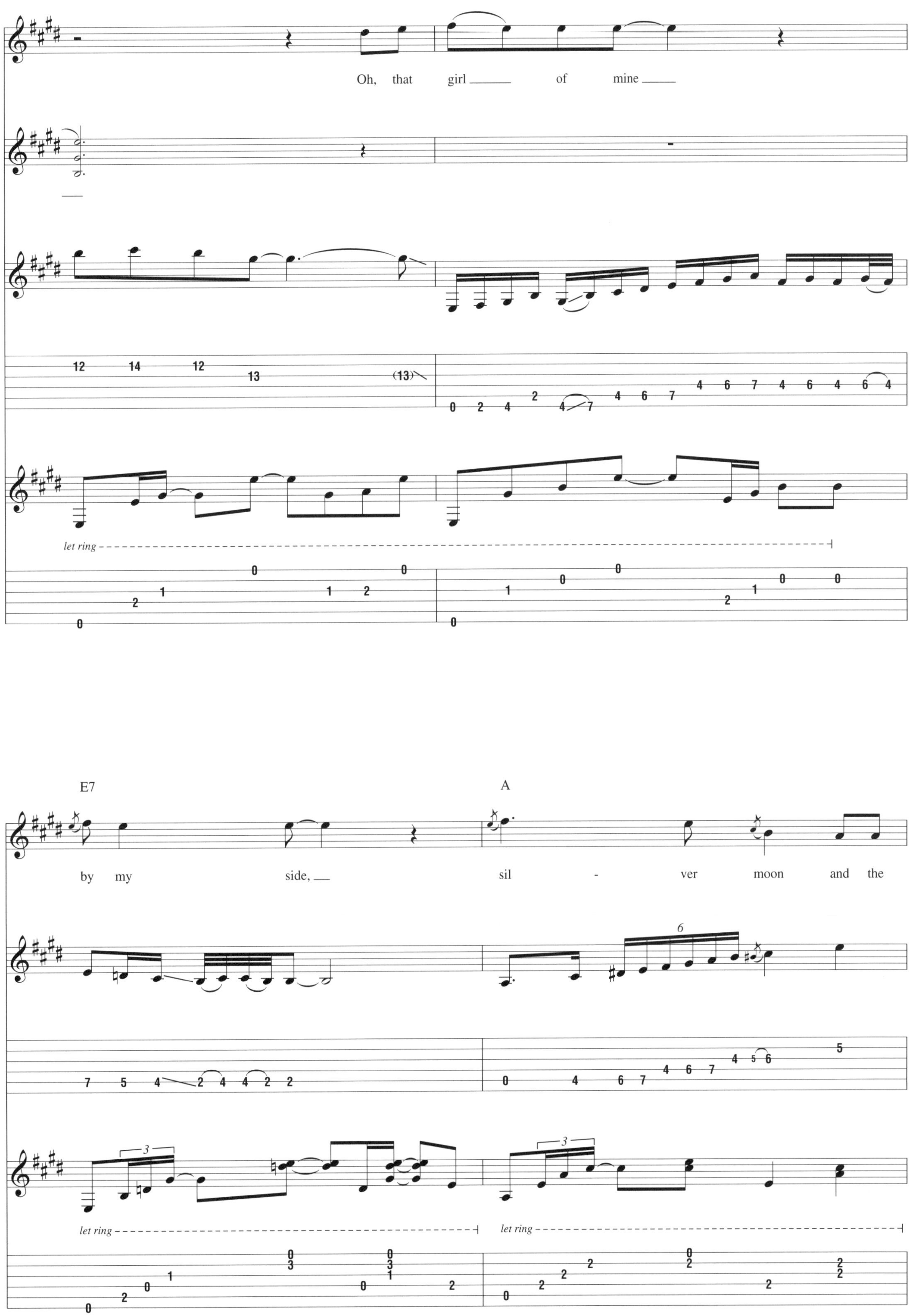
Oh, that girl of mine
let ring
E7
A
by my side, sil - ver moon and the
let ring
let ring

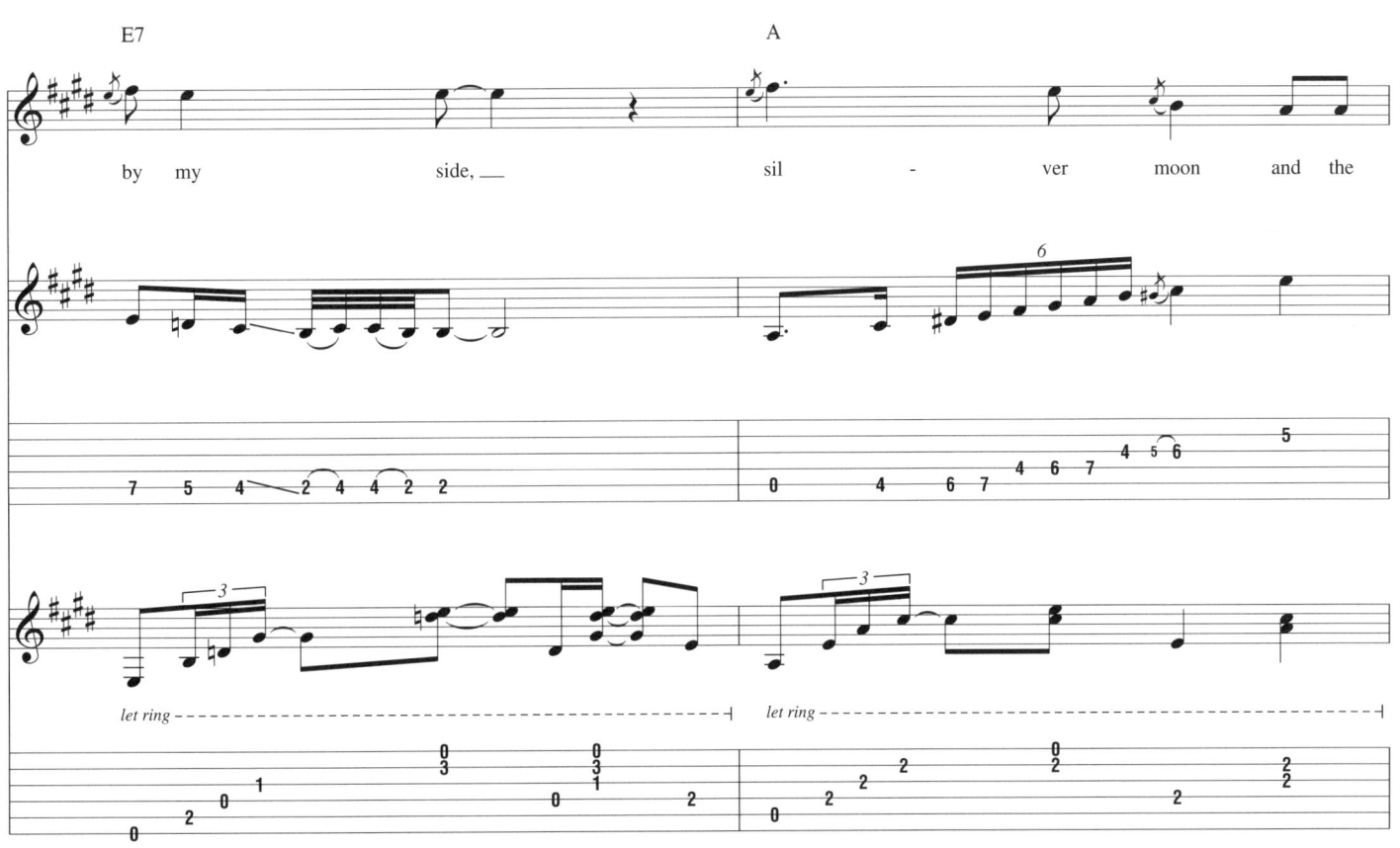

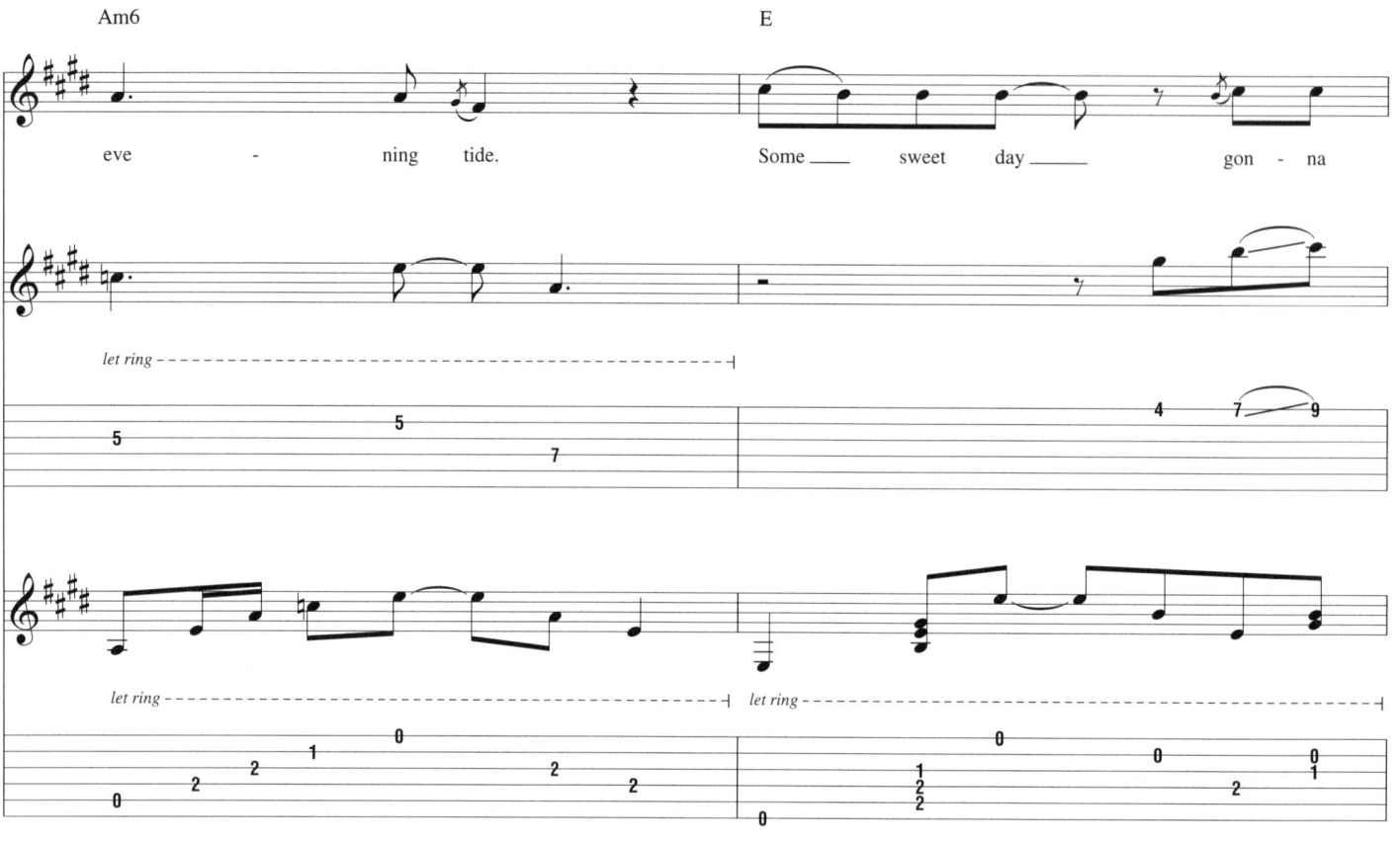

Outro

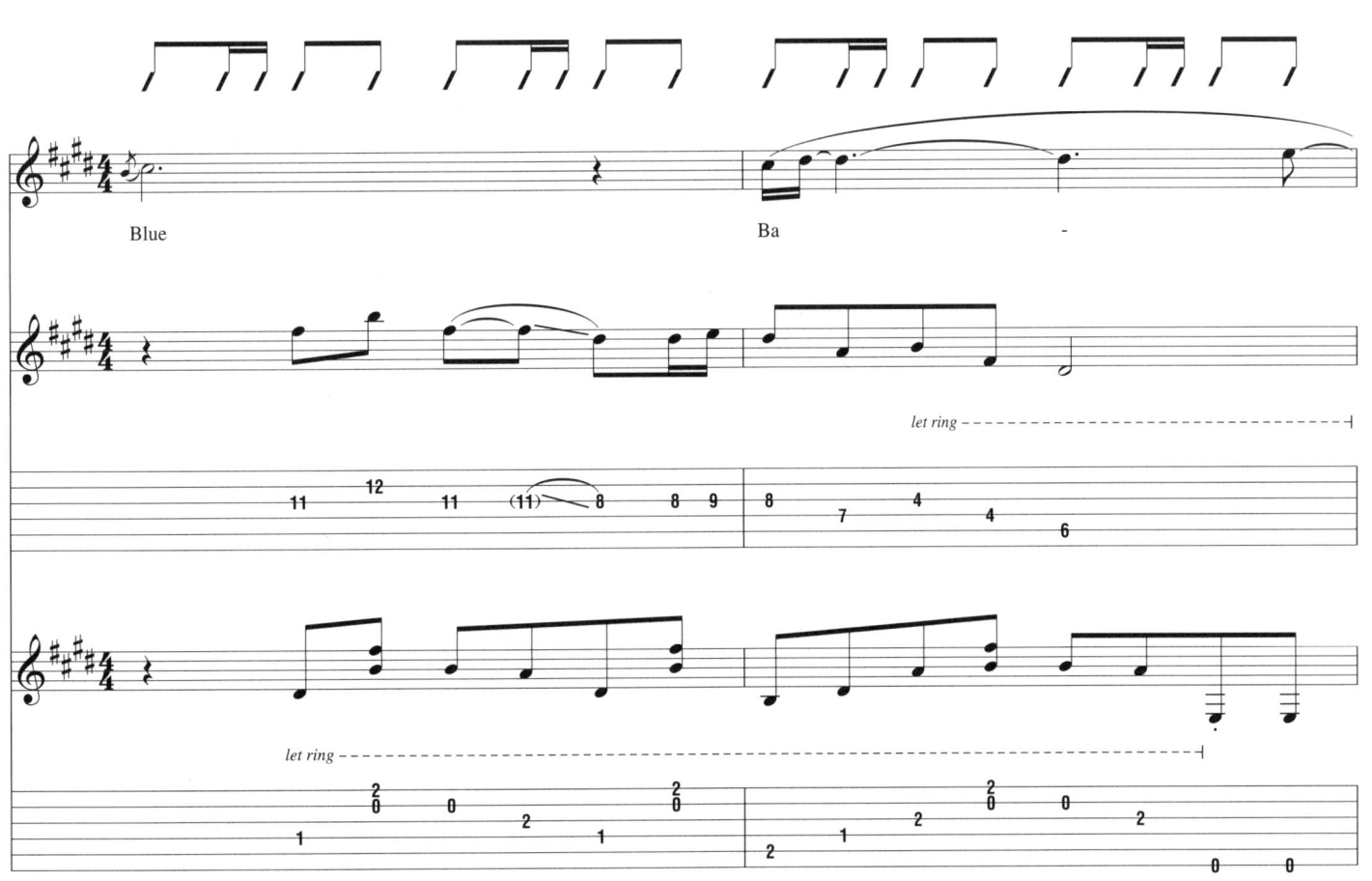

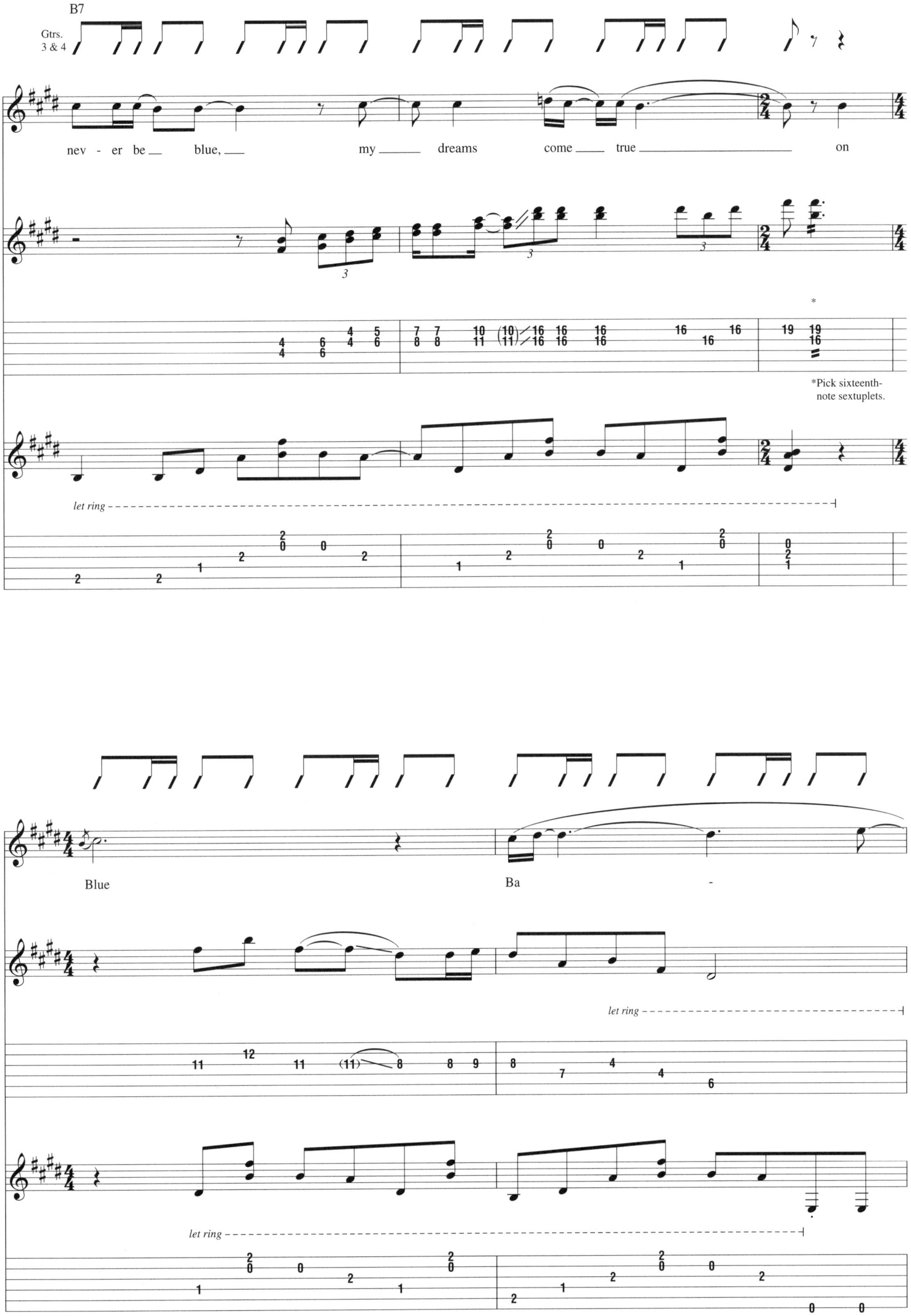
B7
Gtrs. 3 & 4
nev - er be blue, my dreams come true on
*Pick sixteenth-note sextuplets.
let ring
Blue
Ba -
let ring
let ring

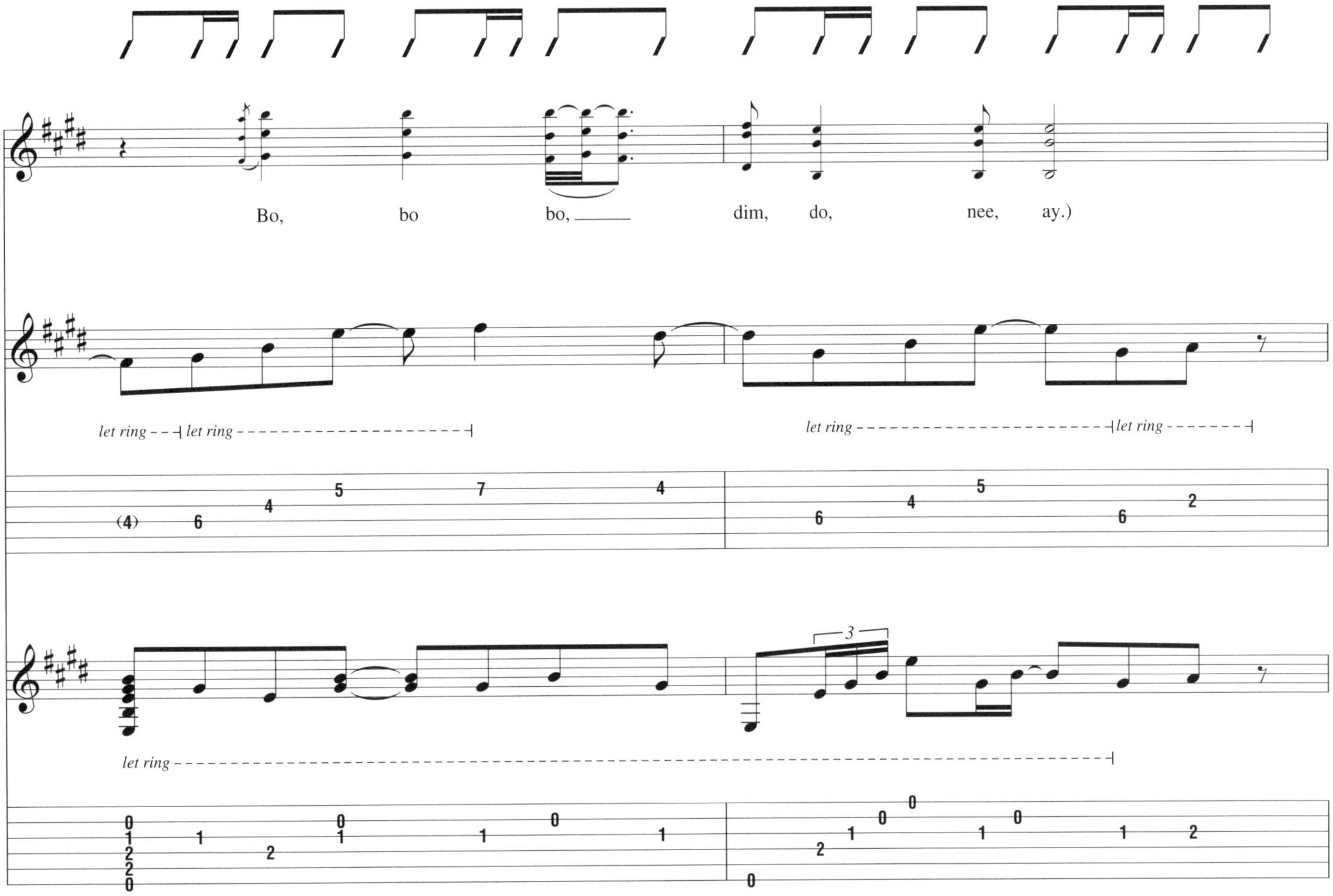
Bo, bo bo, dim, do, nee, ay.)
let ring
let ring
let ring
let ring
let ring

Gtrs. 3 & 4 tacet
E7 D E E7 D E N.C. E
let ring
pp mf
P.M.

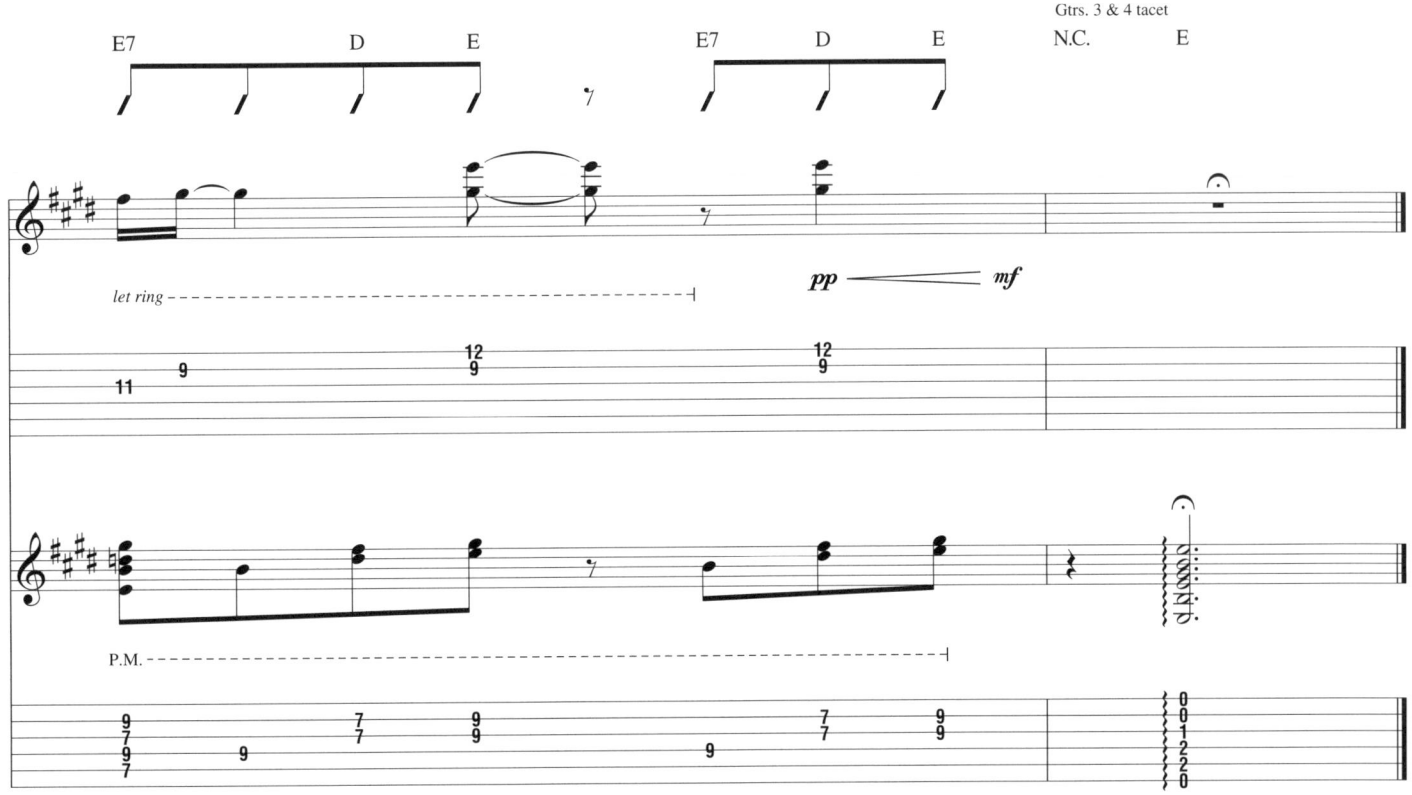

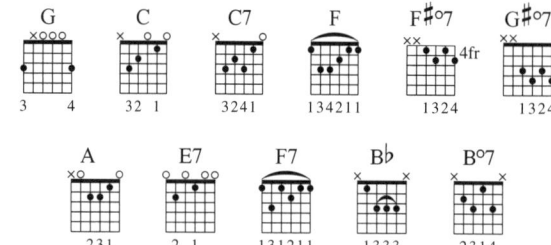
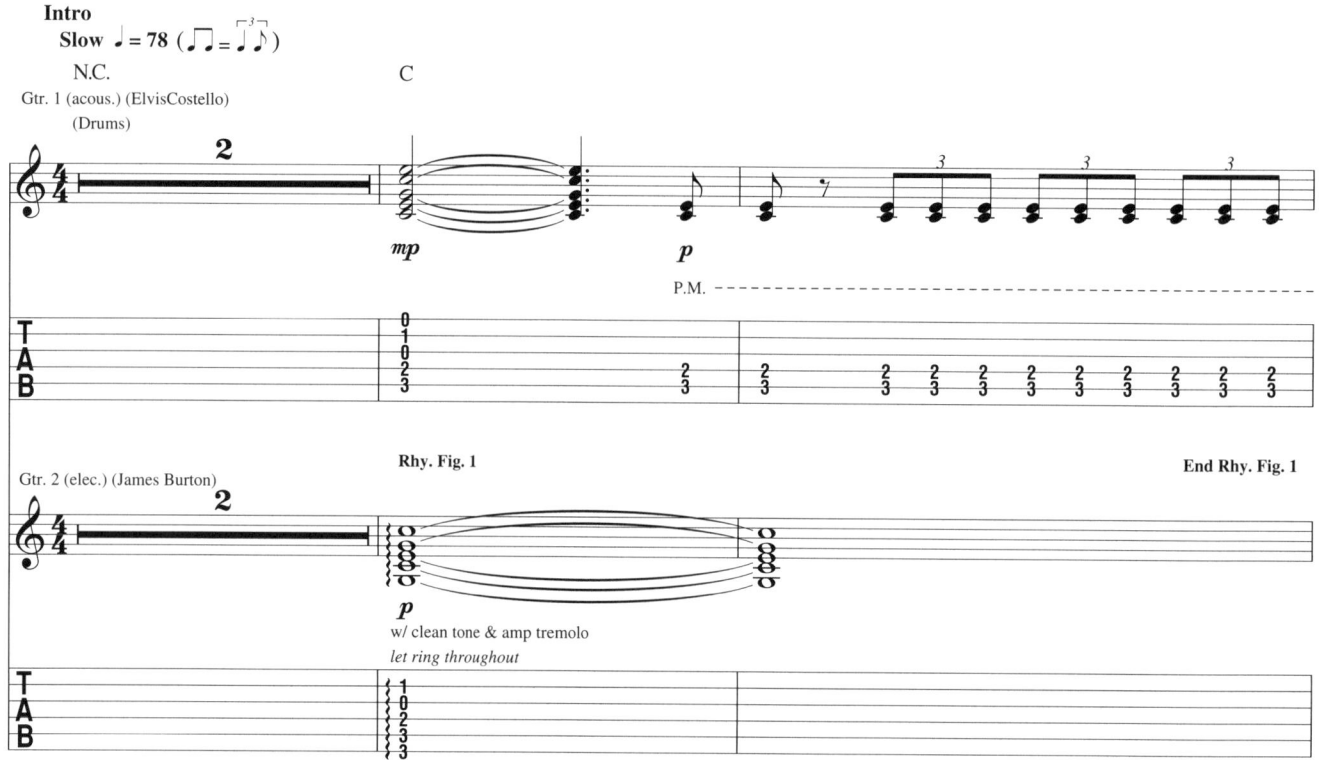

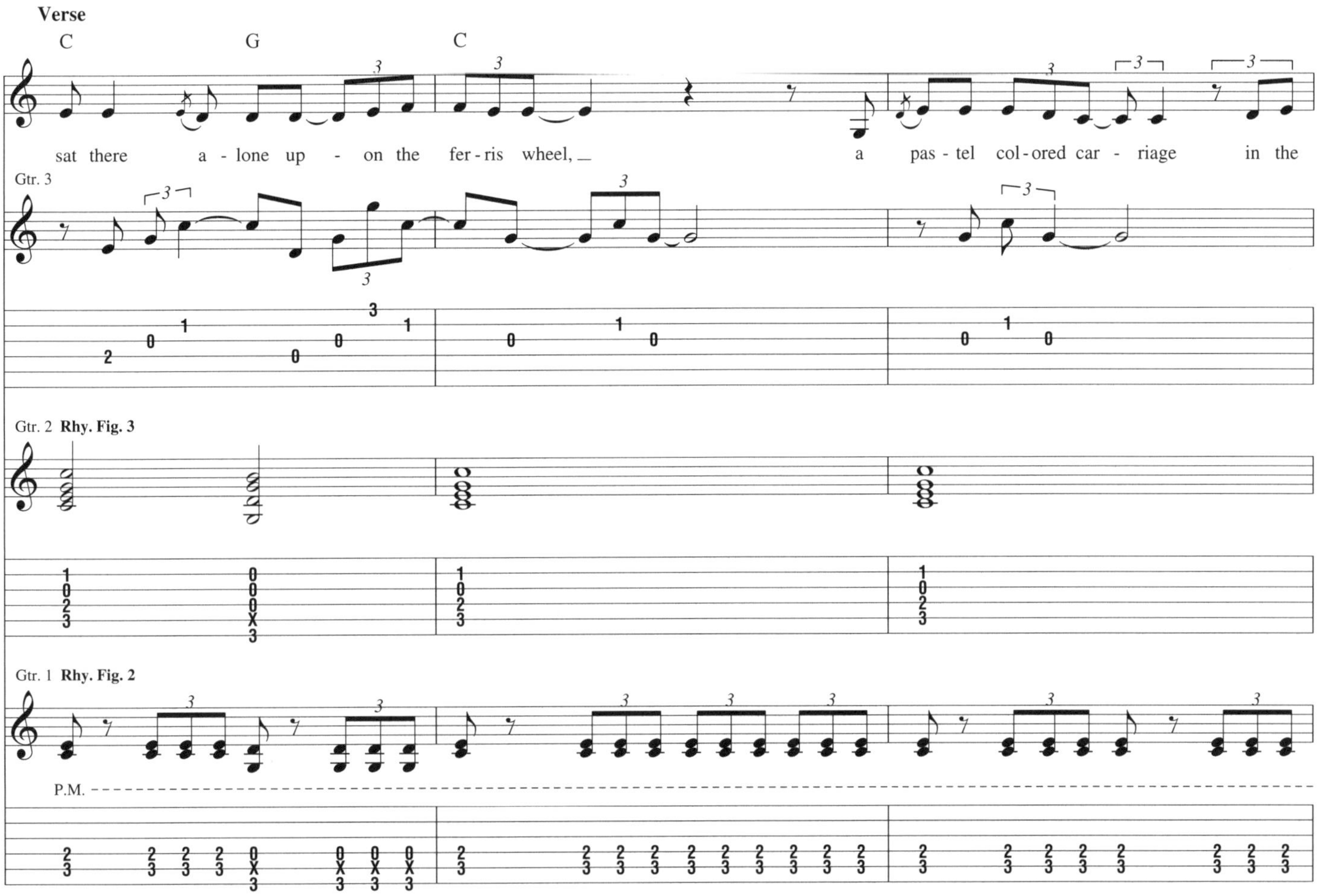
Verse
C
G
C
sat there a - lone up - on the fer - ris wheel, a pas - tel col - ored car - riage in the
Gtr. 3
Gtr. 2 Rhy. Fig. 3
Gtr. 1 Rhy. Fig. 2
P.M.

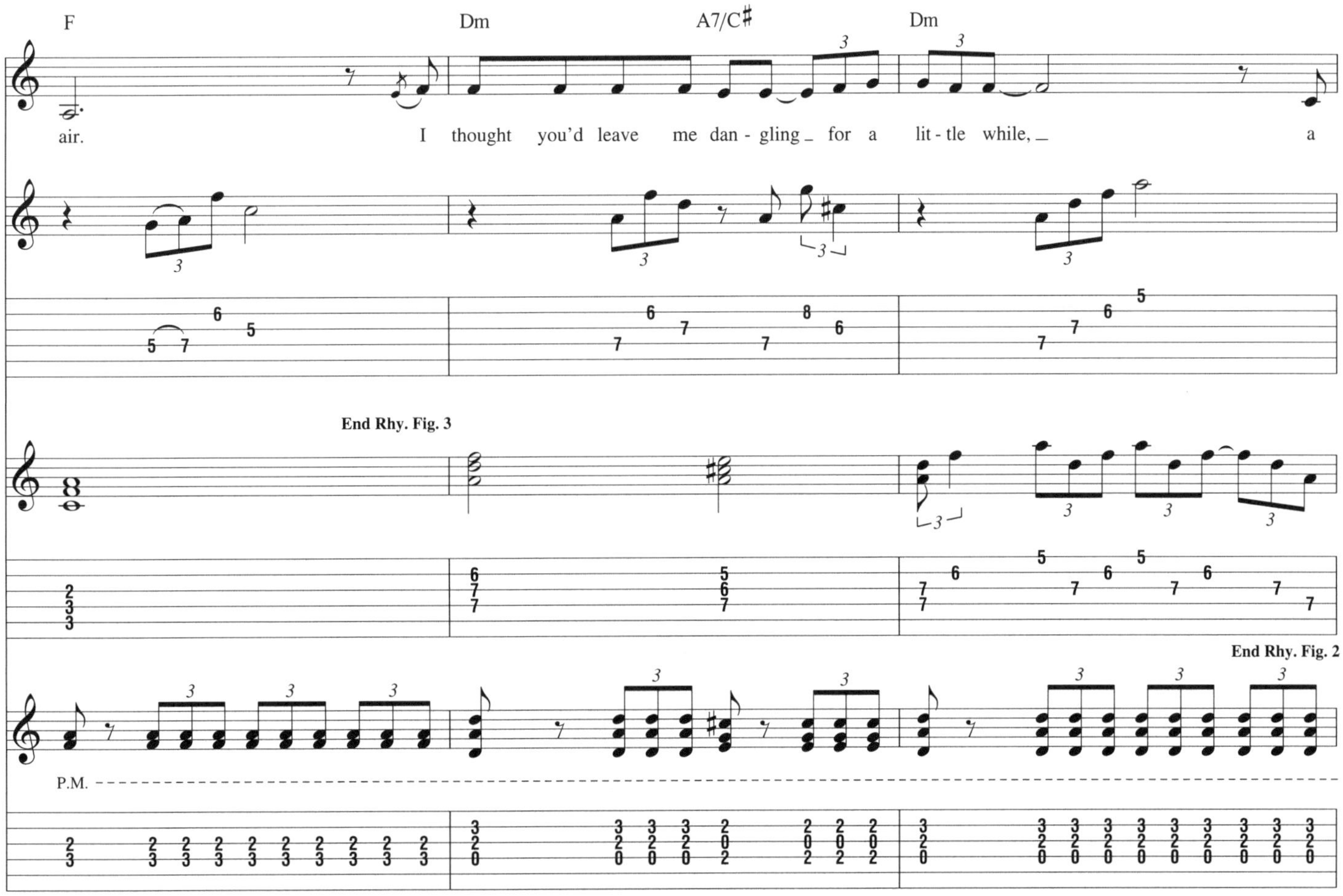
F
Dm
A7/C♯
Dm
air. I thought you'd leave me dan - gling for a lit - tle while, a
End Rhy. Fig. 3
End Rhy. Fig. 2
P.M.

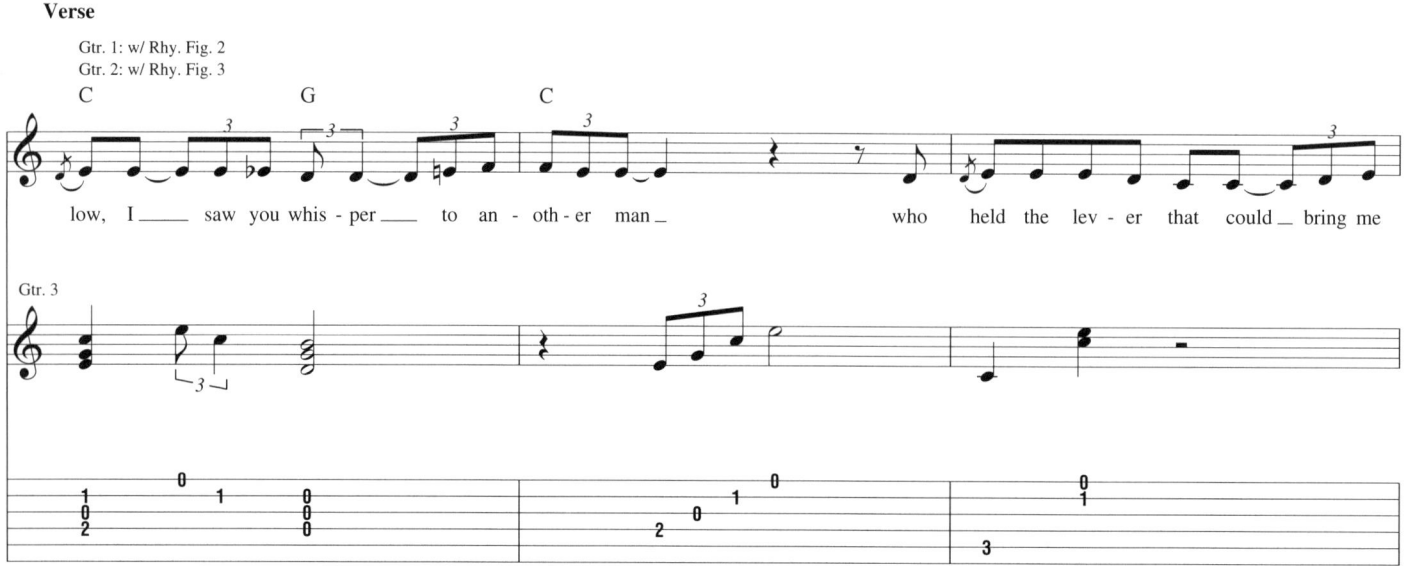

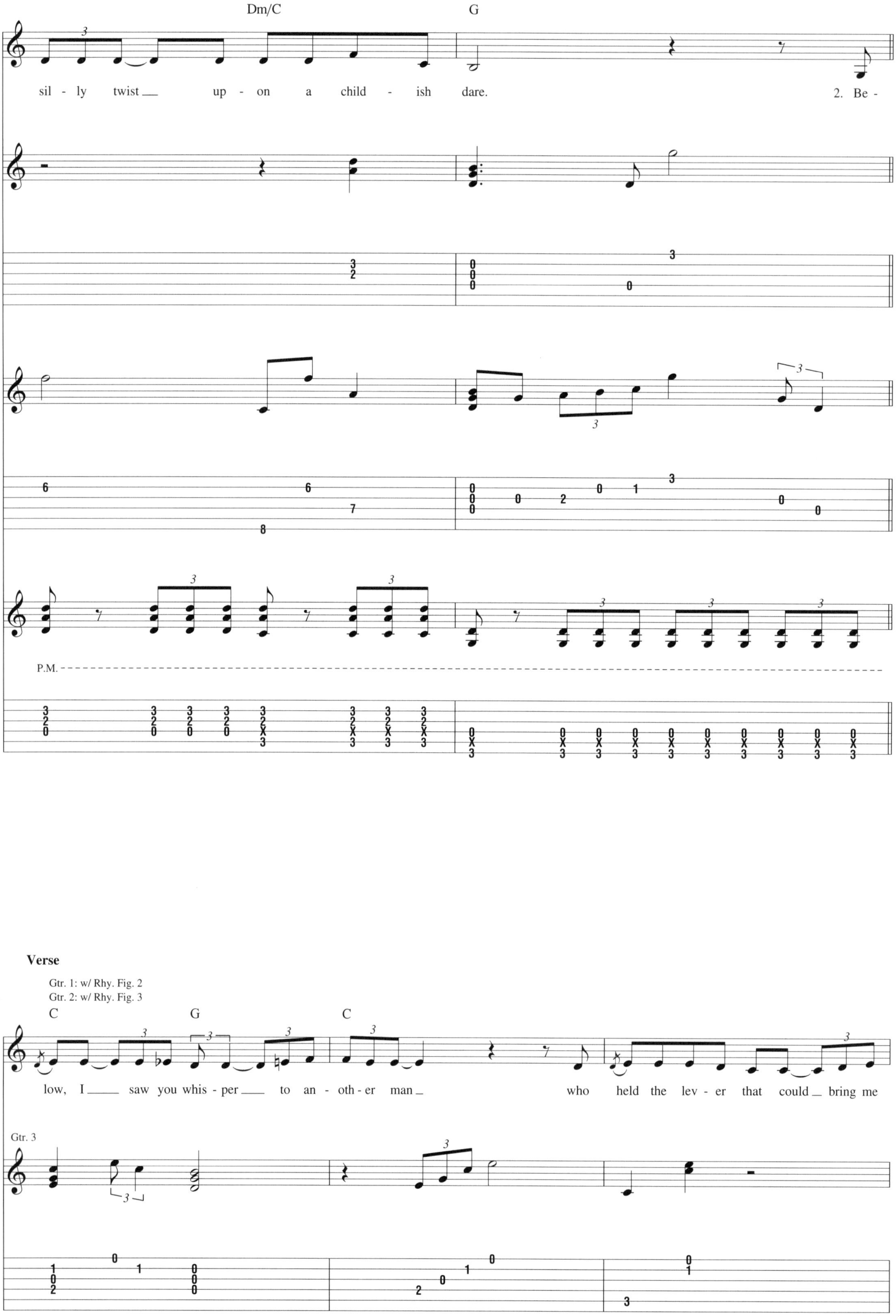
Dm/C
G
sil - ly twist __ up - on a child - ish dare.
2. Be -
P.M.
Verse
Gtr. 1: w/ Rhy. Fig. 2
Gtr. 2: w/ Rhy. Fig. 3
C
G
C
low, I ___ saw you whis - per ___ to an - oth - er man __
who held the lev - er that could __ bring me
Gtr. 3

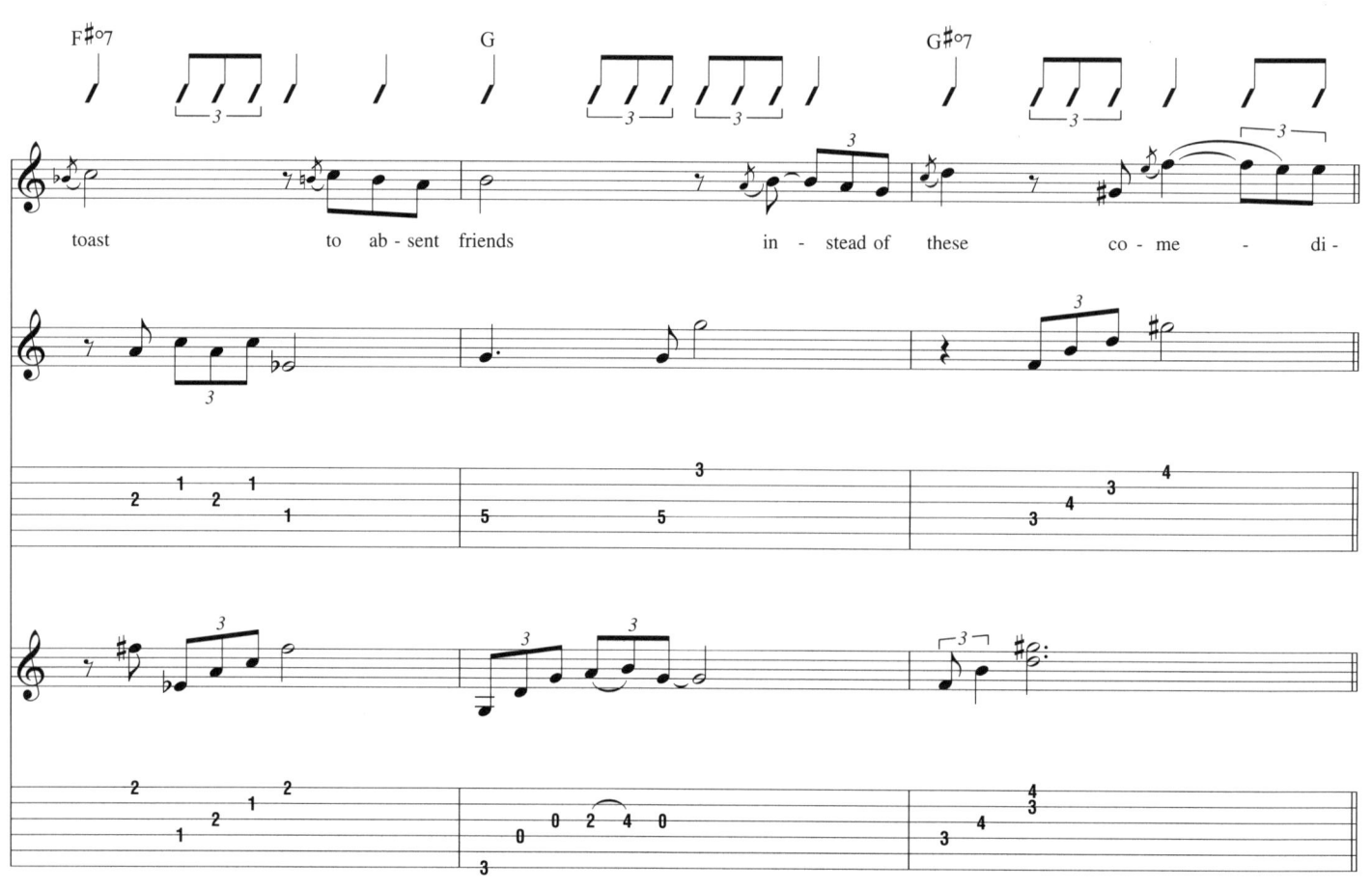

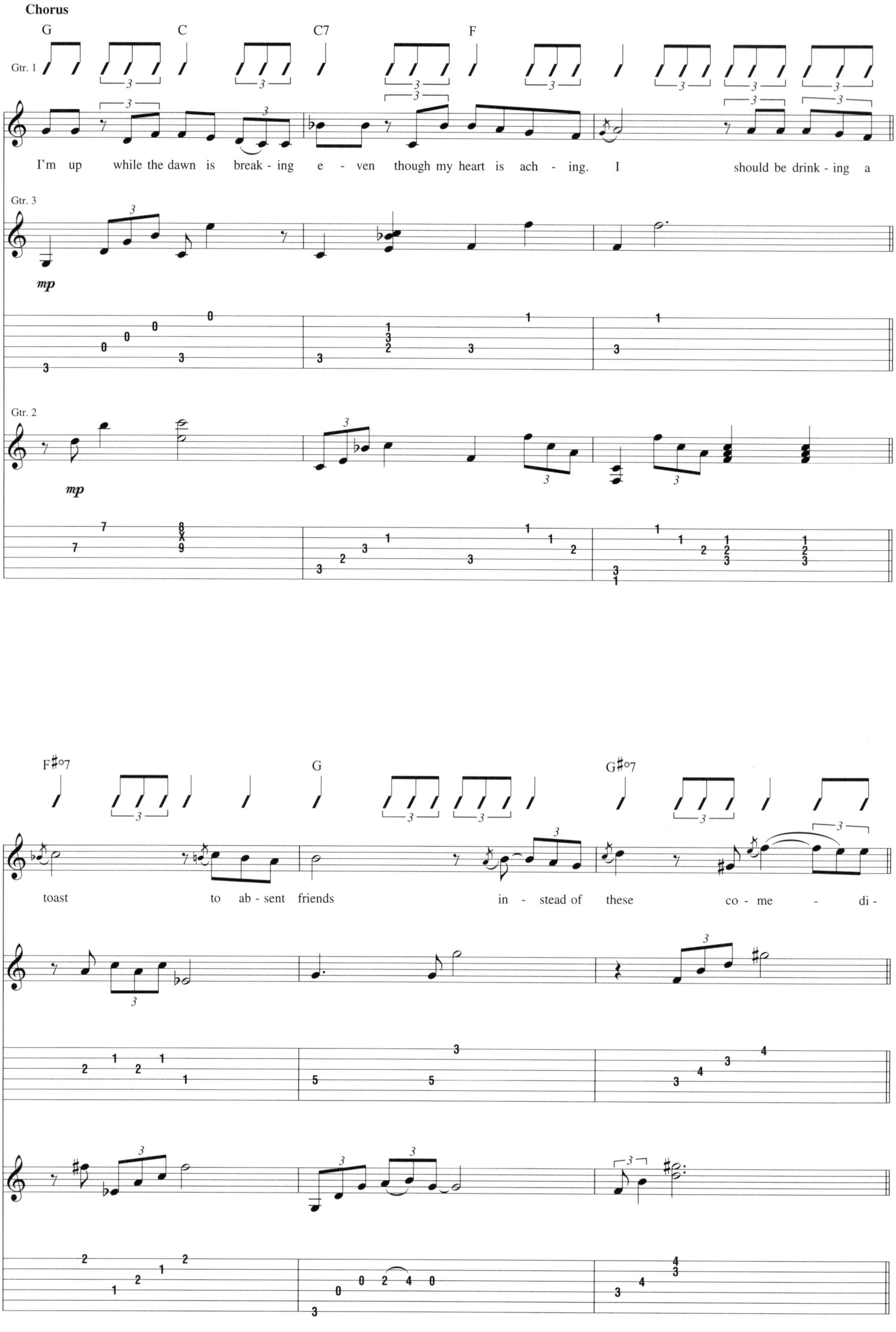
Chorus
G C C7 F
Gtr. 1
I'm up while the dawn is break - ing e - ven though my heart is ach - ing. I should be drink - ing a
Gtr. 3
mp
Gtr. 2
mp
F#°7 G G#°7
toast to ab - sent friends in - stead of these co - me - di -

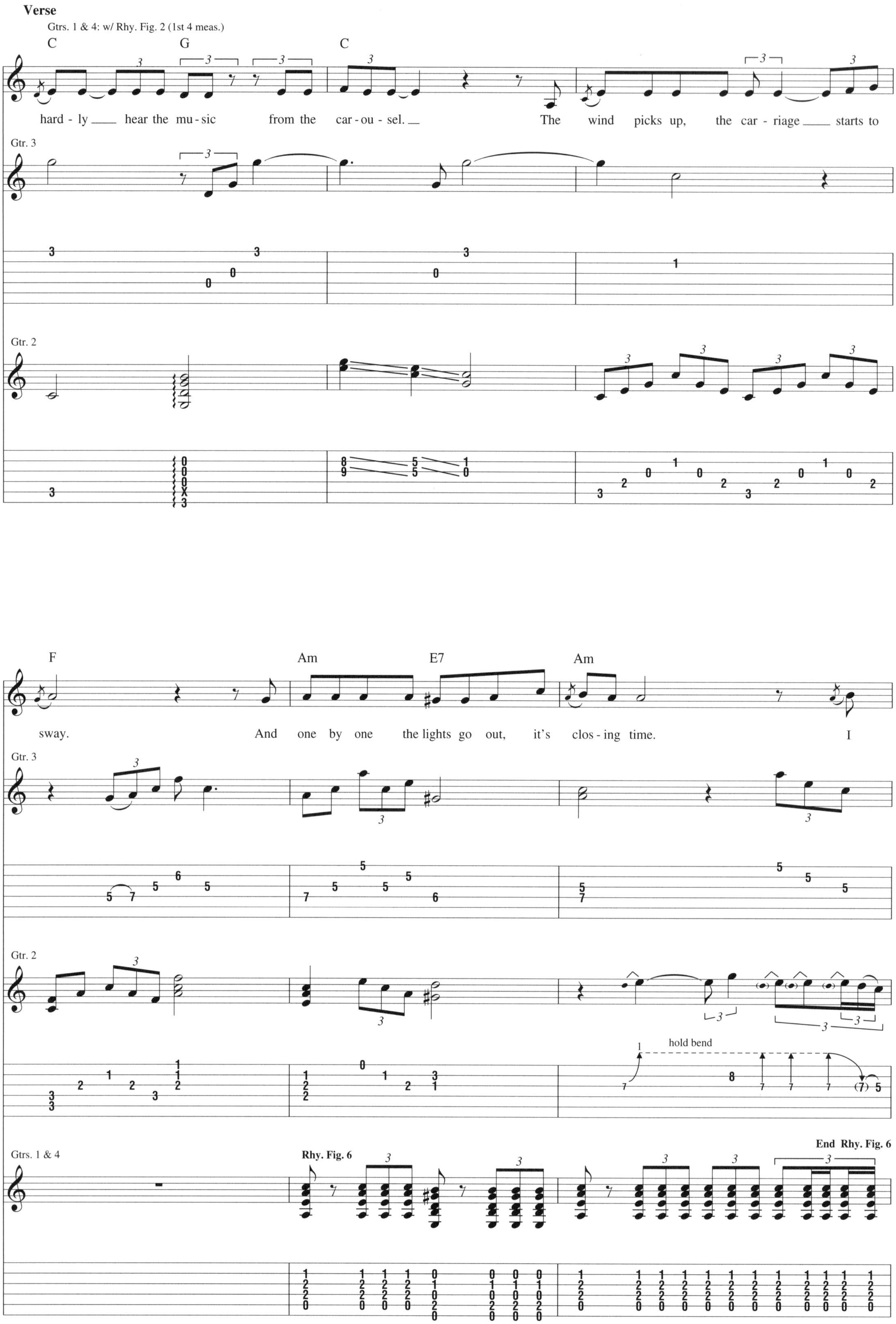
Verse
Gtrs. 1 & 4: w/ Rhy. Fig. 2 (1st 4 meas.)
C G C
hard - ly ___ hear the mu - sic from the car - ou - sel. ___ The wind picks up, the car - riage ___ starts to
Gtr. 3
Gtr. 2
F Am E7 Am
sway. And one by one the lights go out, it's clos - ing time. I
Gtr. 3
Gtr. 2
hold bend
Gtrs. 1 & 4
Rhy. Fig. 6
End Rhy. Fig. 6

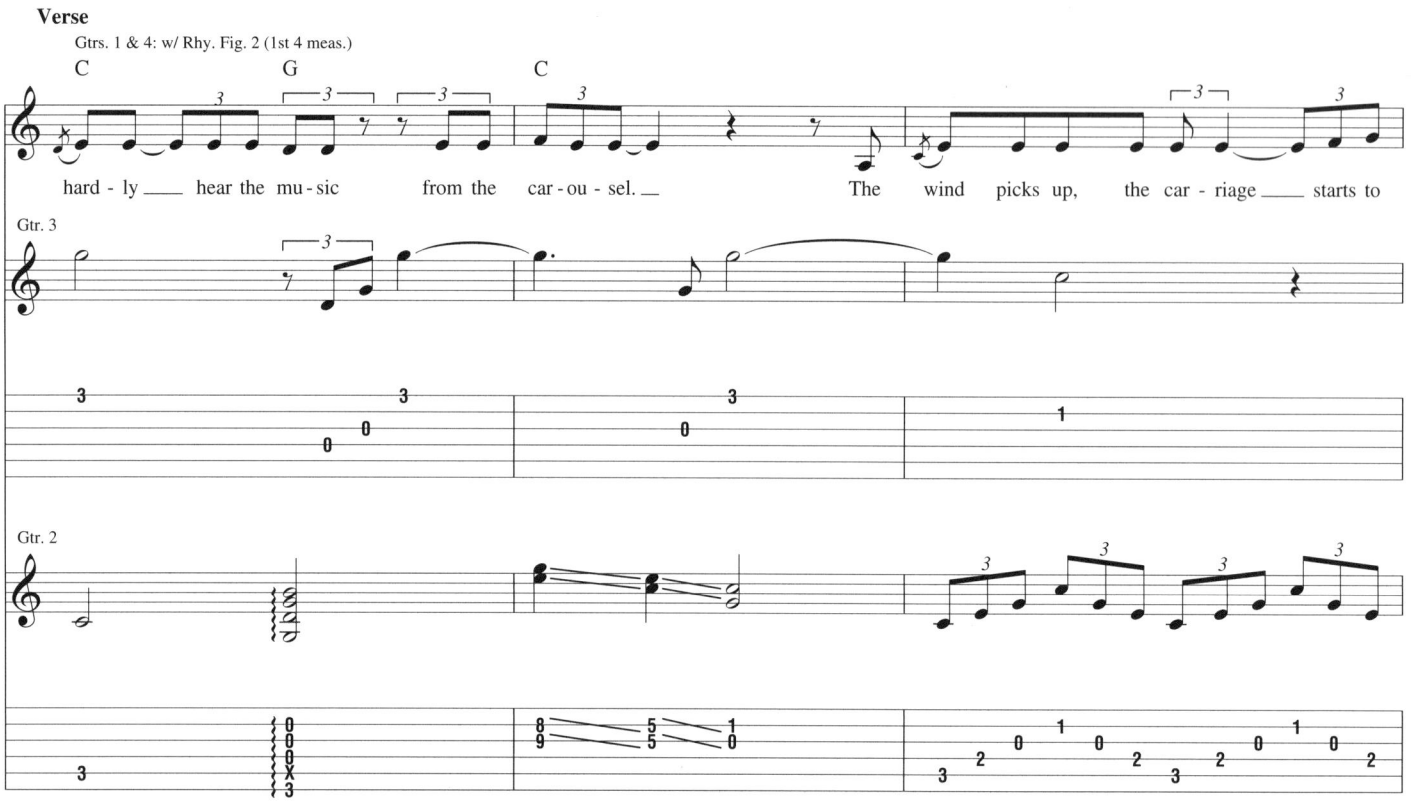

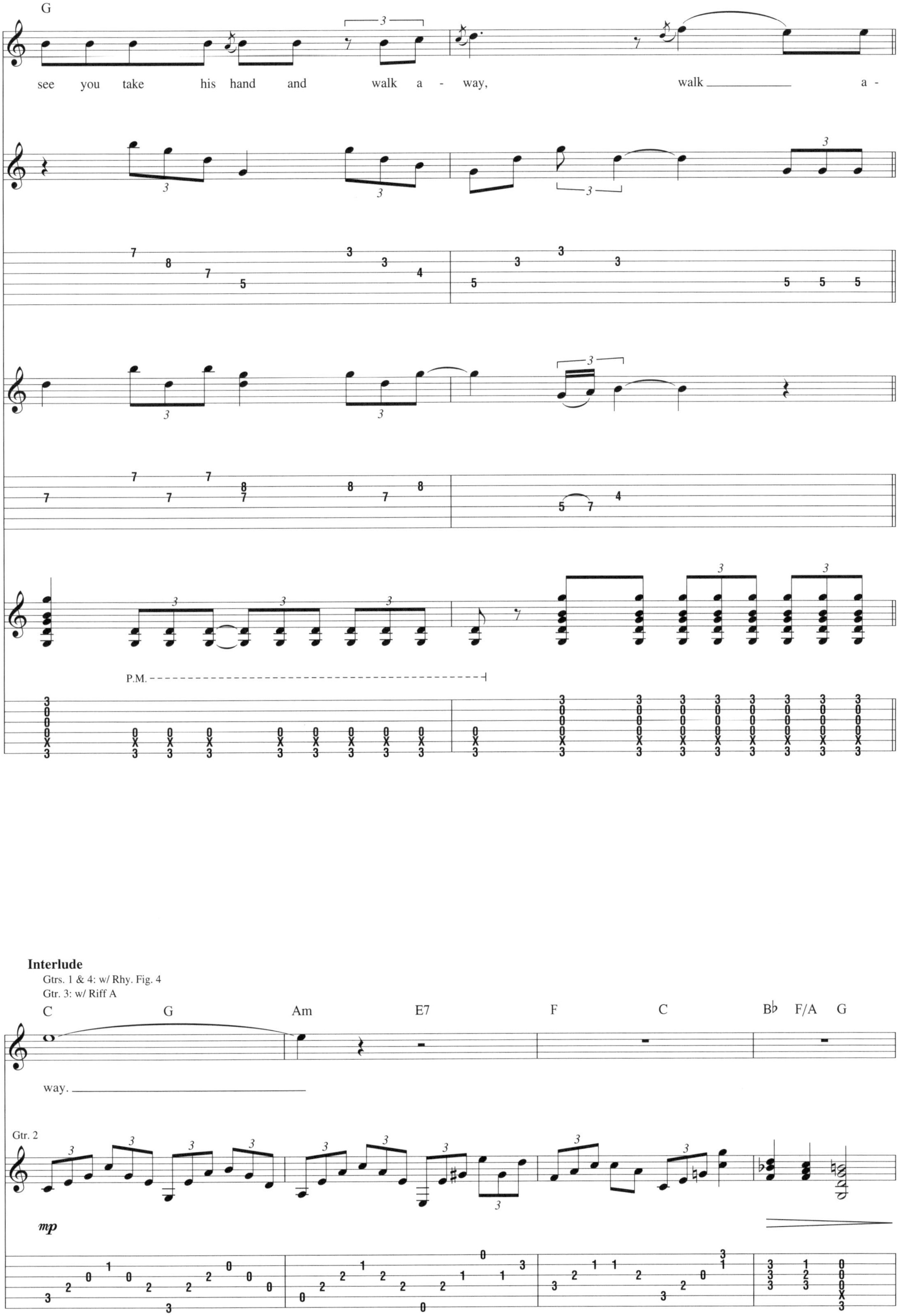
G
see you take his hand and walk a - way, walk a -
P.M.
Interlude
Gtrs. 1 & 4: w/ Rhy. Fig. 4
Gtr. 3: w/ Riff A
C G Am E7 F C B♭ F/A G
way.
Gtr. 2
mp

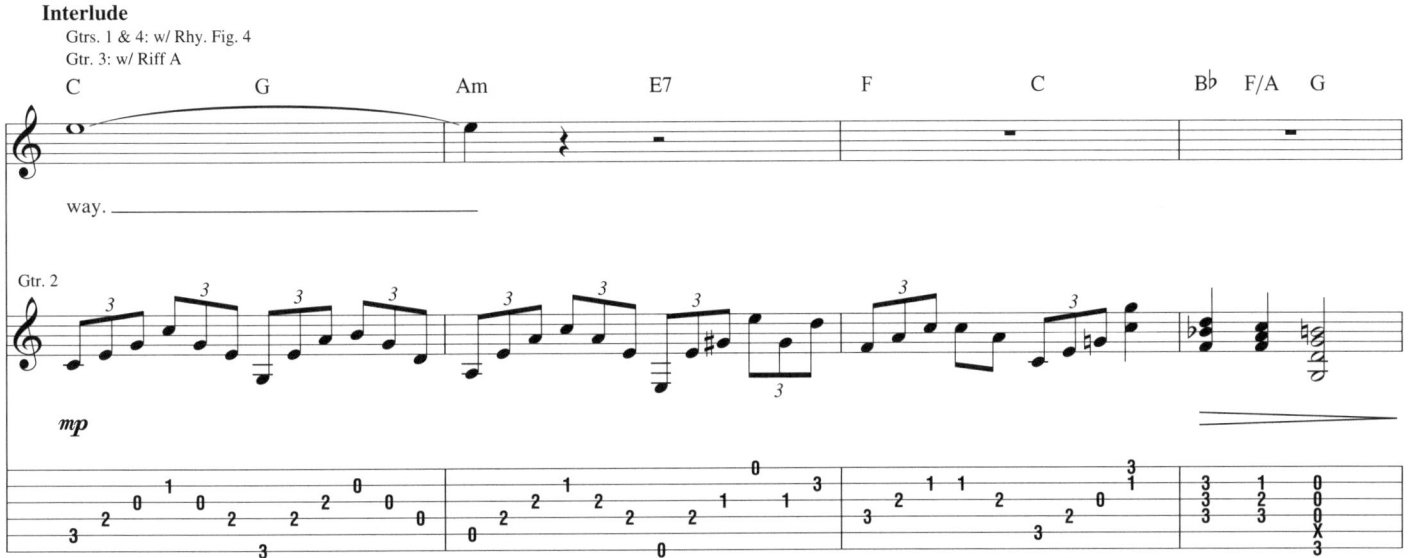

G
Gtrs. 1 & 4
mf
it's the bit - ter way that I was told. And
Gtr. 3
Gtr. 2

Chorus

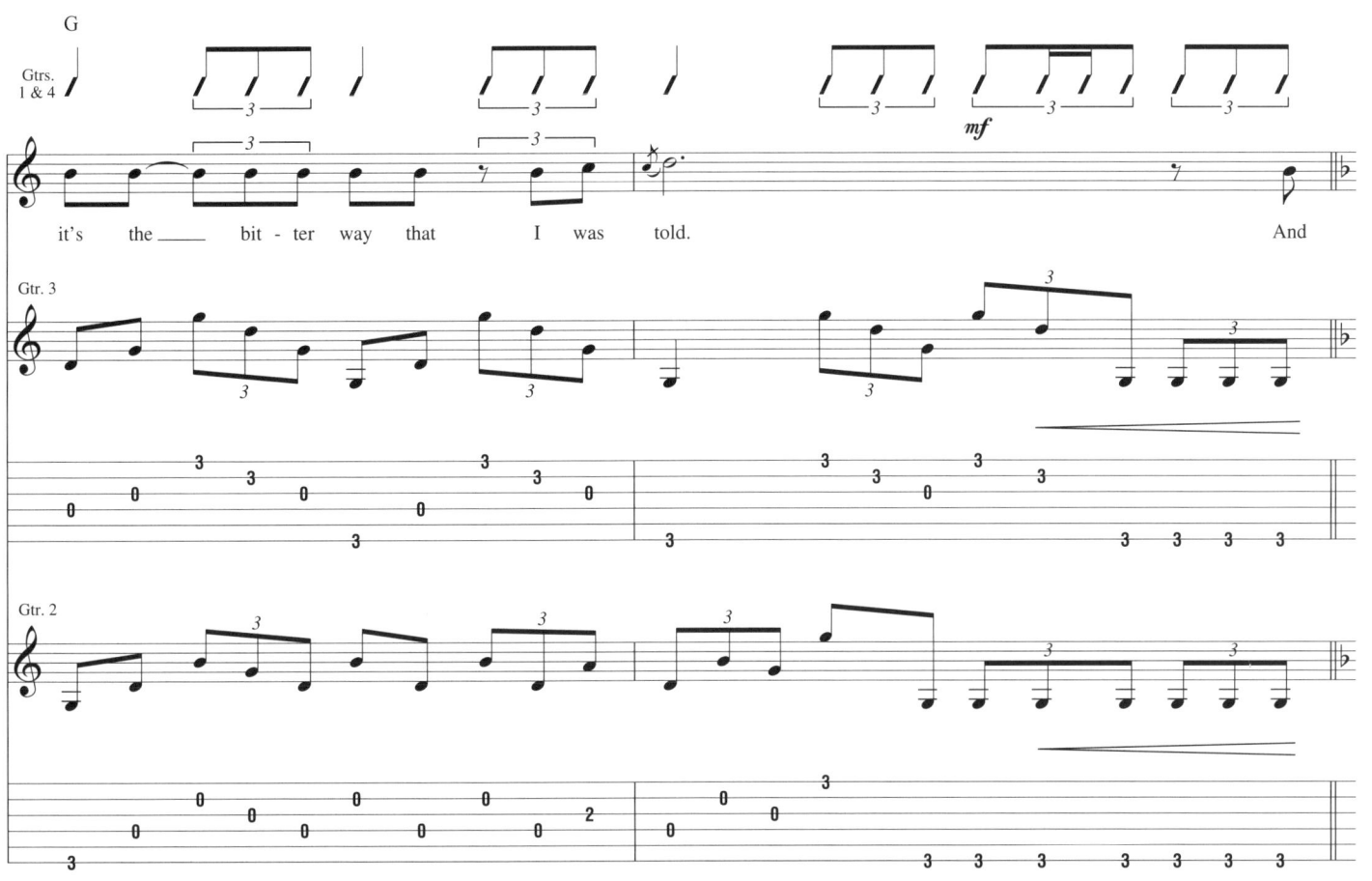

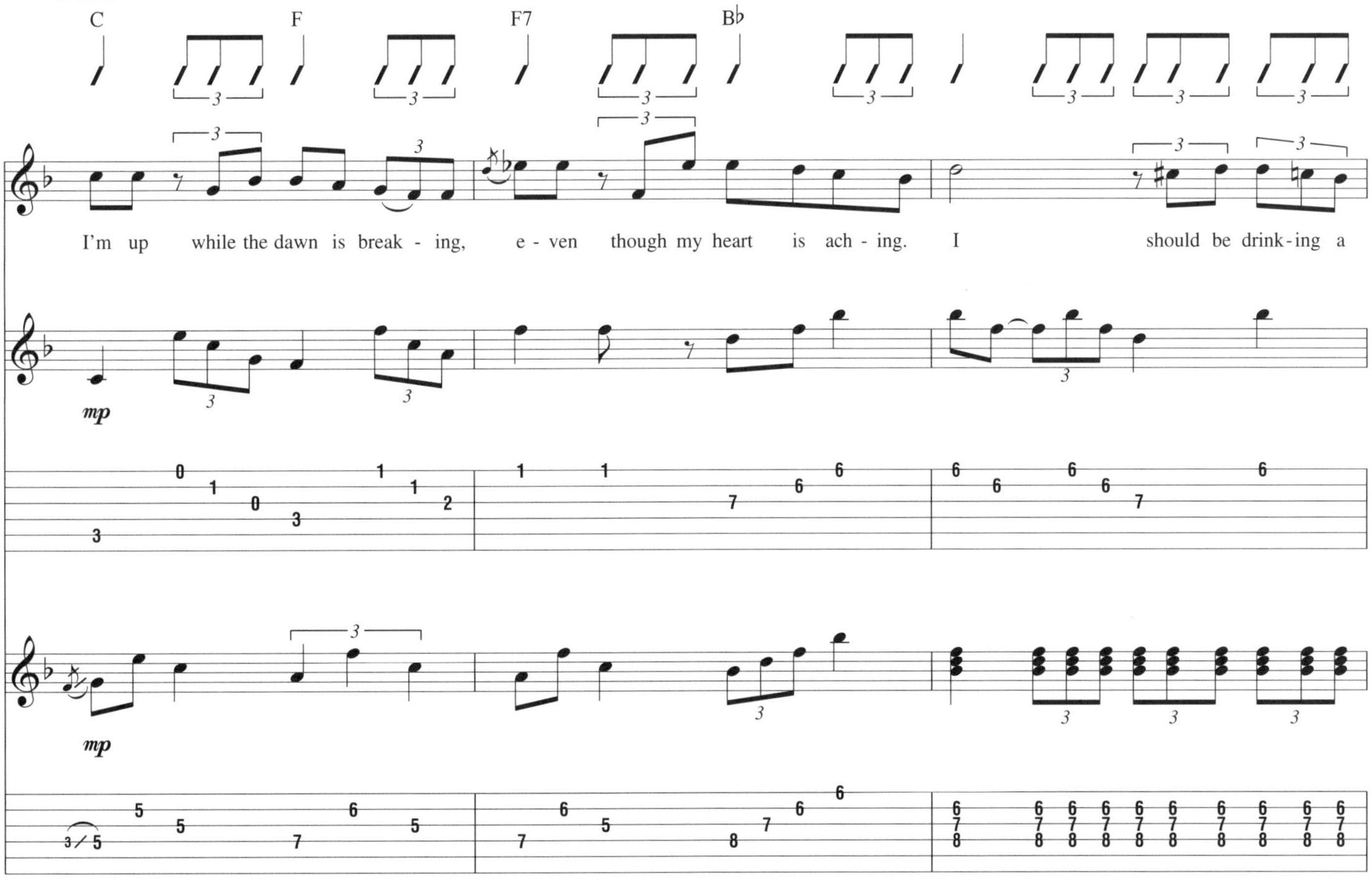
C F F7 B♭
I'm up while the dawn is break - ing, e - ven though my heart is ach - ing. I should be drink-ing a
mp
mp

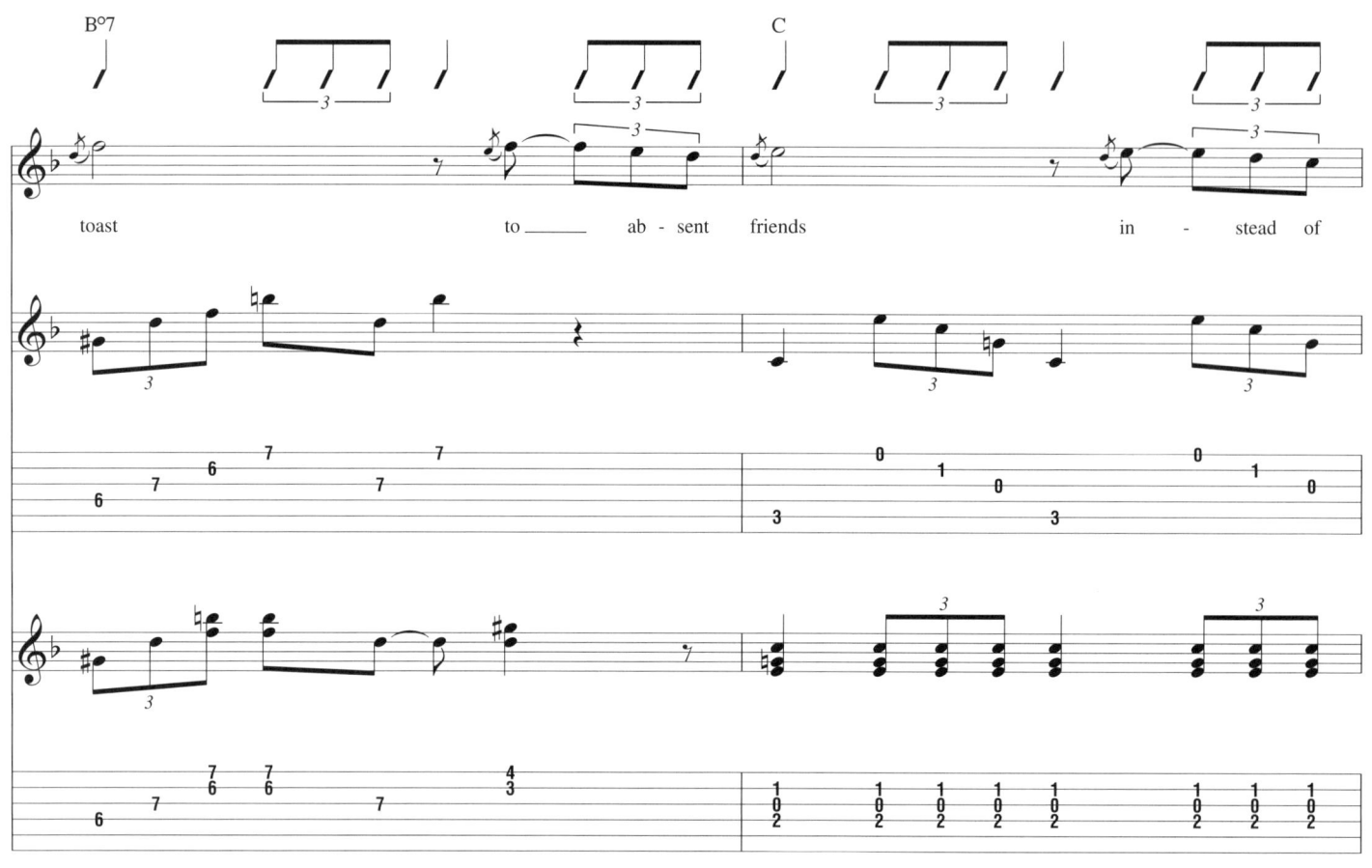

Ooby-Dooby

Words and Music by Wade L. Moore and Richard A. Penner

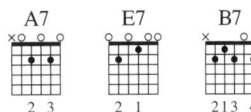

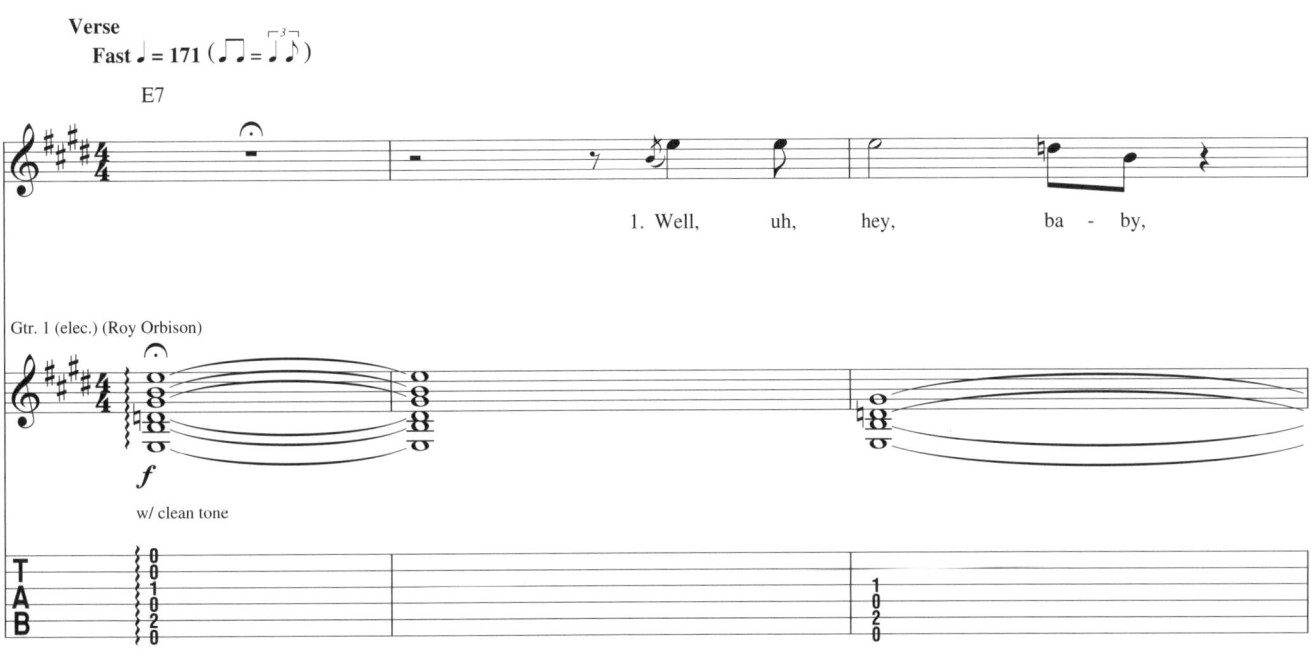

Copyright © 1956 by Peer International Corporation
Copyright Renewed
International Copyright Secured   All Rights Reserved

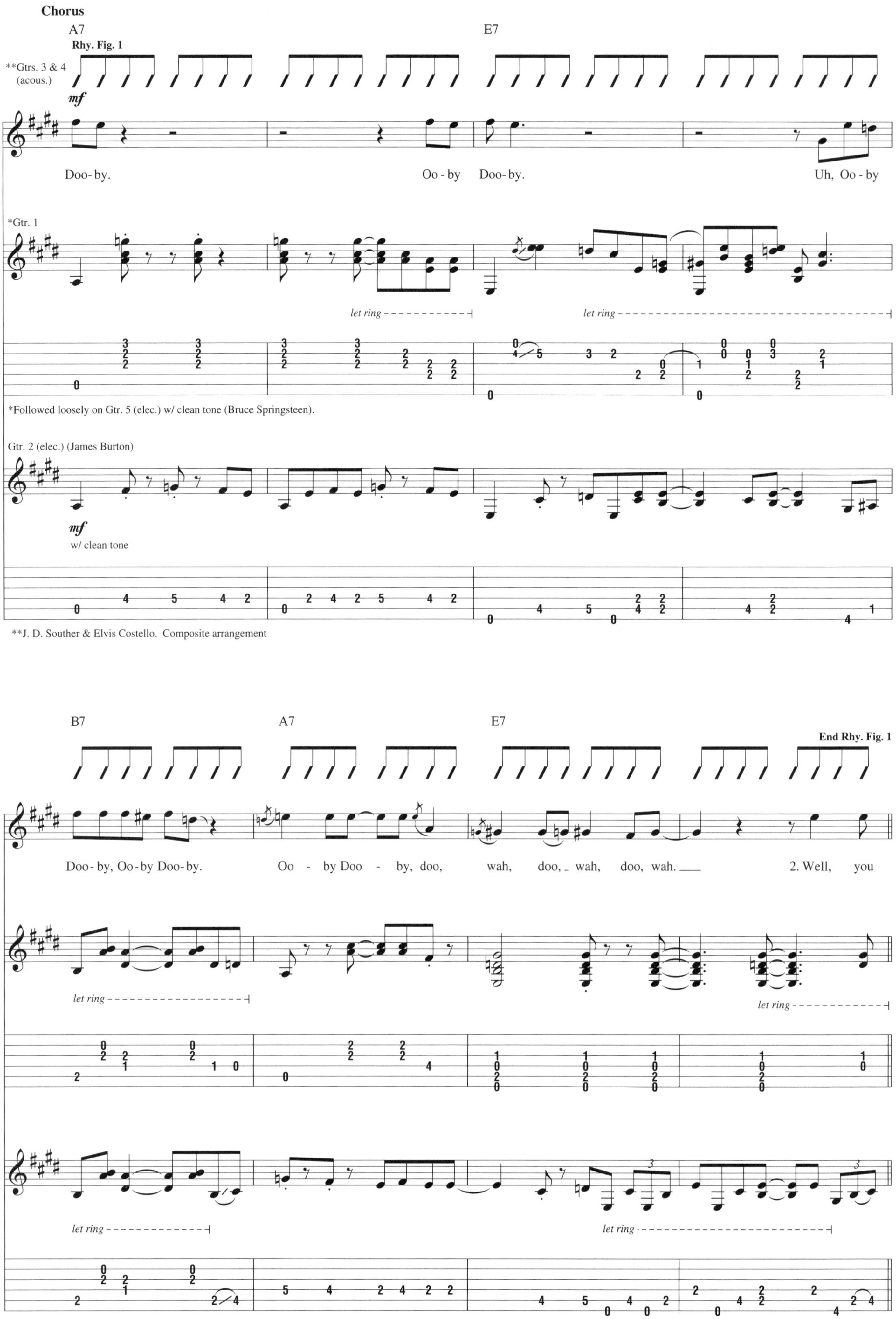
Chorus
A7
E7
Rhy. Fig. 1
**Gtrs. 3 & 4 (acous.)
mf
Doo-by. Oo-by Doo-by. Uh, Oo-by
*Gtr. 1
let ring
let ring
*Followed loosely on Gtr. 5 (elec.) w/ clean tone (Bruce Springsteen).
Gtr. 2 (elec.) (James Burton)
mf
w/ clean tone
**J. D. Souther & Elvis Costello. Composite arrangement
B7
A7
E7
End Rhy. Fig. 1
Doo-by, Oo-by Doo-by. Oo - by Doo - by, doo, wah, doo, wah, doo, wah. 2. Well, you
let ring
let ring
let ring
let ring

Verse

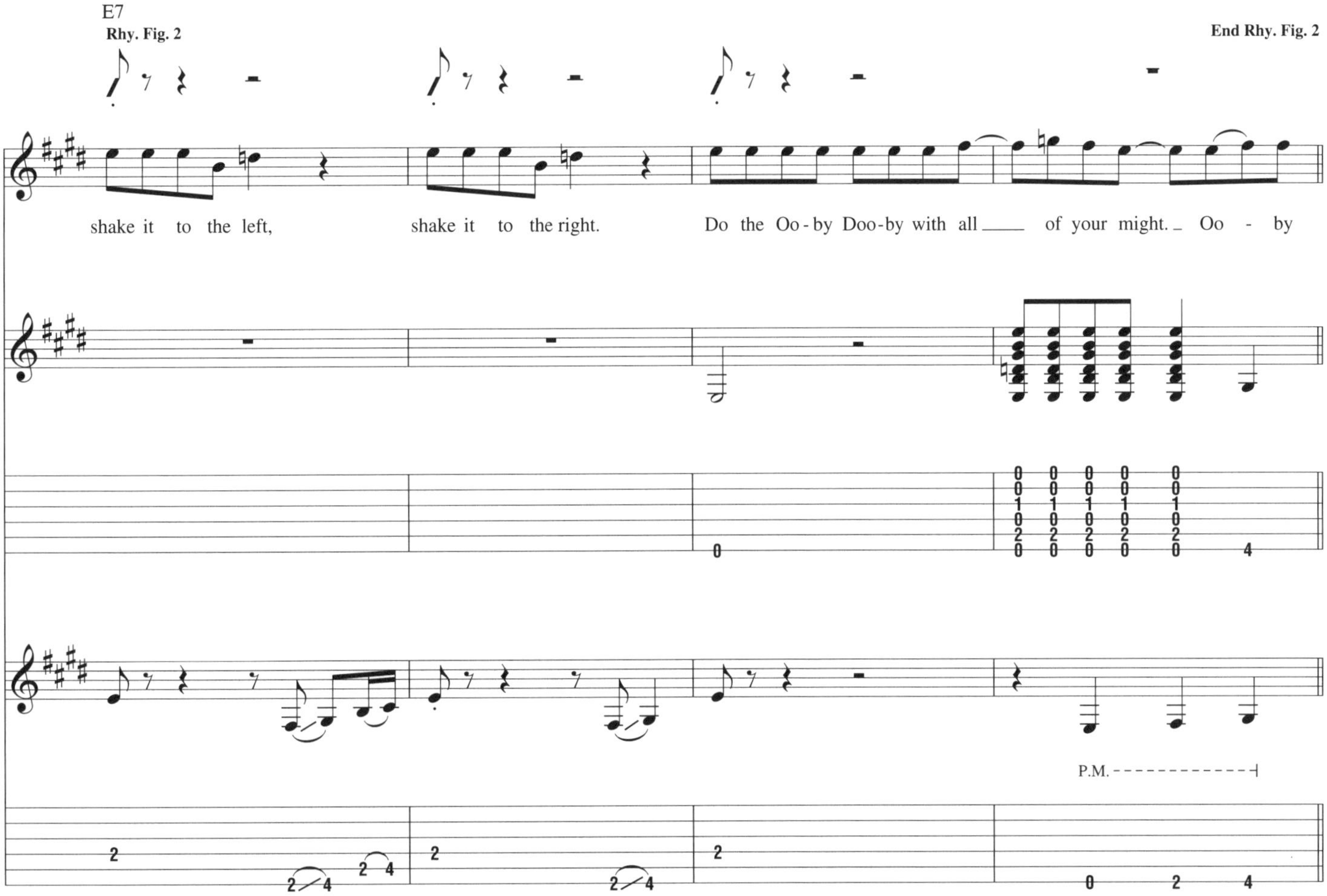
E7
Rhy. Fig. 2
End Rhy. Fig. 2
shake it to the left, shake it to the right. Do the Oo-by Doo-by with all ___ of your might. _ Oo - by
P.M.

Chorus

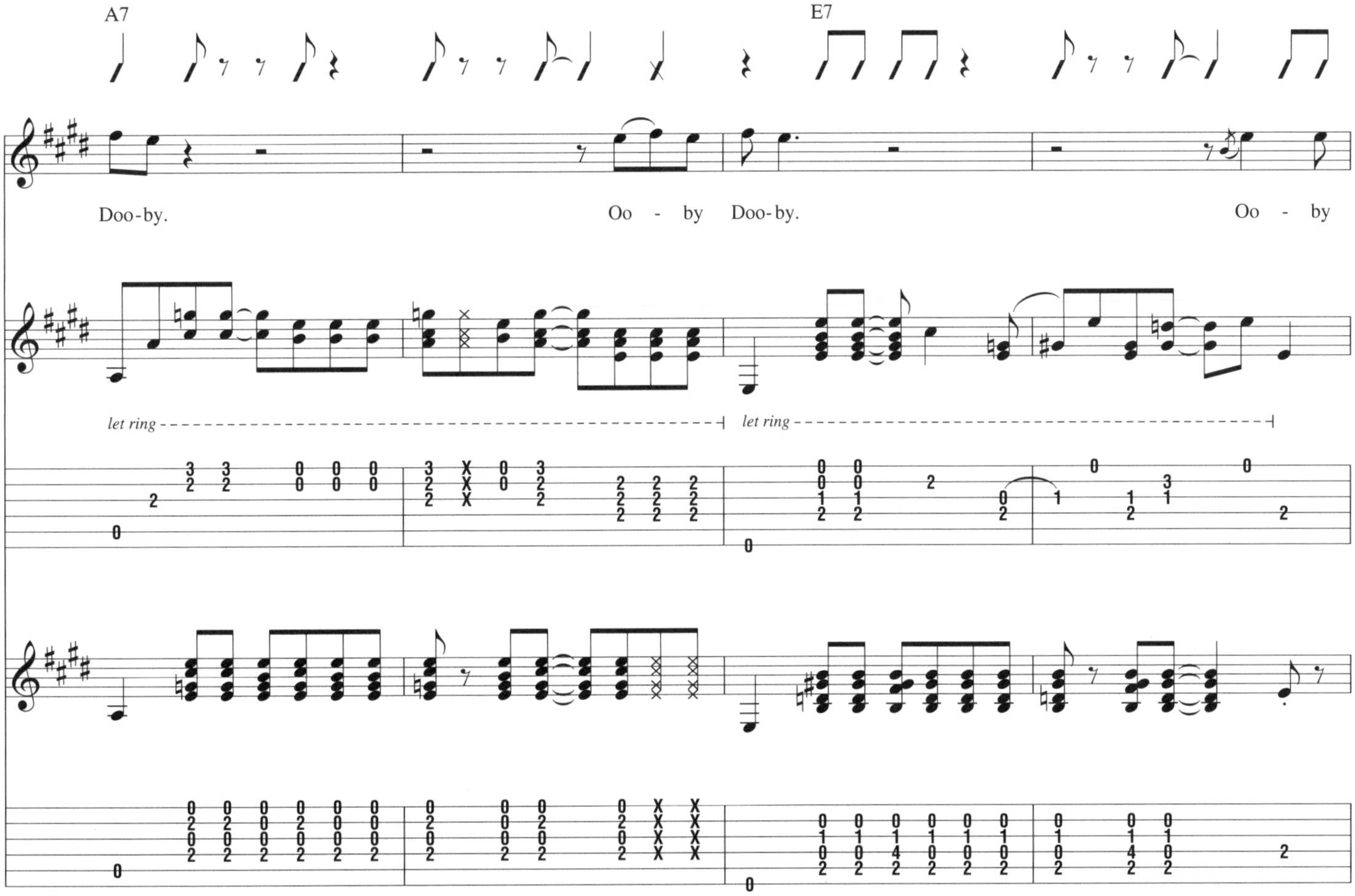
A7
E7
Doo-by. Oo - by Doo-by. Oo - by
let ring
let ring

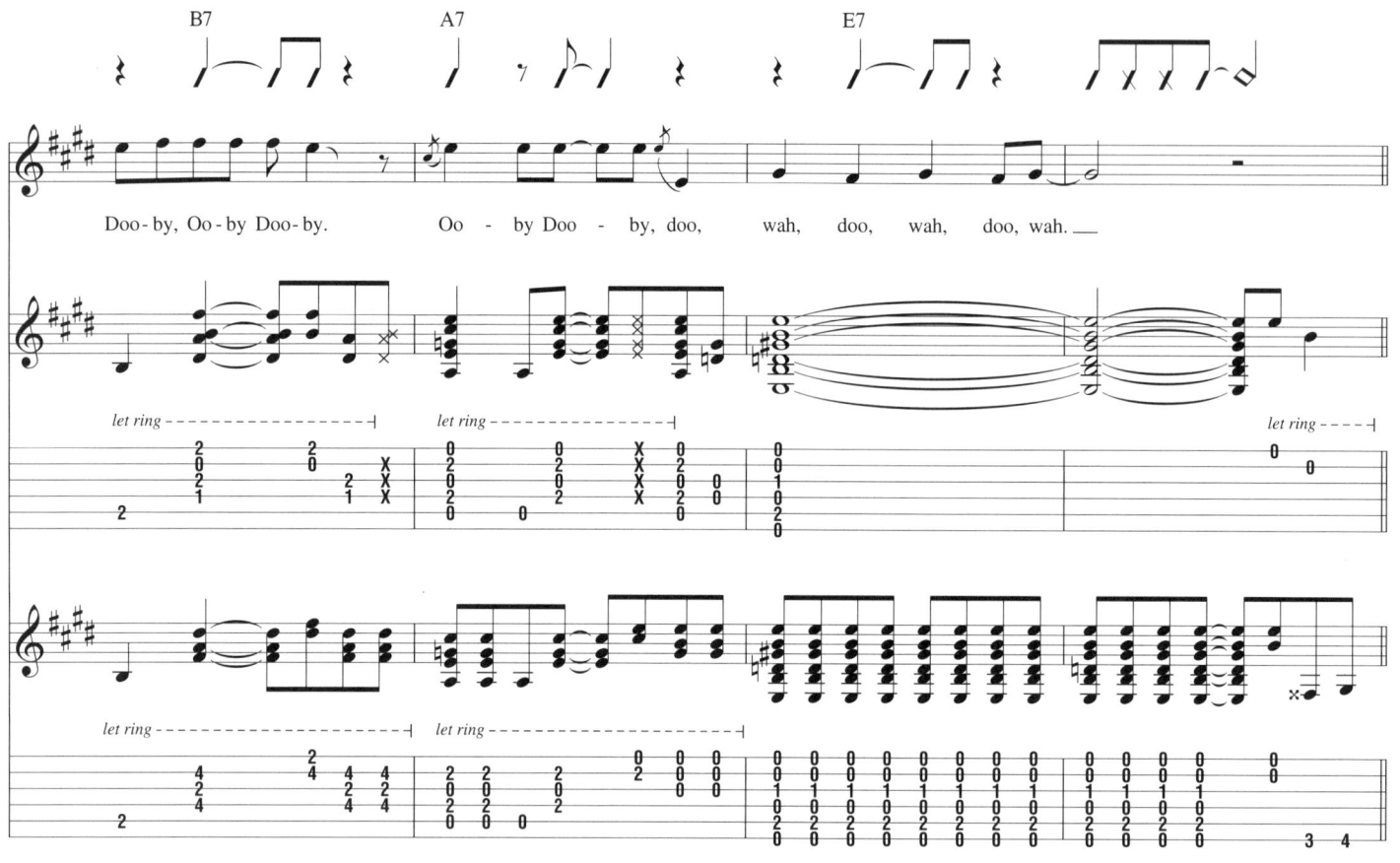

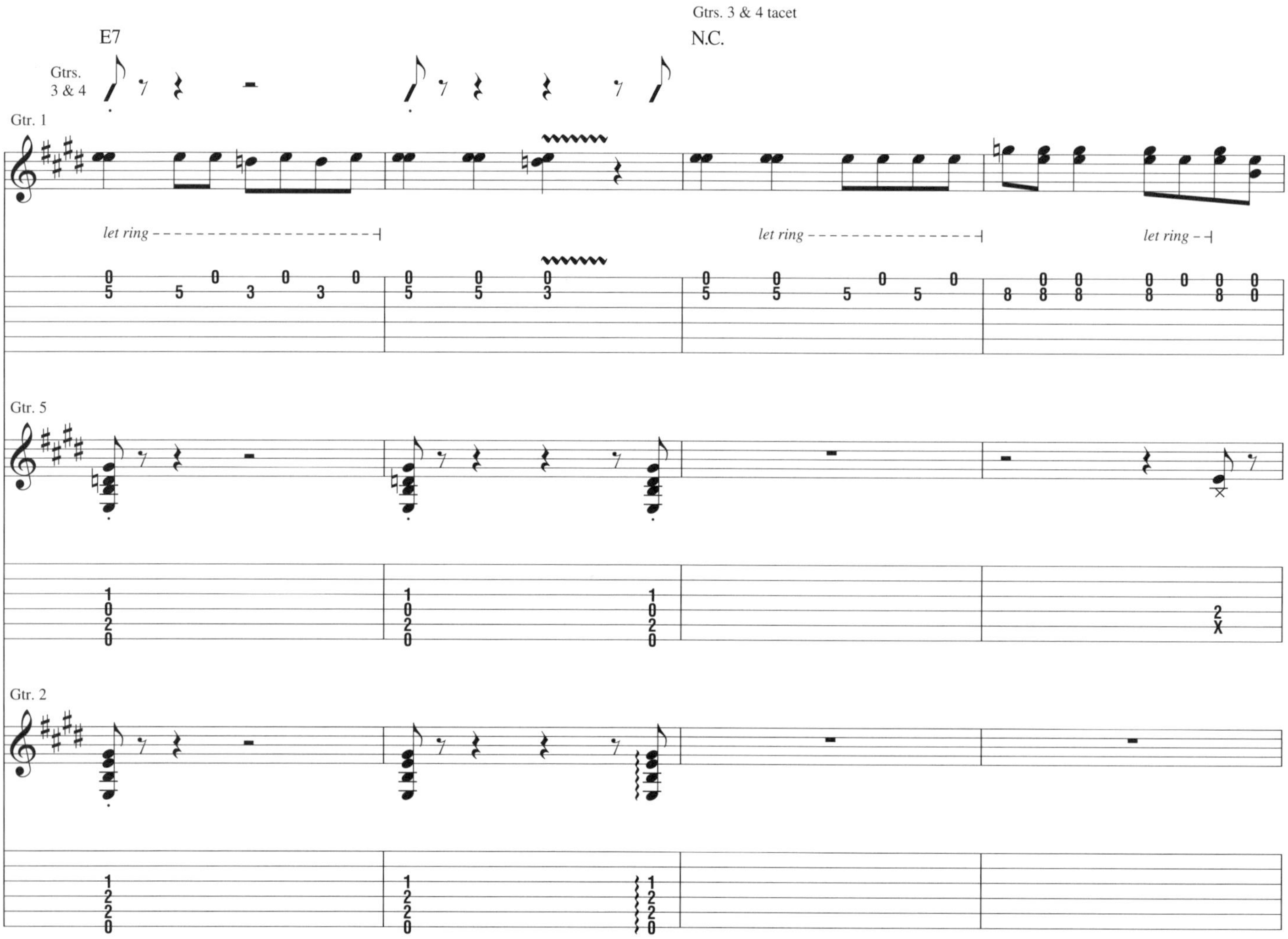

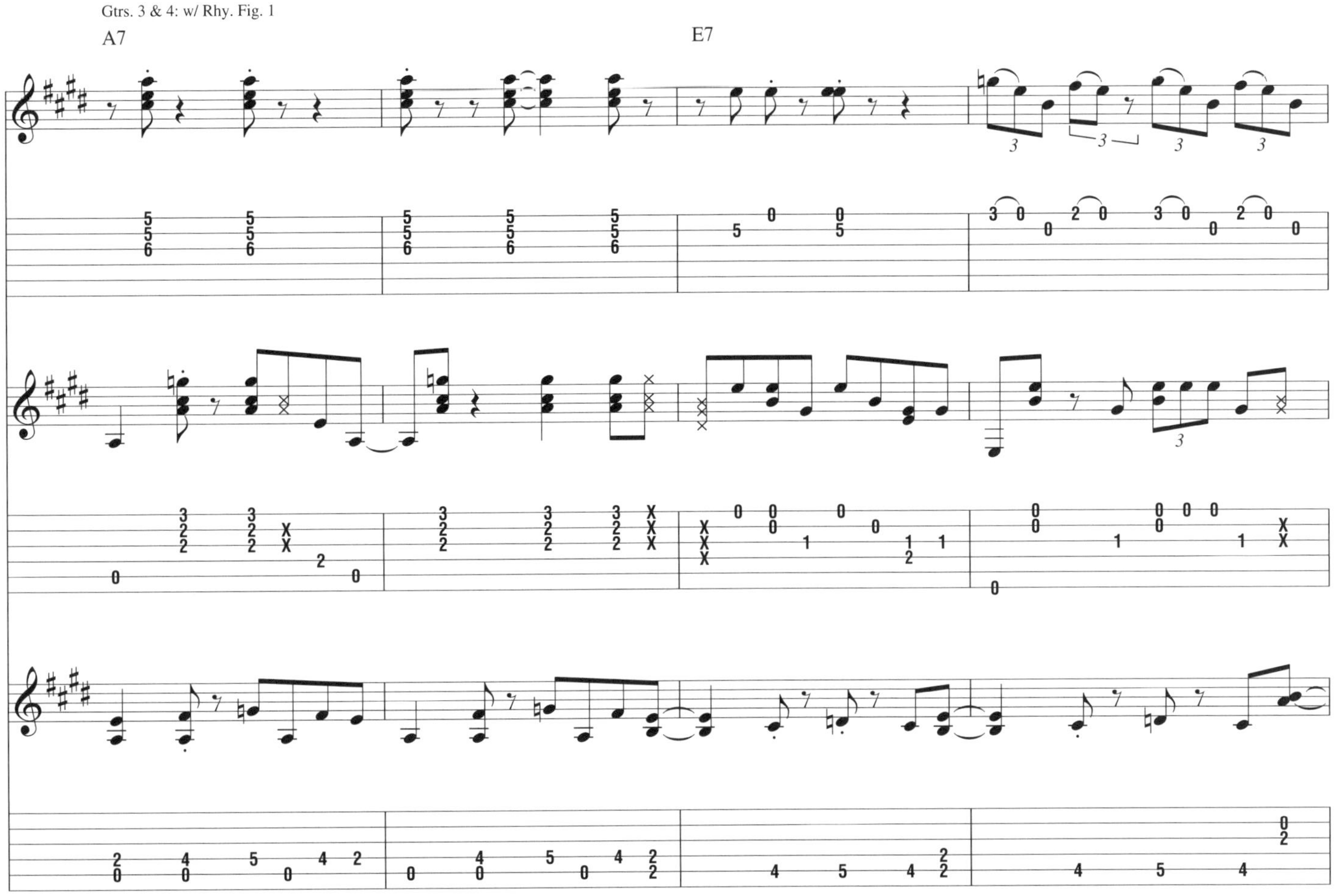
Gtrs. 3 & 4: w/ Rhy. Fig. 1
A7
E7

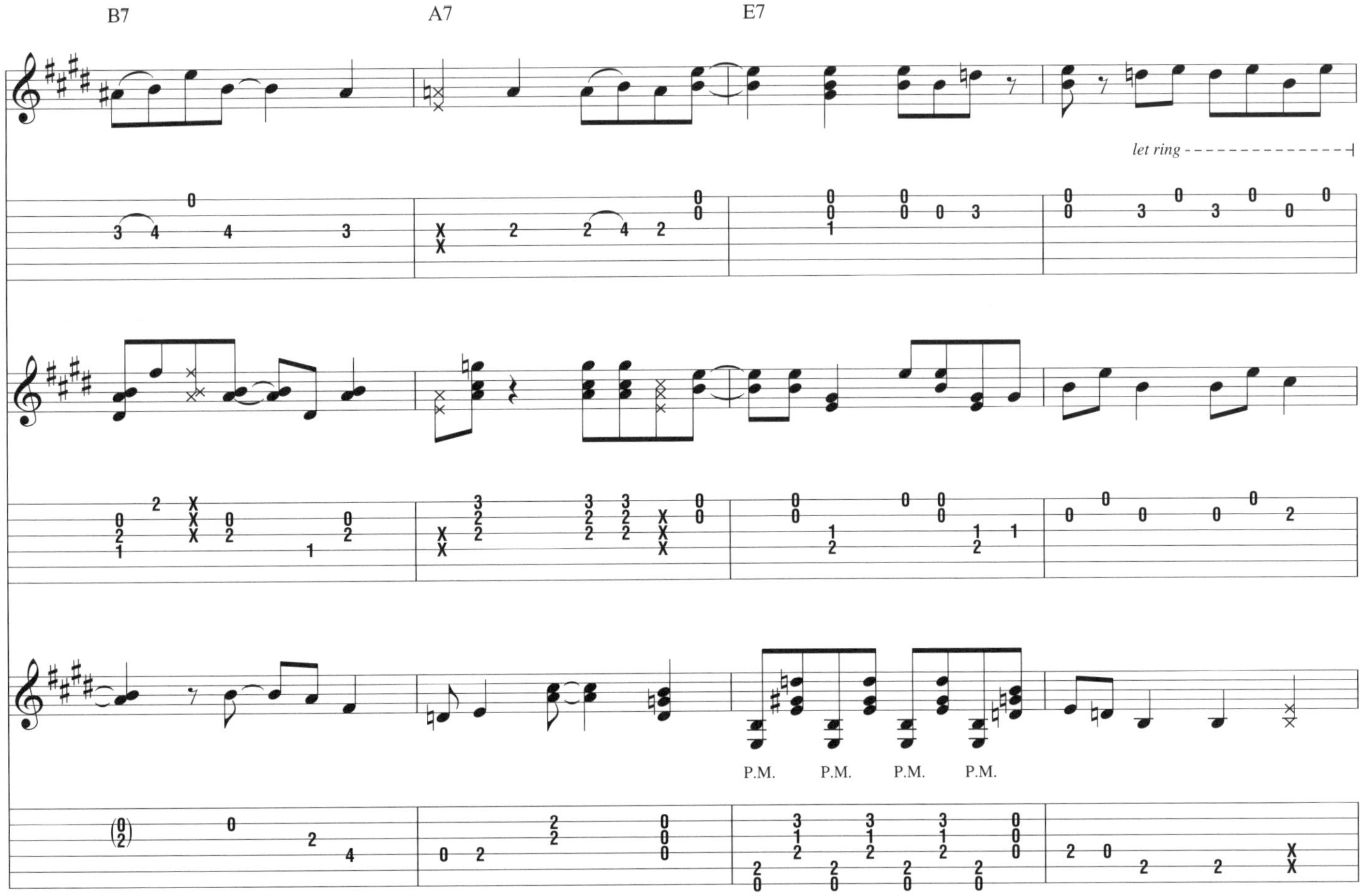
B7
A7
E7
let ring
P.M.
P.M.
P.M.
P.M.

Gtrs. 3 & 4: w/ Rhy. Fig. 2
E7 N.C.
E7 N.C.
E7 N.C.
1/4
let ring

Gtrs. 3 & 4: w/ Rhy. Fig. 1
A7
E7

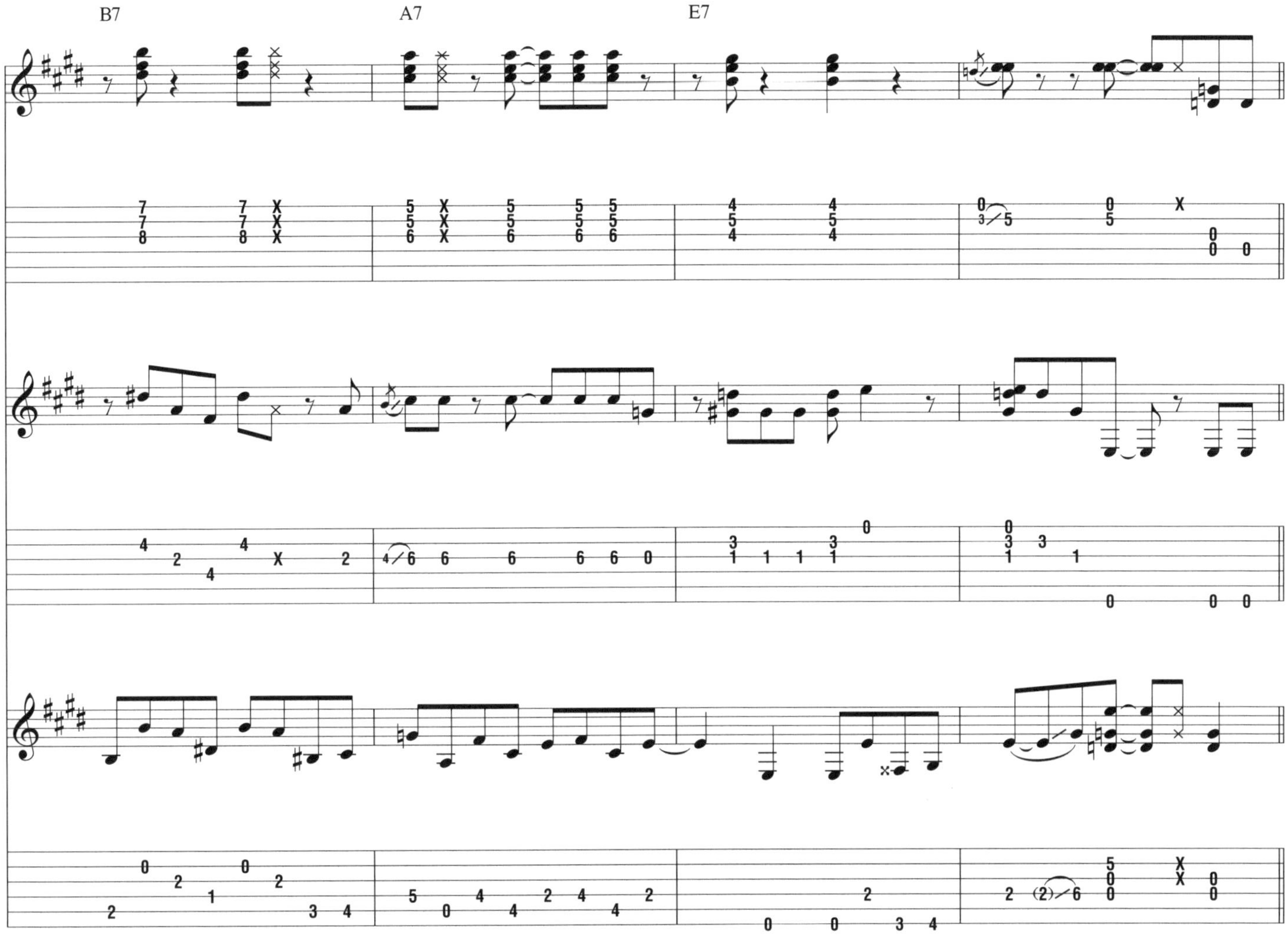

Guitar Solo

*Composite arrangement

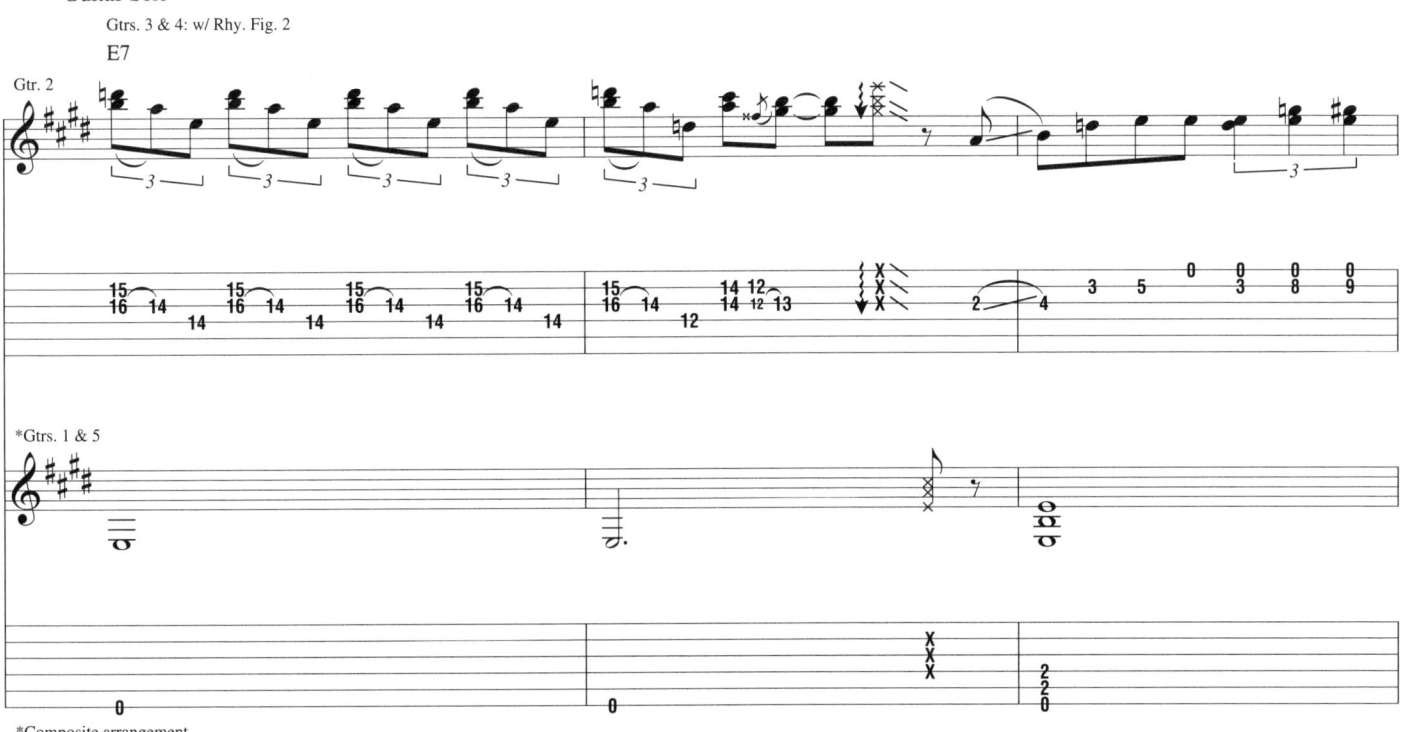

Verse

Chorus

B7 A7 E7
Doo-by, Oo-by Doo-by. Doo - by, doo - by, doo, wah, doo, wah, doo, wah.
let ring
let ring
let ring
let ring
let ring

Guitar Solo

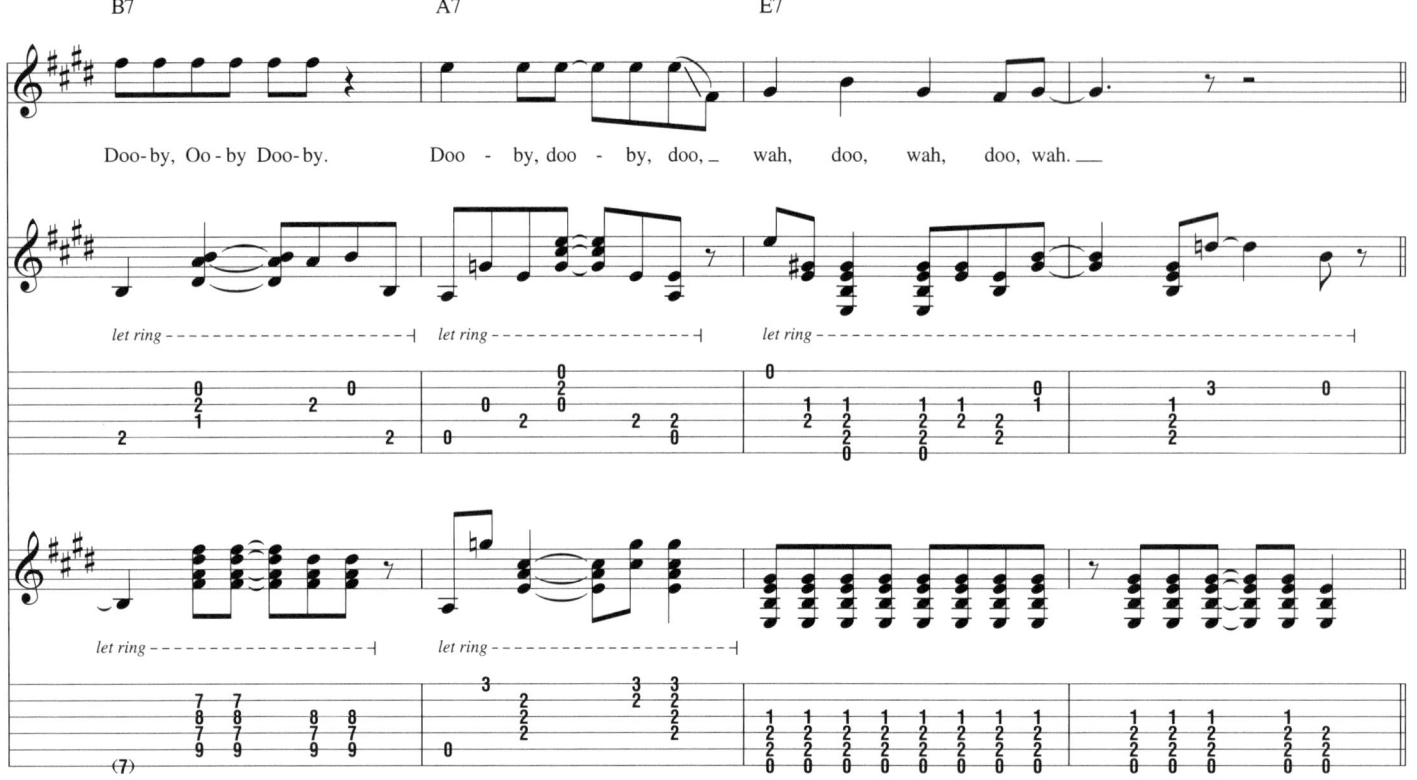

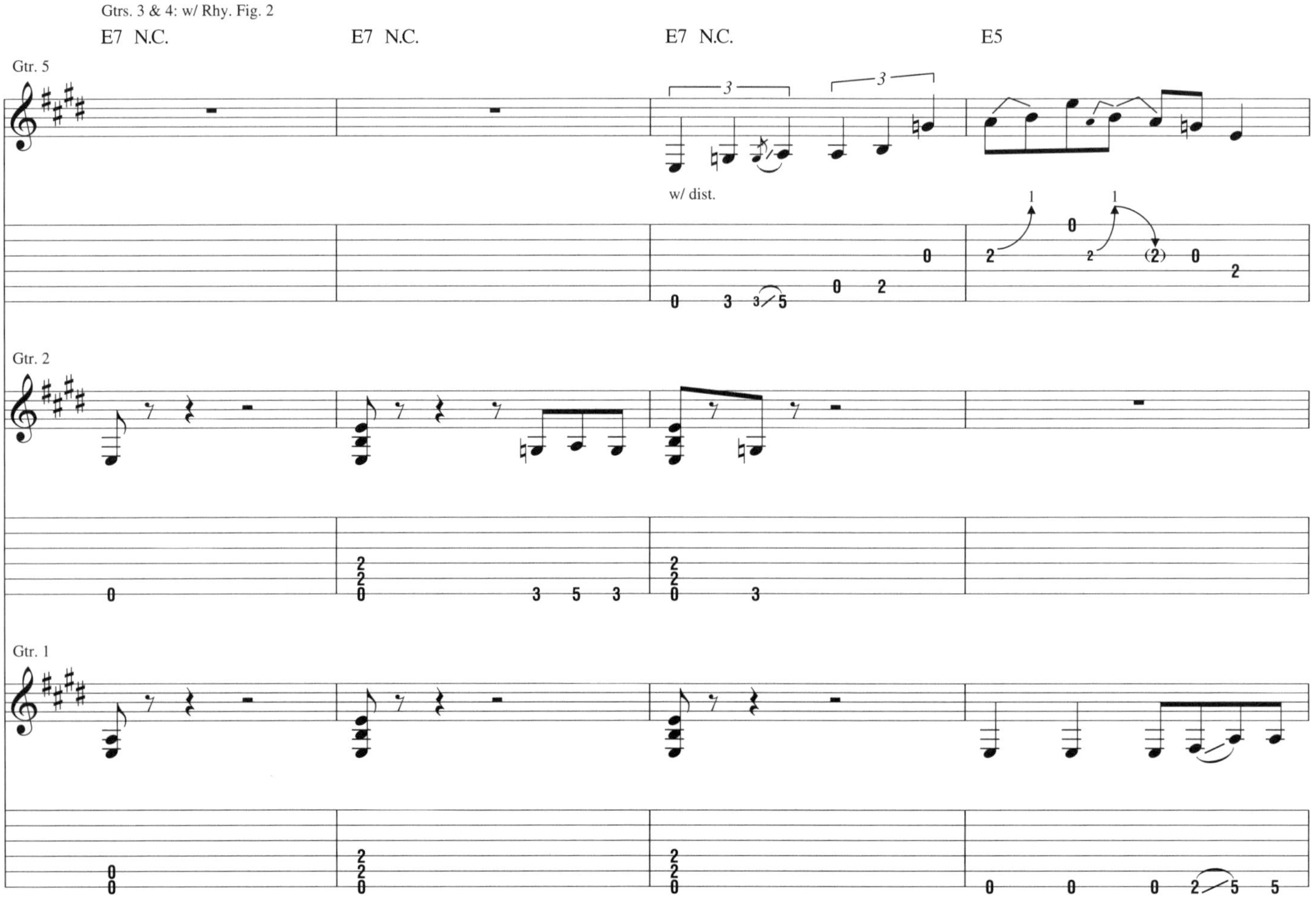
Gtrs. 3 & 4: w/ Rhy. Fig. 2
E7 N.C. E7 N.C. E7 N.C. E5
Gtr. 5
w/ dist.
Gtr. 2
Gtr. 1

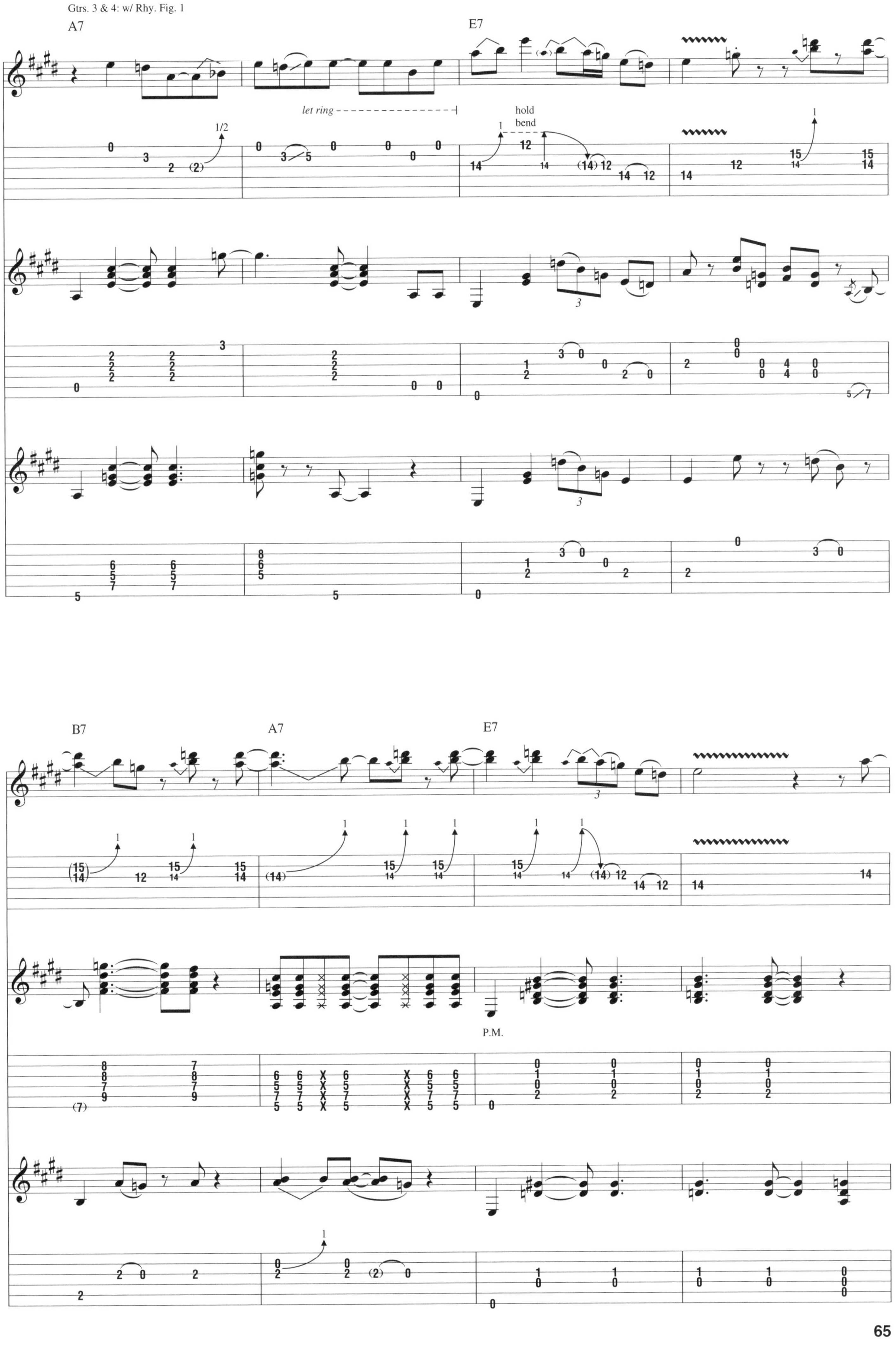
Gtrs. 3 & 4: w/ Rhy. Fig. 1
A7
E7
let ring
hold bend
B7
A7
E7
P.M.

Gtrs. 3 & 4: w/ Rhy. Fig. 2
E7 N.C.
E7 N.C.
E7 N.C.
E7♯9
hold bend
P.M.
*Played as even eighth-notes.

Gtrs. 3 & 4: w/ Rhy. Fig. 1
A7
E7
slight P.M.

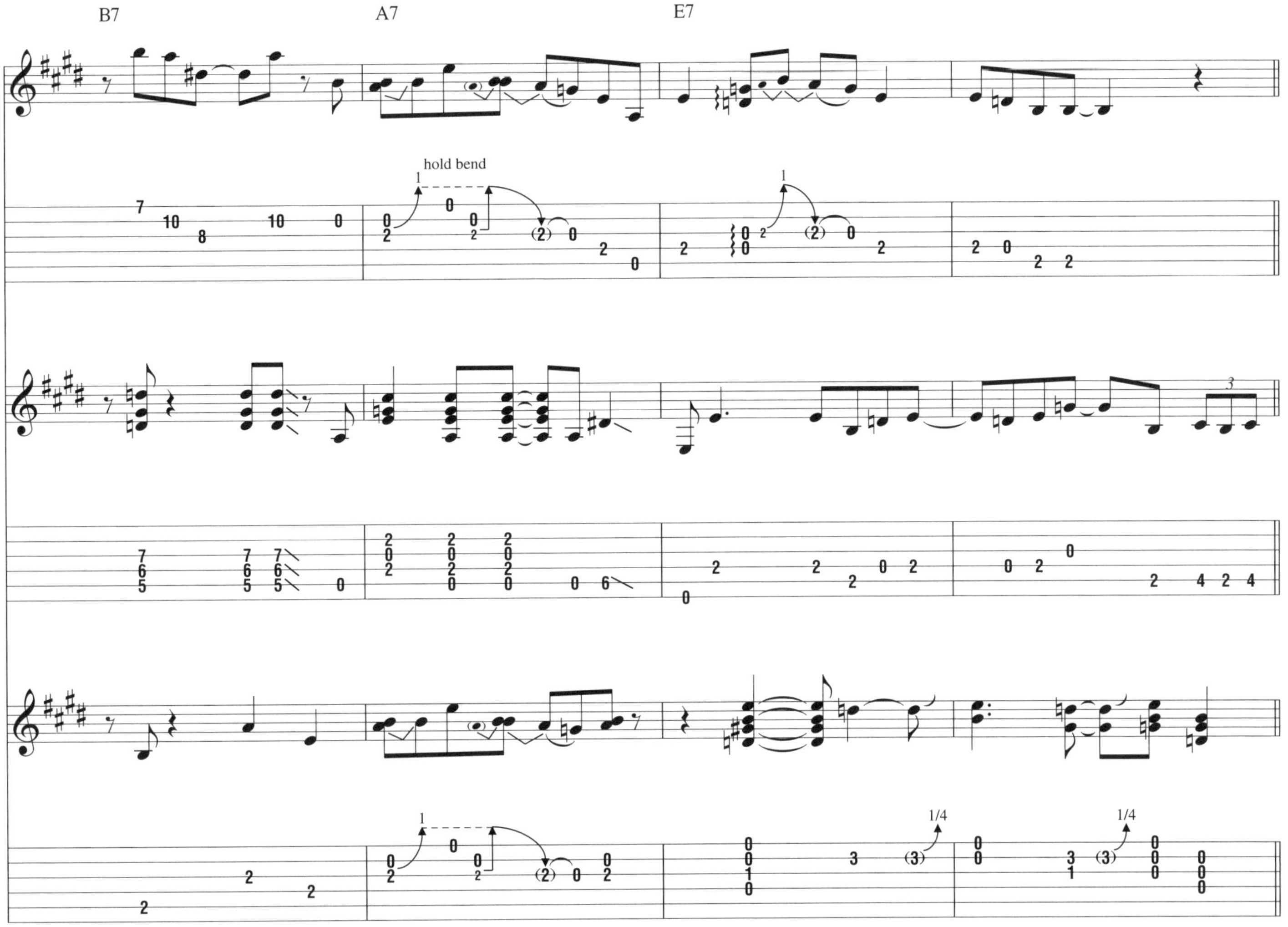

Organ Solo

*Composite arrangement

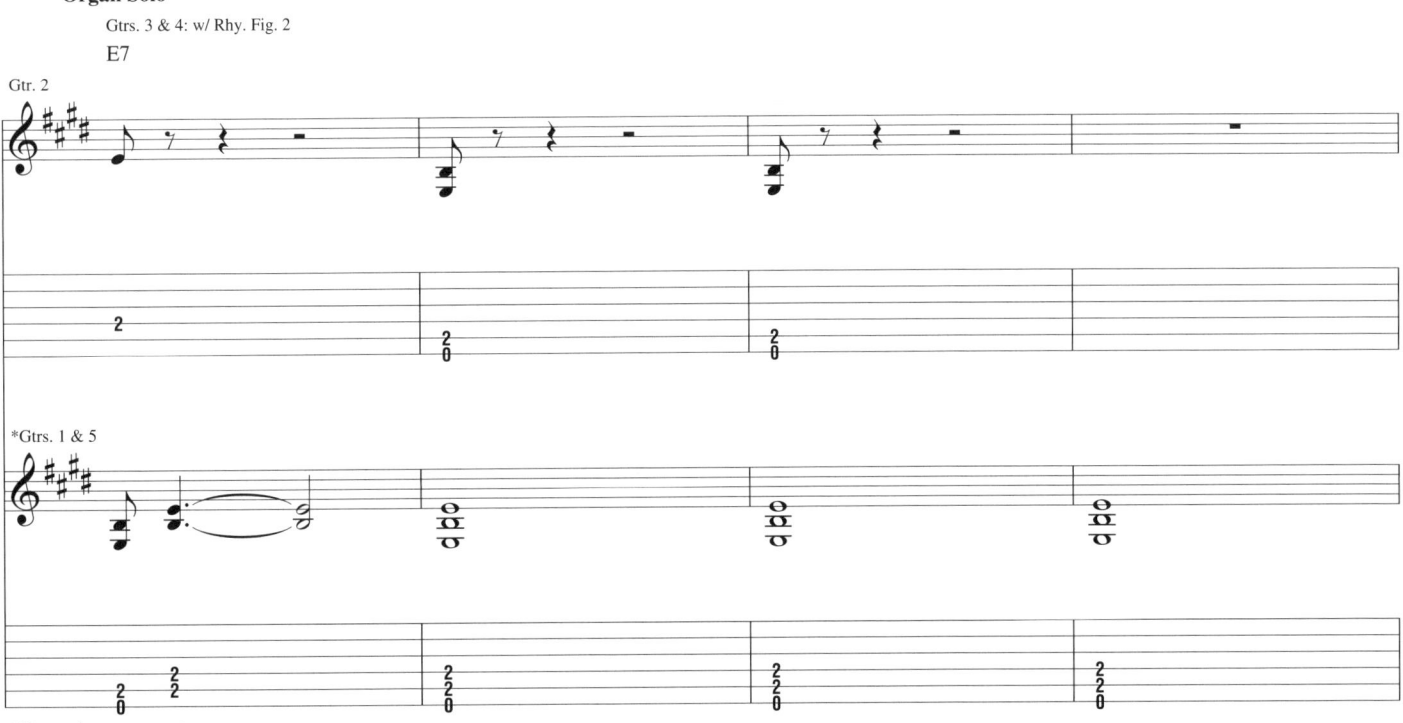

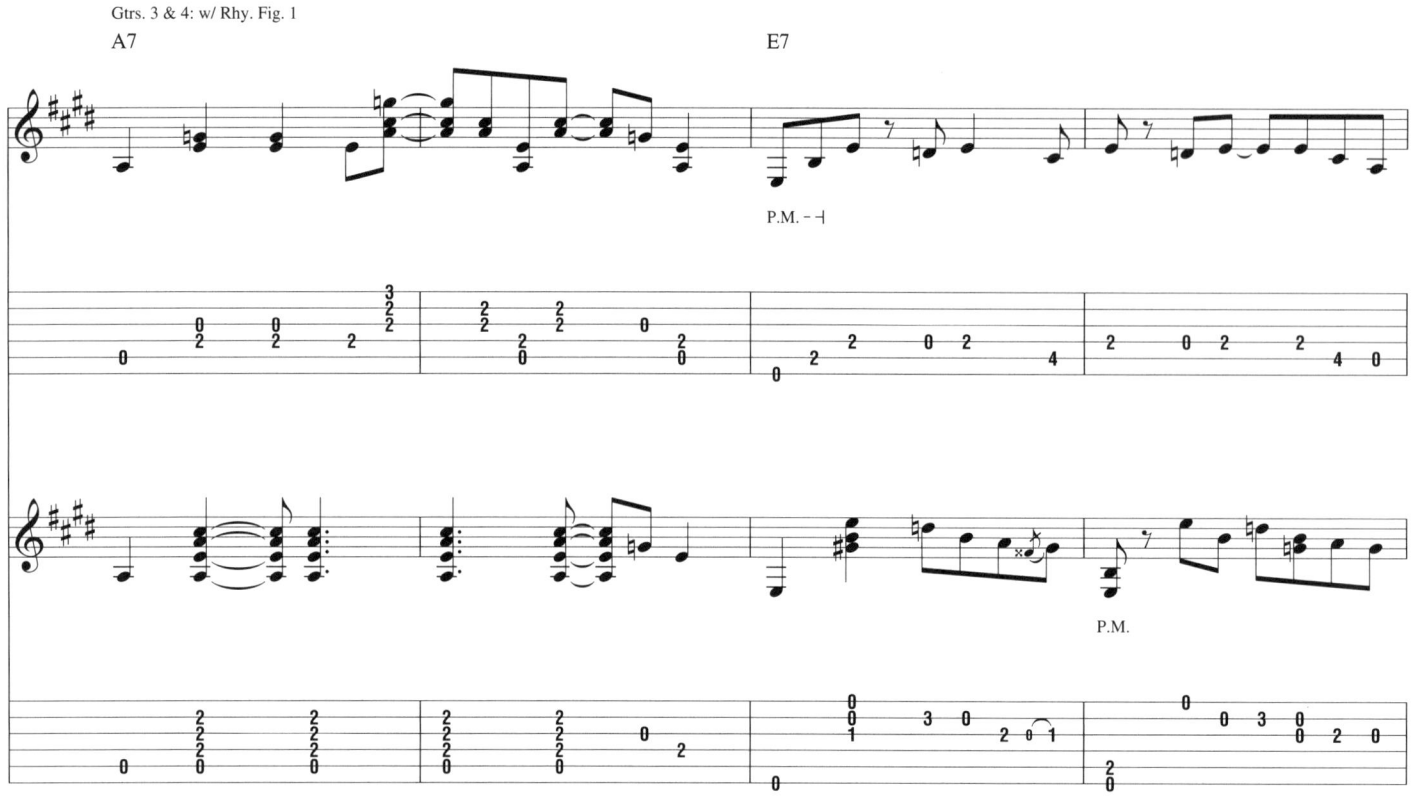

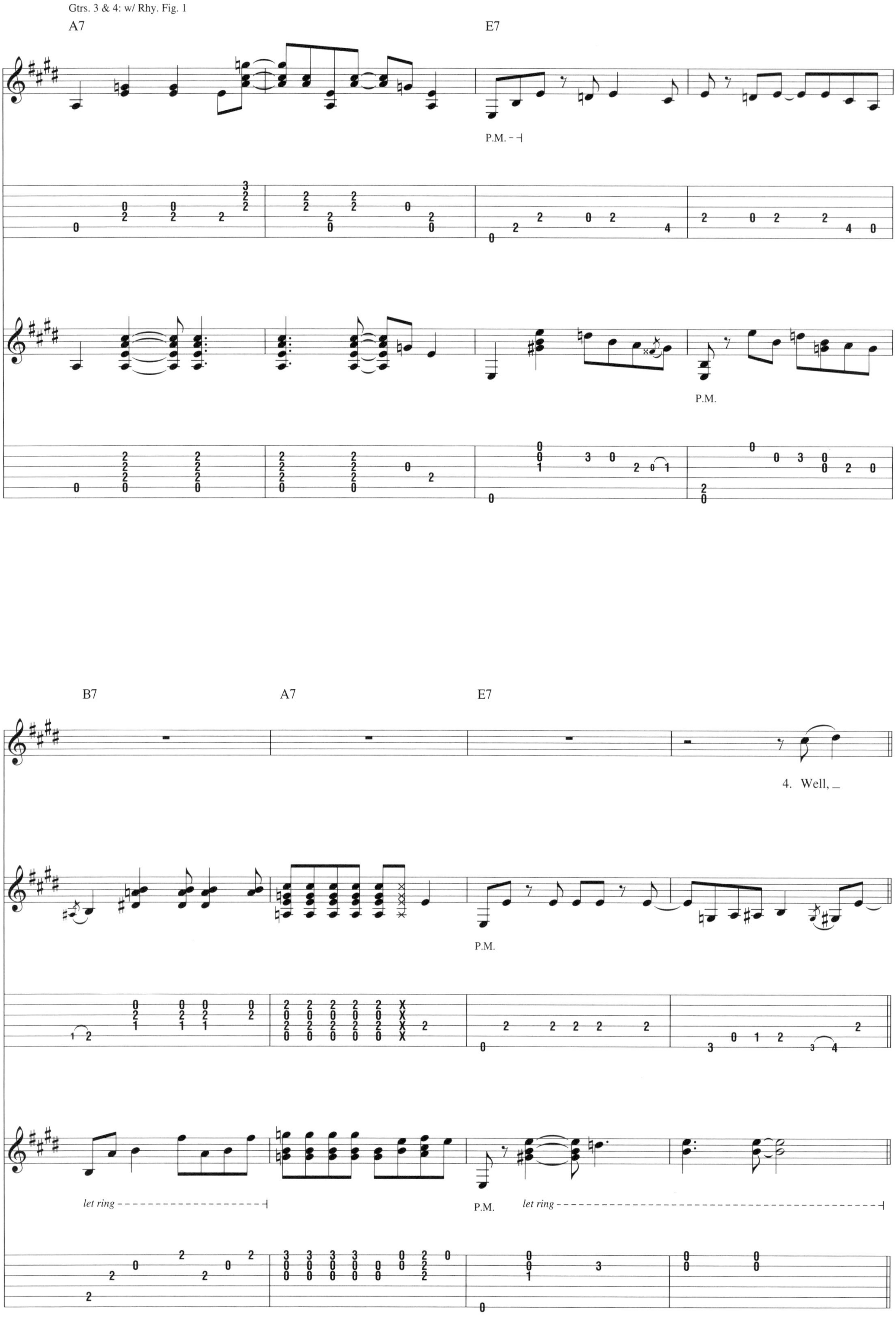
Gtrs. 3 & 4: w/ Rhy. Fig. 1
A7
E7
P.M.
P.M.
B7
A7
E7
4. Well, _
P.M.
let ring
P.M.
let ring

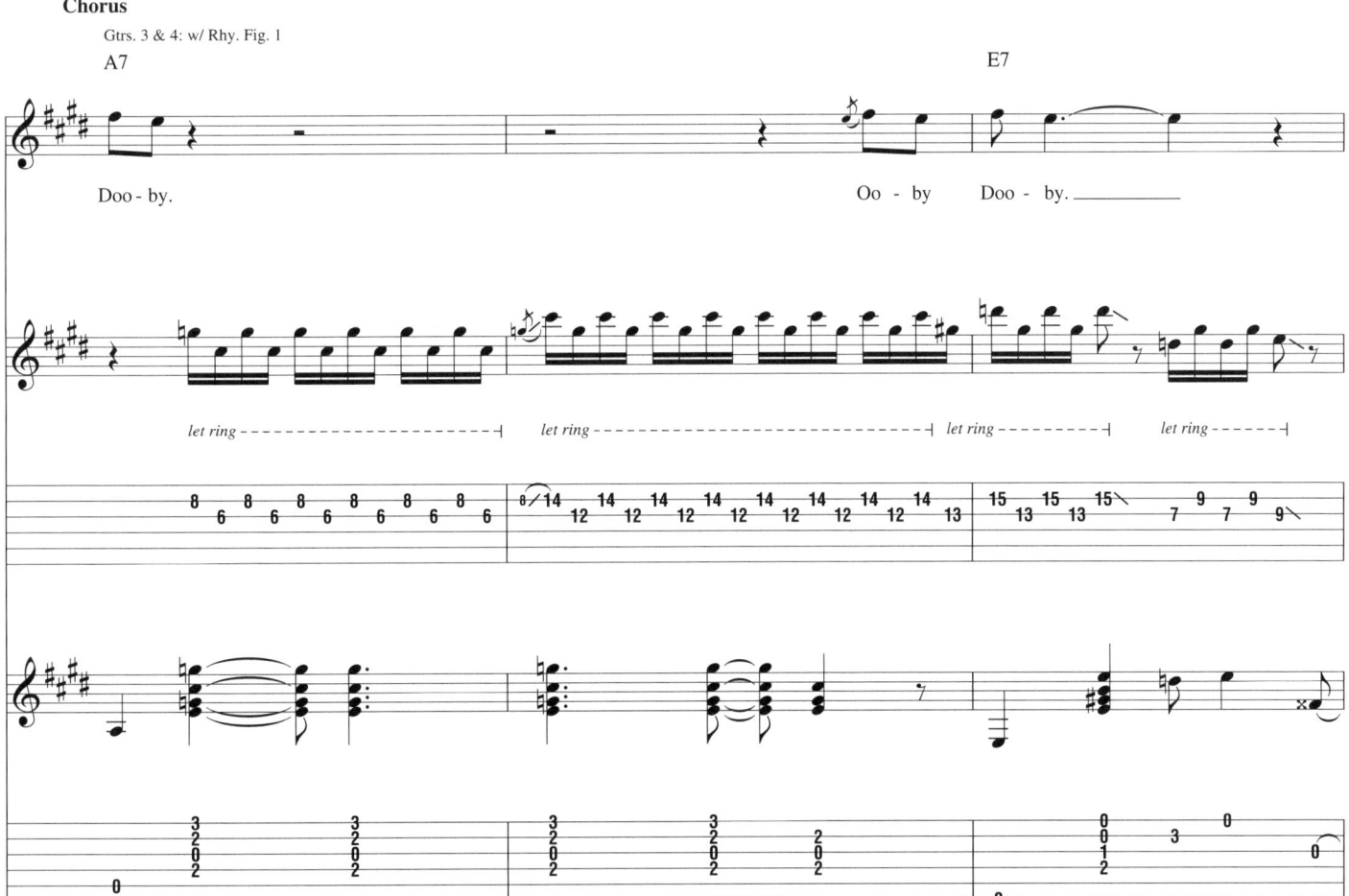

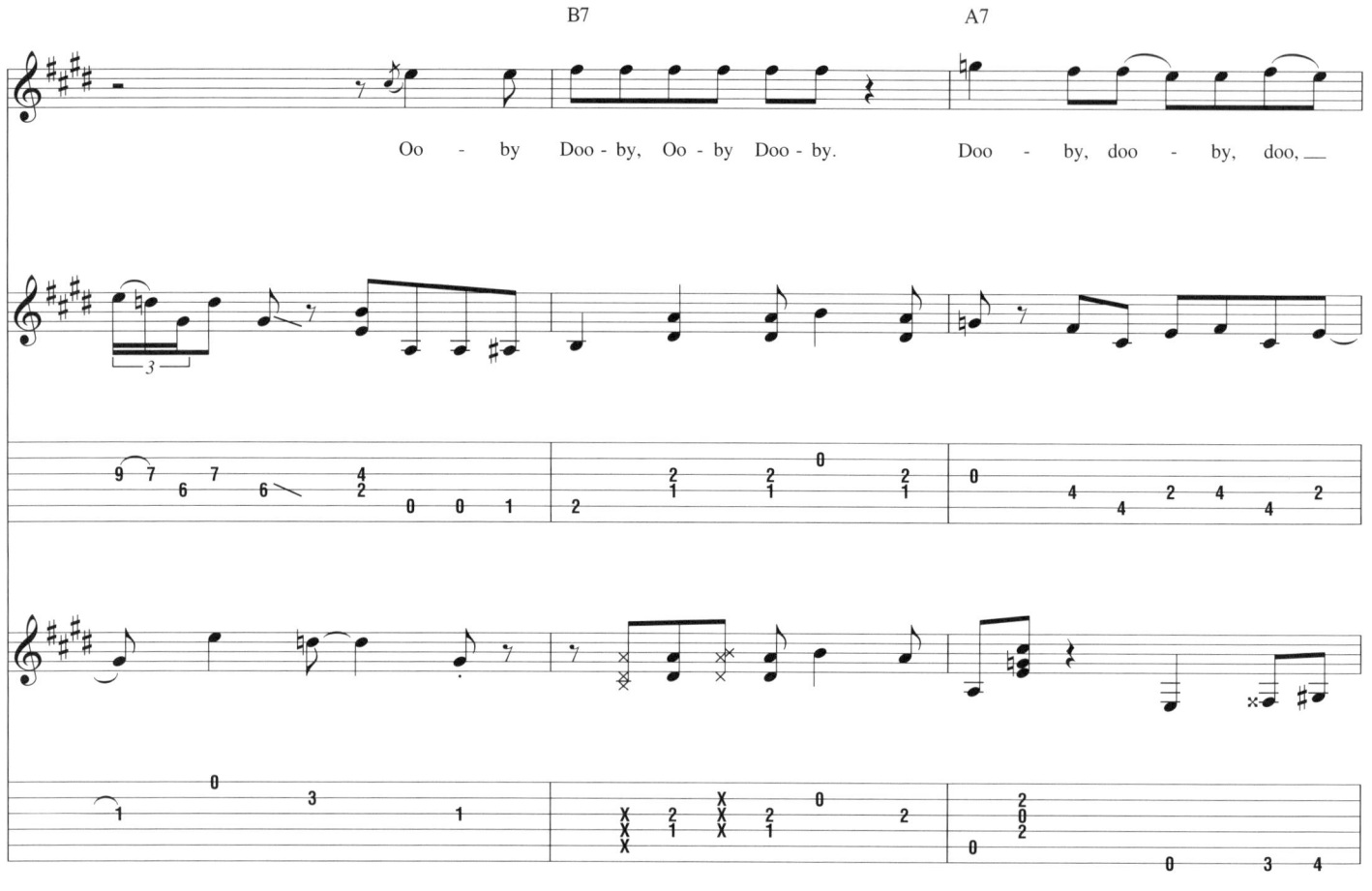

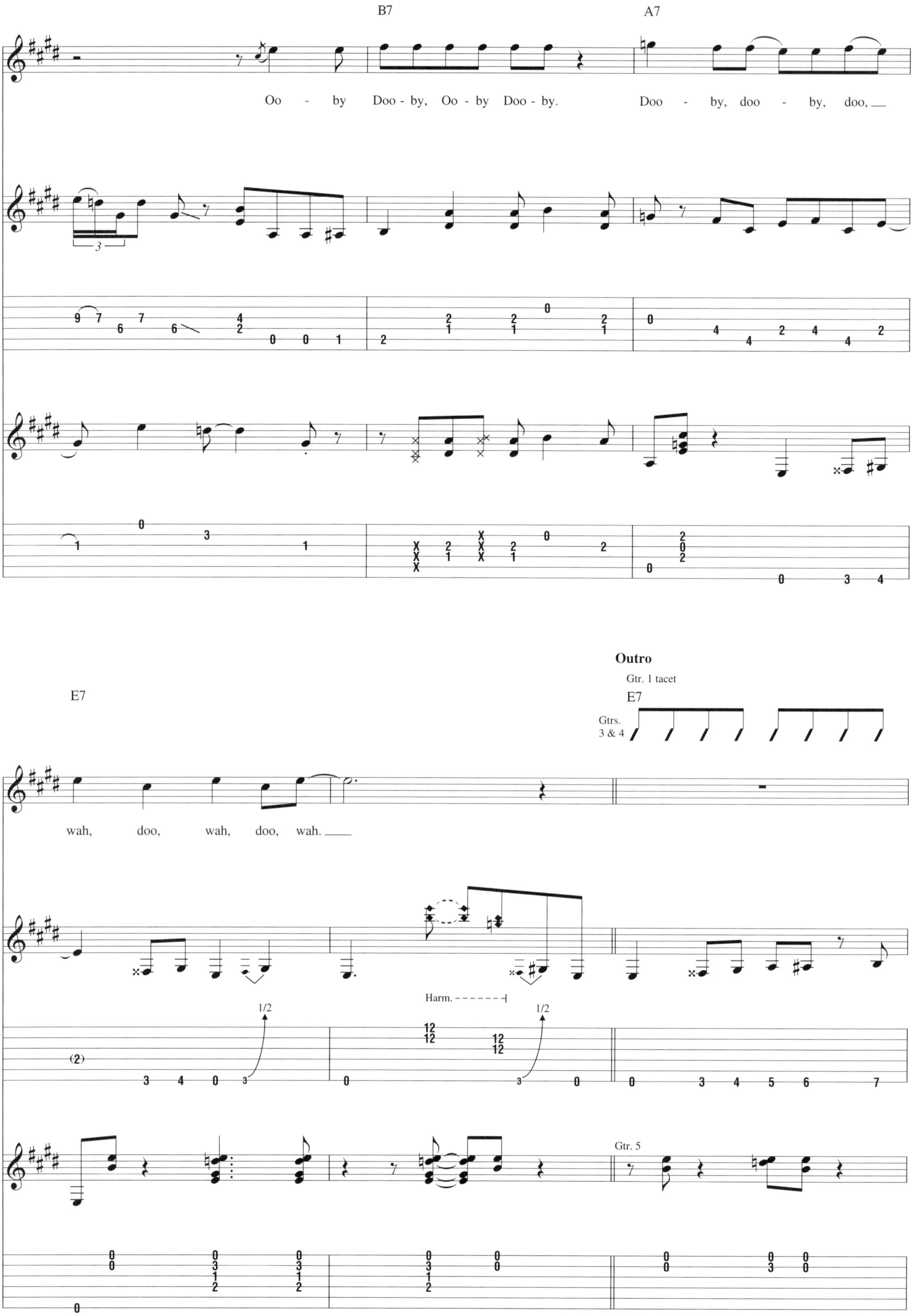
B7
A7
Oo - by Doo - by, Oo - by Doo - by.
Doo - by, doo - by, doo,
E7
wah, doo, wah, doo, wah.
Outro
Gtr. 1 tacet
E7
Gtrs. 3 & 4
Harm.
1/2
Gtr. 5

Free time
Gtr. 2
Gtr. 5
Gtr. 1
Gtr. 5 tacet
steady gliss.

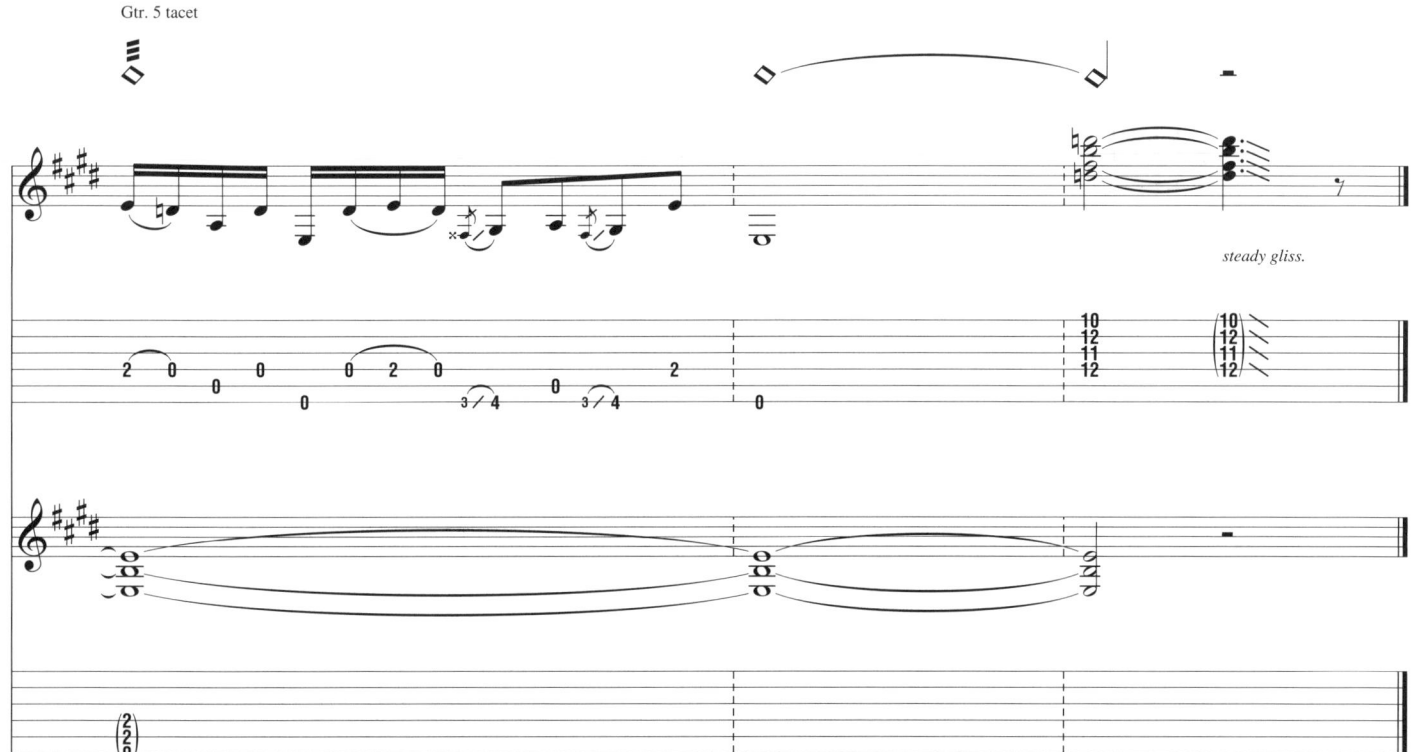

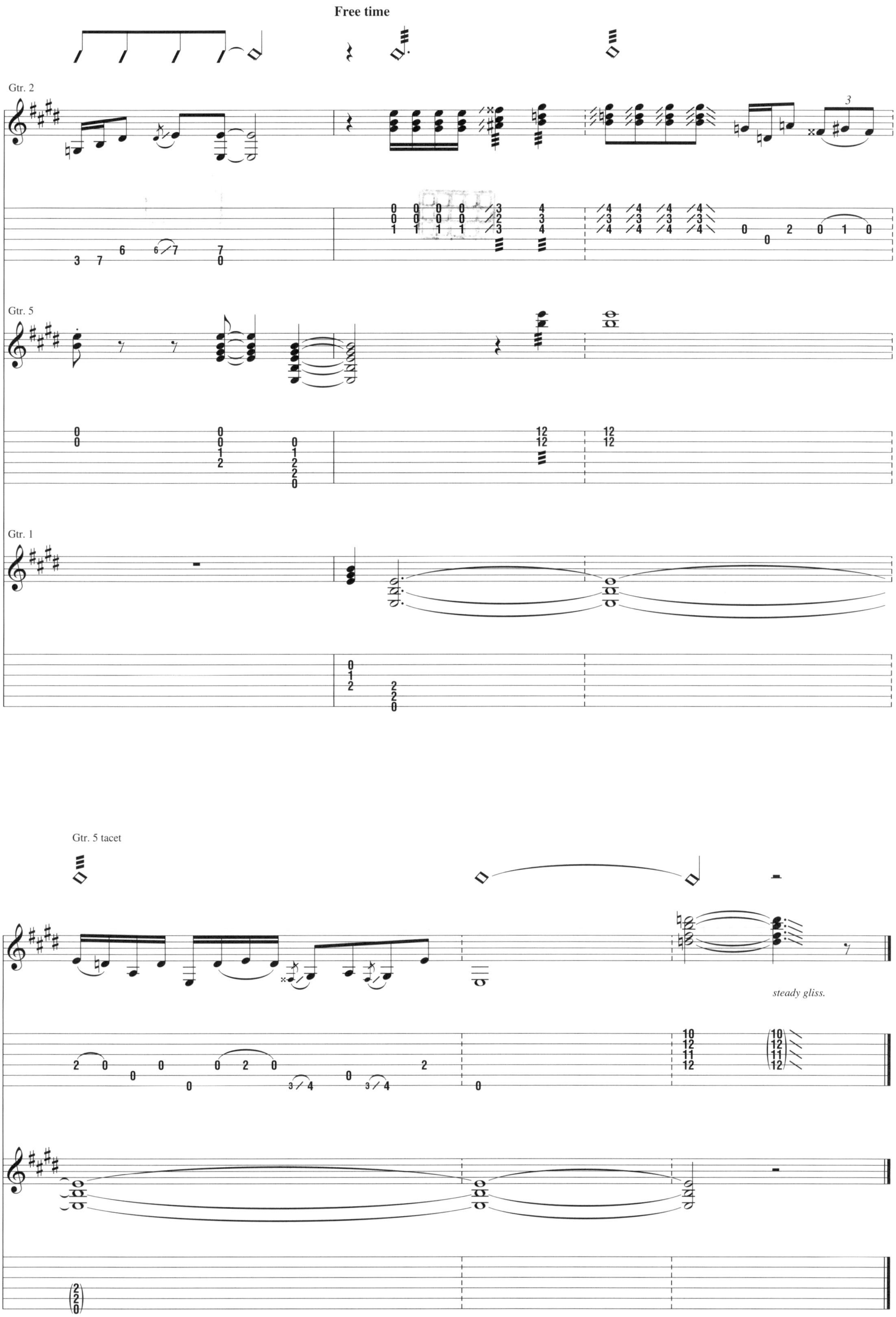

Leah

Words and Music by Roy Orbison

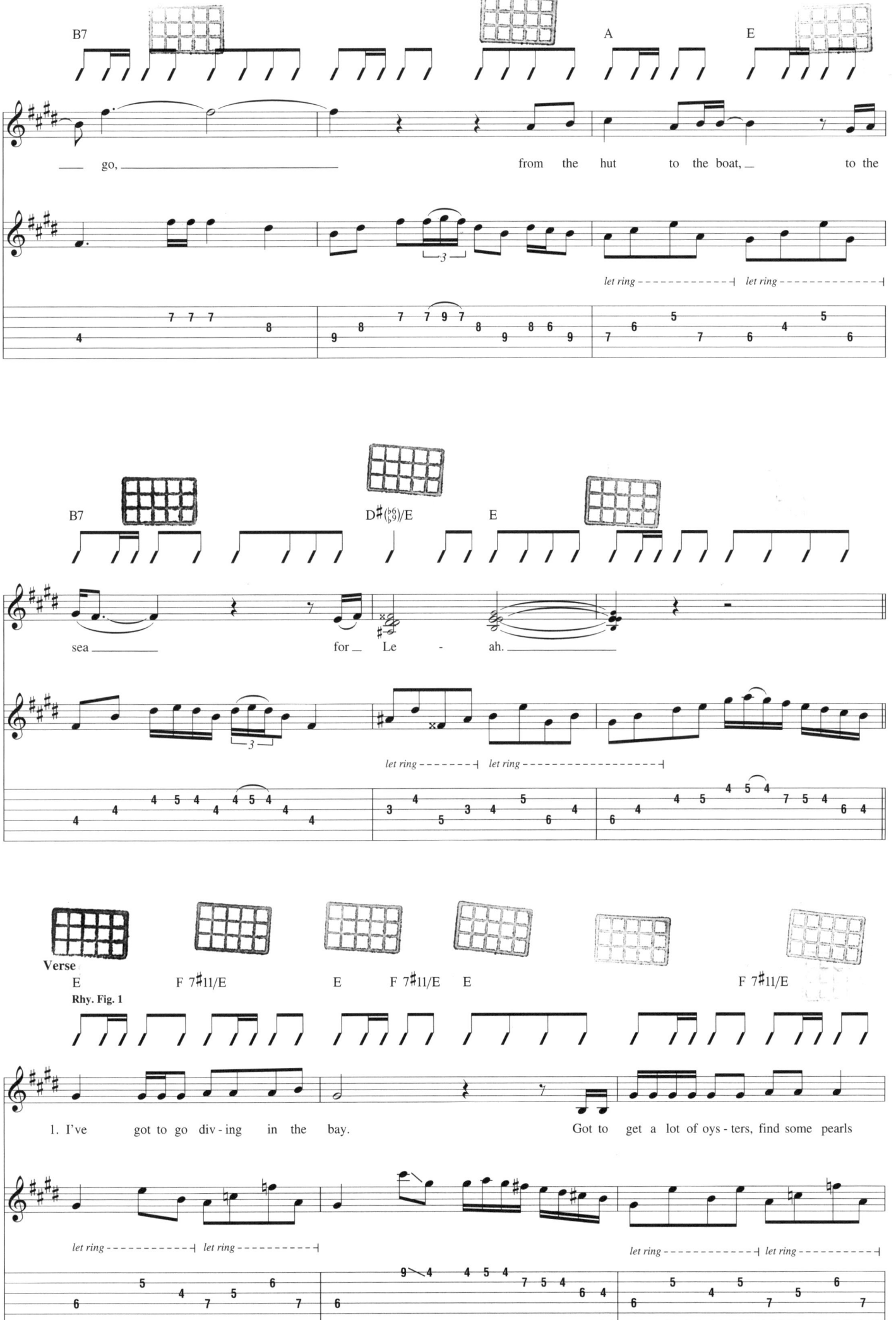

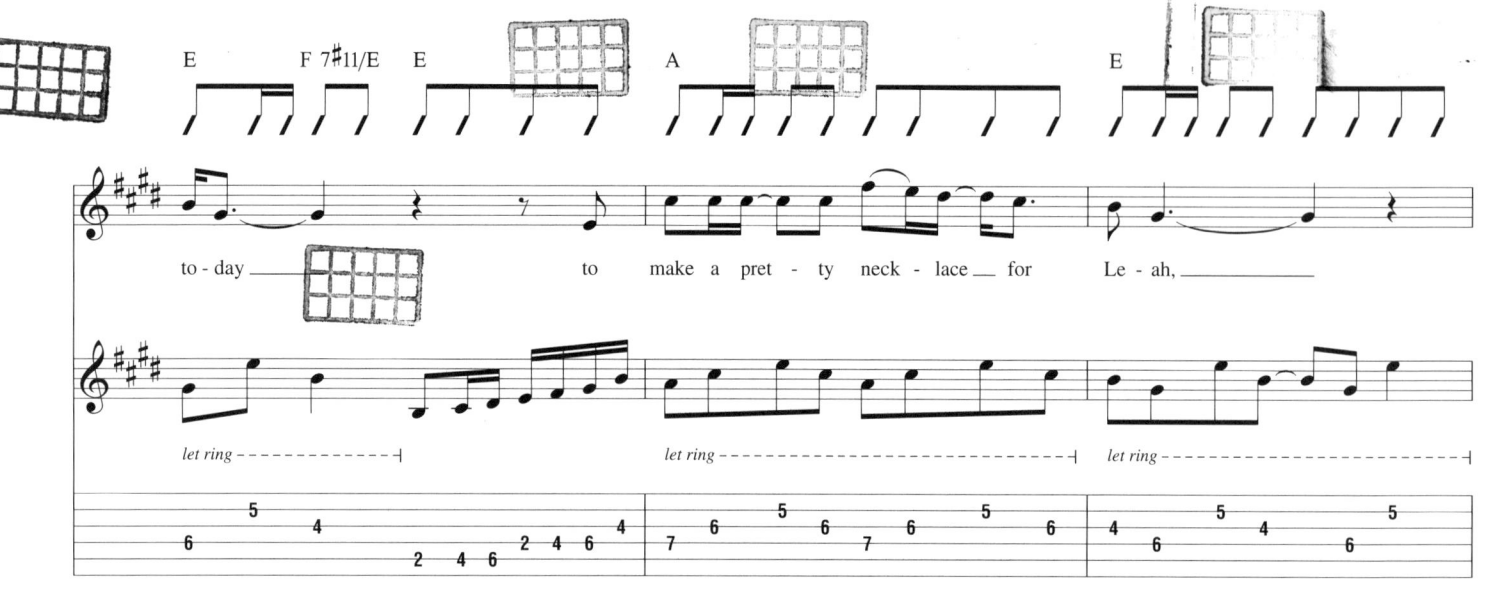

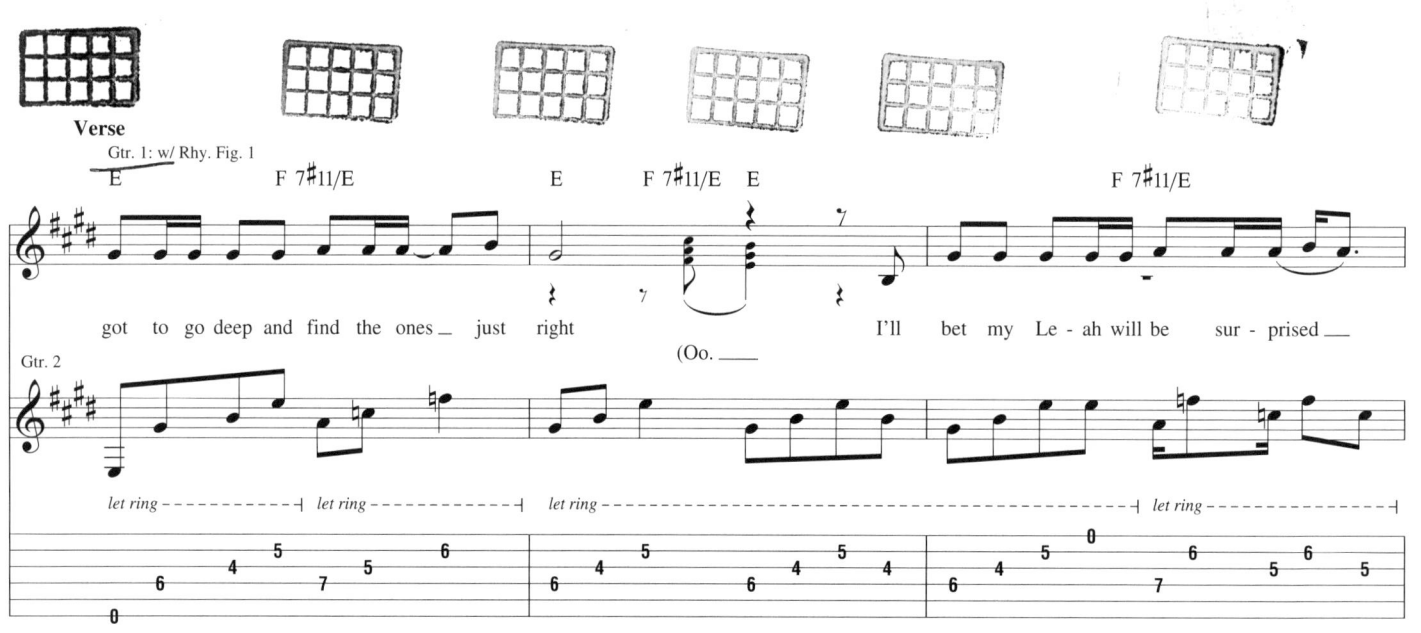

E F 7♯11/E E A E
to - night ___ I'll place the pearls _ a - round _ the on - ly girl for me, __
Oo. ___ Ah. ___
let ring
D♯(♭6 ♭9)/E B7 E E C/G
Le - ah.
Le - ah.) ___
3. But
let ring
Verse
F G♭ F G♭ F G♭
Rhy. Fig. 2
some - thing's wrong, I can - not move _ a - round.
My leg is caught, it's pull - ing __ me __
let ring

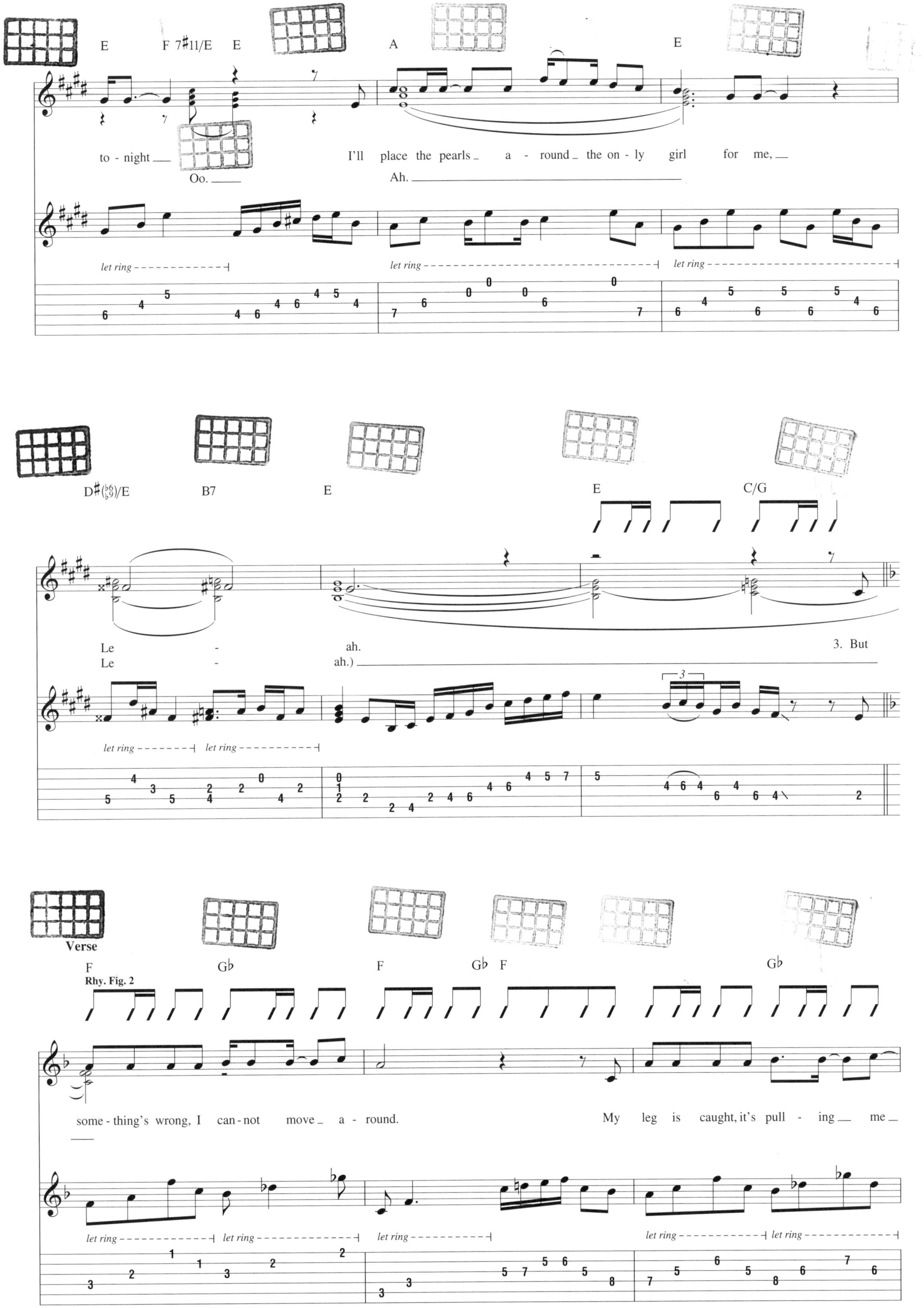

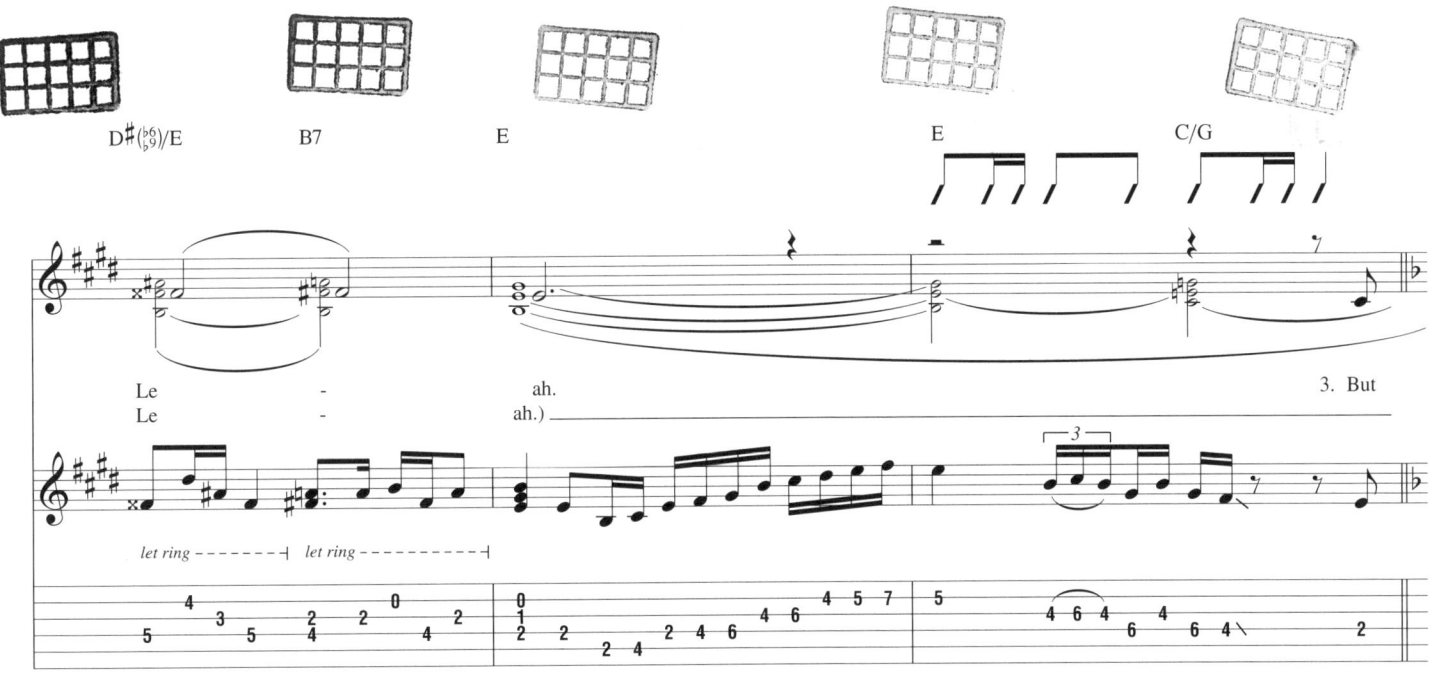

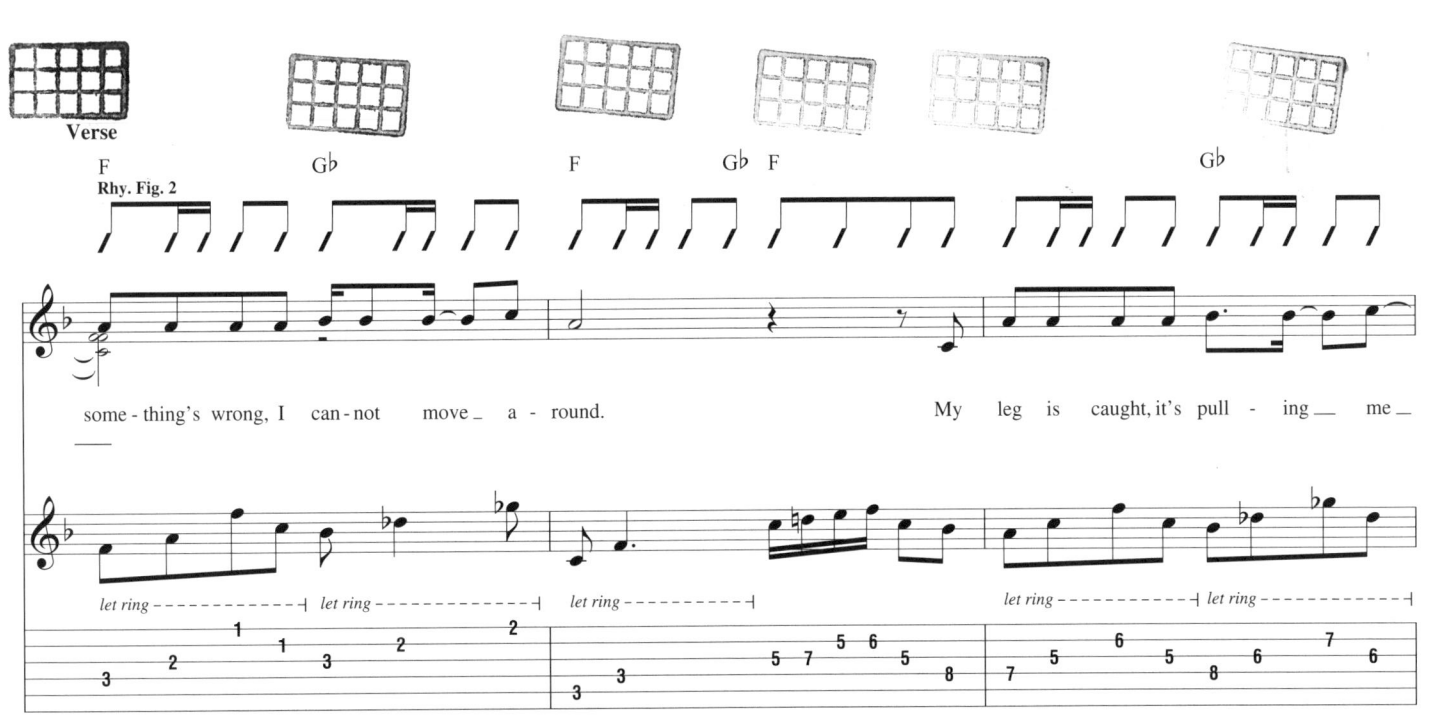

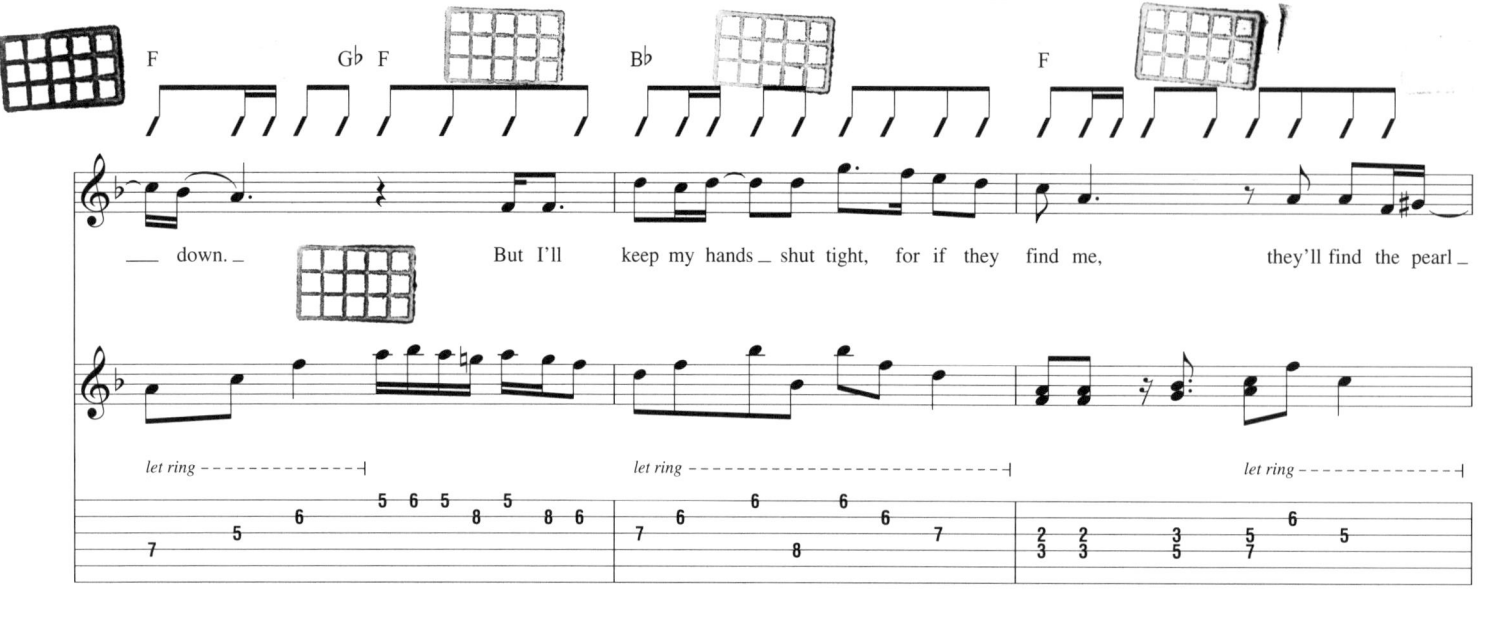
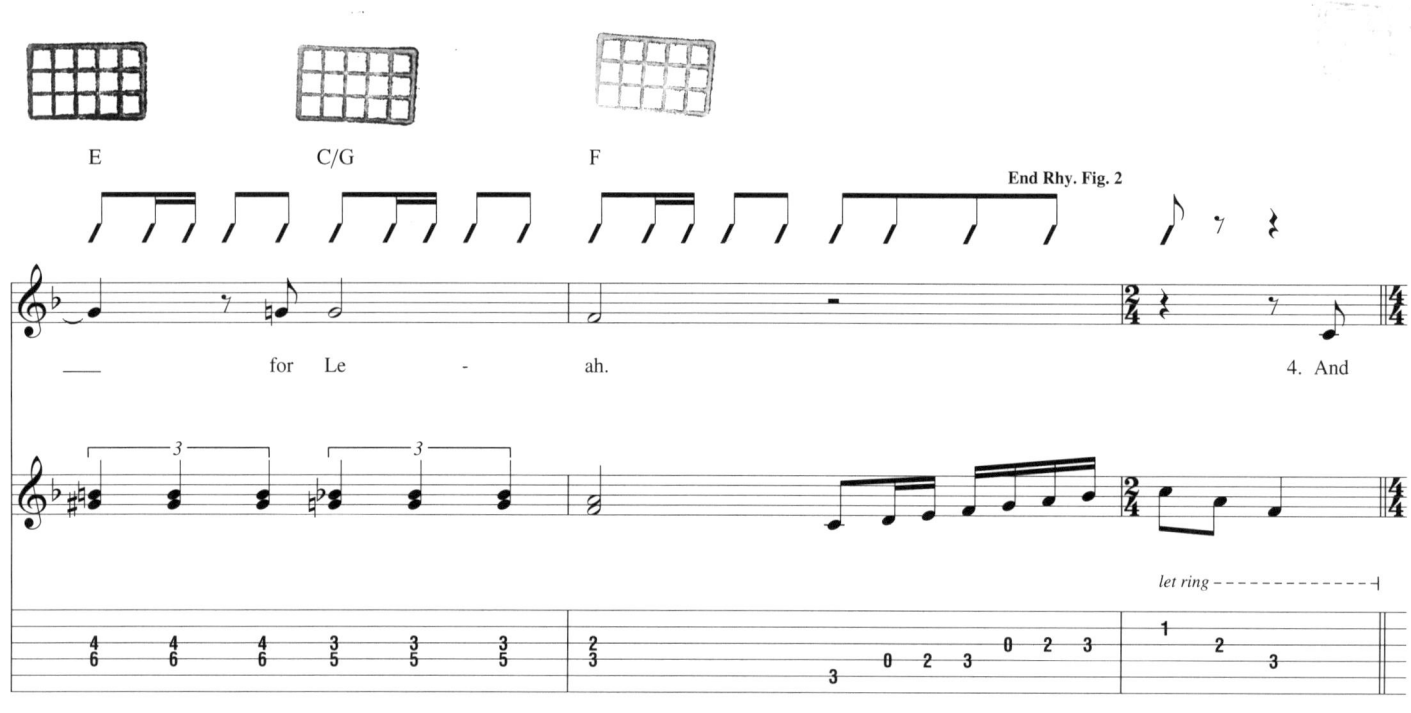
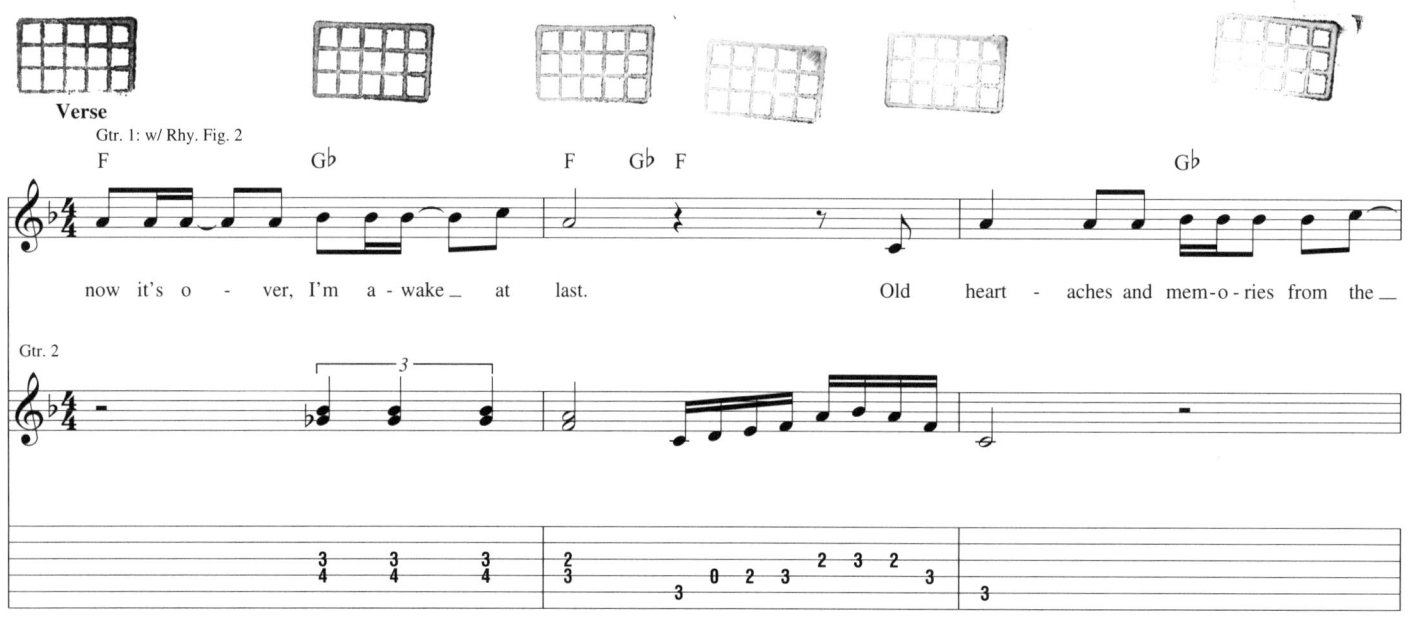

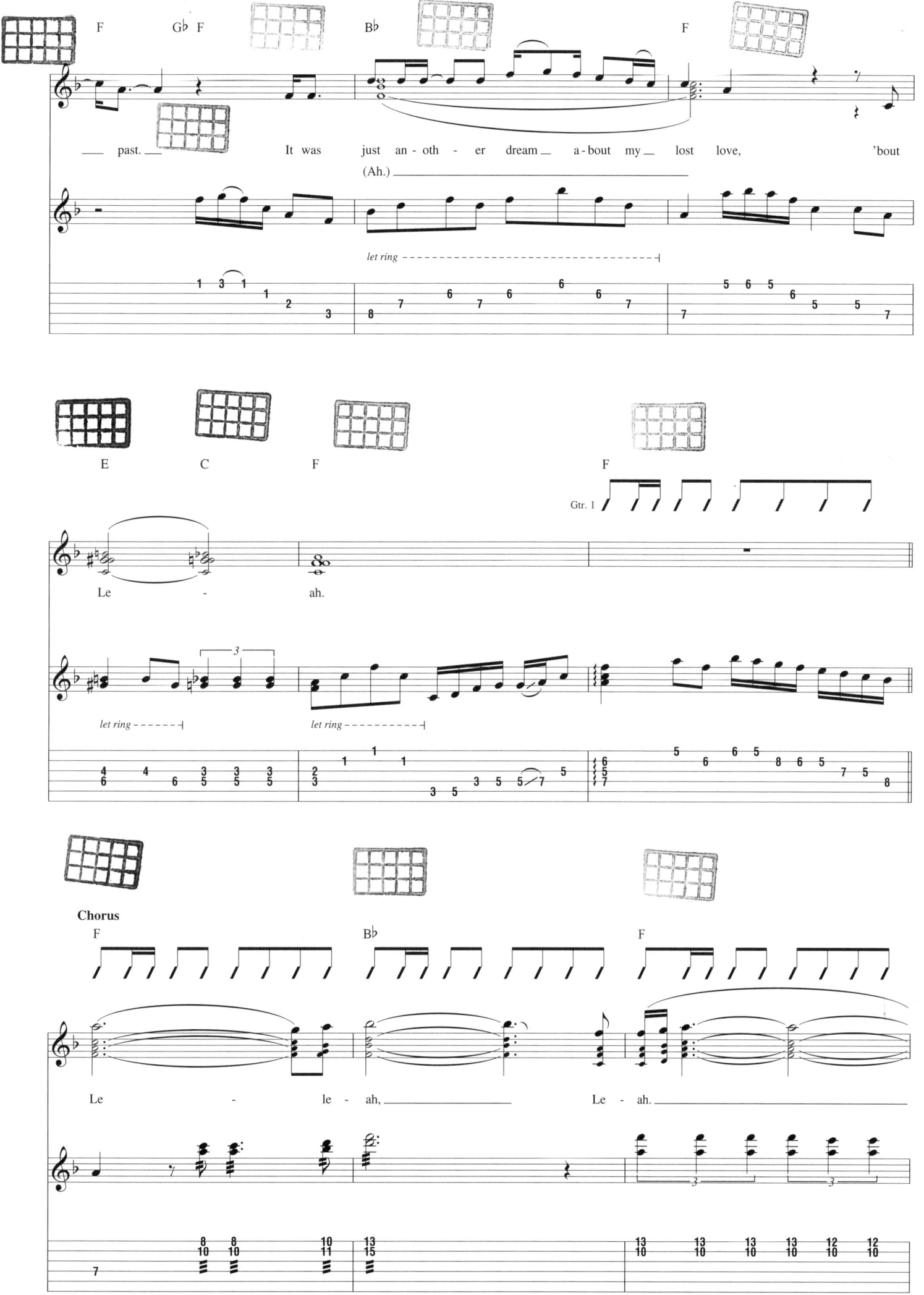

Running Scared

Words and Music by Roy Orbison and Joe Melson

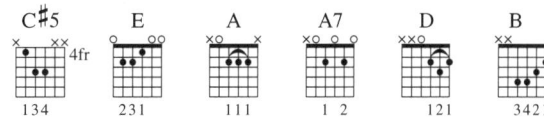

Copyright © 1952 (Renewed 1980) BARBARA ORBISON MUSIC COMPANY, ORBI-LEE MUSIC, R-KEY DARKUS MUSIC and SONY/ATV MUSIC PUBLISHING LLC
All Rights on behalf of SONY/ATV MUSIC PUBLISHING LLC Administered by SONY/ATV MUSIC PUBLISHING LLC, 8 Music Square West, Nashville, TN 37203
All Rights Reserved   Used by Permission

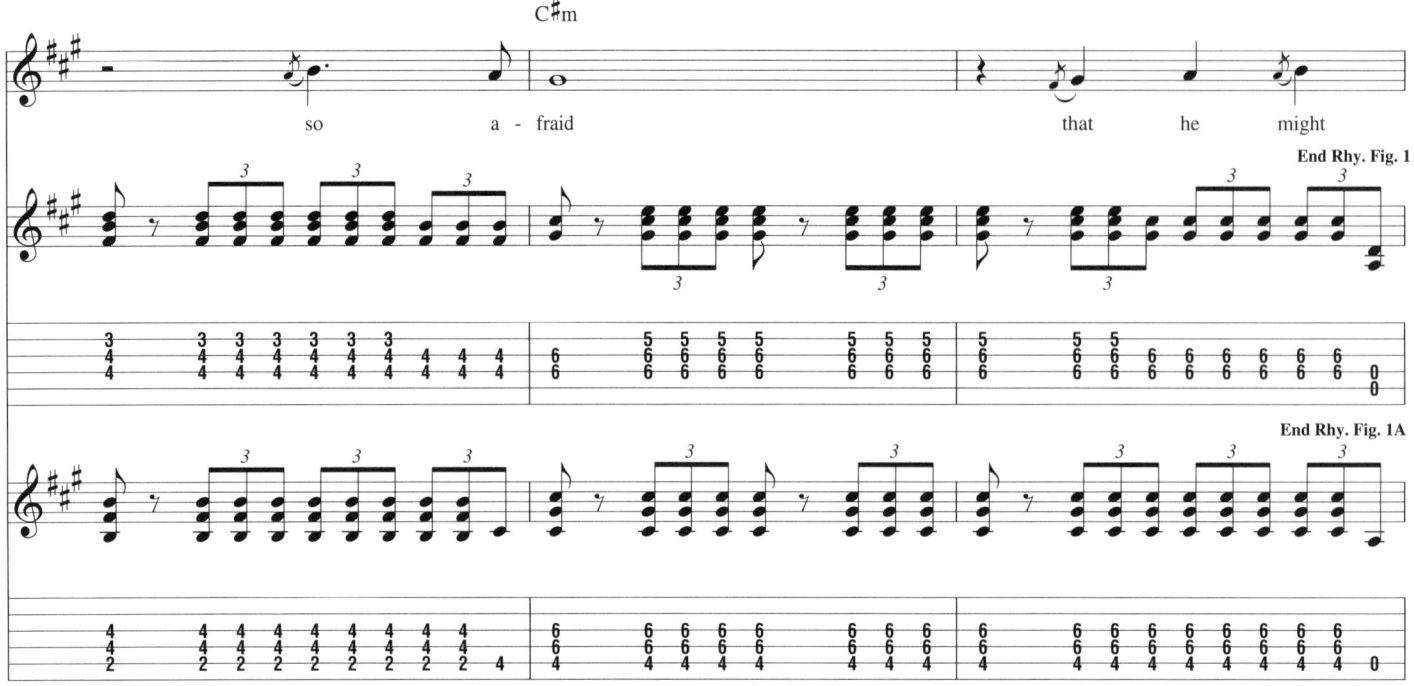
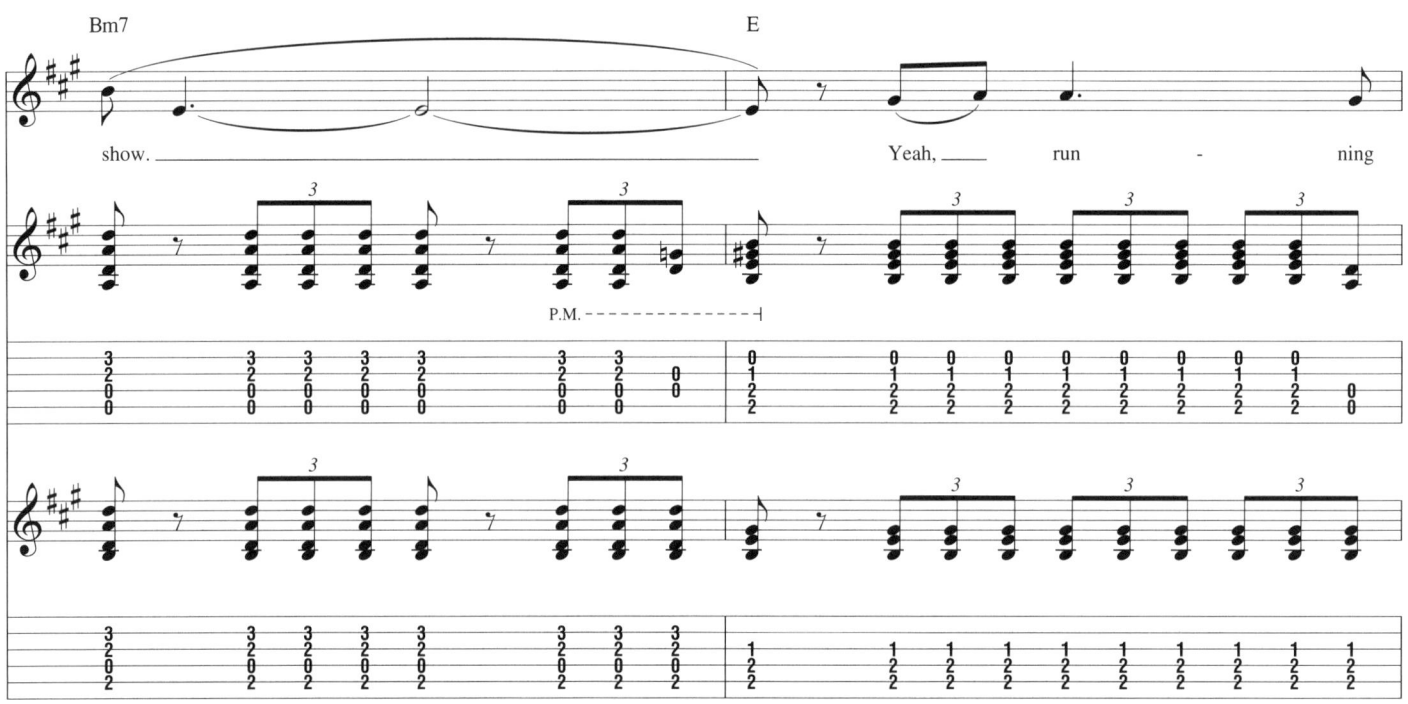
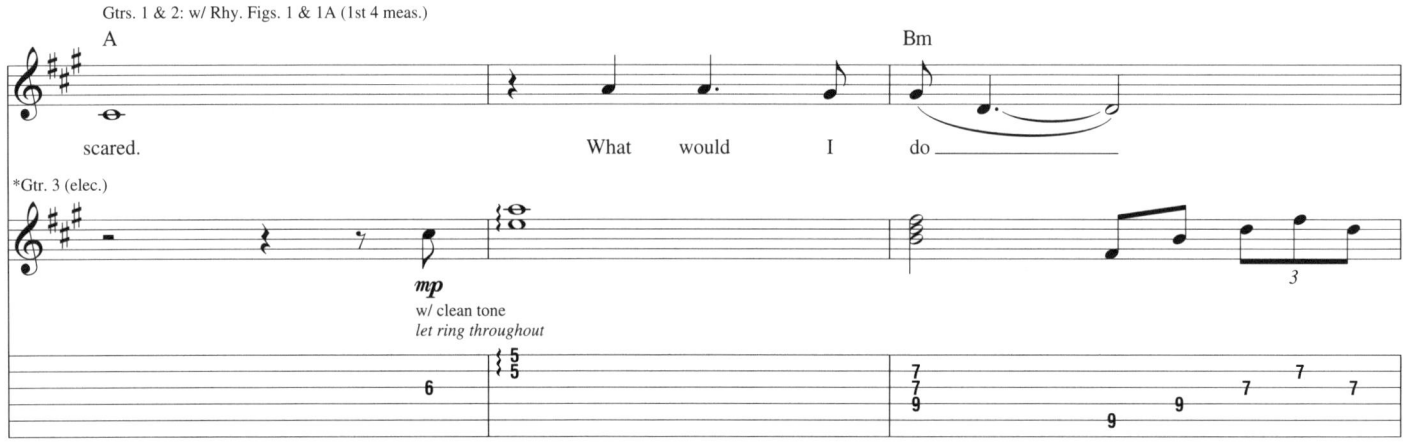

*Two gtrs. arr. for one. (James Burton & Bruce Springsteen)

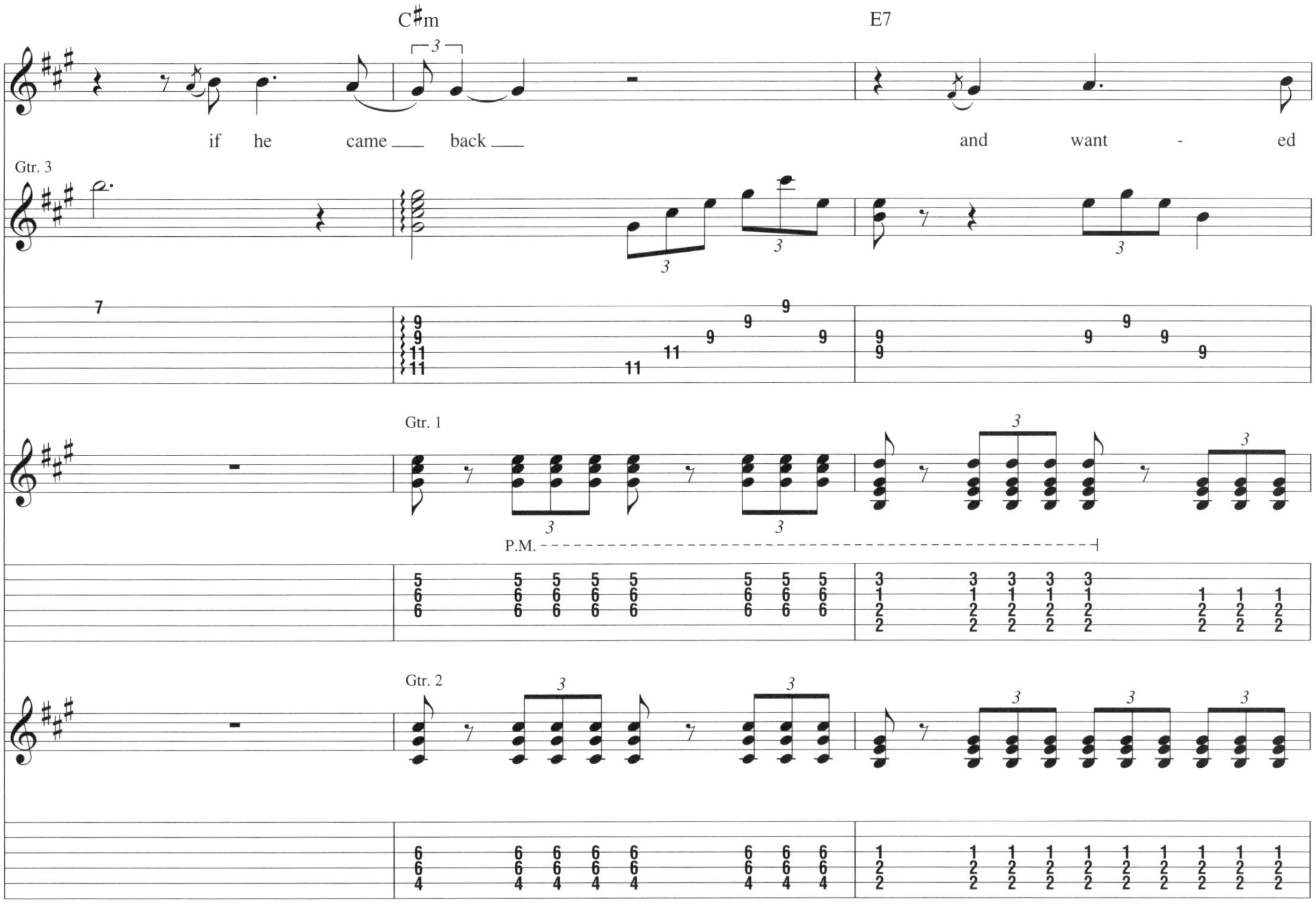
C♯m
E7
if he came back and want - ed
Gtr. 3
Gtr. 1
P.M.
Gtr. 2

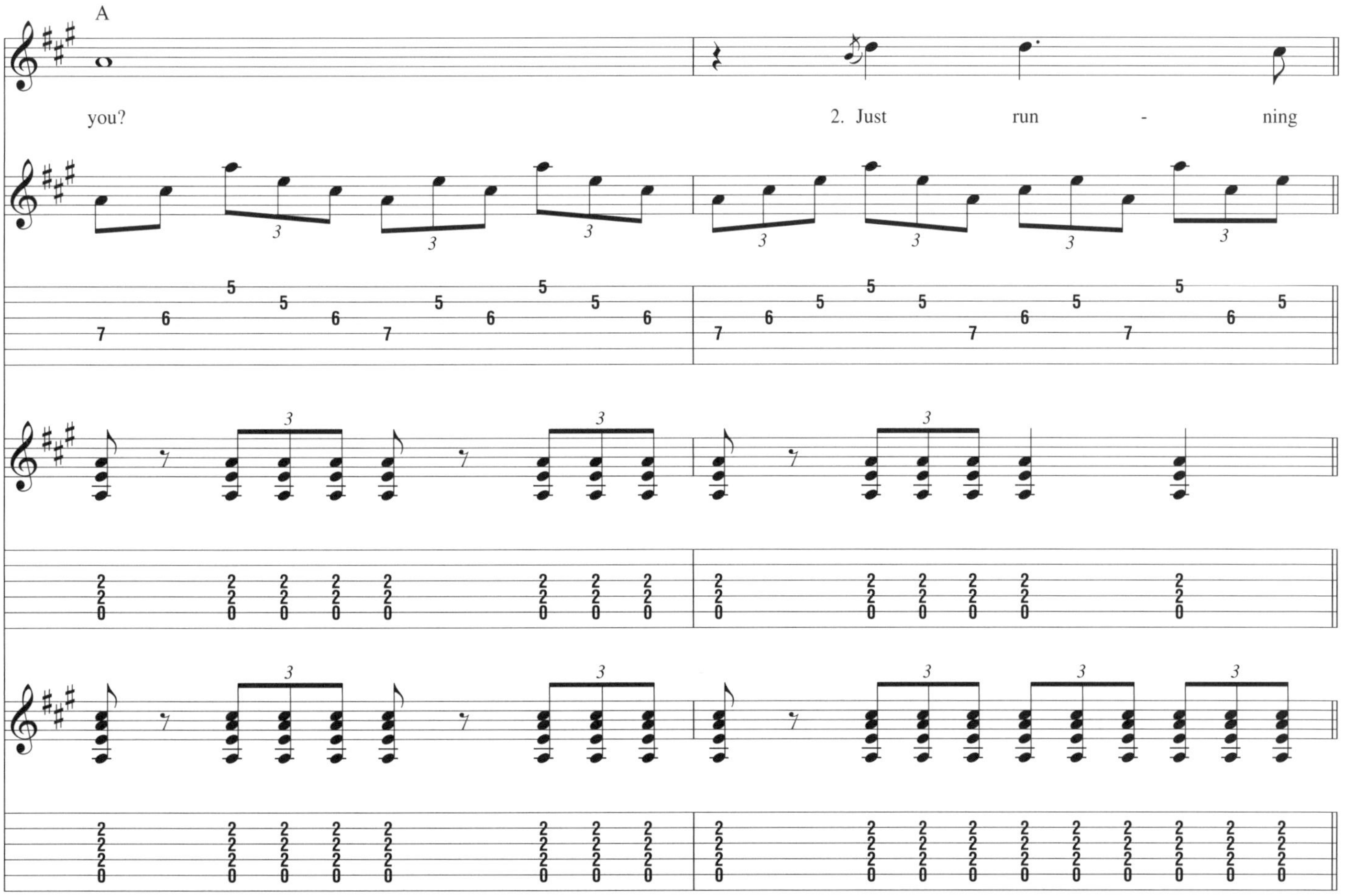
A
you?
2. Just run - ning

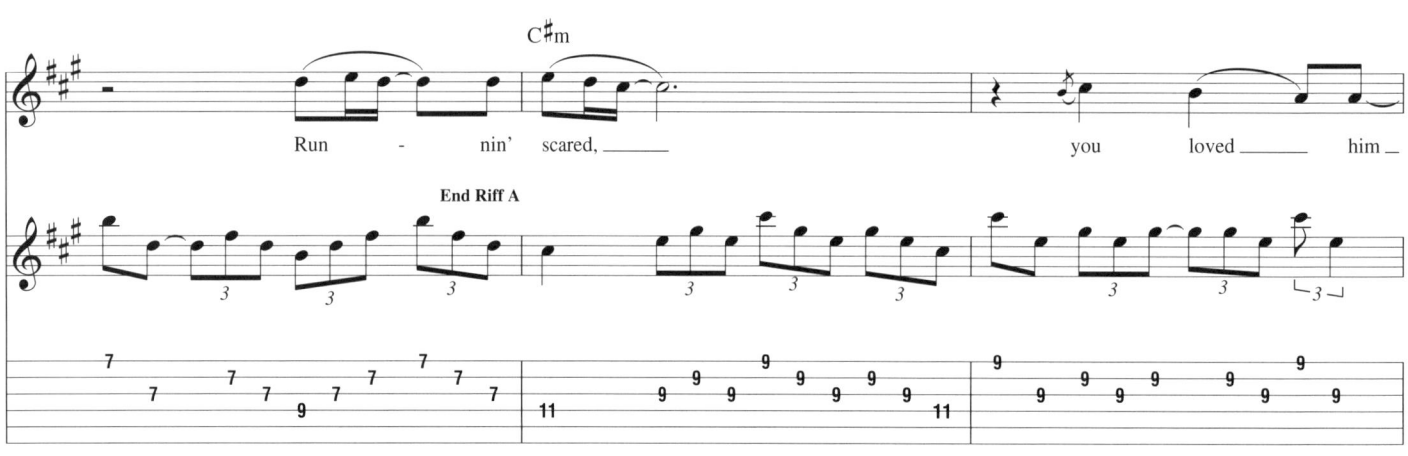
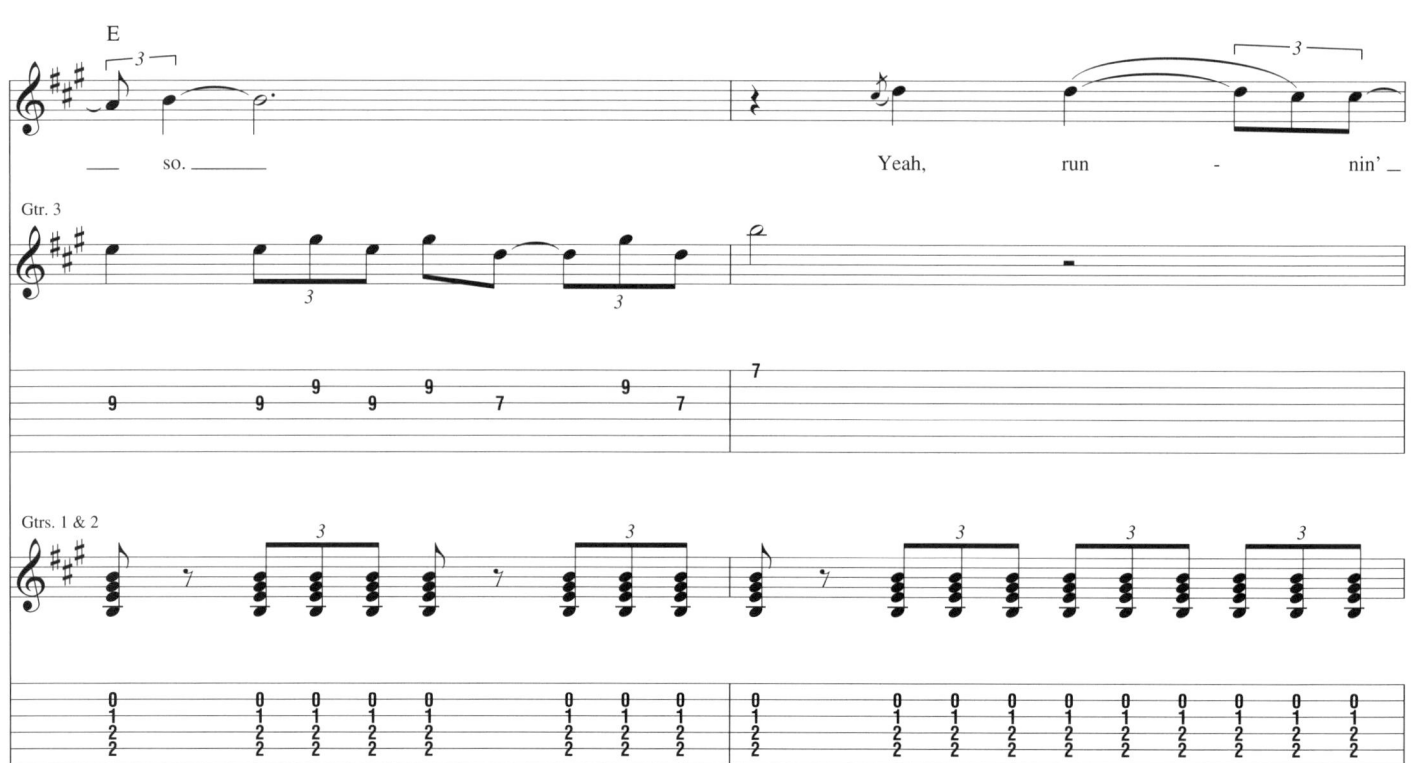

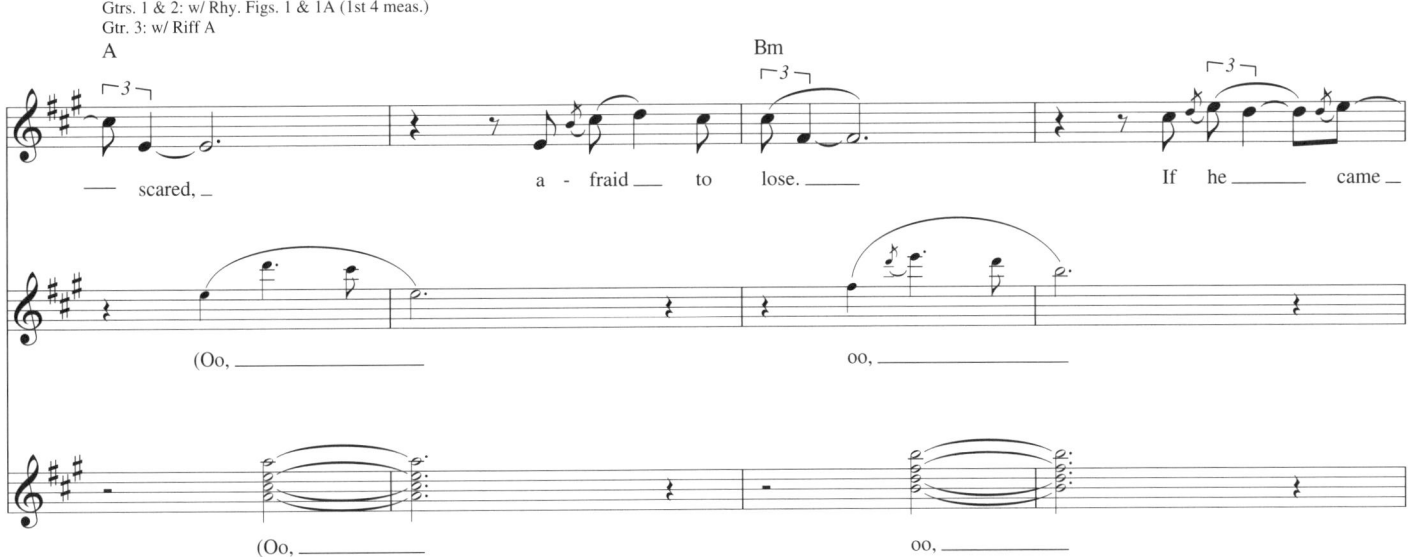

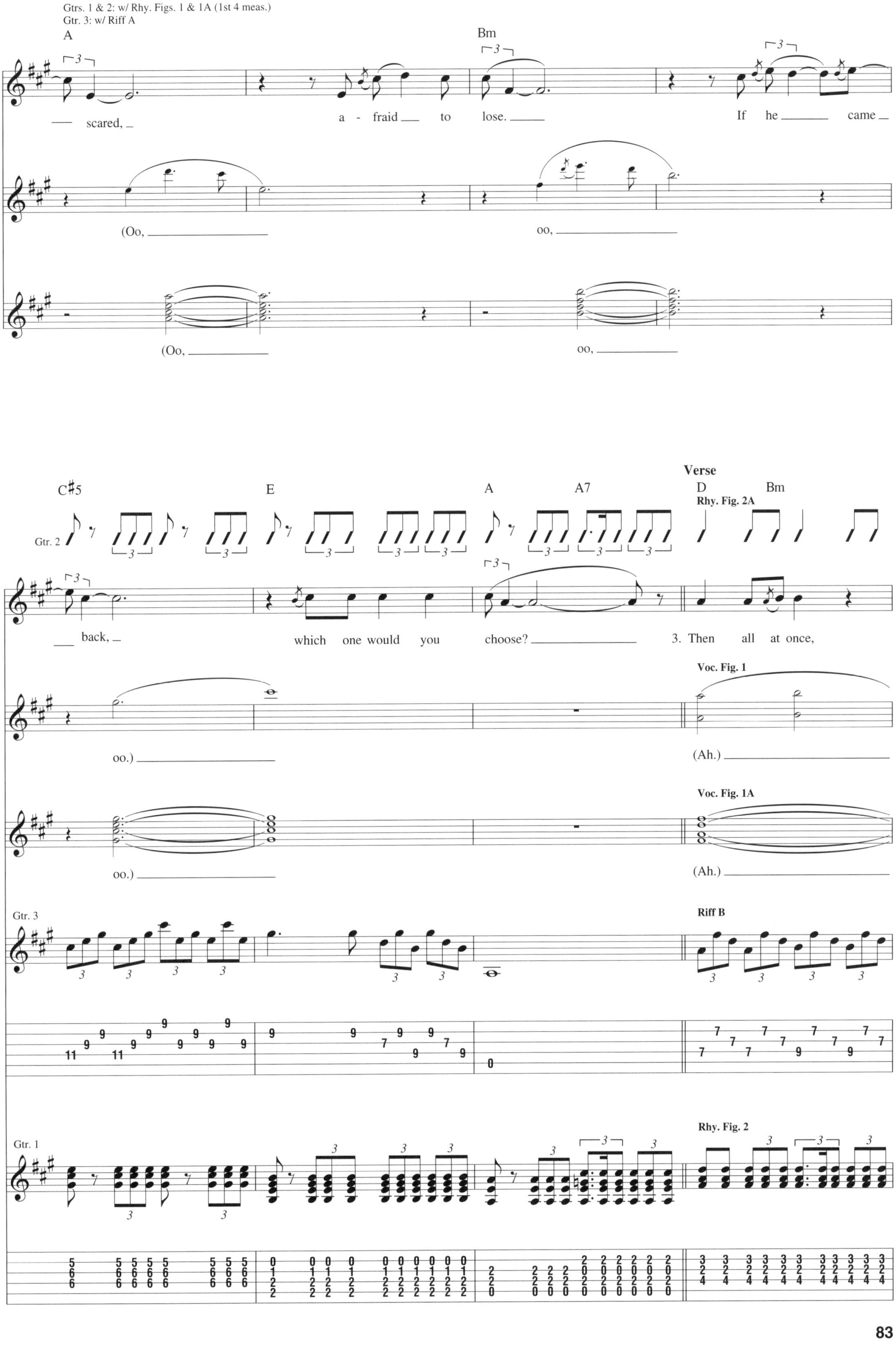
Gtrs. 1 & 2: w/ Rhy. Figs. 1 & 1A (1st 4 meas.)
Gtr. 3: w/ Riff A
A
Bm
scared,
a - fraid to lose.
If he came
(Oo,
oo,
(Oo,
oo,
C♯5
E
A
A7
Verse
D
Bm
Rhy. Fig. 2A
Gtr. 2
back,
which one would you
choose?
3. Then all at once,
Voc. Fig. 1
oo.)
(Ah.)
Voc. Fig. 1A
oo.)
(Ah.)
Gtr. 3
Riff B
Gtr. 1
Rhy. Fig. 2

D
Bm
D
Bm
End Voc. Fig. 2A
he was stand - ing there,
so
End Voc. Fig. 1
End Voc. Fig. 1A
End Riff B
End Rhy. Fig. 2
Bkgd. Voc.: w/ Voc. Figs. 1 & 1A
Gtrs. 1 & 2: w/ Rhy. Figs. 2 & 2A (1 2/3 times)
Gtr. 3: w/ Riff B (1 2/3 times)
D
Bm
D
Bm
D
Bm
sure of him - self, his head in the air.
And
D
Bm
D
Bm
my heart was break - ing. Which one would it be?
(Ah,
(Ah,

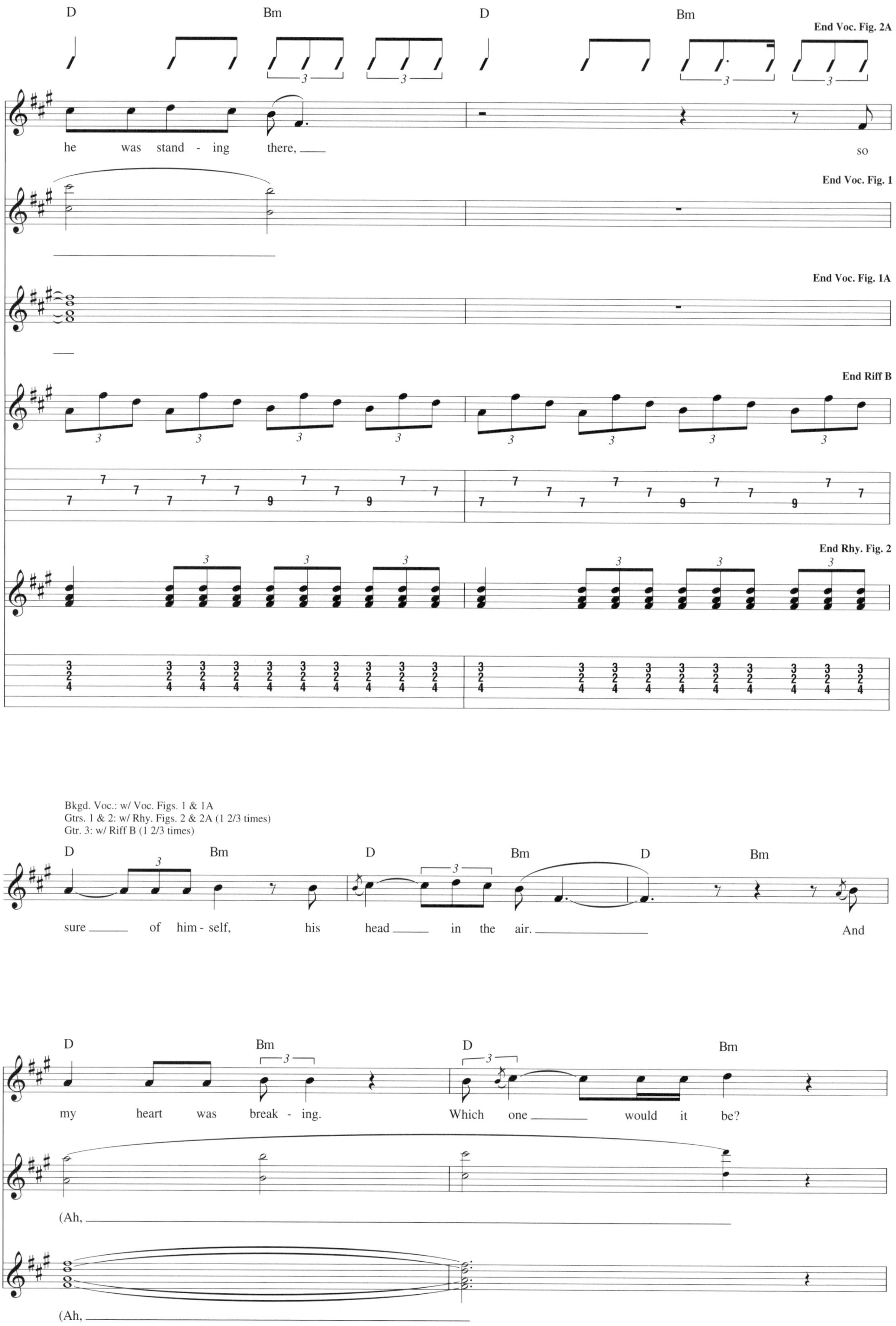

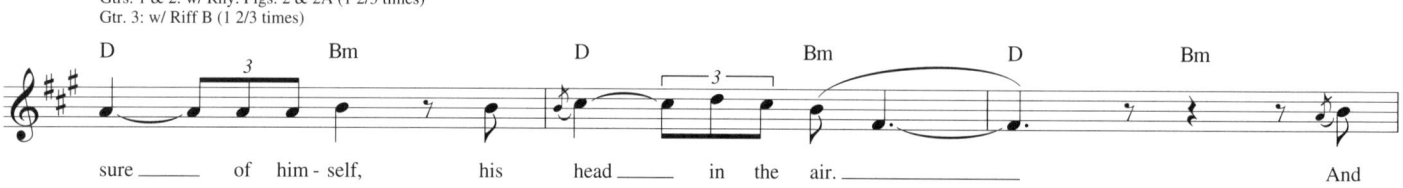

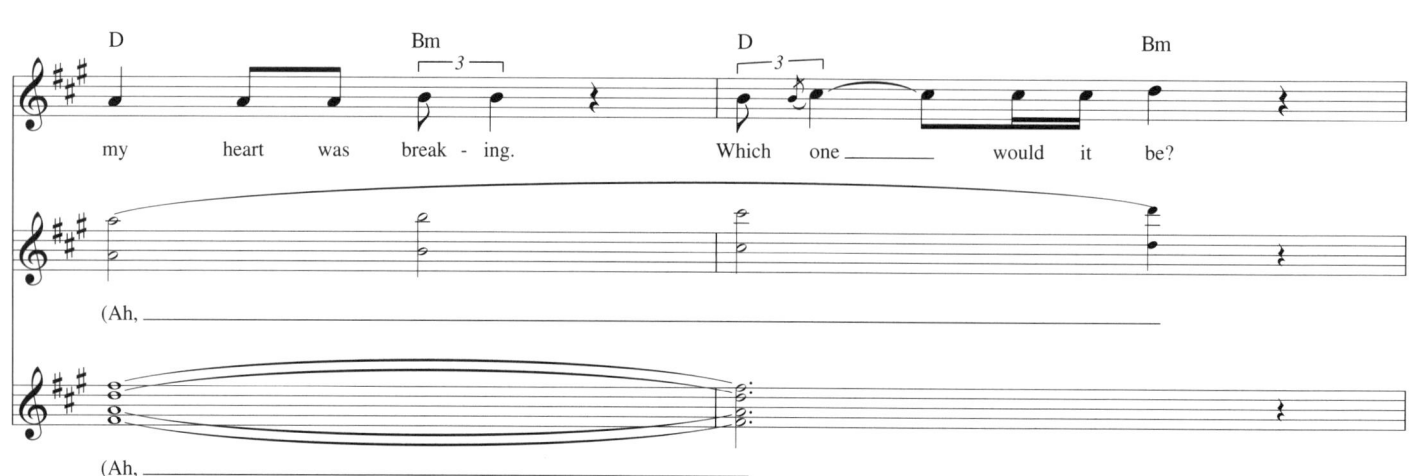

Up Town

Words and Music by Roy Orbison and Joe Melson

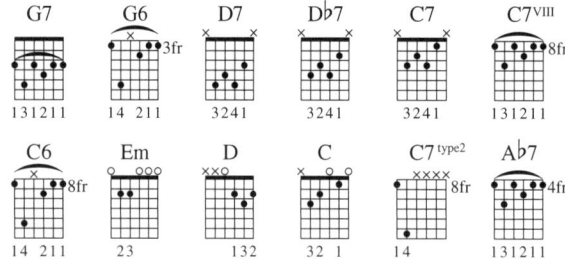

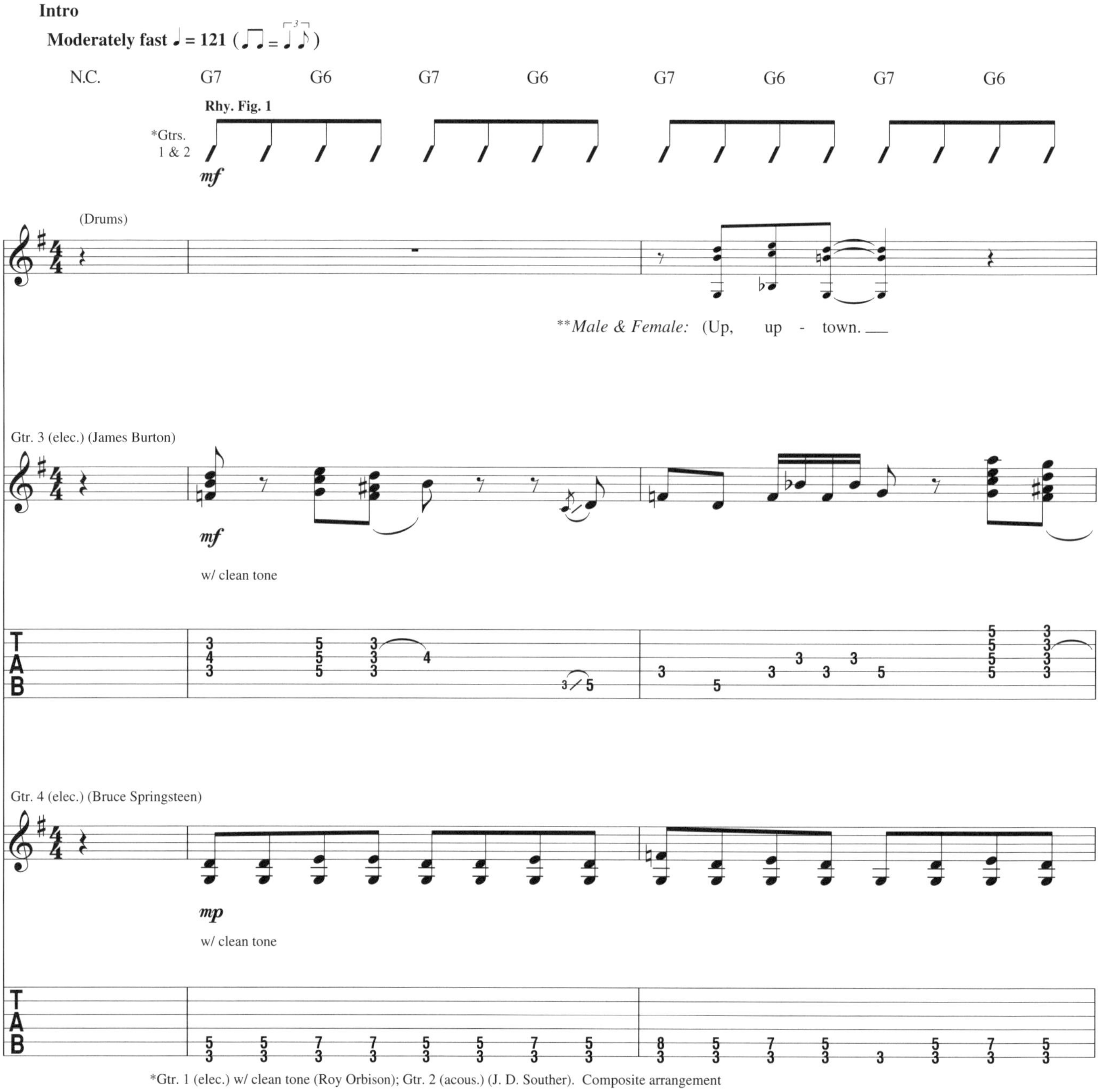

Intro
Moderately fast ♩ = 121

Verse
G7 G6 G7 G6 G7 G6 G7 G6 G7 G6 G7 G6
End Rhy. Fig. 1
Rhy. Fig. 2
*Gtrs. 1, 2 & 4
1. Up - town in
Voc. Fig. 1
End Voc. Fig. 1
Up, up - town.
Up, up - town.
Up, up - town.)
1/4
(cont. in slashes)
*Composite arrangement
Bkgd. Voc.: w/ Voc. Fig. 1
D7 D♭7 C7 G7 G6 G7 G6 G7 G6 G7 G6
End Rhy. Fig. 2
pent-house num - ber three.
Up - town,
Gtr. 3
1
1/4

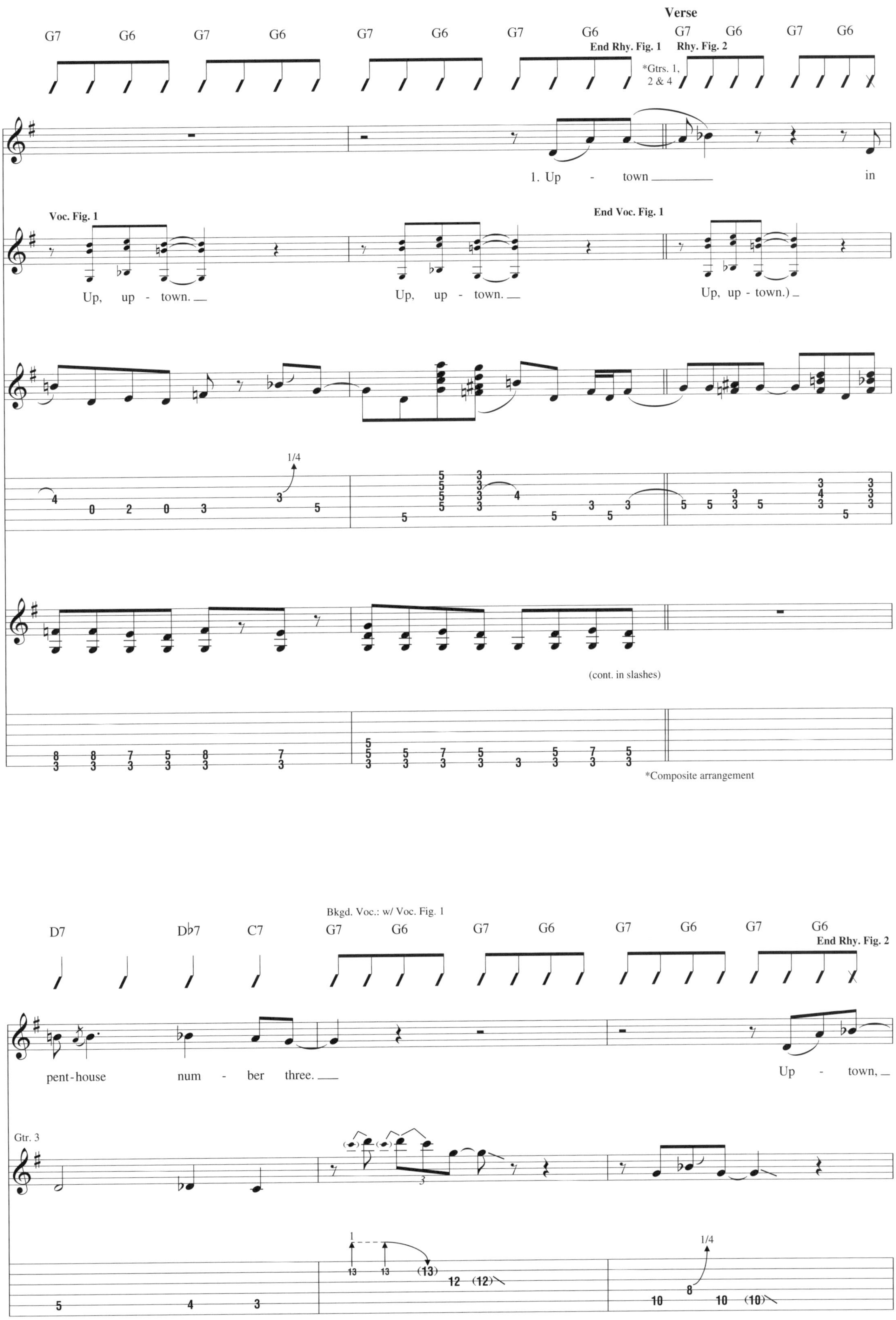

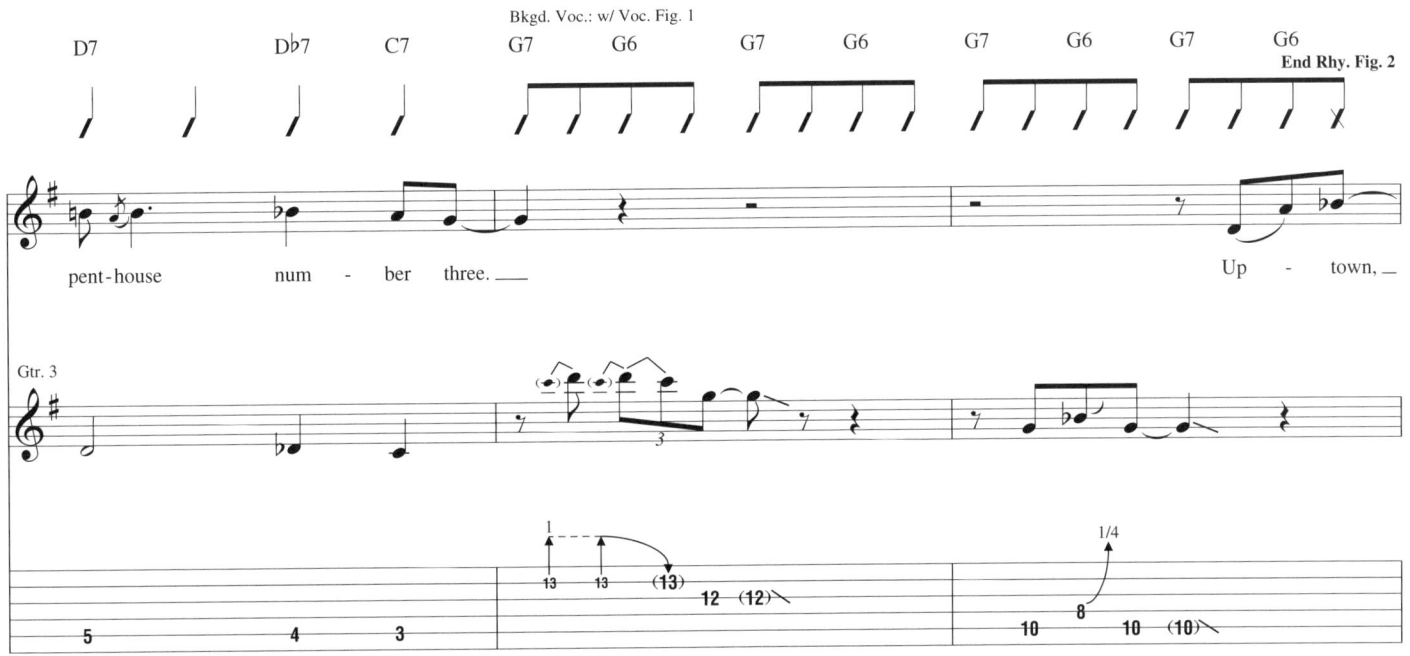

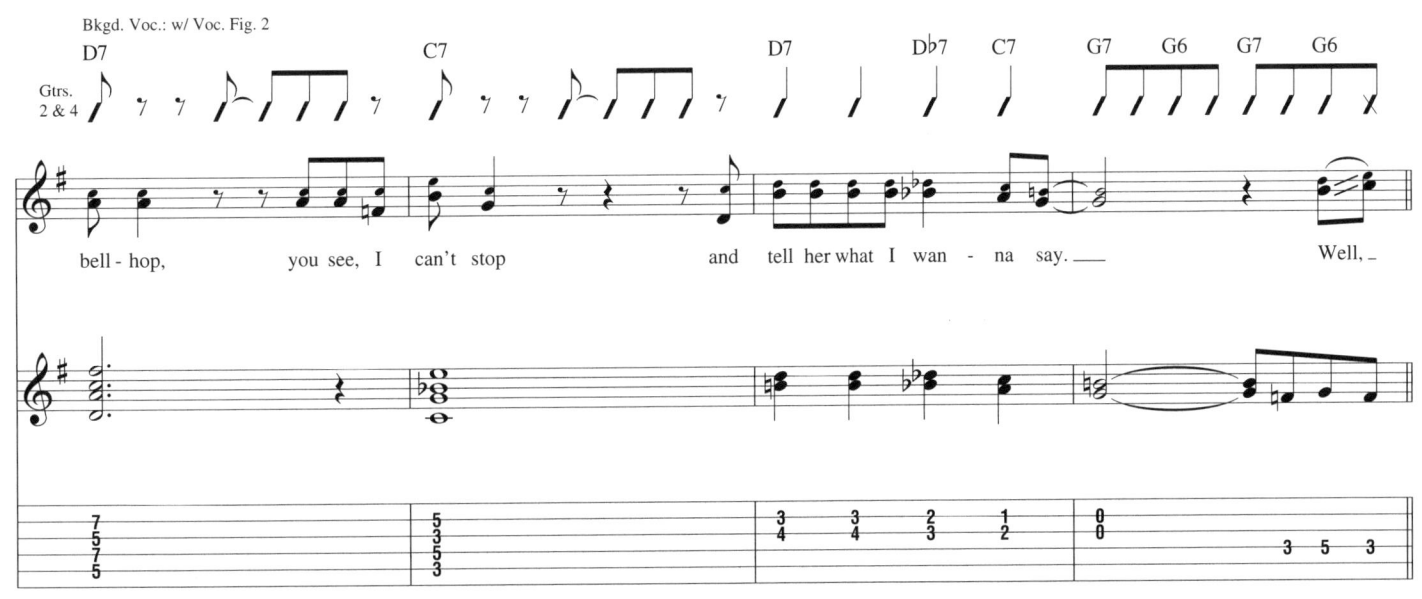

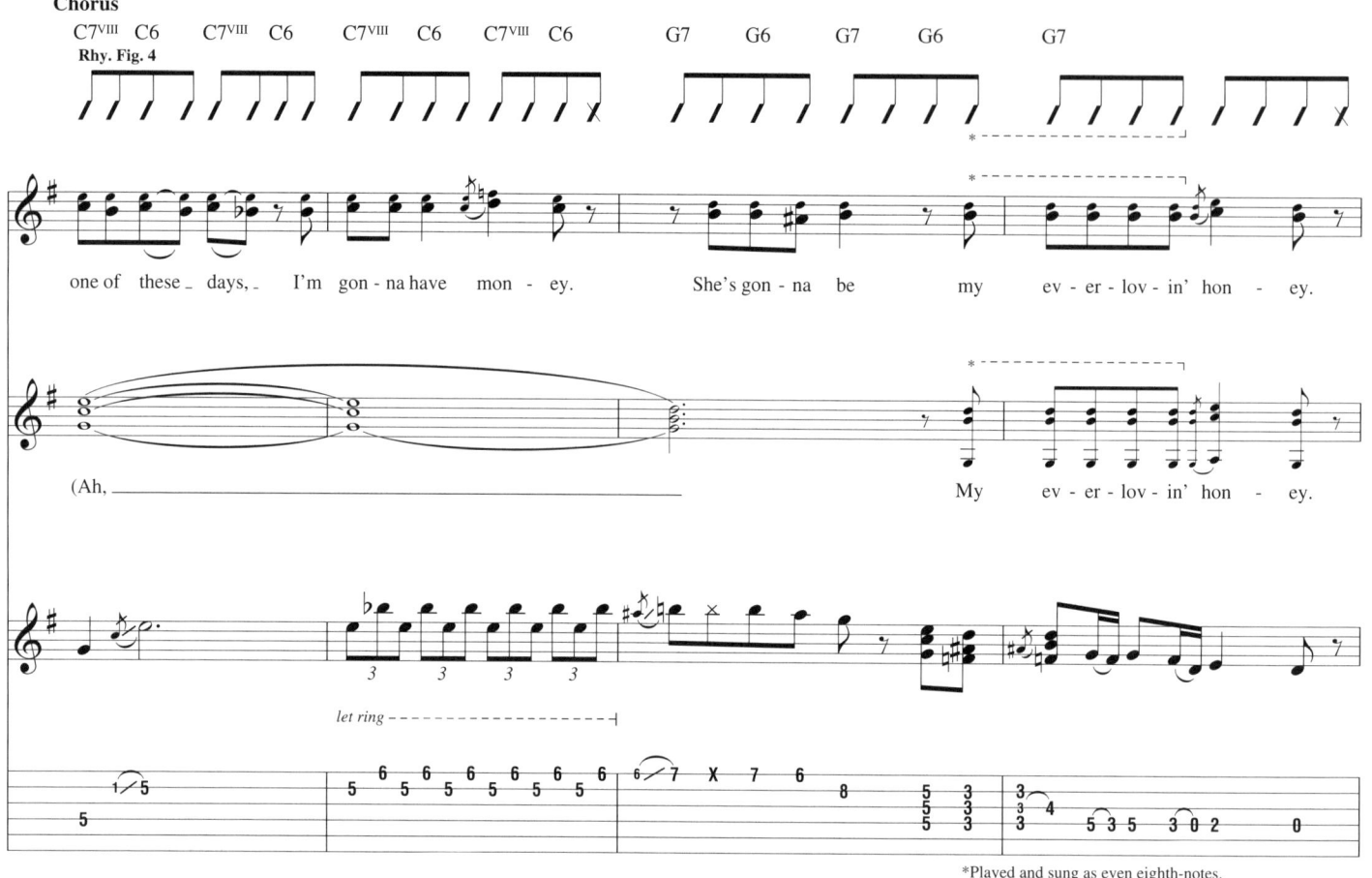

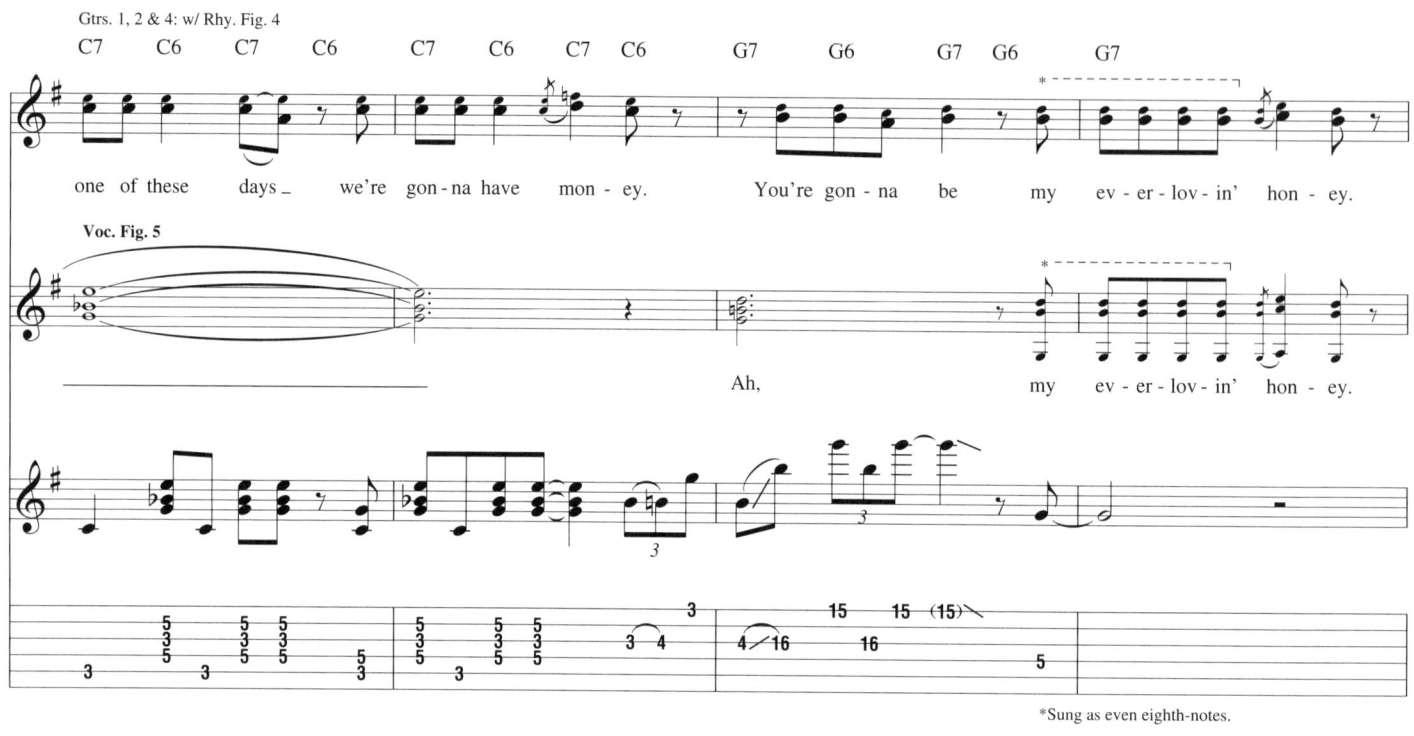

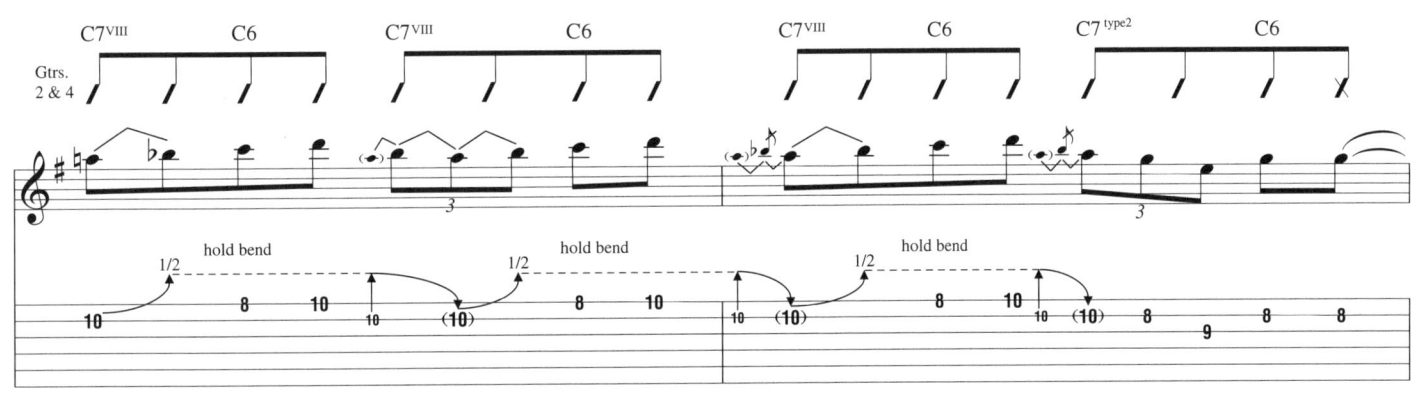

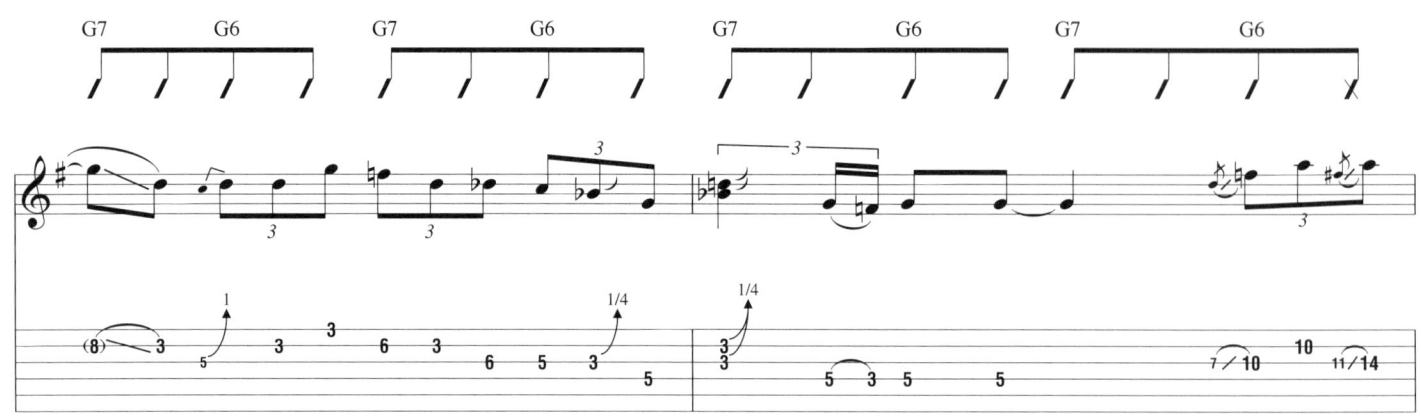
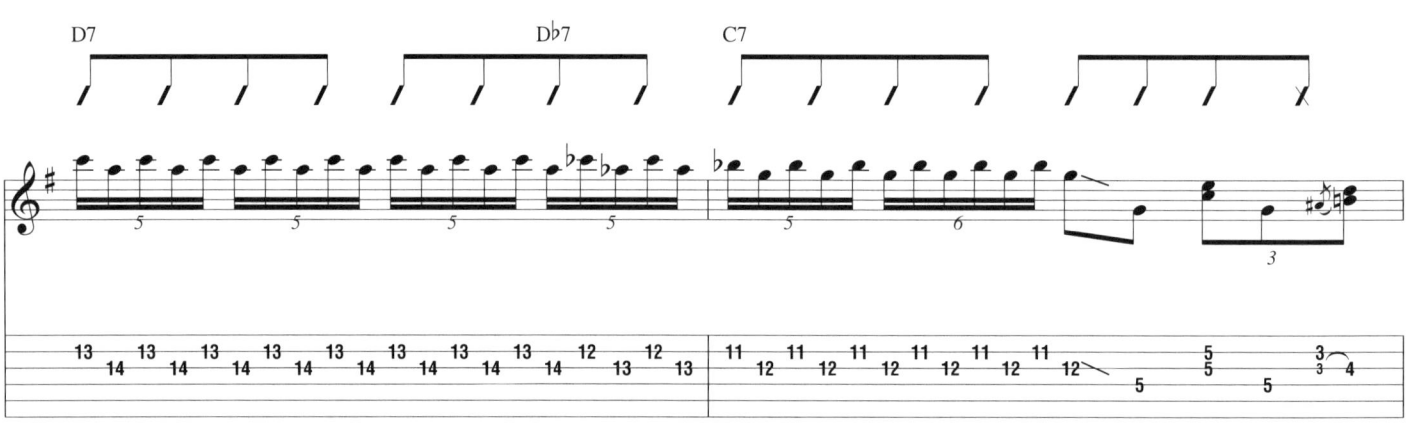
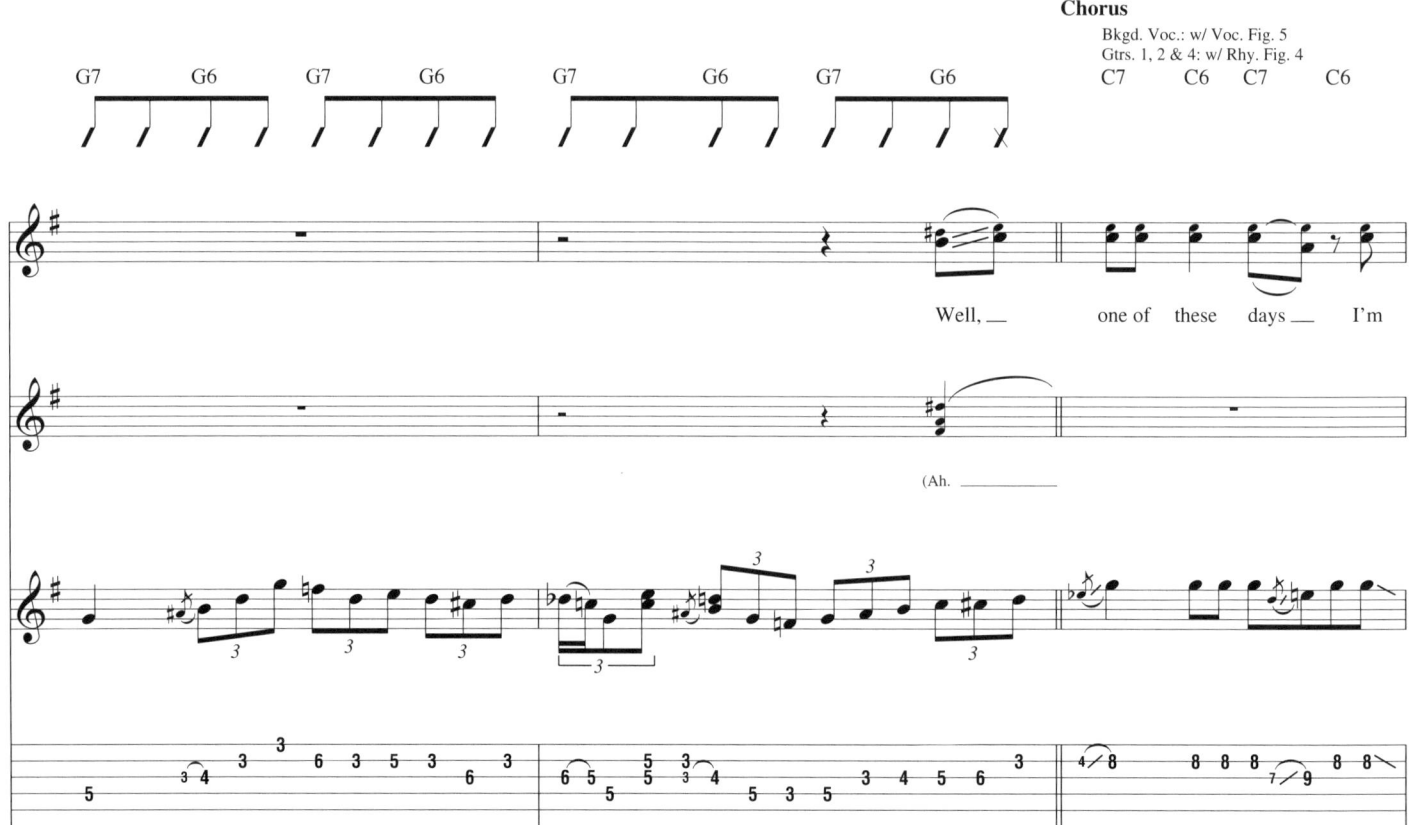

94

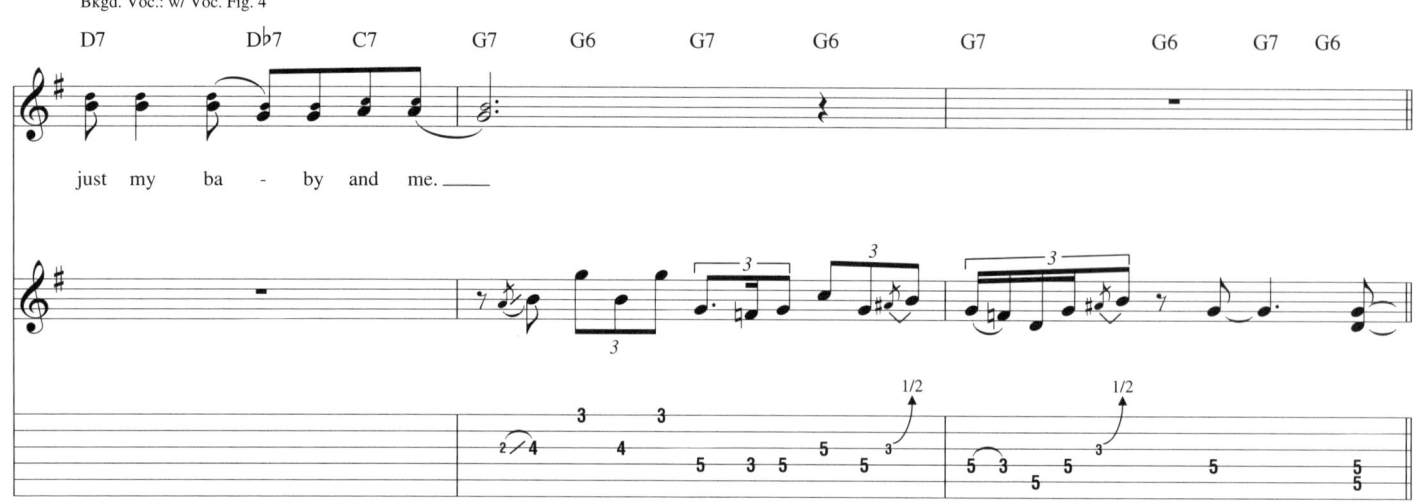
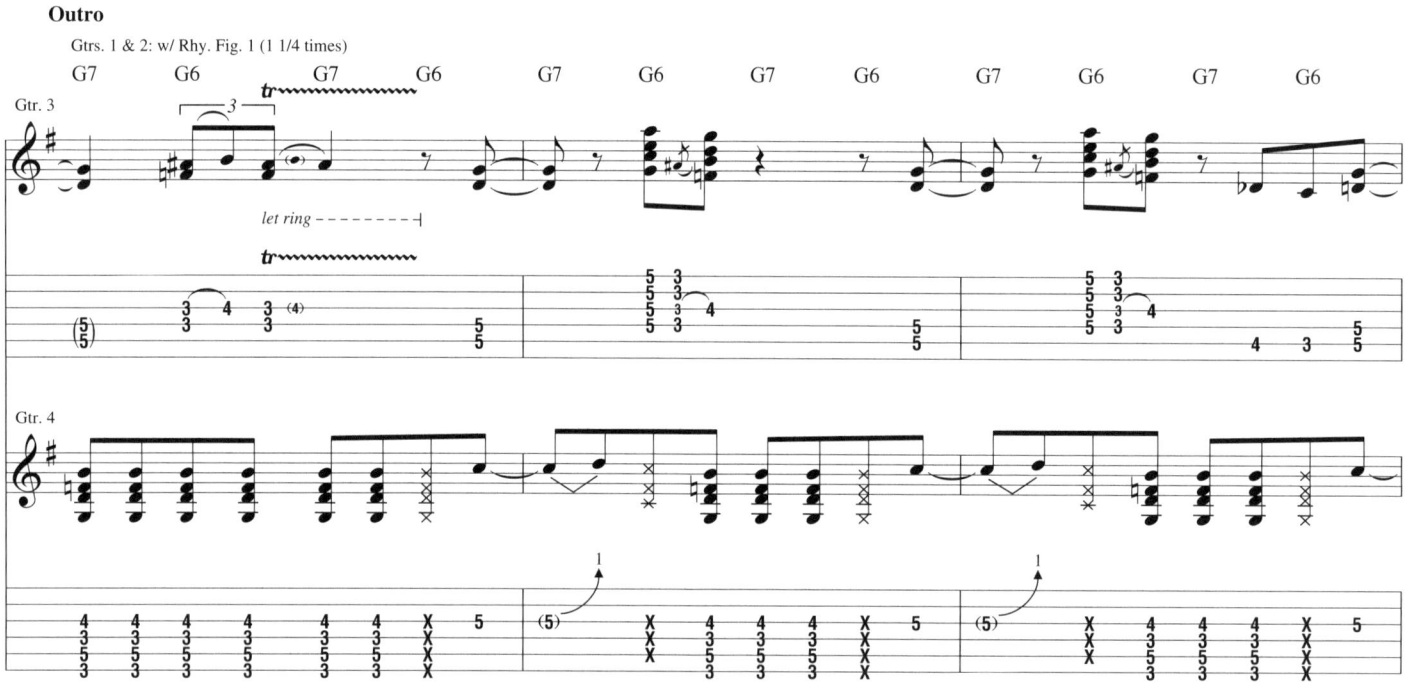

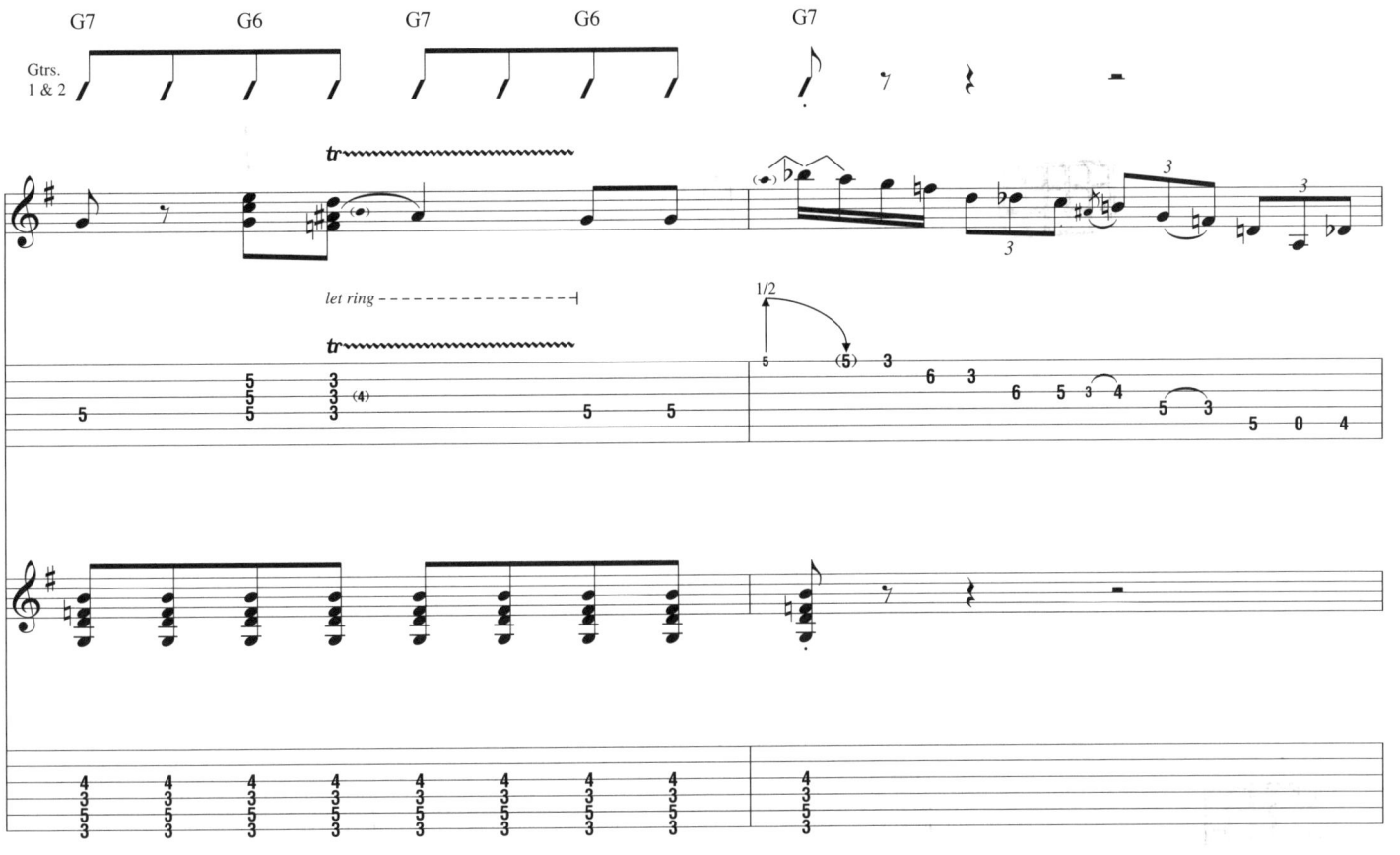

In Dreams
Words and Music by Roy Orbison

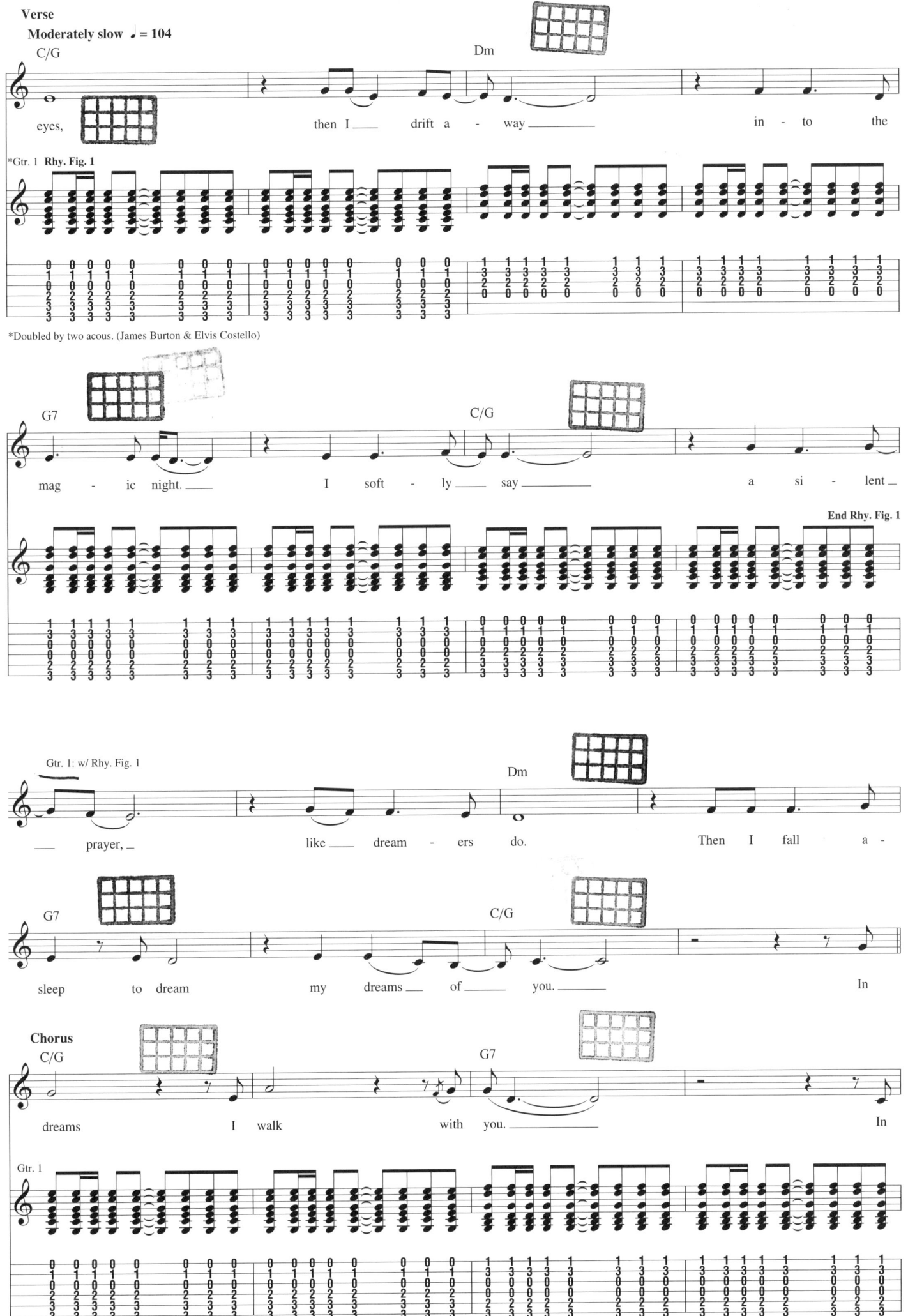

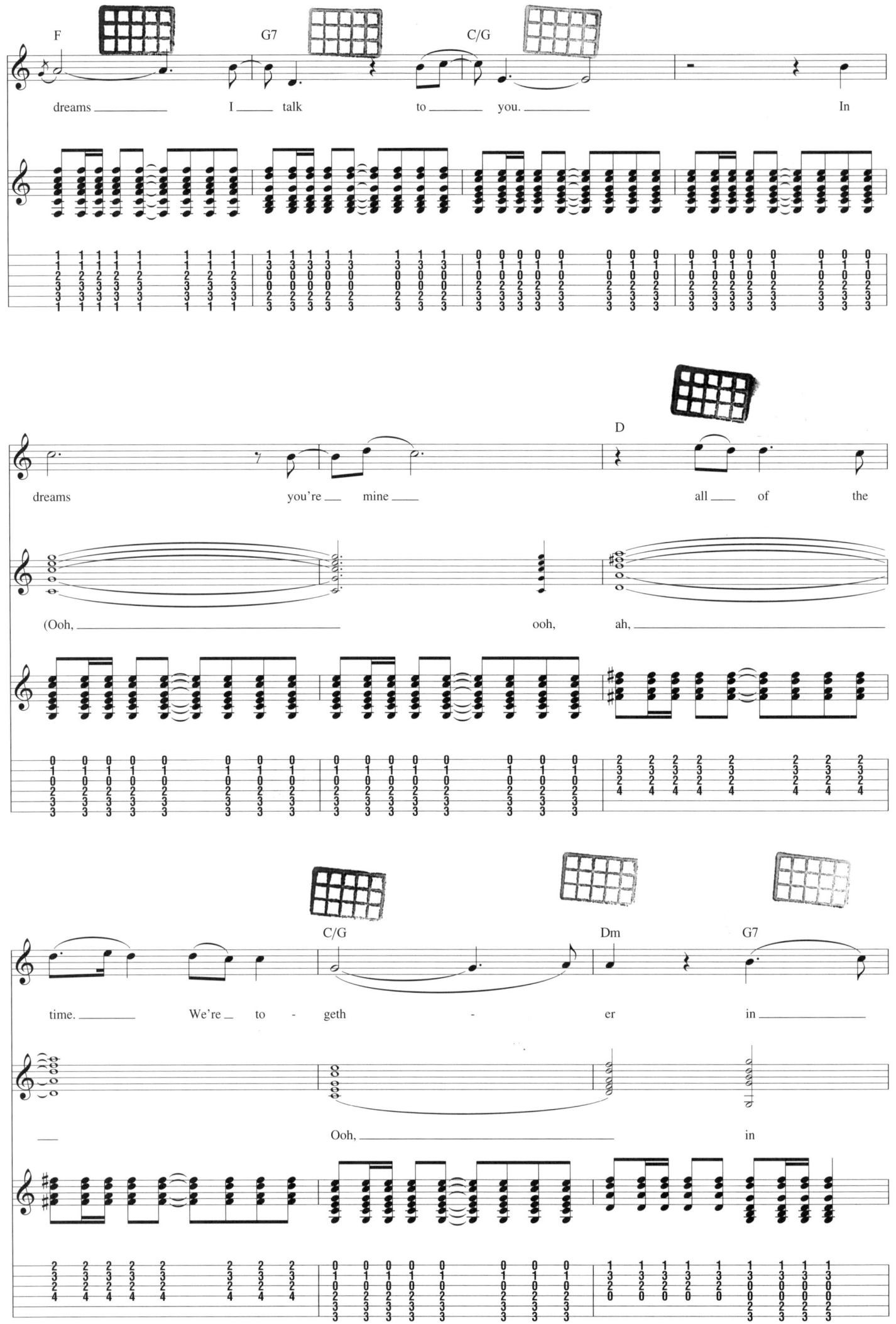

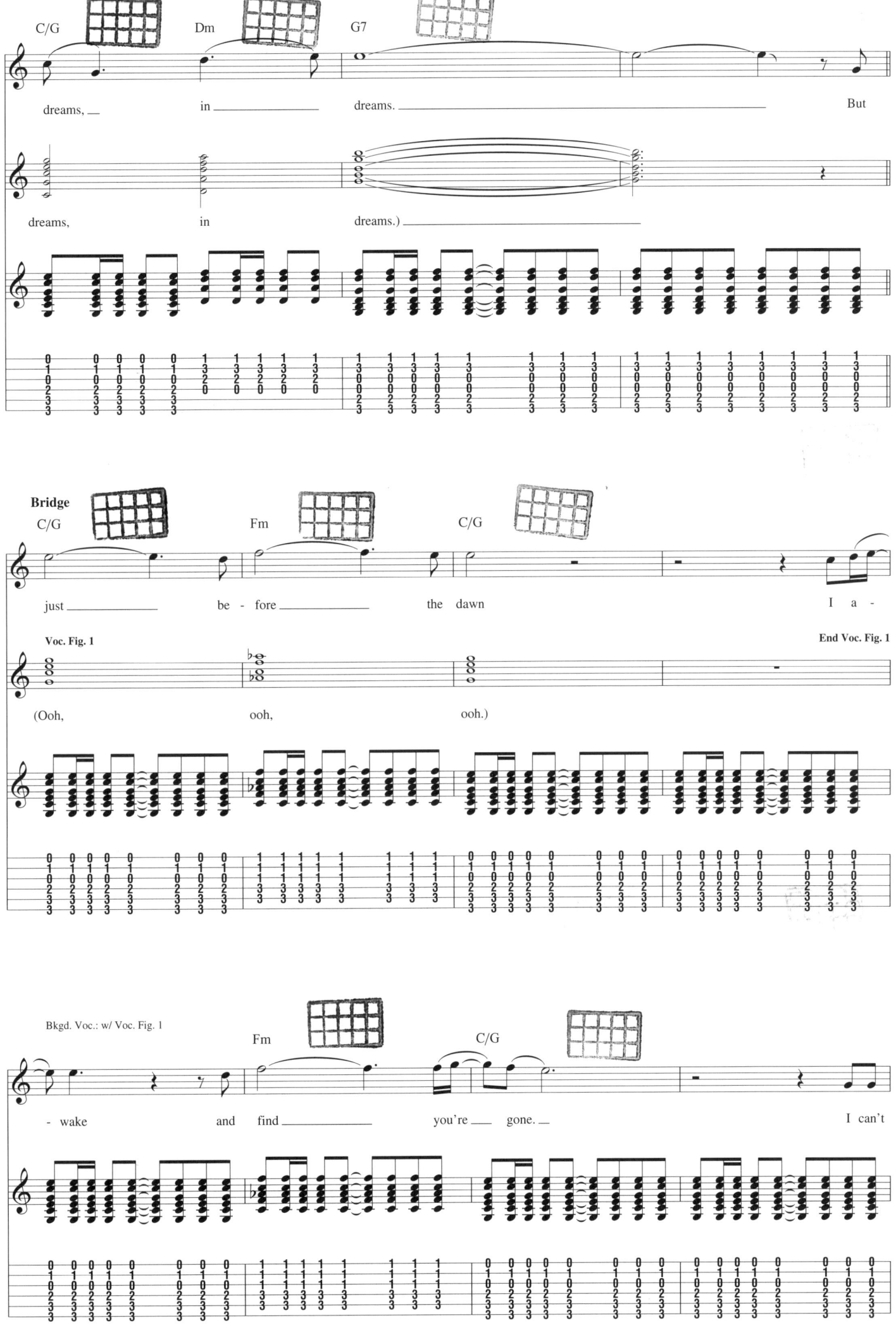

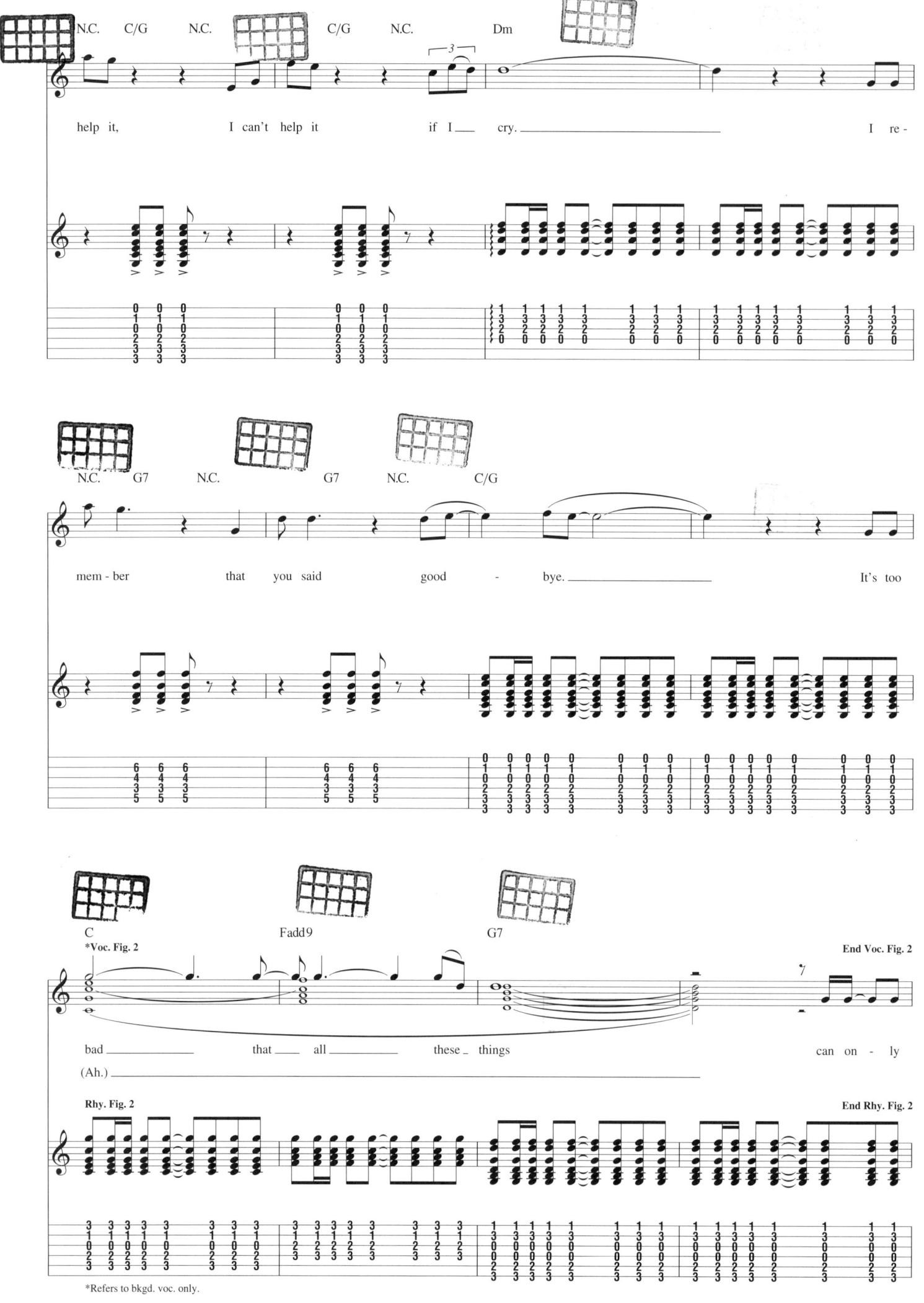

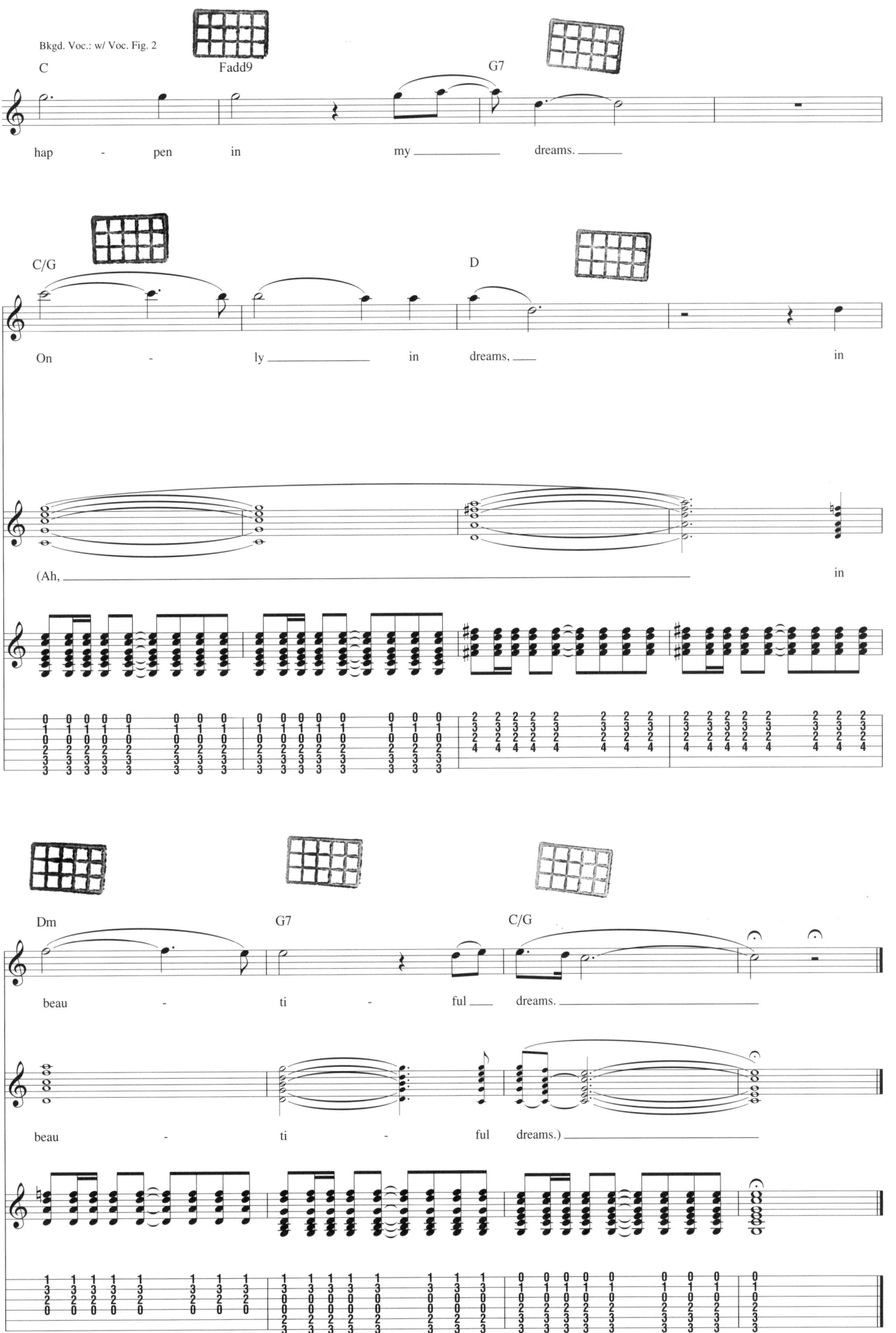

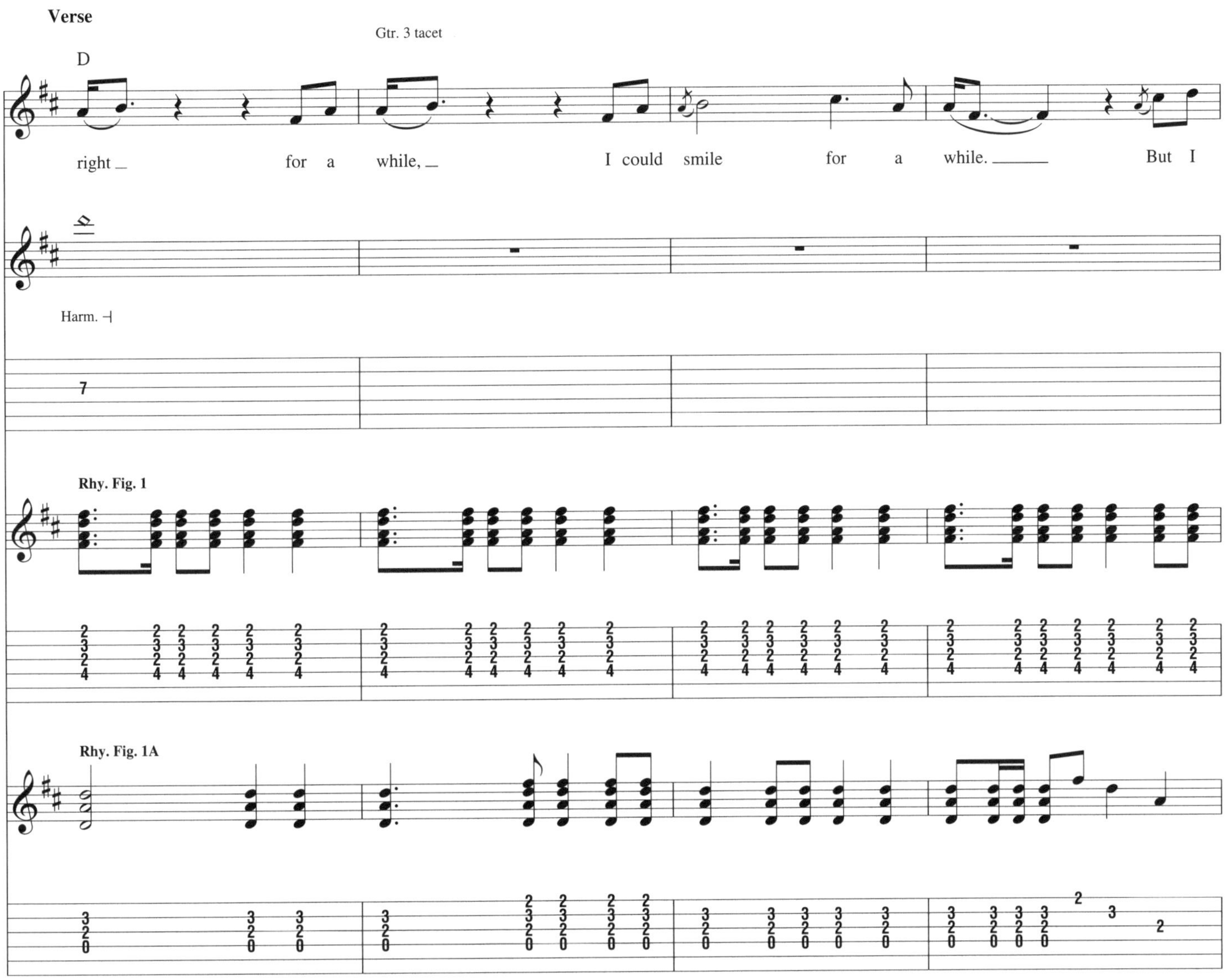
Verse
Gtr. 3 tacet
D
right for a while, I could smile for a while. But I
Harm.
Rhy. Fig. 1
Rhy. Fig. 1A

D+
G
N.C.
Gm
saw you last night, you held my hand so tight as you stopped to say hel - lo. You
Gtr. 1
End Rhy. Fig. 1
Gtr. 2
End Rhy. Fig. 1A

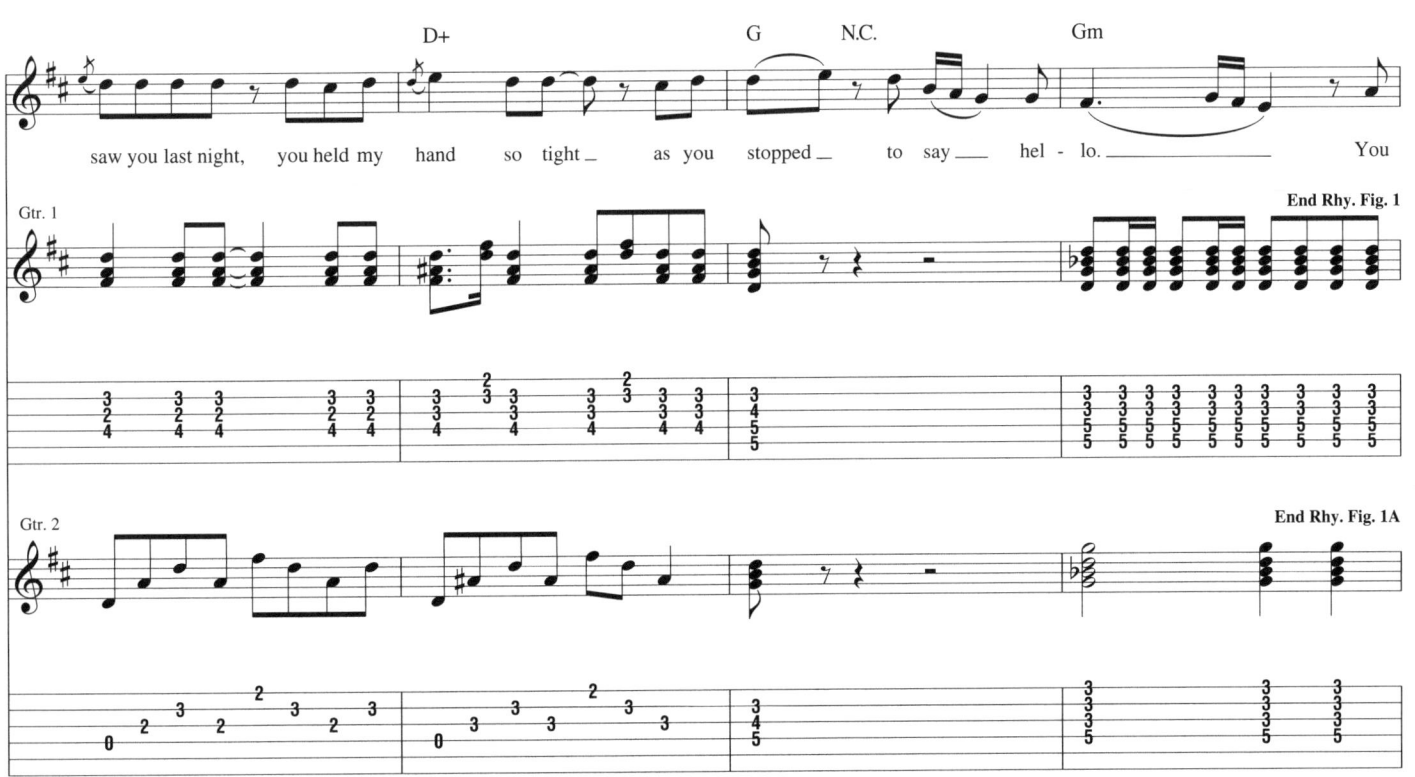

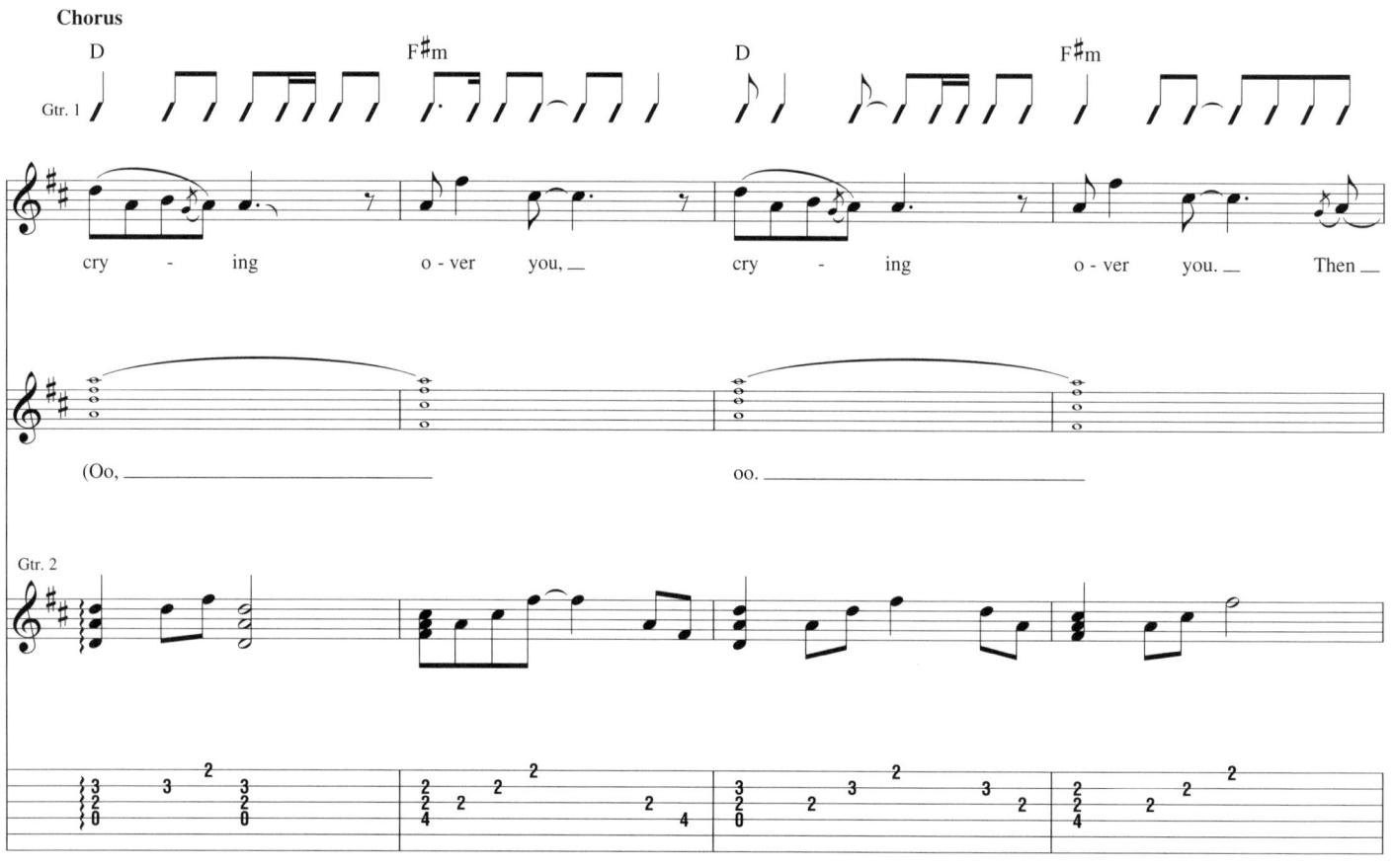

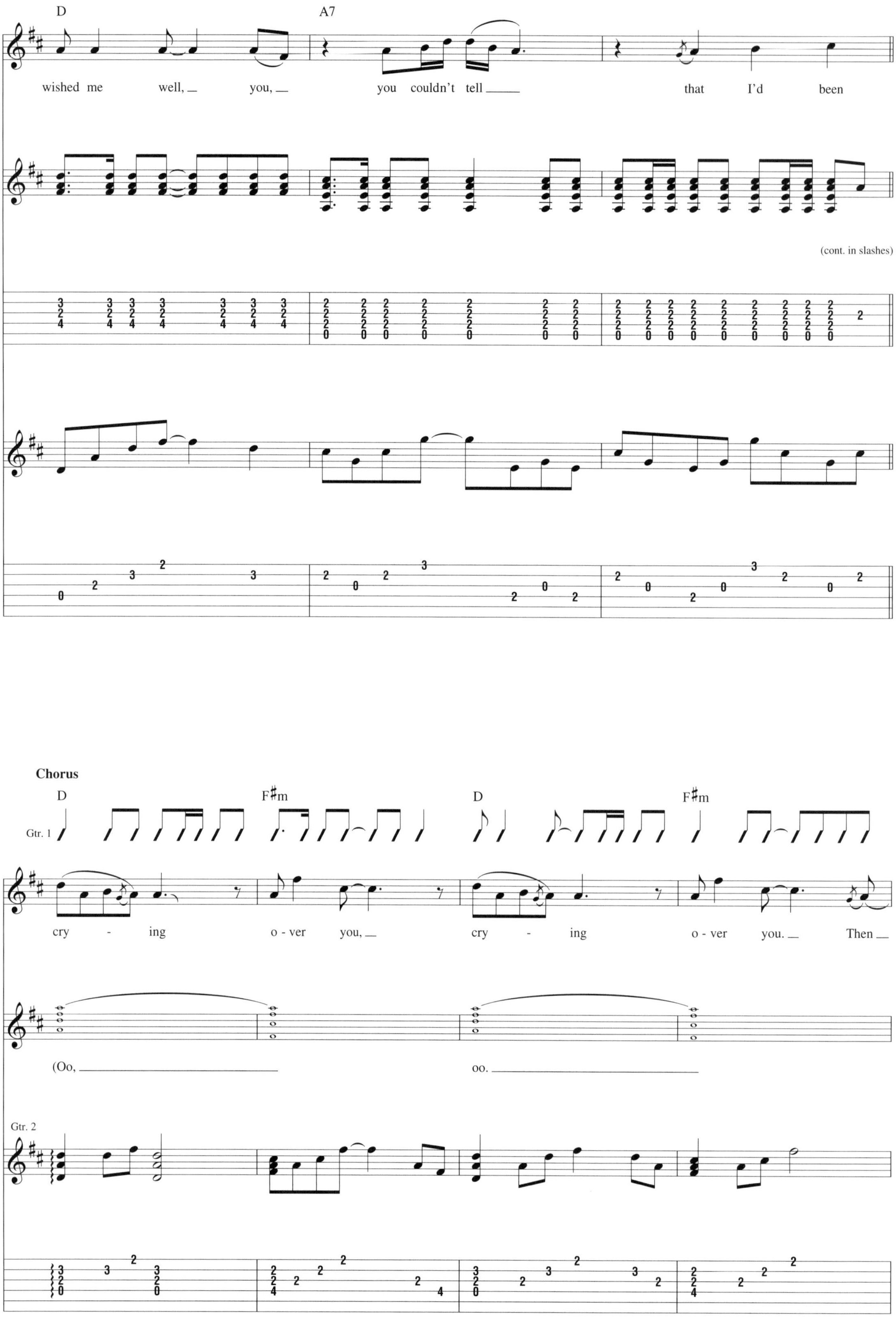
D
A7
wished me well, you, you couldn't tell that I'd been
(cont. in slashes)
Chorus
D
F♯m
D
F♯m
Gtr. 1
cry - ing o - ver you, cry - ing o - ver you. Then
(Oo, oo.
Gtr. 2

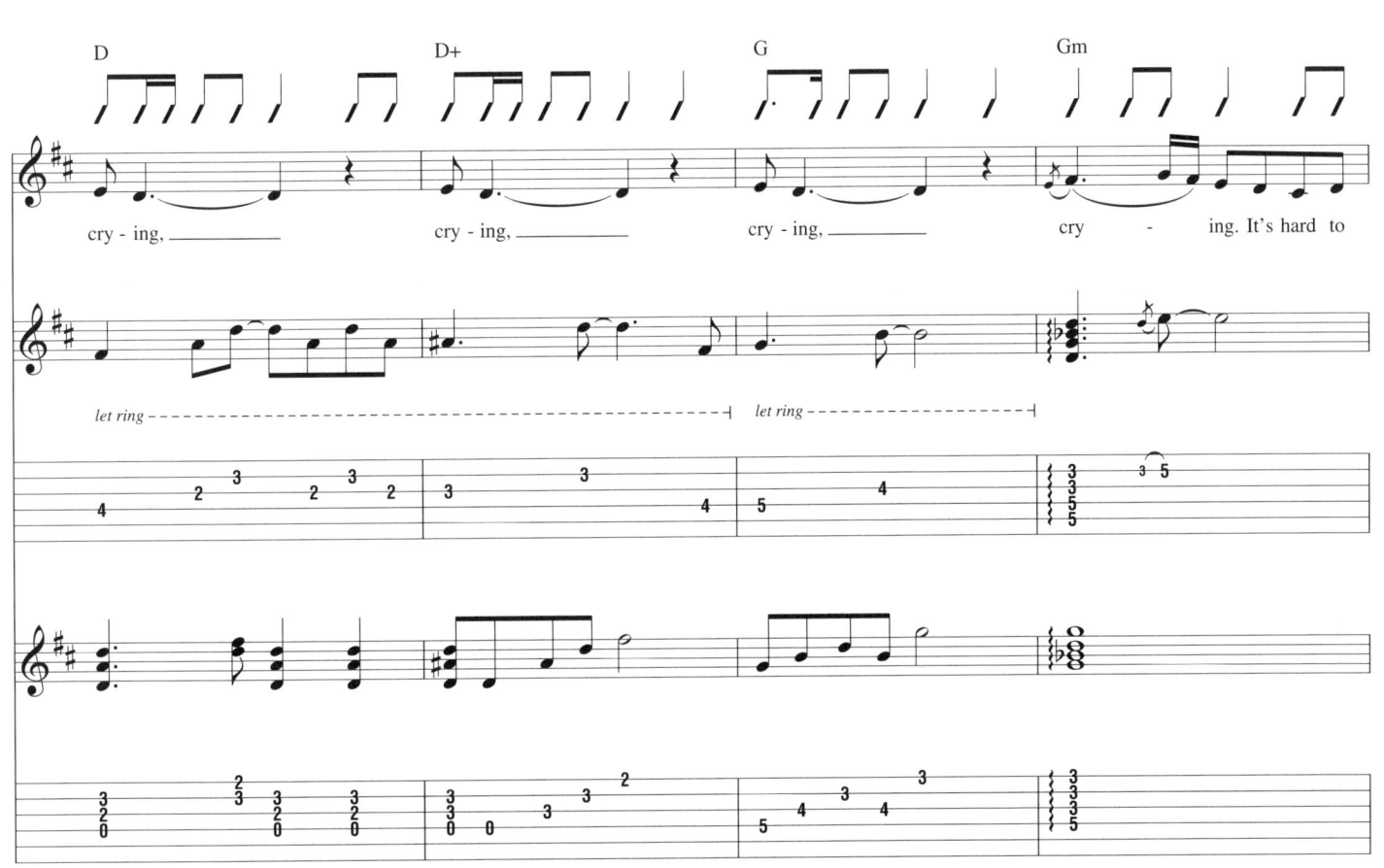

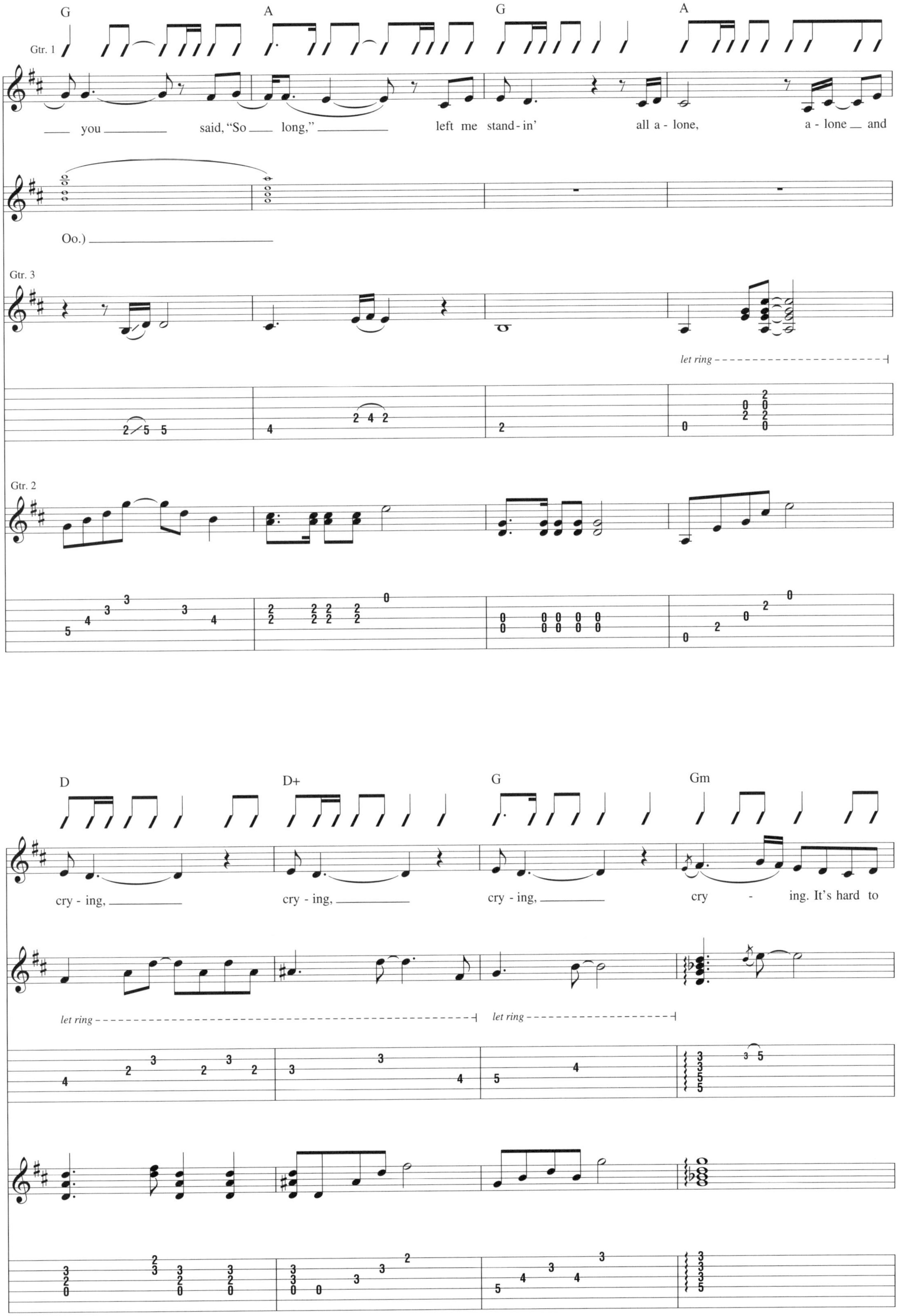
G A G A
Gtr. 1
you said, "So long," left me stand-in' all a-lone, a-lone and
Oo.)
Gtr. 3
let ring
Gtr. 2
D D+ G Gm
cry-ing, cry-ing, cry-ing, cry - ing. It's hard to
let ring
let ring

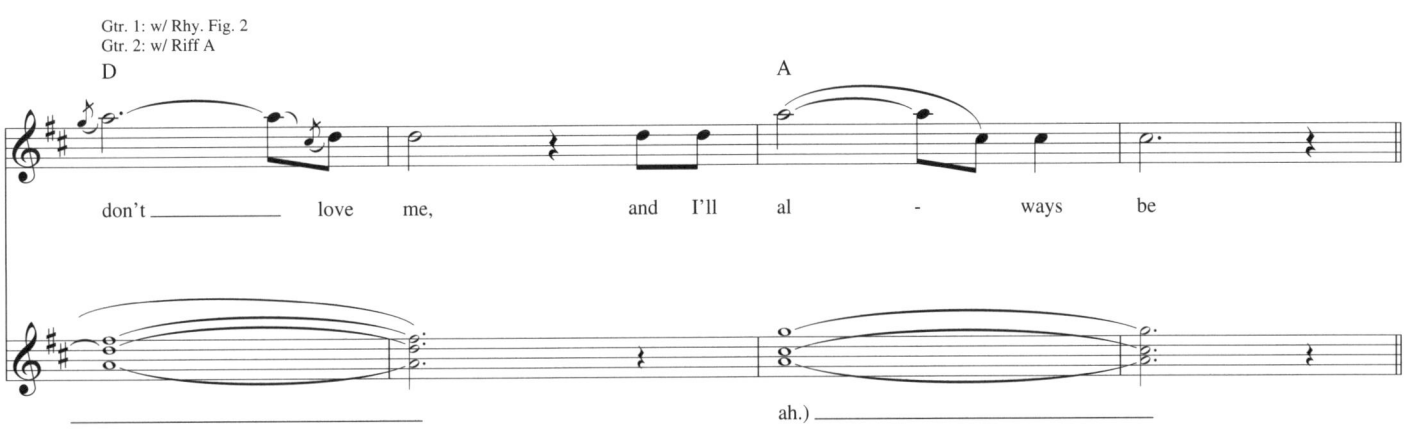

109

G
A
G
A
Yes, now you're gone and from this mo-ment on I'll be
oo,
oo,
Gtr. 2
Gtr. 1
(cont. in slashes)

D
D+
G
Gm
Gtr. 1
crying, crying, crying cry - ing, and
Ah,
ah,
Gtr. 2

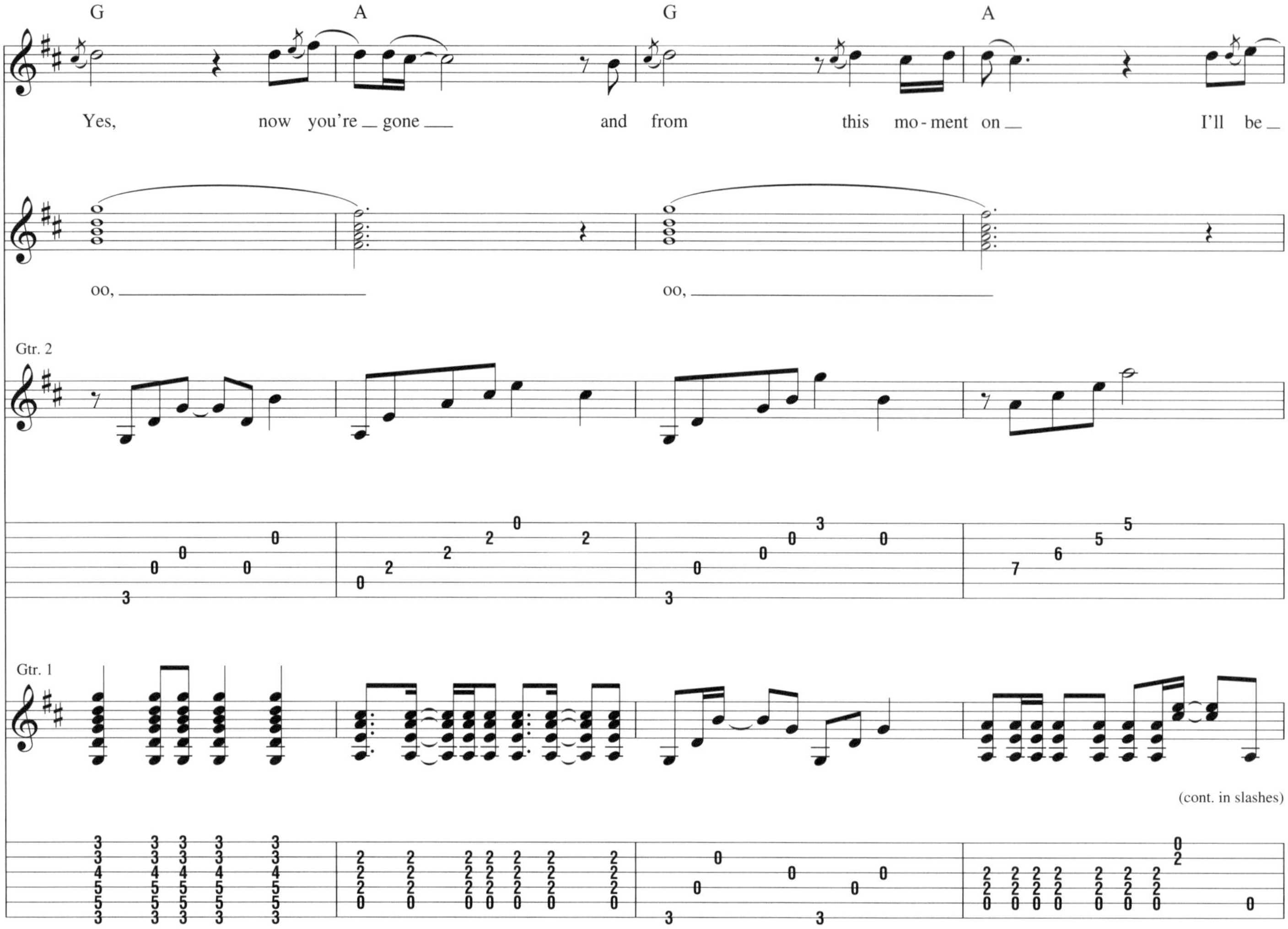

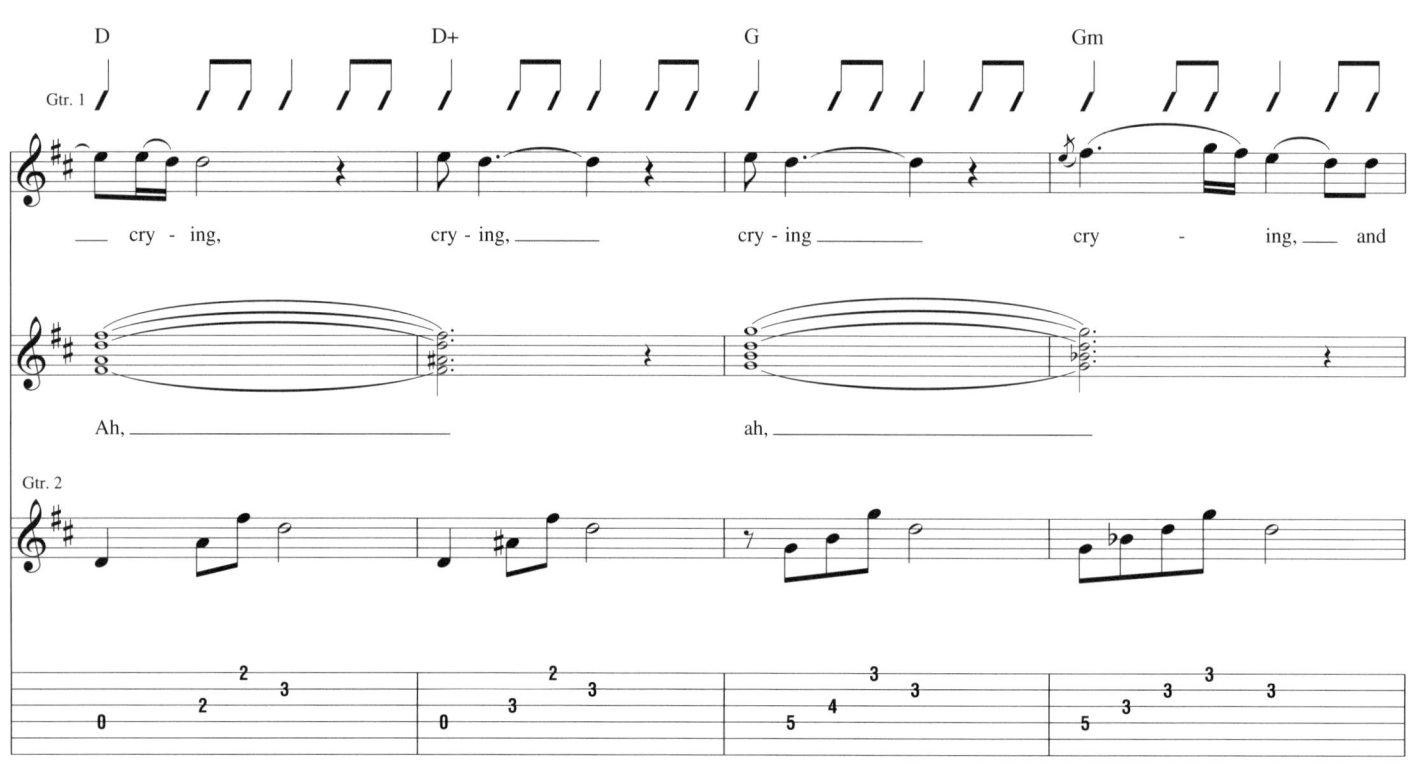

D
Bm
G
A
(cont. in slashes)
cry - ing, cry - ing o - ver
ah, ah, ah,

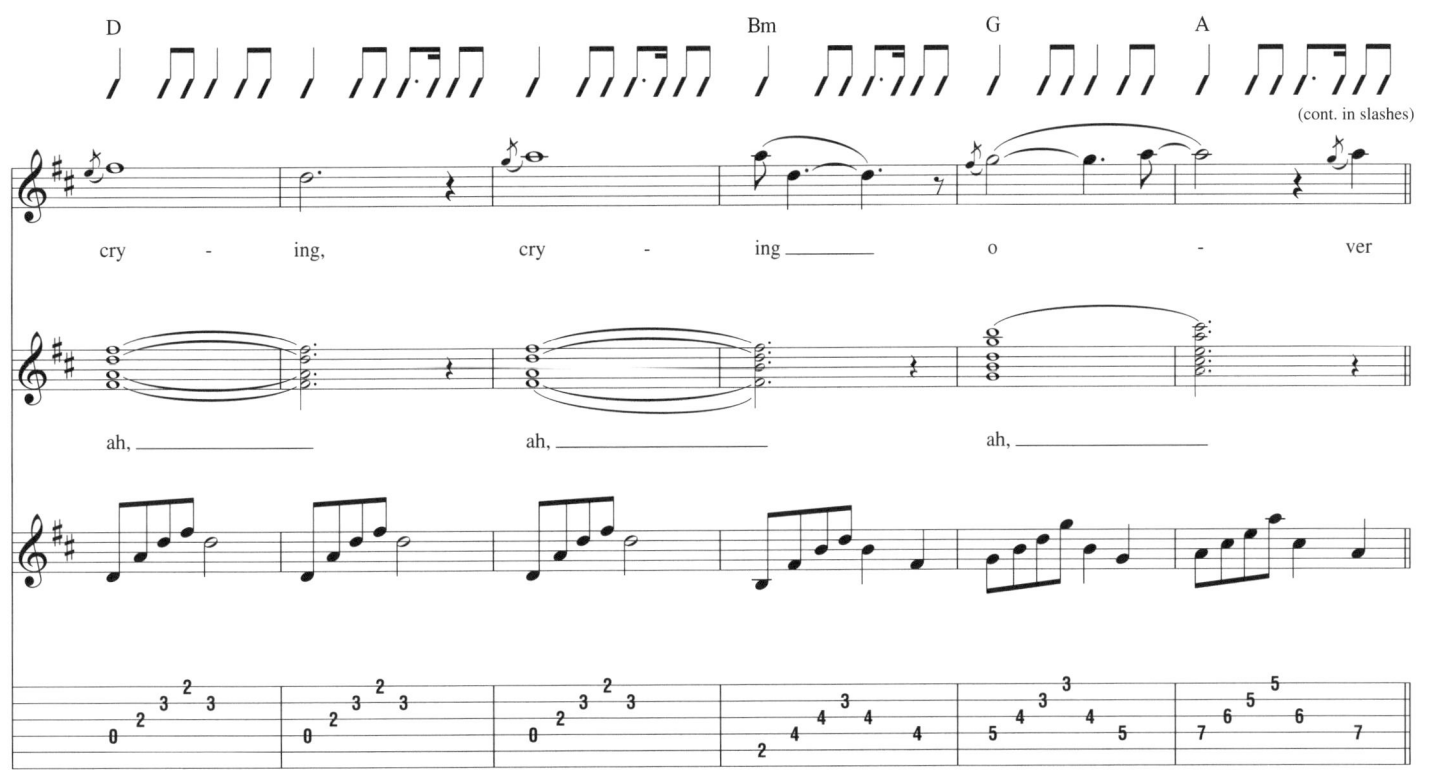

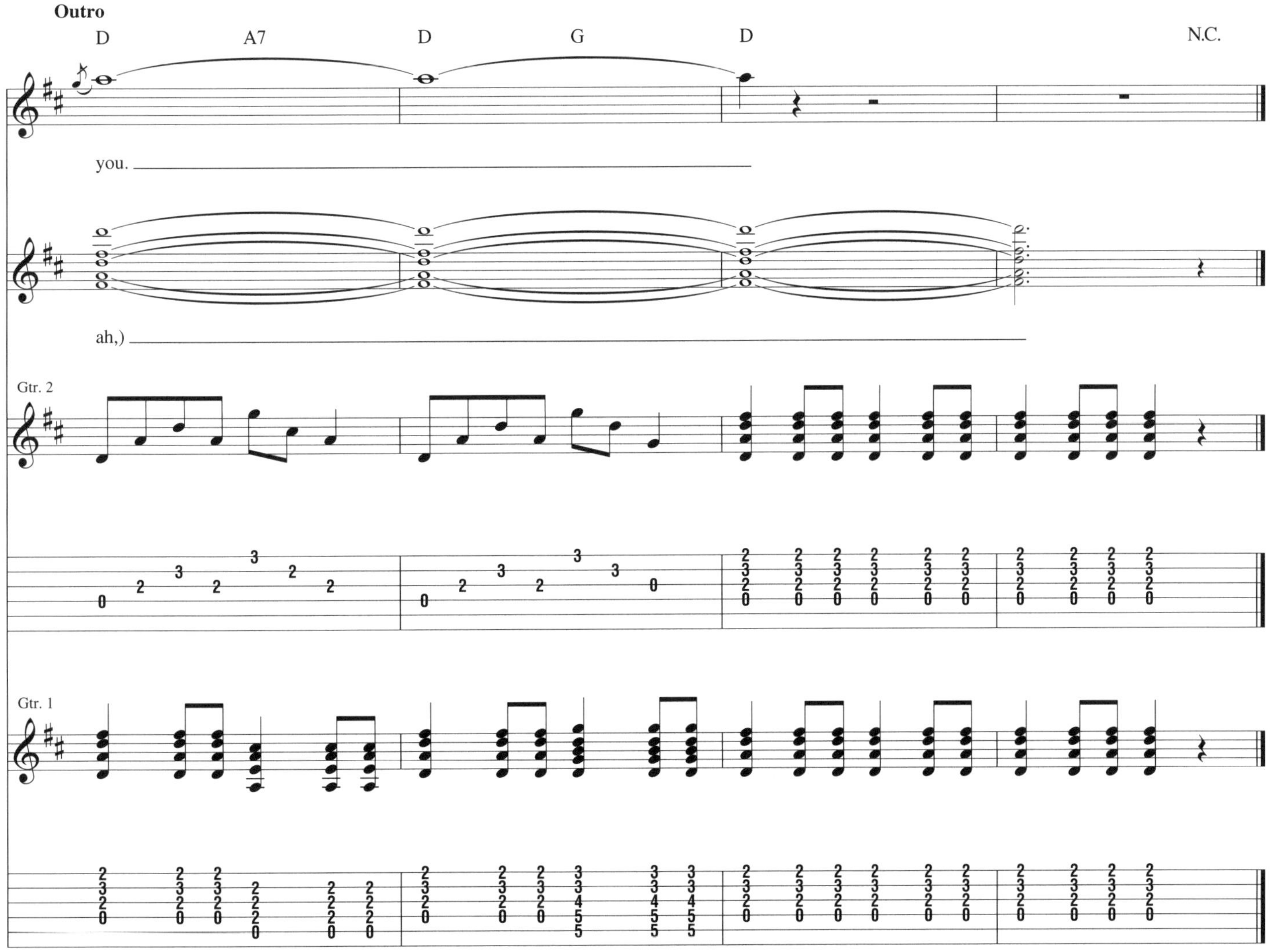
Outro
D
A7
D
G
D
N.C.
you.
ah,)
Gtr. 2
Gtr. 1

Candy Man

Words and Music by Beverly Ross and Frederick Neil

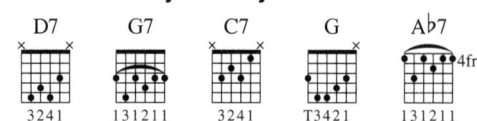
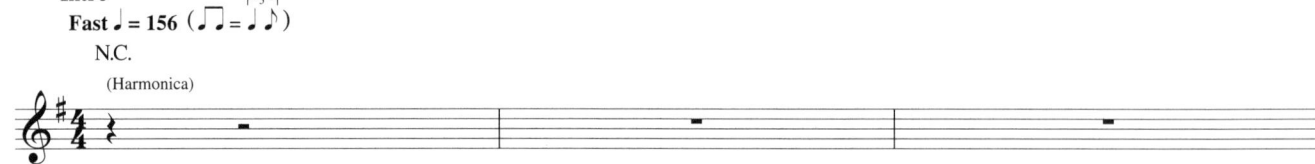

Copyright © 1961 by Unichappell Music Inc.
Copyright Renewed
International Copyright Secured All Rights Reserved

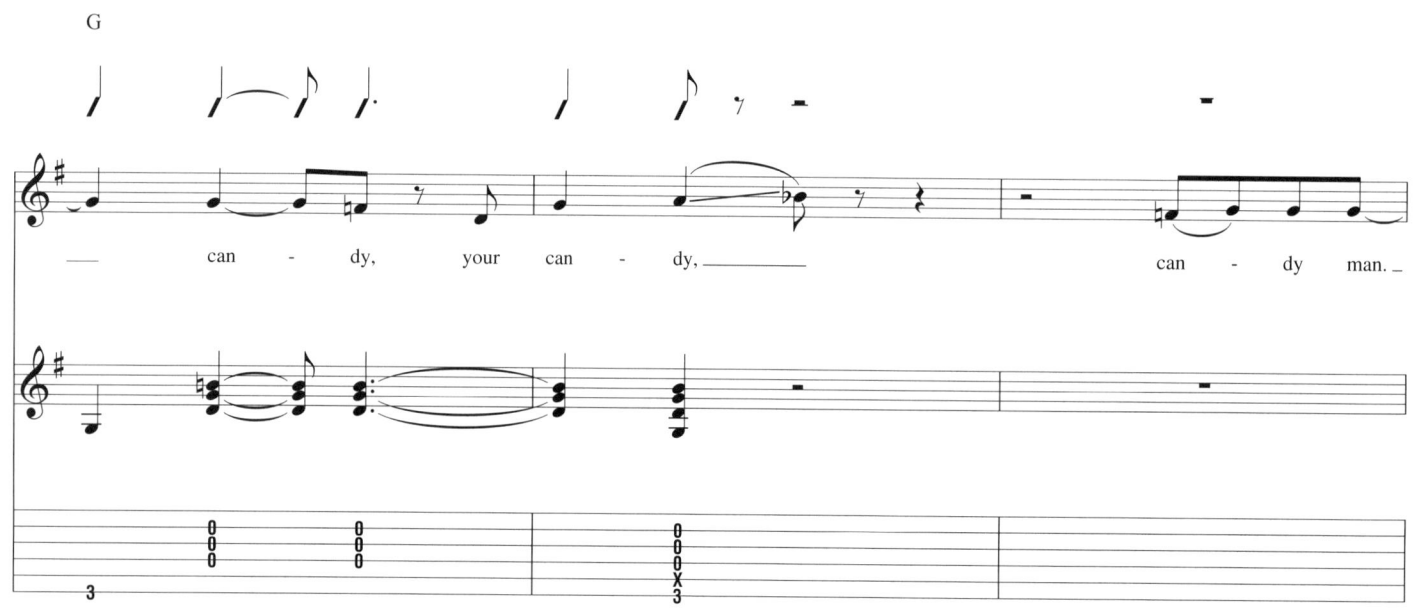

Verse

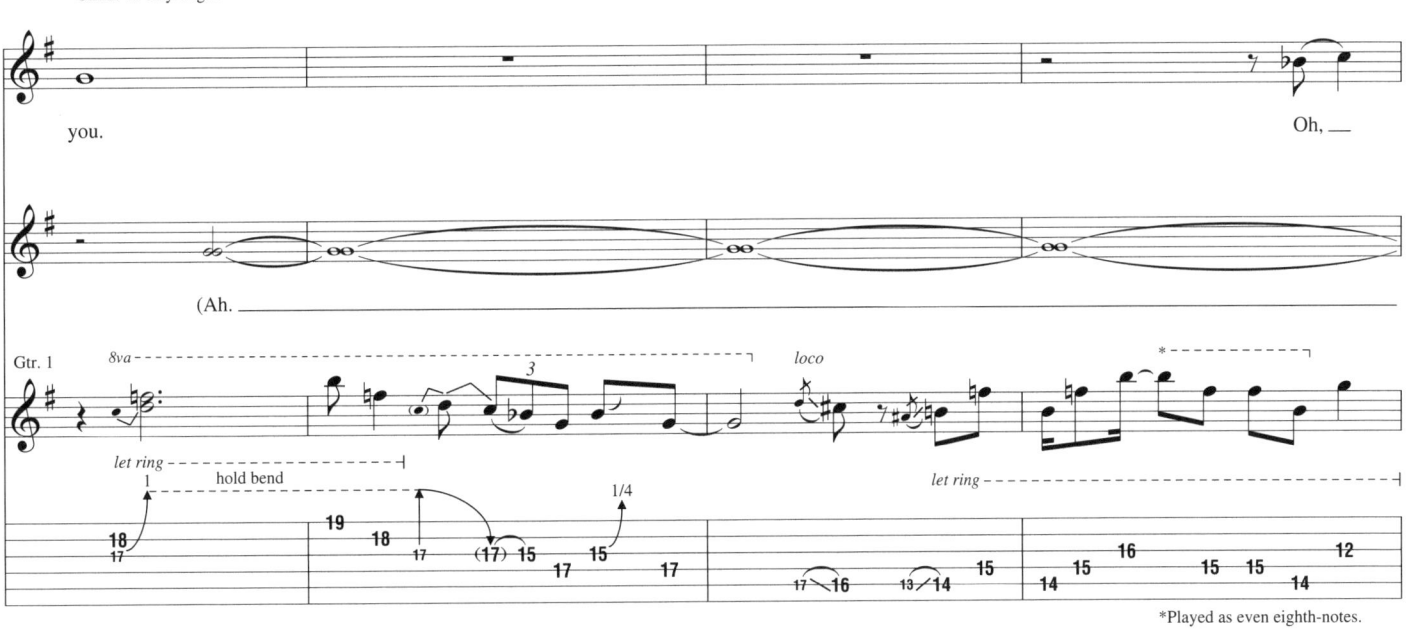
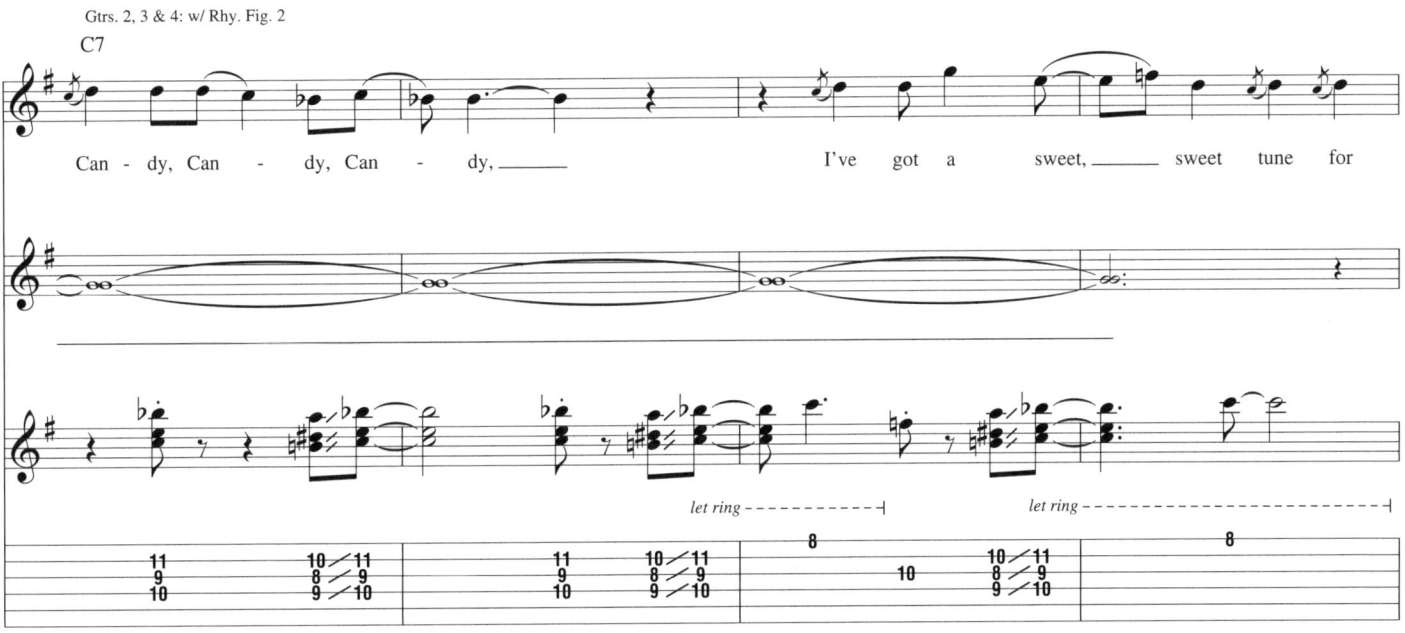
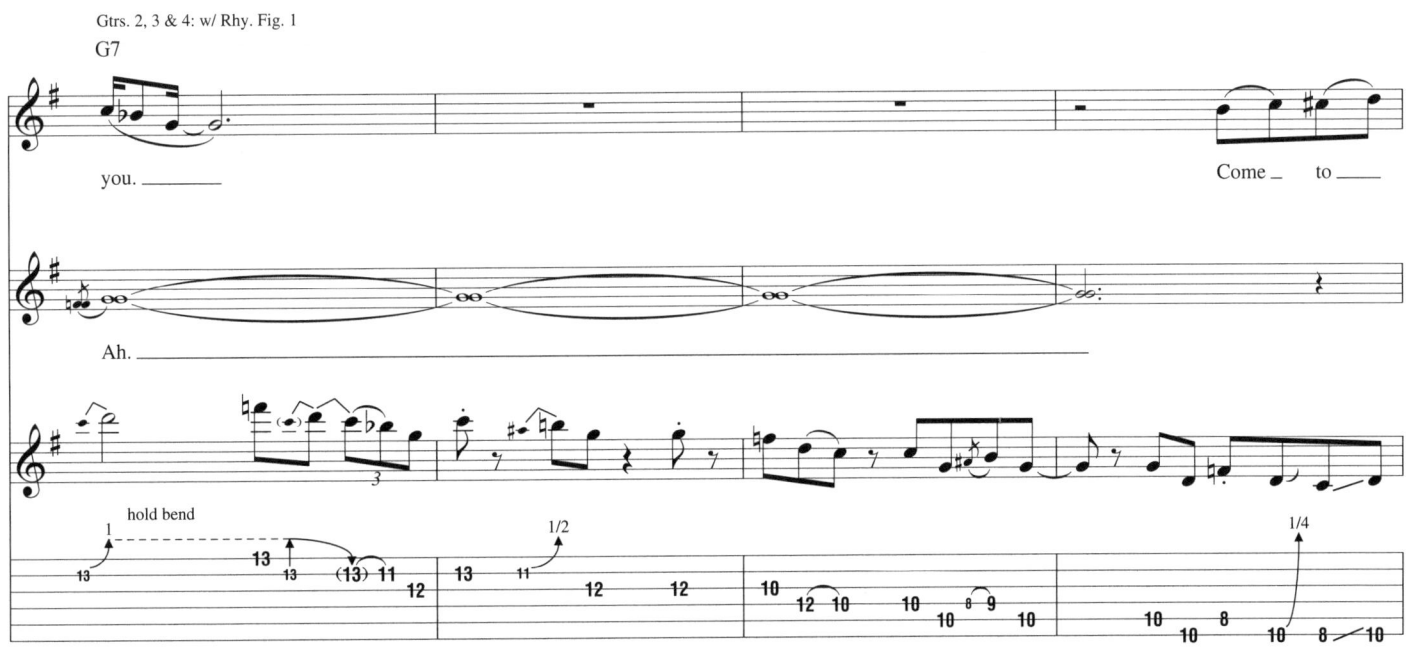

122

Go, Go, Go

Words and Music by Roy Orbison

*Bass arr. for gtr.

**Doubled by two acous. gtrs. (Tom Waits & T Bone Burnett).

***T=Thumb on 6th string

†Chord symbols reflect basic harmony.

Copyright © 1956 (Renewed 1985) ROY ORBISON MUSIC COMPANY and BARBARA ORBISON MUSIC COMPANY
All Rights Reserved   Used by Permission

1/2
let ring
T
let ring
T

Gtr. 4 (elec.) (James Burton)
mf
w/ clean tone
w/ pick & fingers
let ring
Gtr. 3
1
let ring
Gtr. 2
let ring
T
let ring
T

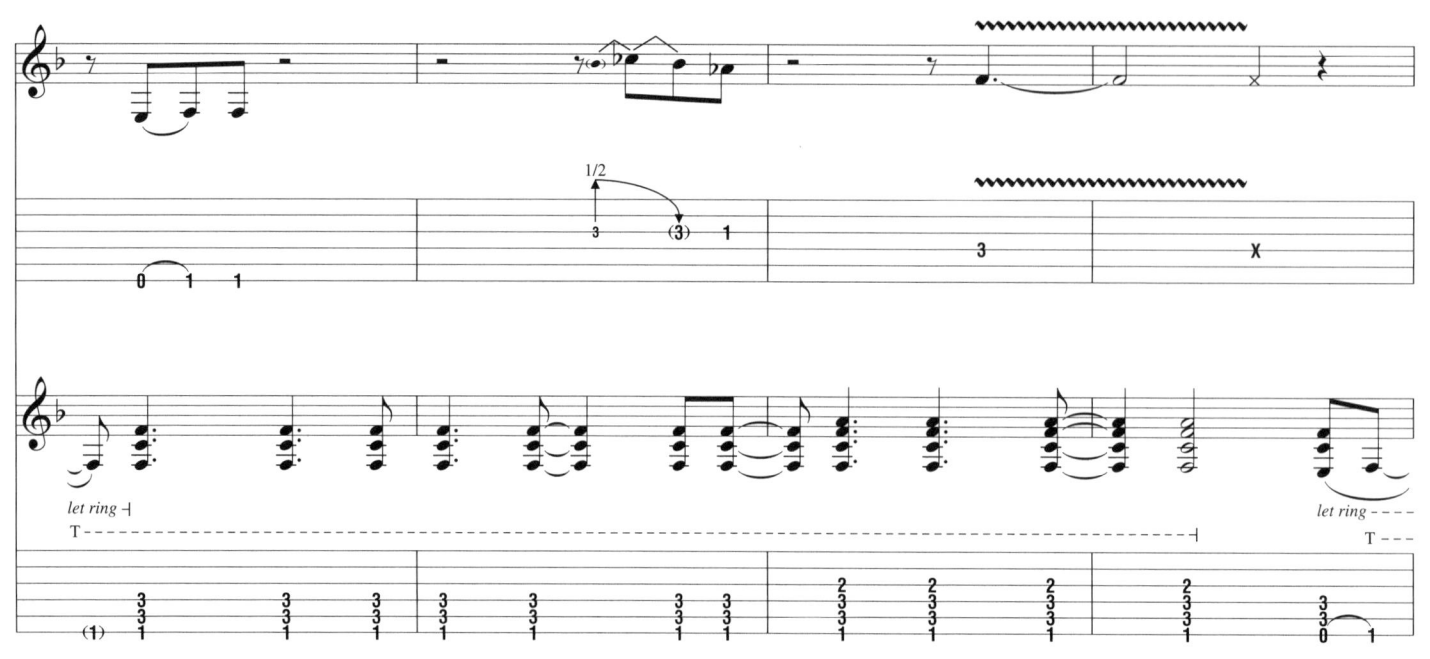

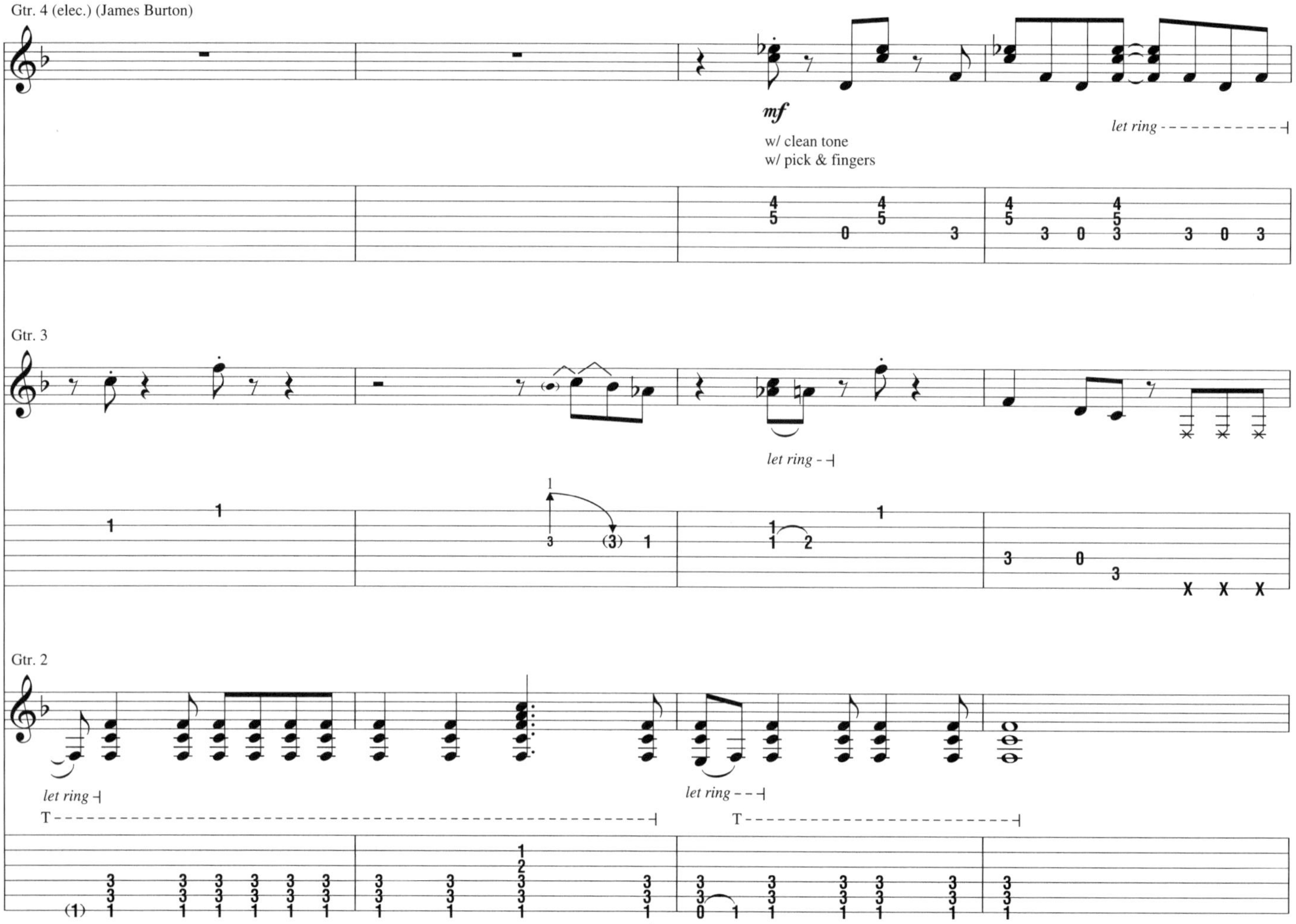

B♭
F
roll, move on down the line. We're gon - na
Gtr. 4
P.M. P.M. P.M. P.M. P.M. P.M. P.M. P.M. P.M. P.M. P.M.
Gtr. 3
P.M. P.M. P.M. P.M. P.M.
1/4
Gtr. 2
Rhy. Fig. 2
T T T T

C
B♭
F
do right, do right all the time. 2. Yeah,
P.M. P.M. P.M. P.M. P.M. P.M. P.M.
P.M. P.M. P.M.
1/2
End Rhy. Fig. 2
T T T

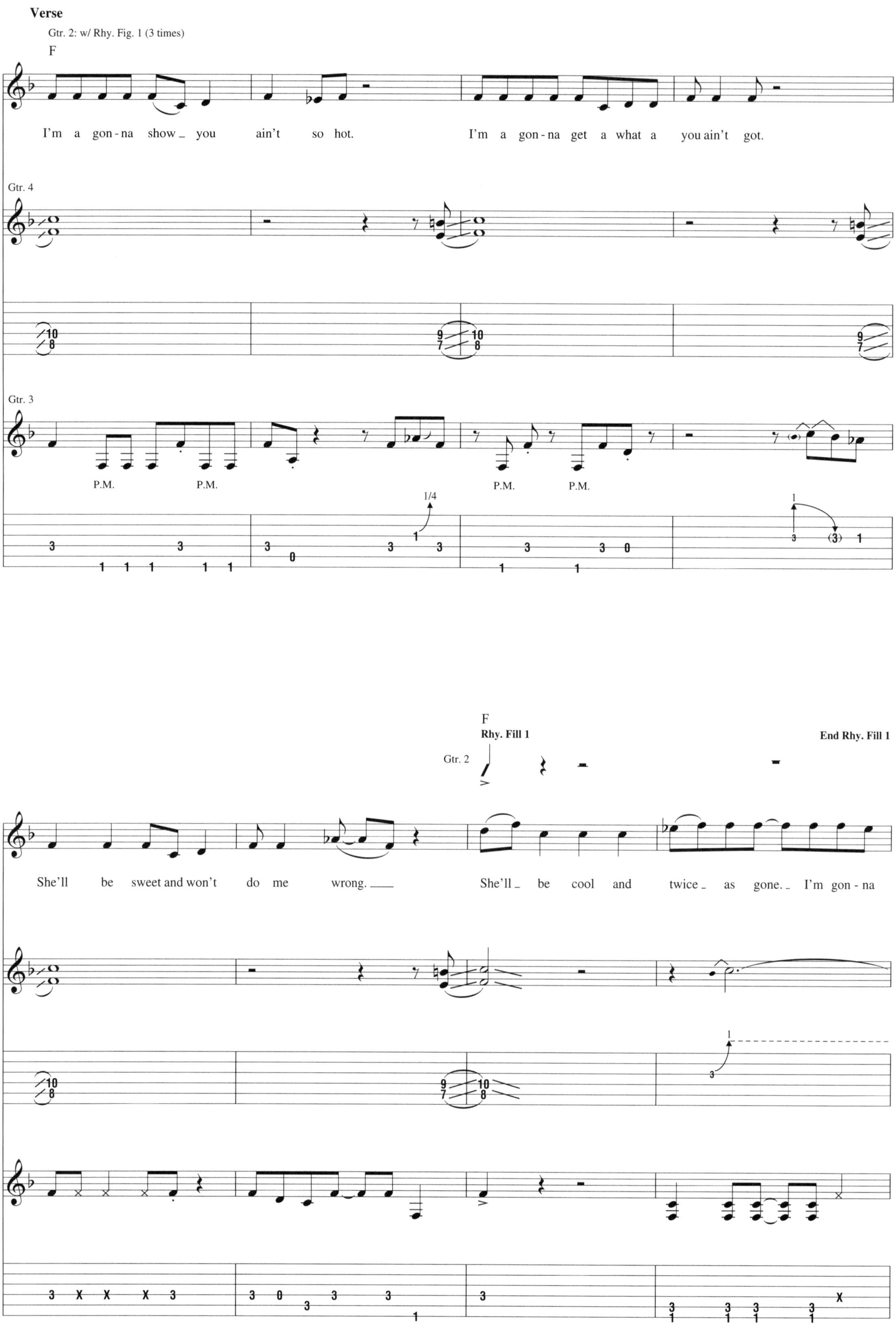
Verse
Gtr. 2: w/ Rhy. Fig. 1 (3 times)
F
I'm a gon-na show _ you ain't so hot. I'm a gon-na get a what a you ain't got.
Gtr. 4
Gtr. 3
P.M.
P.M.
P.M.
P.M.
1/4
F
Rhy. Fill 1
End Rhy. Fill 1
Gtr. 2
She'll be sweet and won't do me wrong. ___ She'll _ be cool and twice _ as gone. _ I'm gon-na

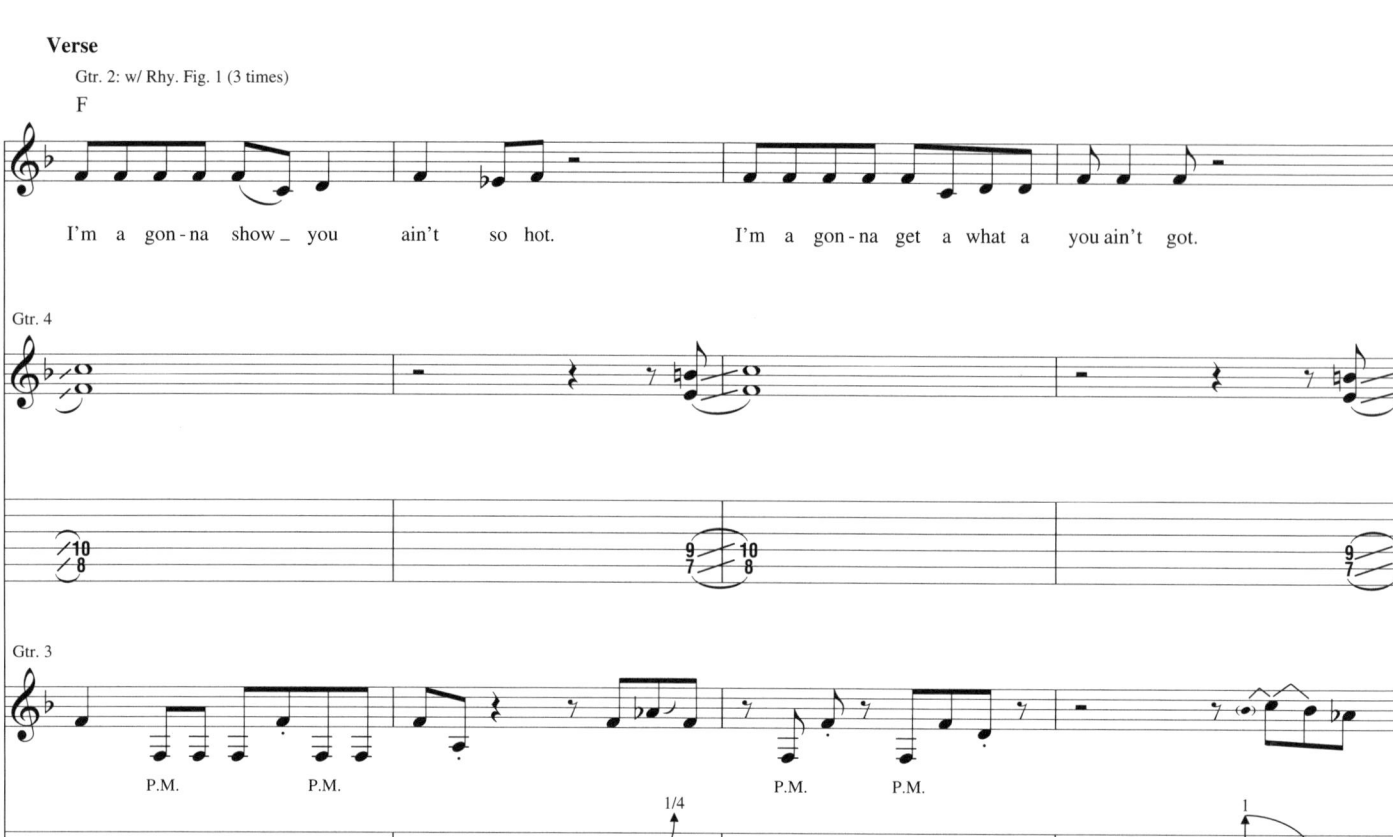

Verse

131

Guitar Solo

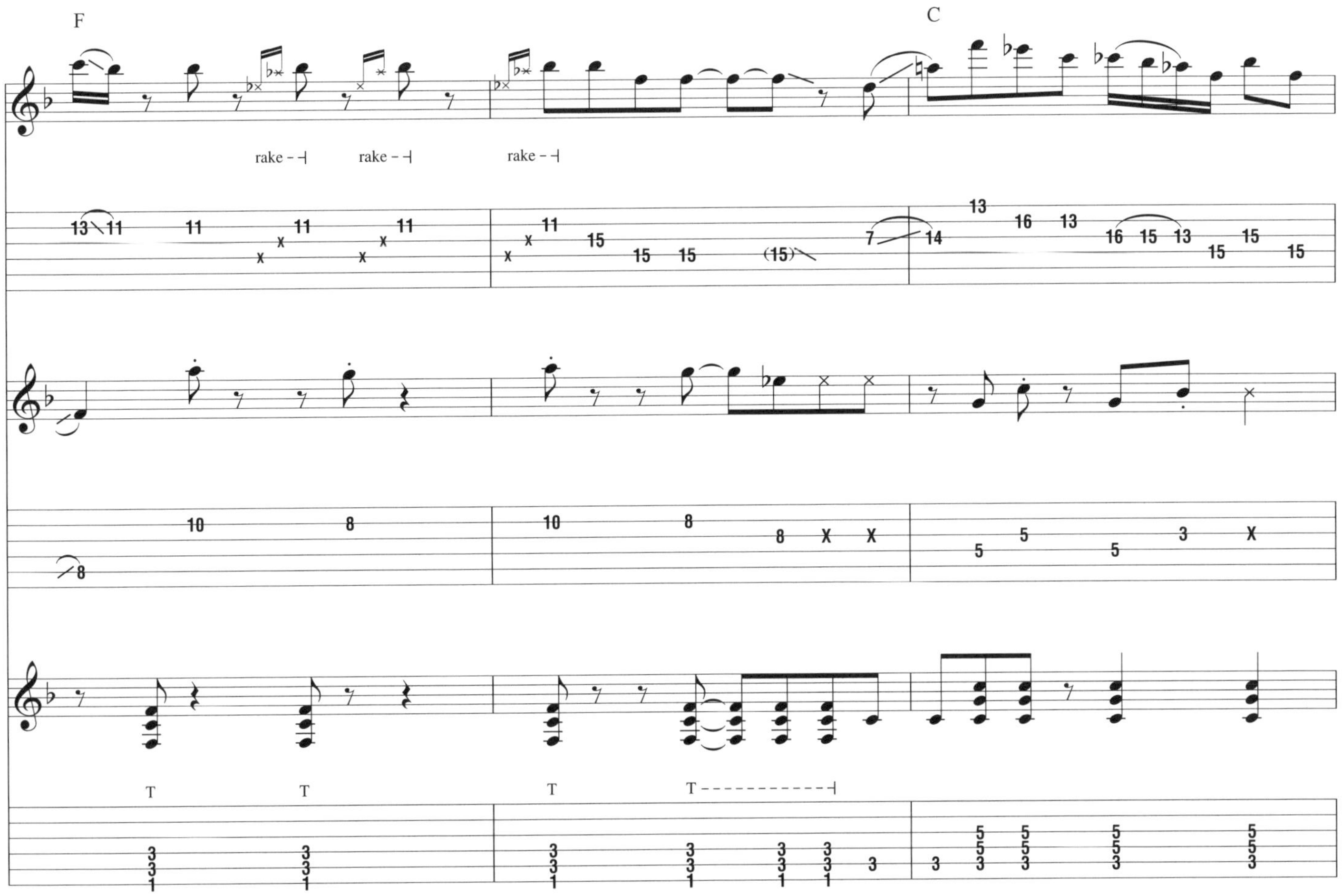
F
C
rake
rake
rake
T
T
T
T

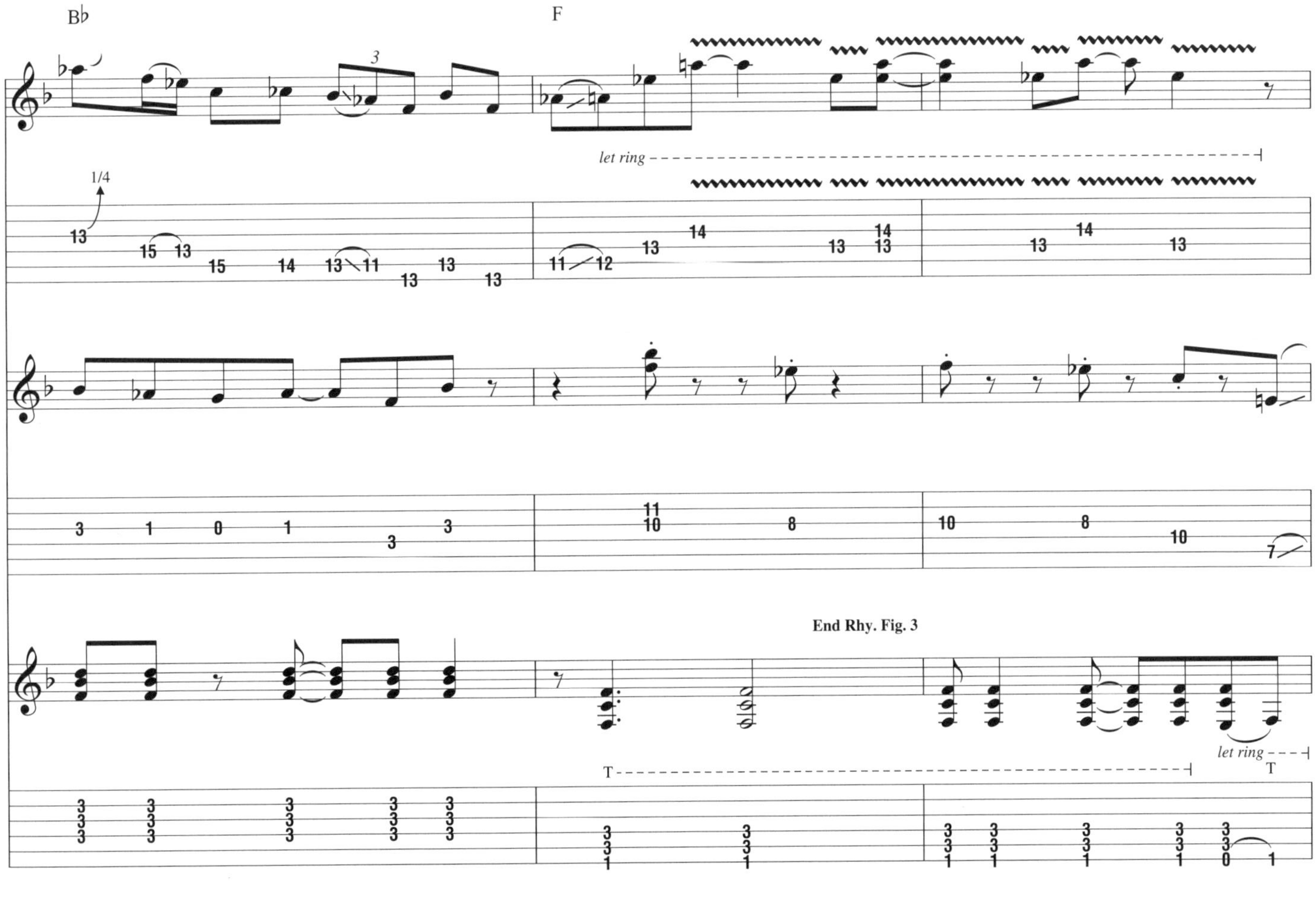
B♭
F
1/4
3
let ring
End Rhy. Fig. 3
T
let ring
T

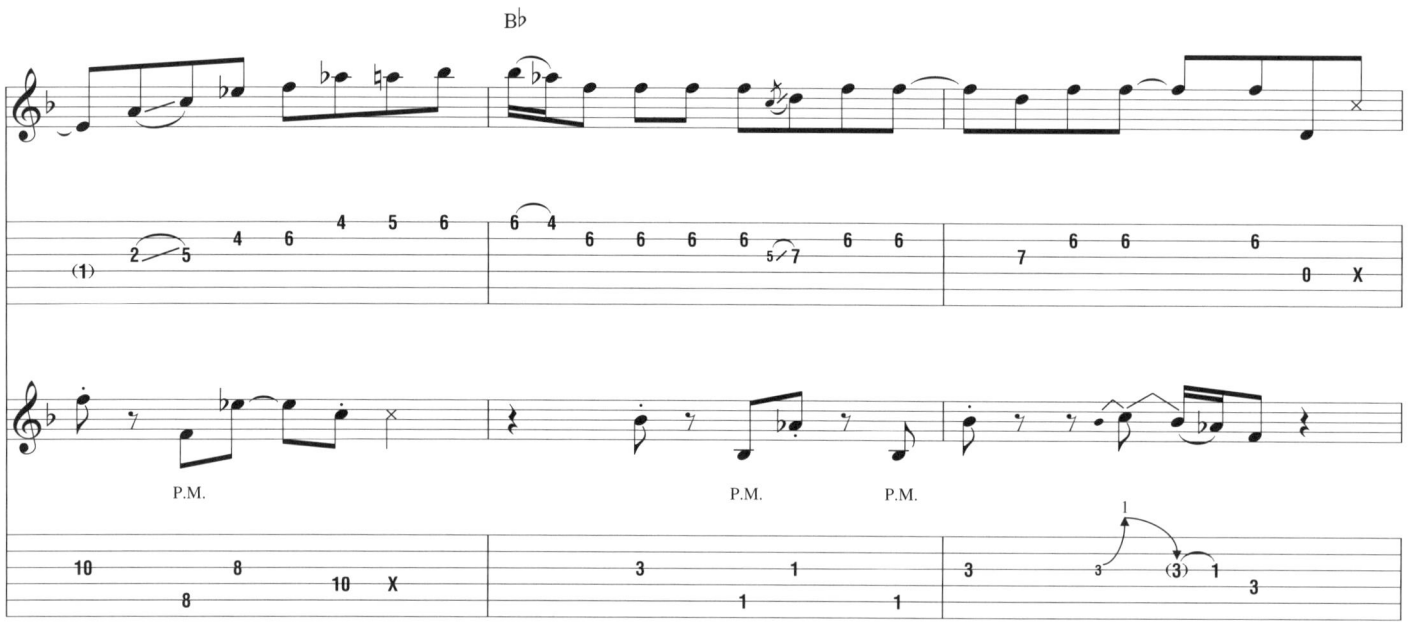
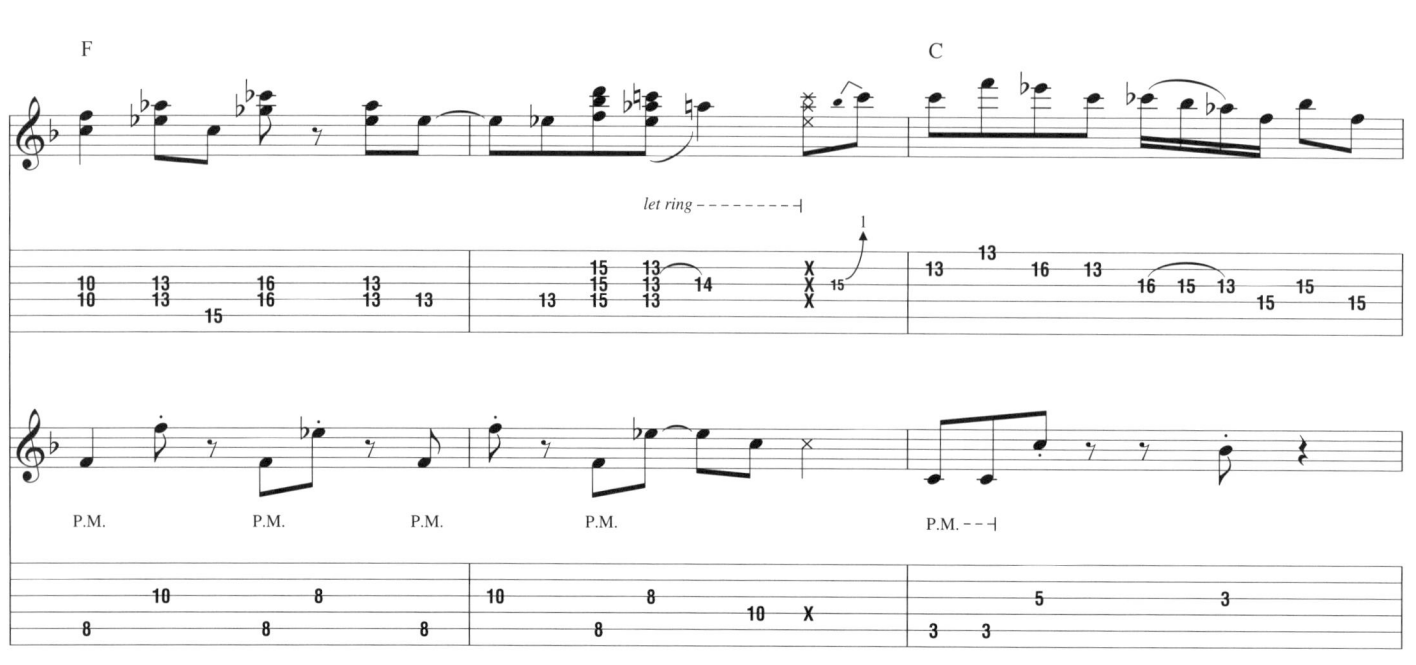

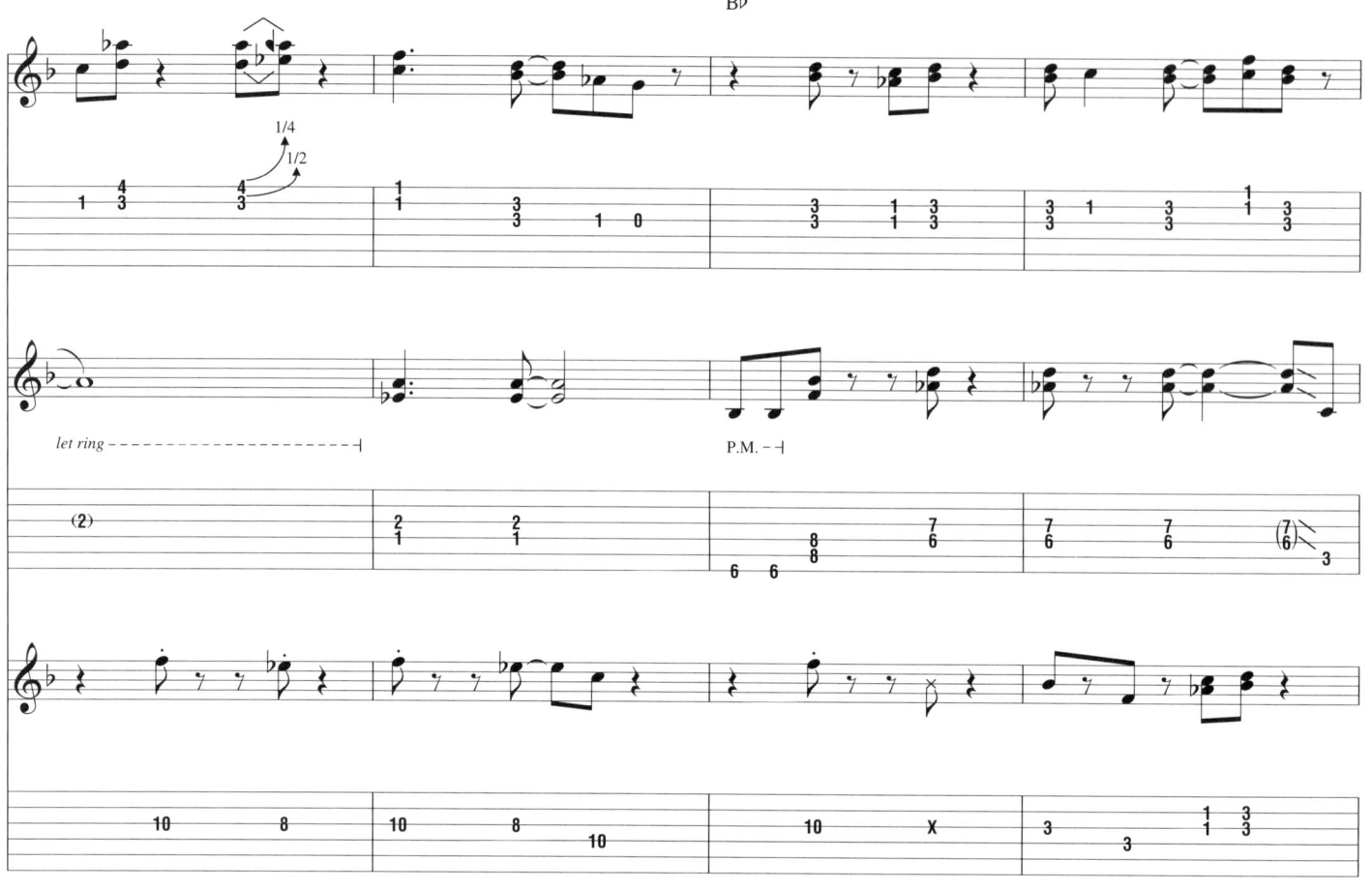

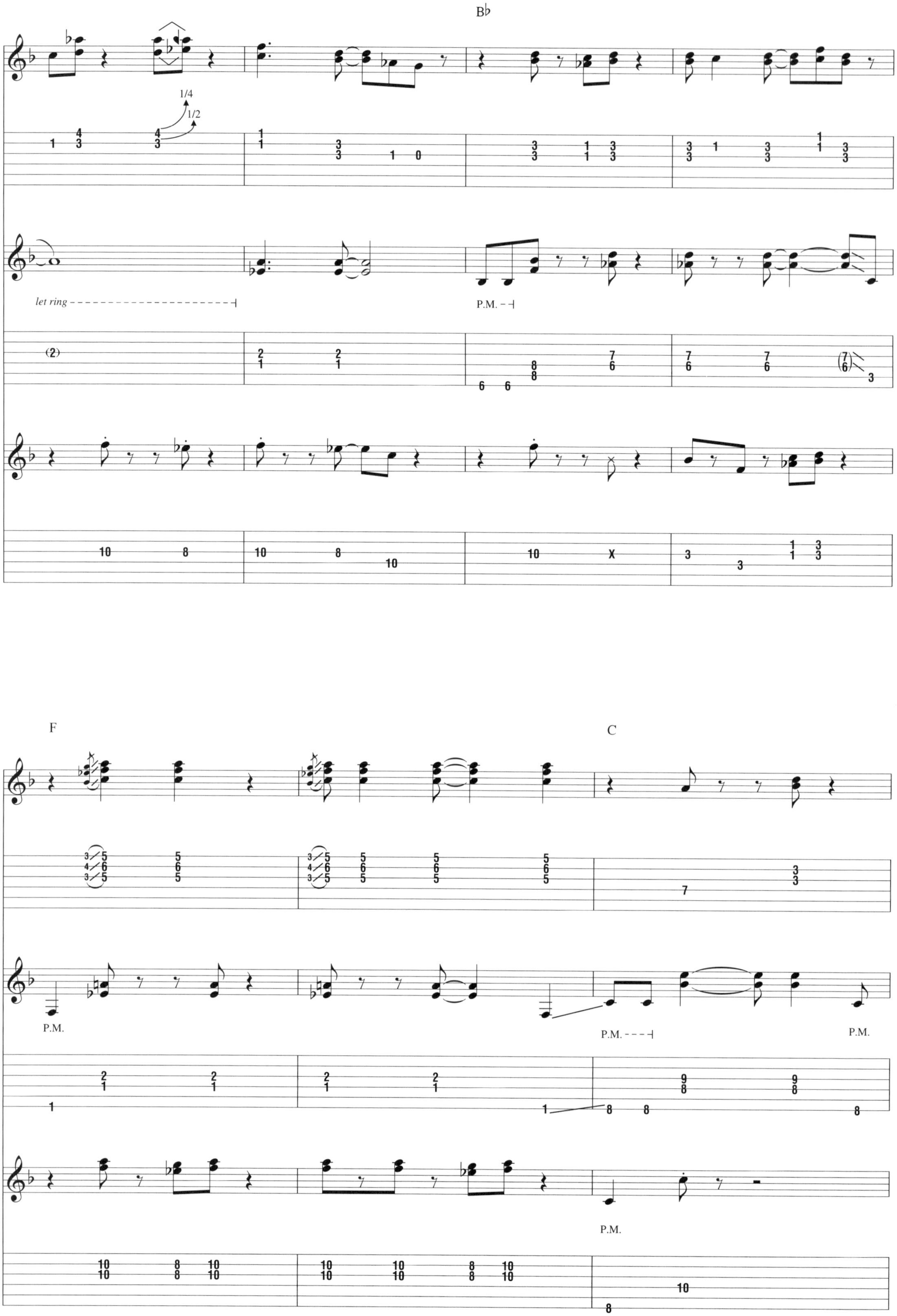
B♭
1/4
1/2
let ring
P.M.
F
C
P.M.
P.M.
P.M.
P.M.

Interlude

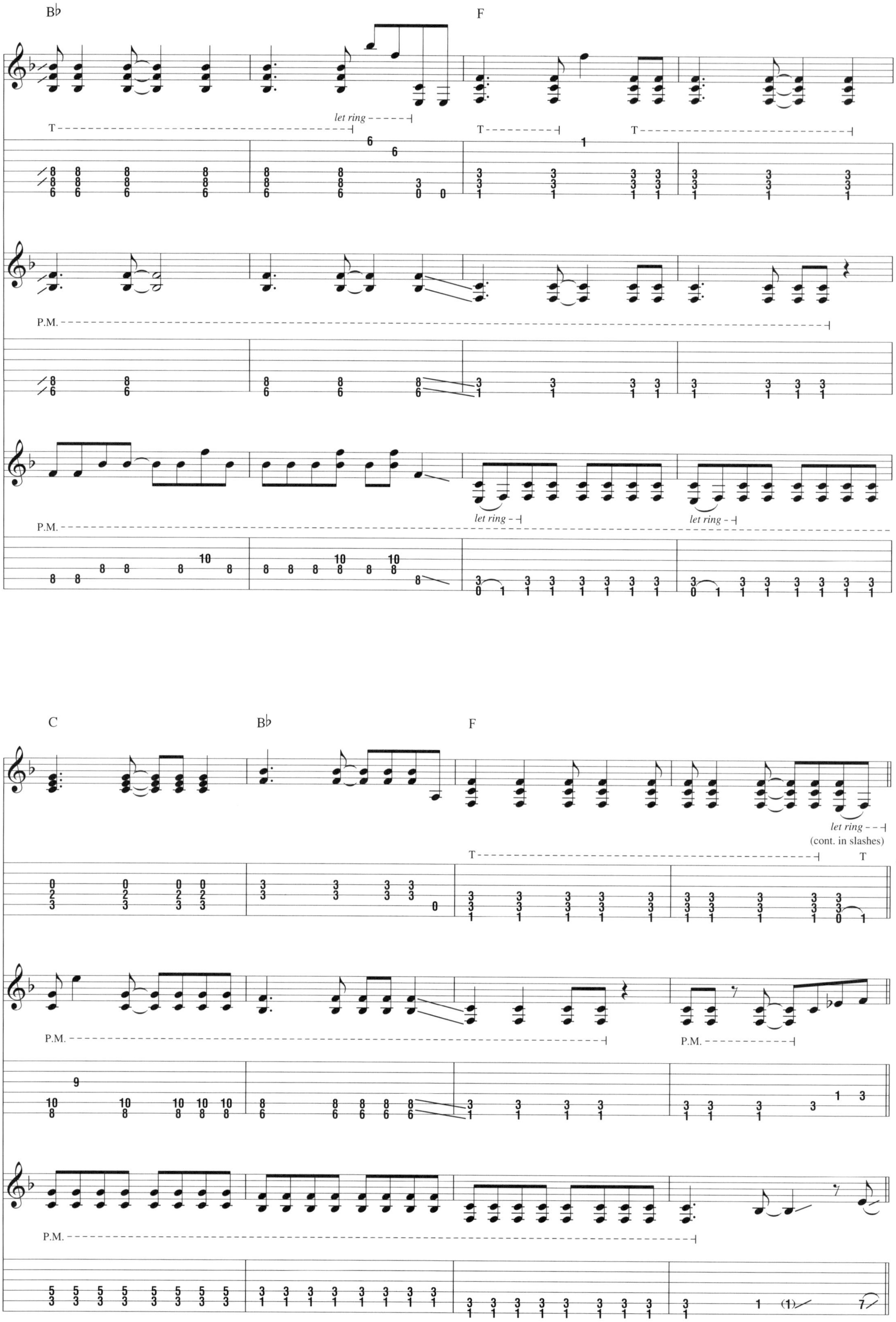
B♭
F
let ring
T
P.M.
C
B♭
F
let ring
(cont. in slashes)
T
P.M.

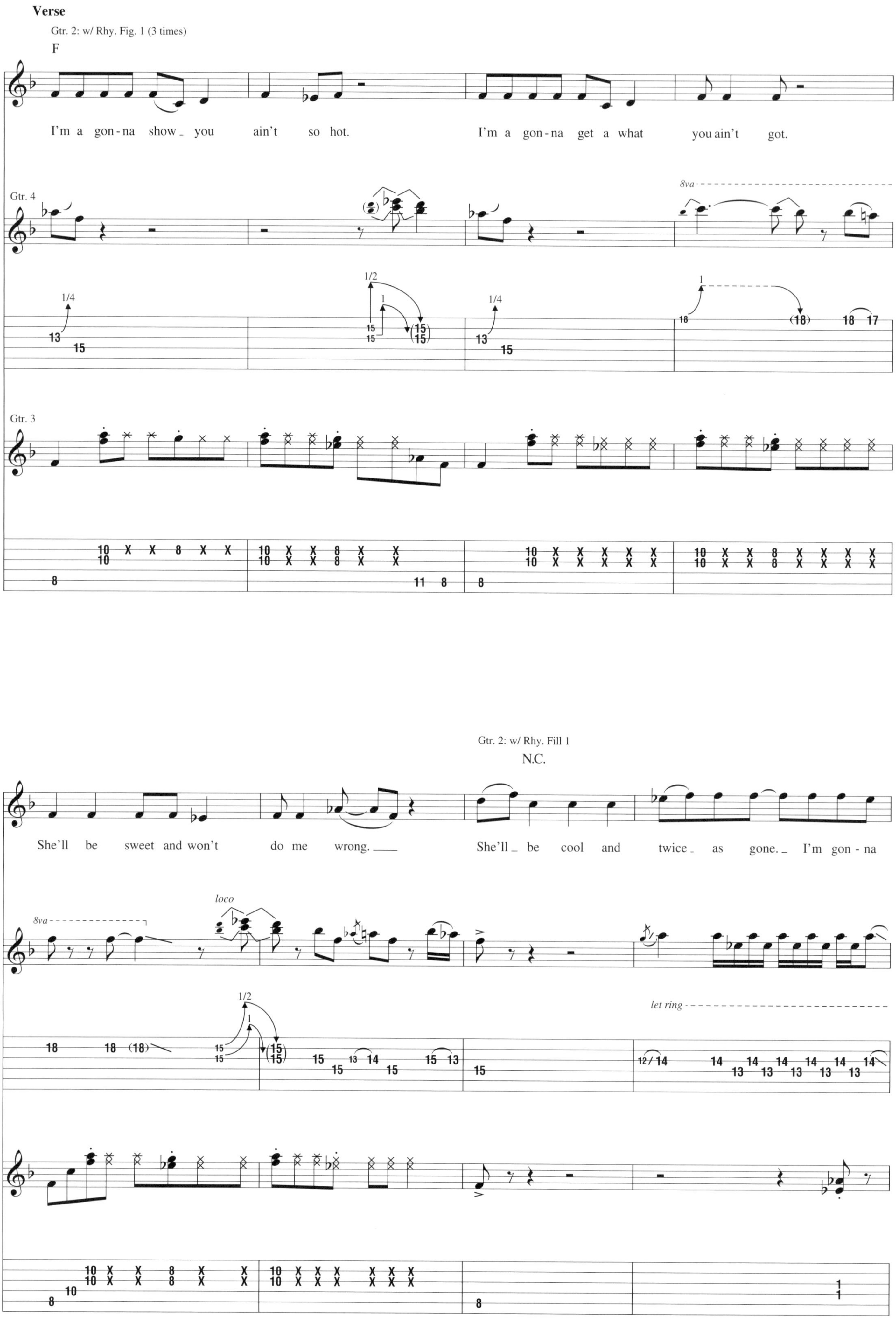
Verse
Gtr. 2: w/ Rhy. Fig. 1 (3 times)
F
I'm a gon-na show _ you ain't so hot. I'm a gon-na get a what you ain't got.
Gtr. 4
8va
1/4
1/2
1
Gtr. 3
Gtr. 2: w/ Rhy. Fill 1
N.C.
She'll be sweet and won't do me wrong. __ She'll _ be cool and twice _ as gone. _ I'm gon-na
loco
let ring

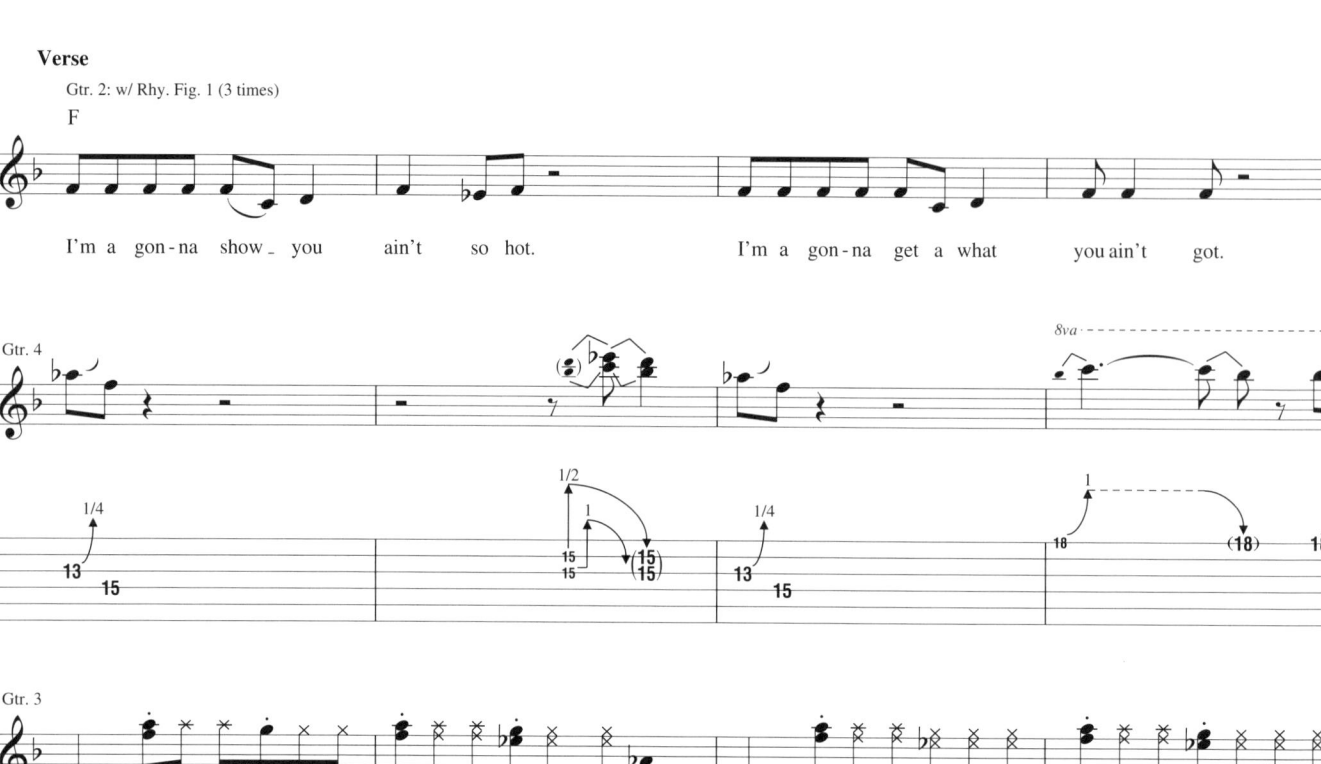

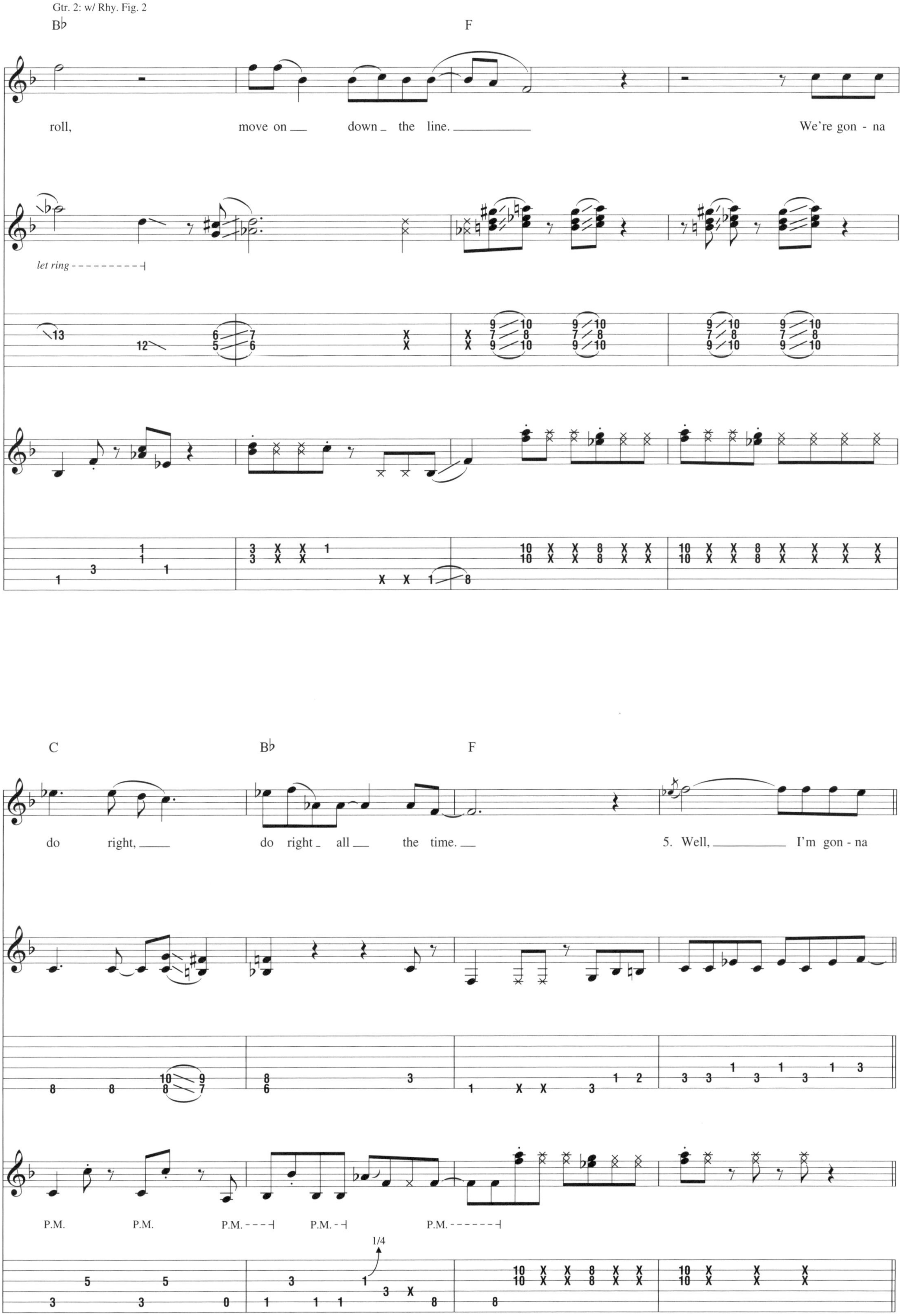
Gtr. 2: w/ Rhy. Fig. 2
B♭
F
roll, move on down the line. We're gon - na
let ring
C
B♭
F
do right, do right all the time. 5. Well, I'm gon - na
P.M.
P.M.
P.M.
P.M.
P.M.
1/4

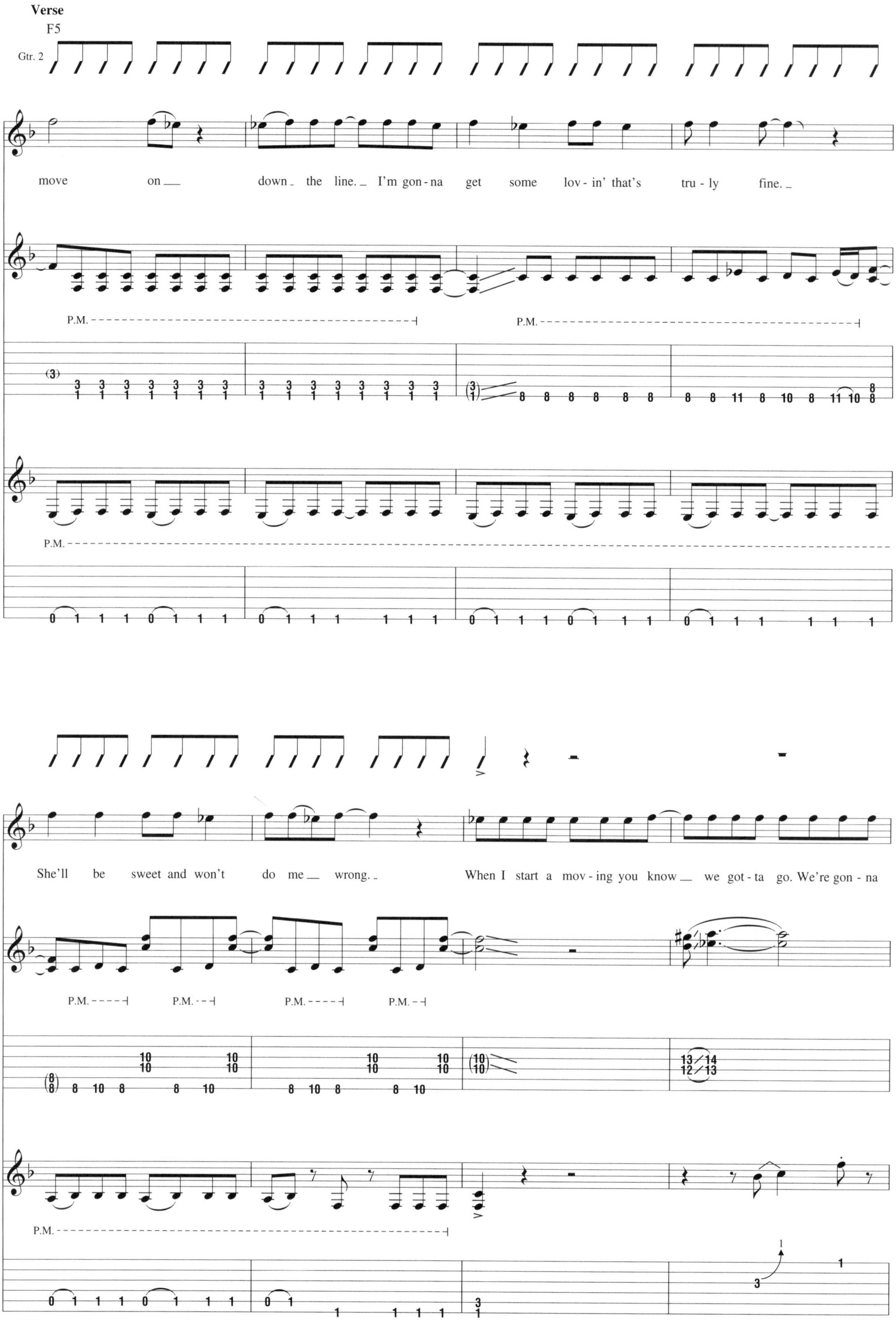
Verse
F5
Gtr. 2
move on down the line. I'm gon-na get some lov-in' that's tru-ly fine.
She'll be sweet and won't do me wrong.
When I start a mov-ing you know we got-ta go. We're gon-na
P.M.

C
B♭
F
do right, do right all the time.
let ring
1/2
C
⑤
3fr
Gtr. 2
C
B♭
We're gon - na do right, do right all the time.
Gtr. 4
mf
P.M.
let ring
let ring
Gtr. 3
P.H.
mf
1/4
1

Pitch: F

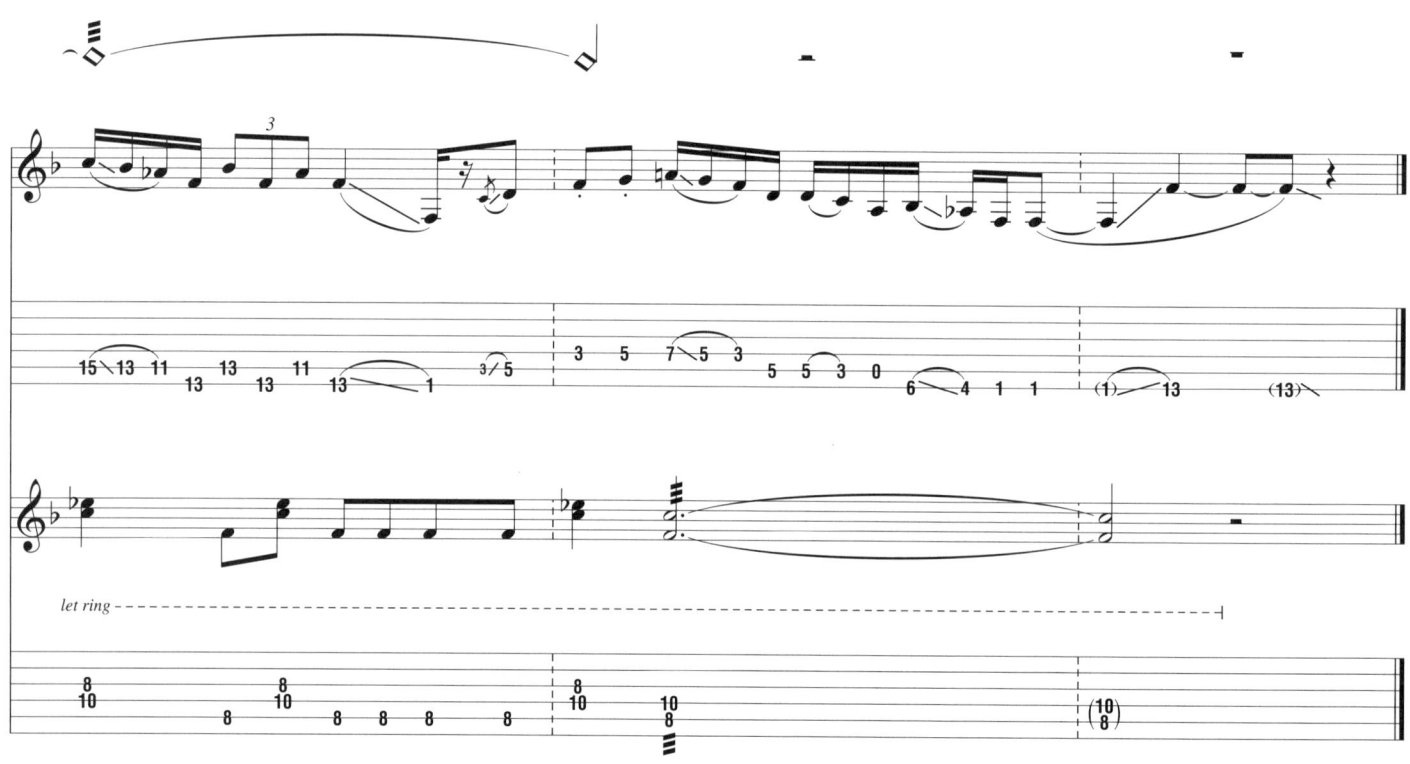

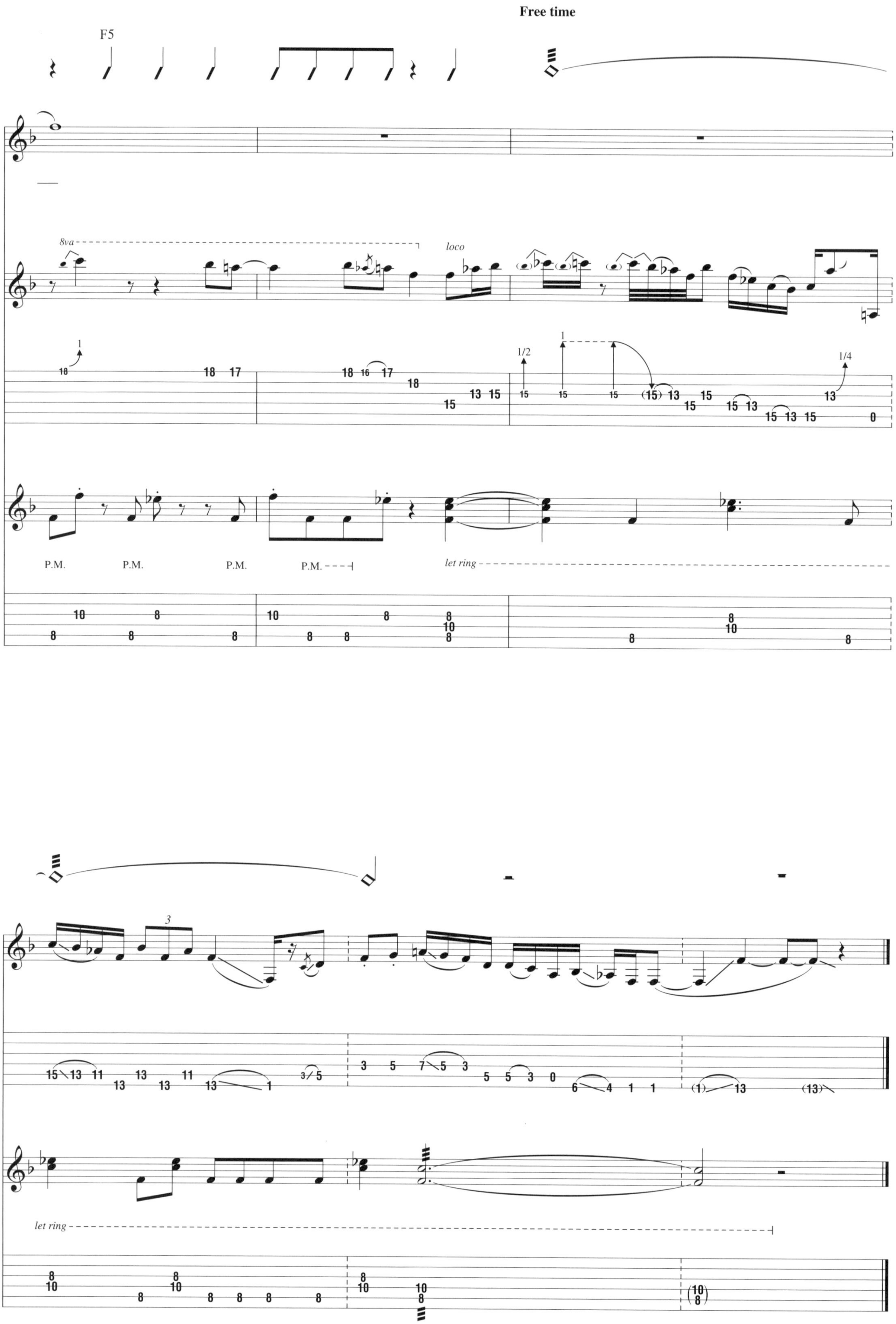
Free time
F5
8va
loco
P.M.
P.M.
P.M.
P.M.
let ring
let ring

Mean Woman Blues
Words and Music by Claude DeMetruis

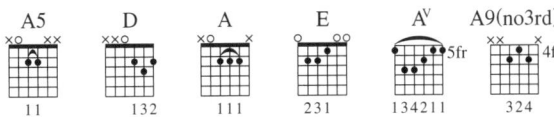

Copyright © 1957; Renewed 1985 Gladys Music (ASCAP)
Worldwide Rights for Gladys Music Administered by Cherry Lane Music Publishing Company, Inc.
International Copyright Secured   All Rights Reserved

*Chord symbols reflect basic harmony.

150

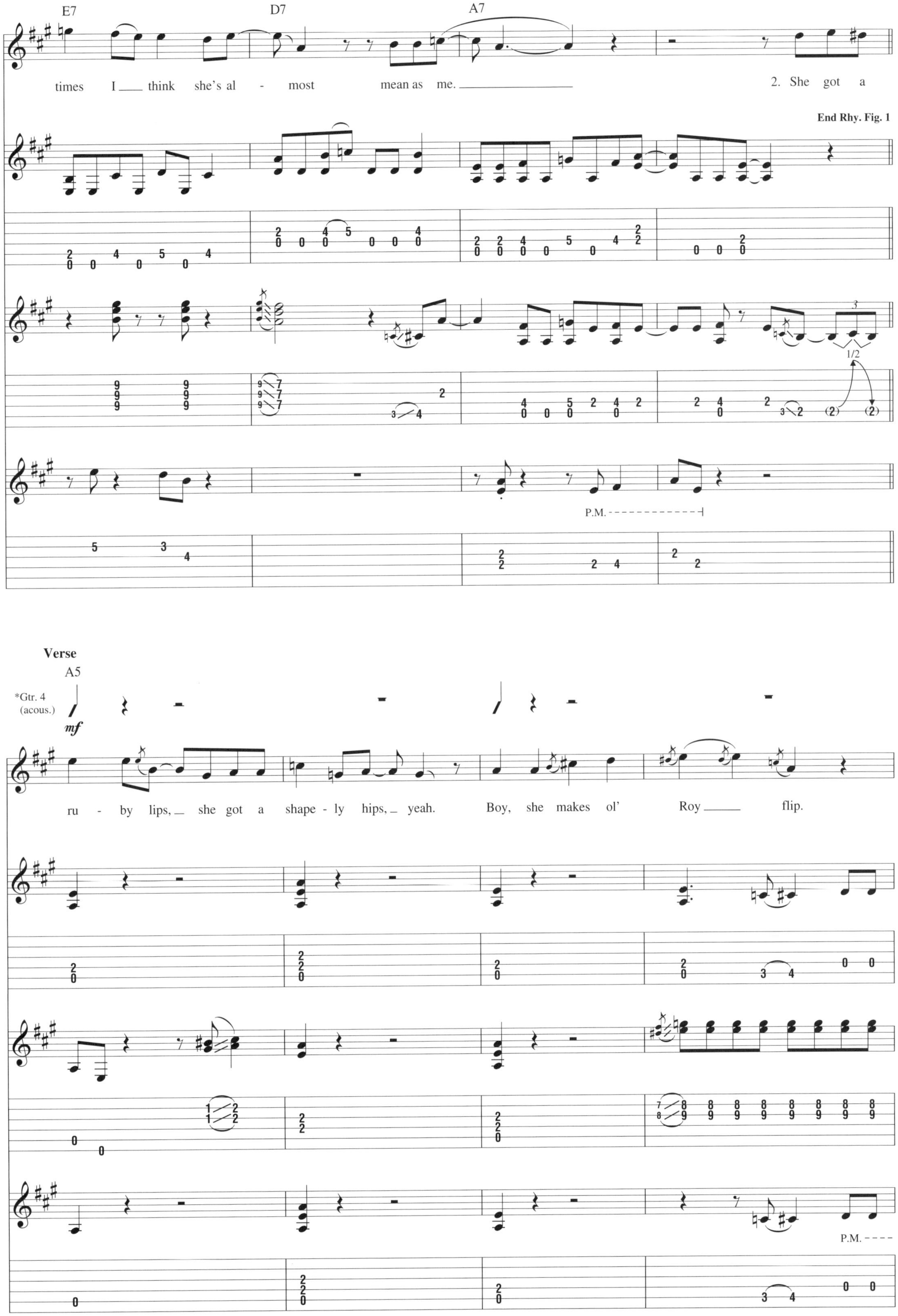
E7
D7
A7
times I think she's al - most mean as me.
2. She got a
End Rhy. Fig. 1
1/2
P.M.
Verse
A5
*Gtr. 4 (acous.)
mf
ru - by lips, she got a shape - ly hips, yeah. Boy, she makes ol' Roy flip.
P.M.

*Elvis Costello

Gtr. 1: w/ Rhy. Fig. 1
D
A
E
Rhy. Fig. 2A
Gtr. 4
I got a wom - an, mean as ___ she can be. ___ Some -
Voc. Fig. 1
(Oo, ___
Gtr. 2
Gtr. 3
Rhy. Fig. 2
P.M.
D
A
End Rhy. Fig. 2A
times I ___ think she's al - most mean as me. ___
3. Yeah, ___ and I ___
End Voc. Fig. 1
oo.) ___
End Rhy. Fig. 2
P.M.

Verse
A
___ ain't brag - gin', ___ it's un - der - stood. Ev - 'ry - thing I do, well, I sure do it good. Yeah, I ___
Gtr. 1
Rhy. Fig. 3
End Rhy. Fig. 3
Gtr. 2
1/2
1/2
Gtr. 3
Rhy. Fig. 3A
End Rhy. Fig. 3A
Bkgd. Voc.: w/ Voc. Fig. 1
Gtr. 1: w/ Rhy. Fig. 1
Gtrs. 3 & 4: w/ Rhy. Figs. 2 & 2A
D7
A7
___ got a wom - an, mean as ___ she can be. Uh, some -
1
1/2
1/4

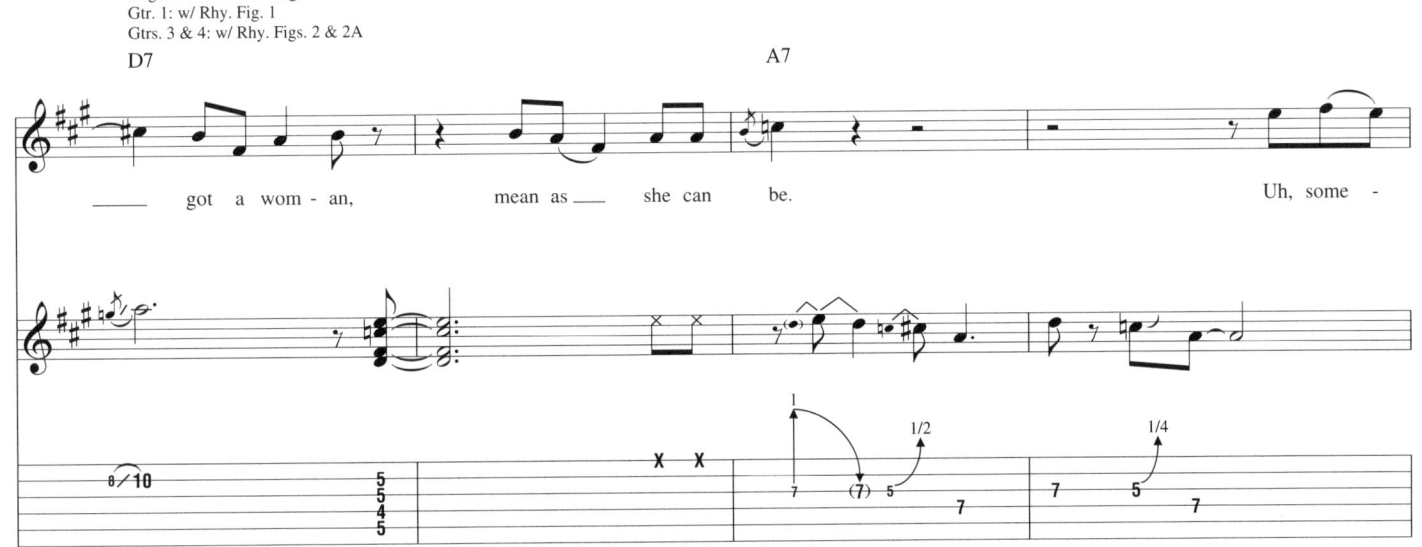

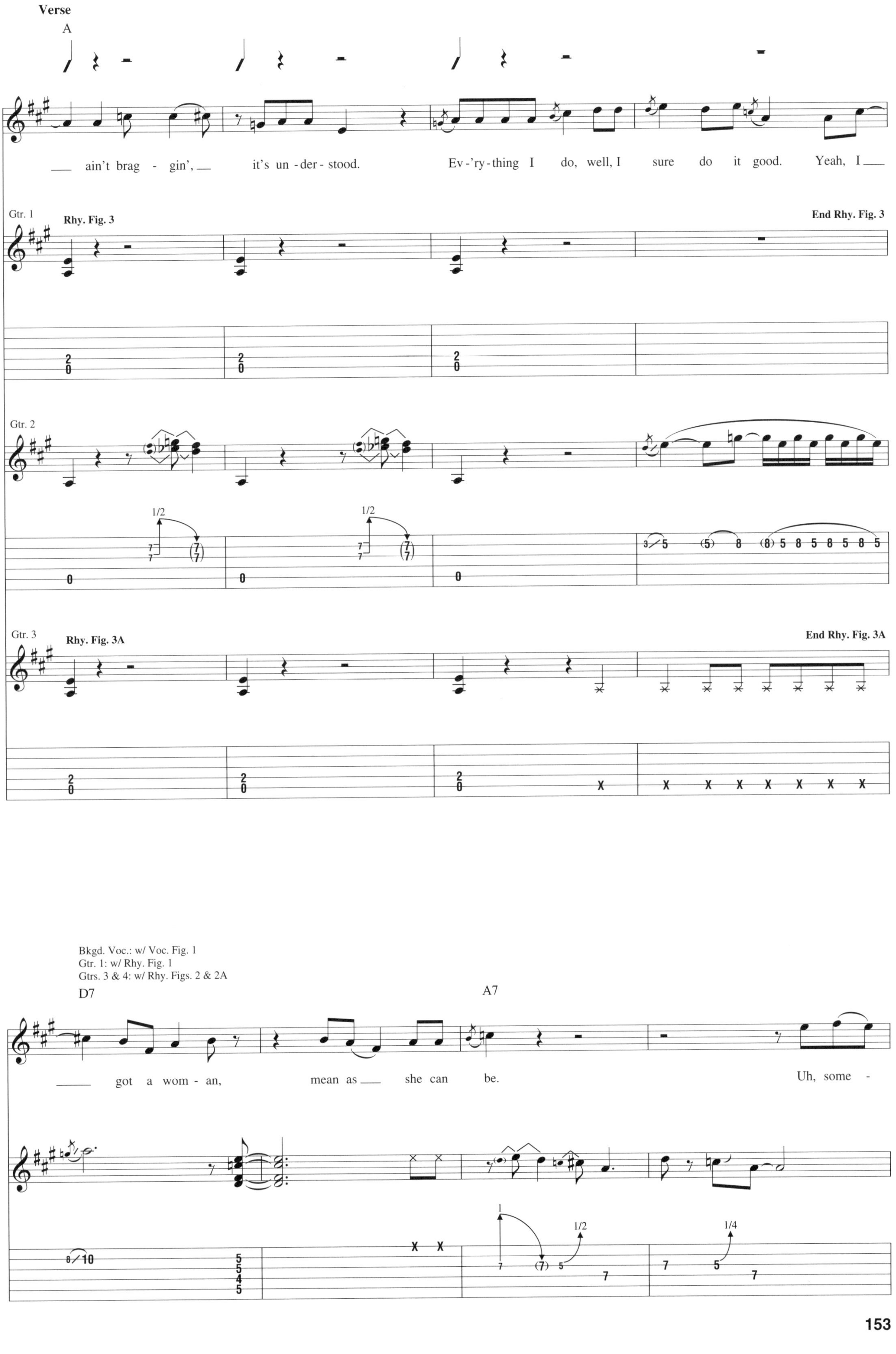

E7
D7
A7
times I think she's al - most mean as me.
Well.
Guitar Solo
A
Rhy. Fig. 5
Gtr. 4
Gtr. 2
Gtr. 1
Rhy. Fig. 4
End Rhy. Fig. 4
Gtr. 3
Gtr. 1: w/ Rhy. Fig. 1
Gtr. 3 tacet
D
A
Gtr. 2

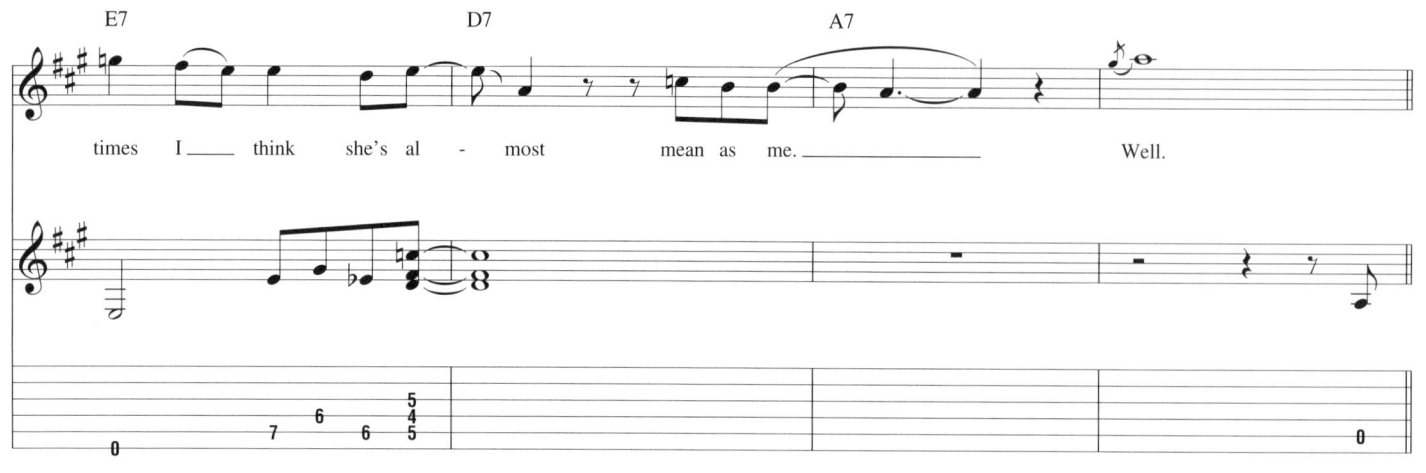

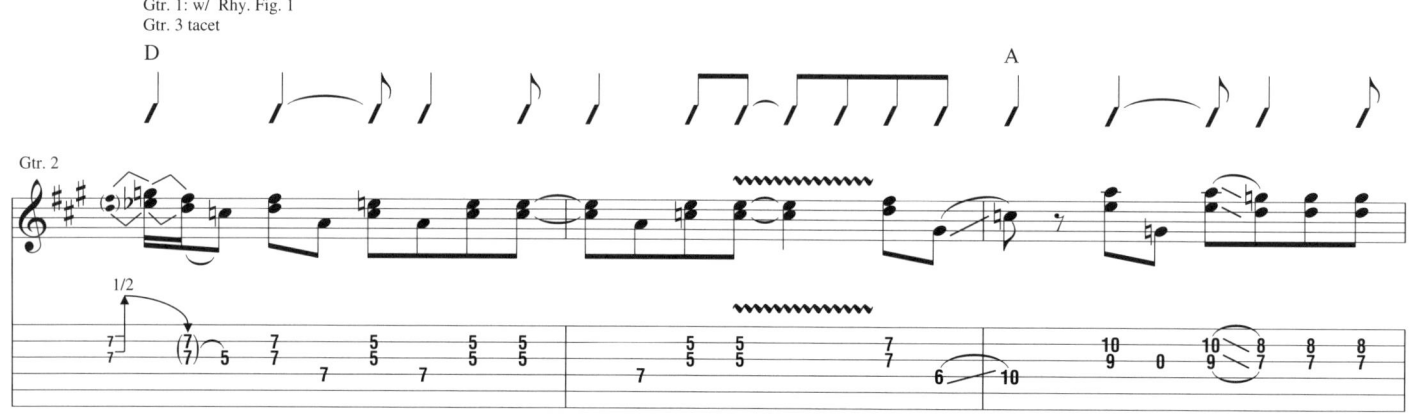

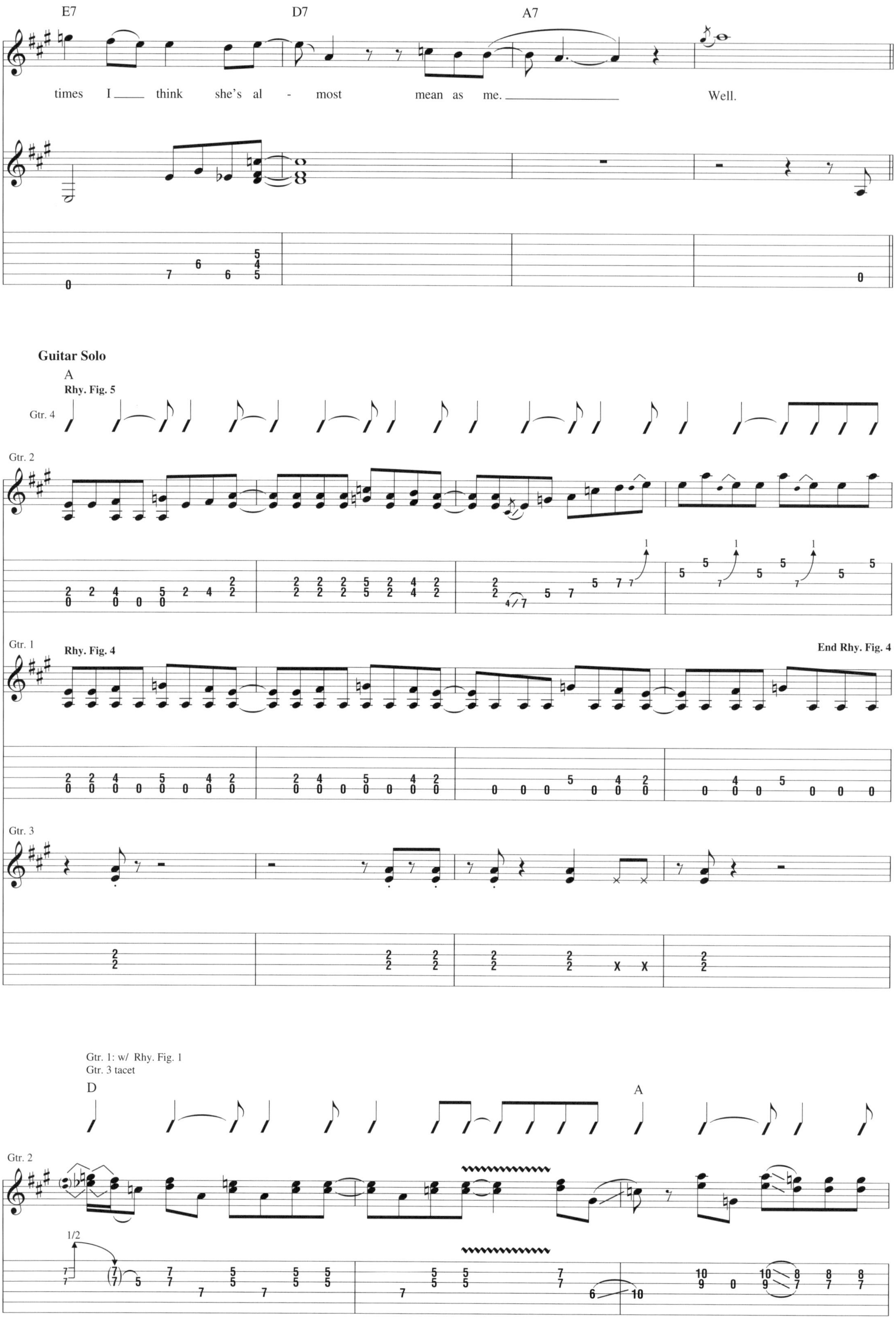

D7
A7
4. She got a
Verse
Gtrs. 1 & 3: w/ Rhy. Figs. 3 & 3A
Gtr. 4 tacet
A5
Gtr. 4
ru - by lips, she got a shape - ly hips, yeah. Boy, she makes ol' Roy flip.
tr
Gtr. 1: w/ Rhy. Fig. 1
Gtr. 4: w/ Rhy. Fig. 2A
D7
A7
I got a wom - an mean as she can be. Uh, some -
(Sha, la, la, la, sha, la, la, la. Sha, la, la, la, sha, la, la, la.
Gtr. 2
P.M.
Gtr. 3
P.M.
P.M.

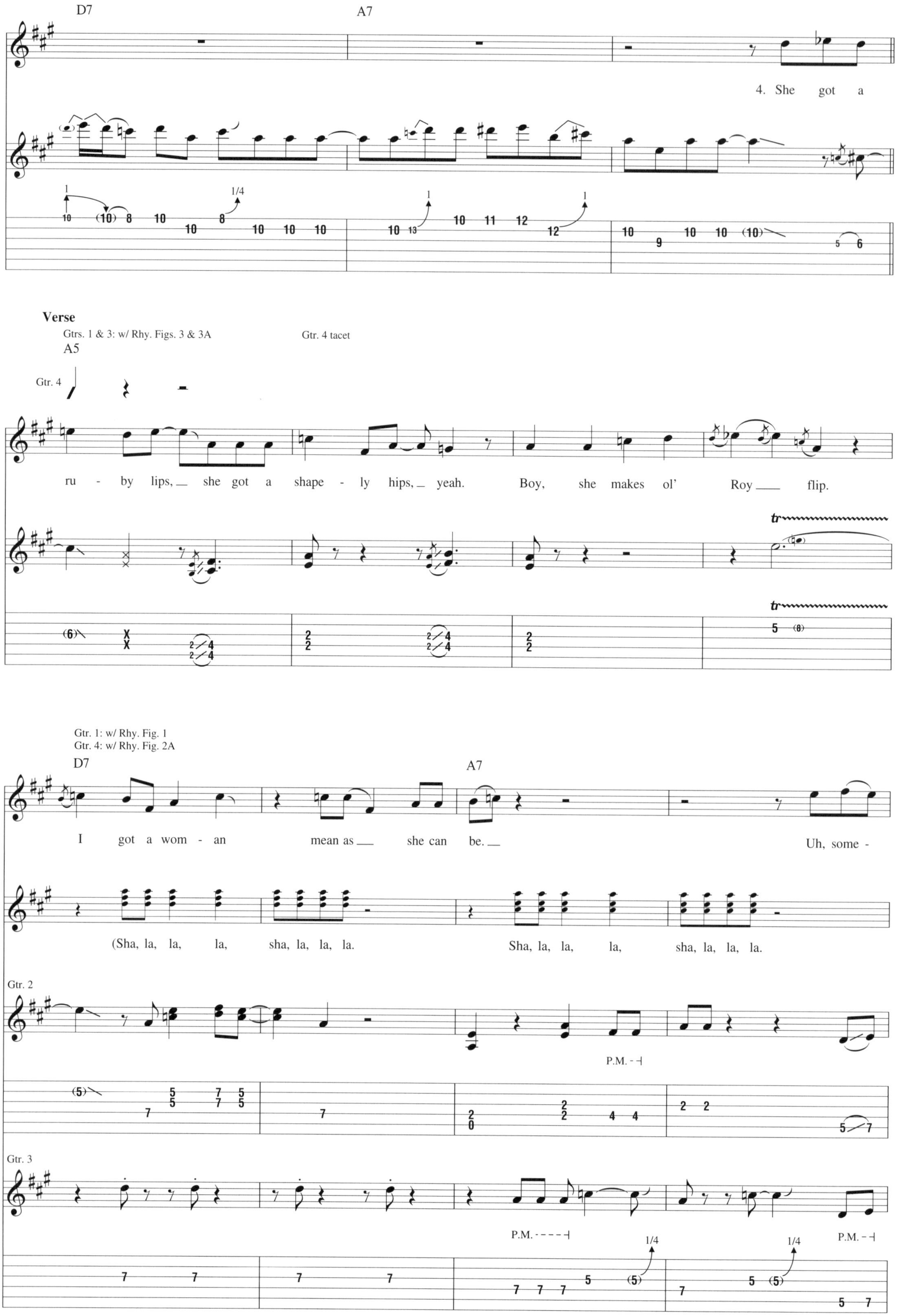

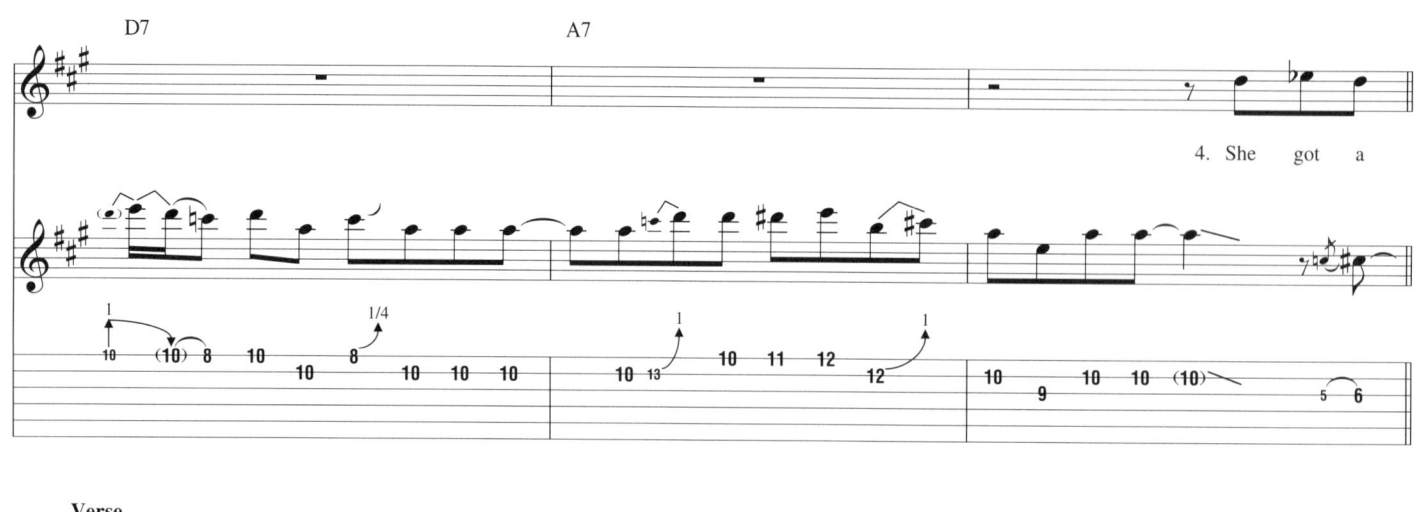

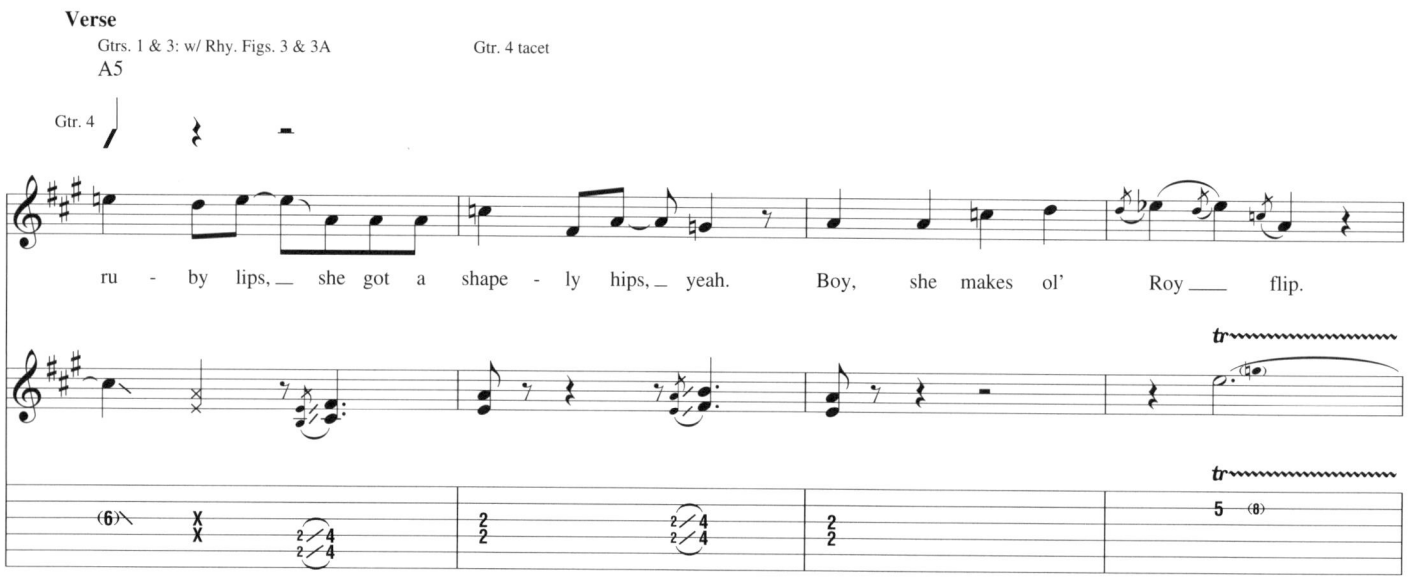

Gtrs. 2 & 4 tacet
A
A9(no3rd)
yeah, yeah, yeah.
A lit - tle low - er now.
p
P.M.
P.M.

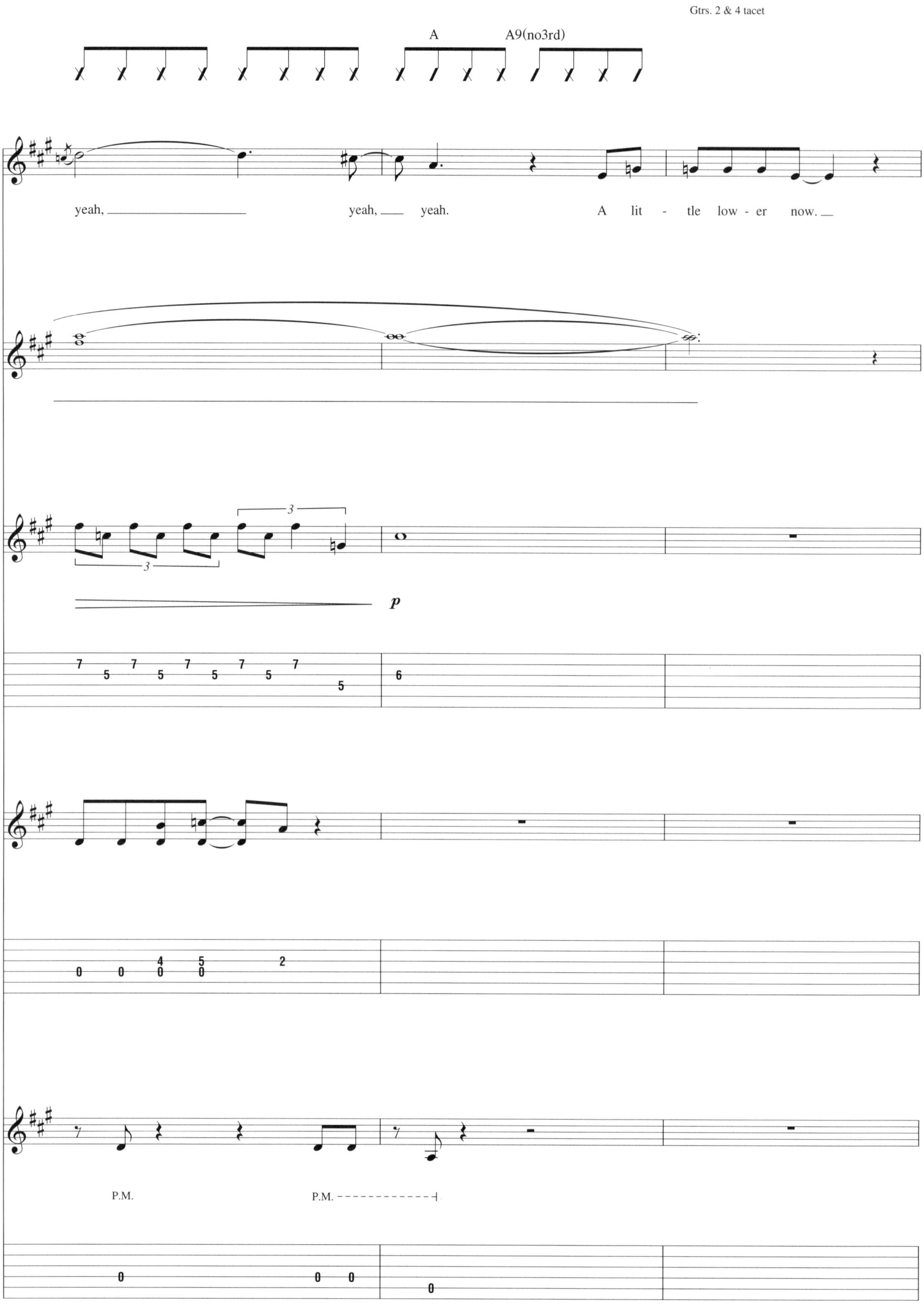

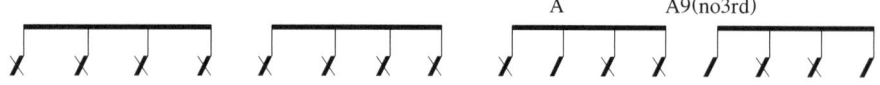

A7
Ah,
Sha, la, la, la, sha, la, la, la. Sha, la, la, la, sha, la, la, la.
Gtr. 3
Gtr. 1

D7
A7
oo.
Tongue roll: Lll!
Sha, la, la, la, sha, la, la, la. Sha, la, la, la, sha, la, la, la.

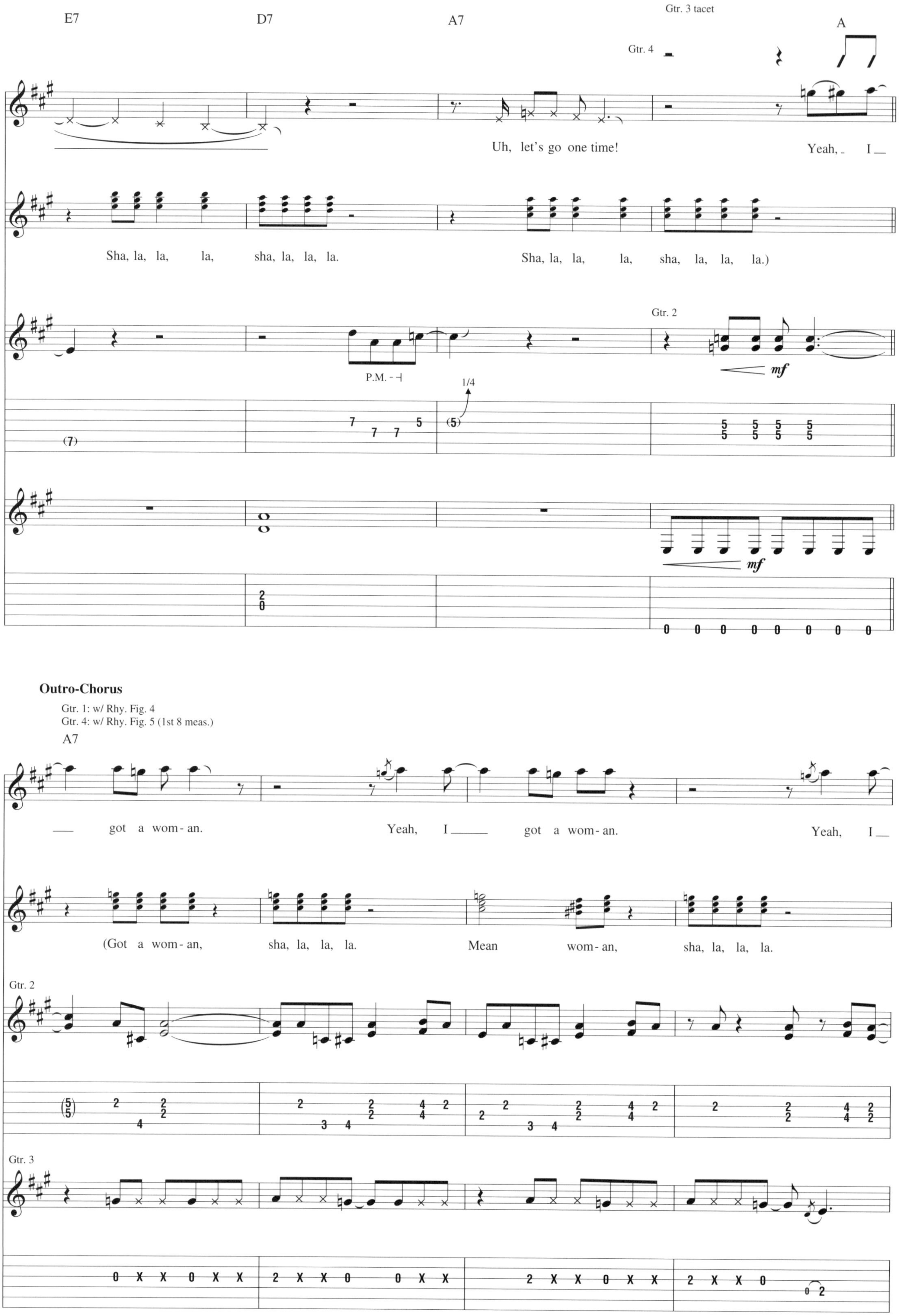

E7
D7
A7
Gtr. 3 tacet
A
Gtr. 4
Uh, let's go one time!
Yeah, I
Sha, la, la, la, sha, la, la, la.
Sha, la, la, la, sha, la, la, la.)
Gtr. 2
P.M.
1/4
mf
mf
Outro-Chorus
Gtr. 1: w/ Rhy. Fig. 4
Gtr. 4: w/ Rhy. Fig. 5 (1st 8 meas.)
A7
got a wom-an.
Yeah, I got a wom-an.
Yeah, I
(Got a wom-an, sha, la, la, la.
Mean wom-an, sha, la, la, la.
Gtr. 2
Gtr. 3

(All I Can Do Is) Dream You

Words and Music by Billy Burnette and David Malloy

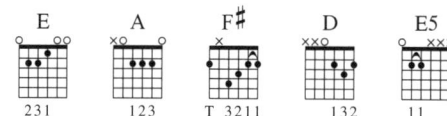

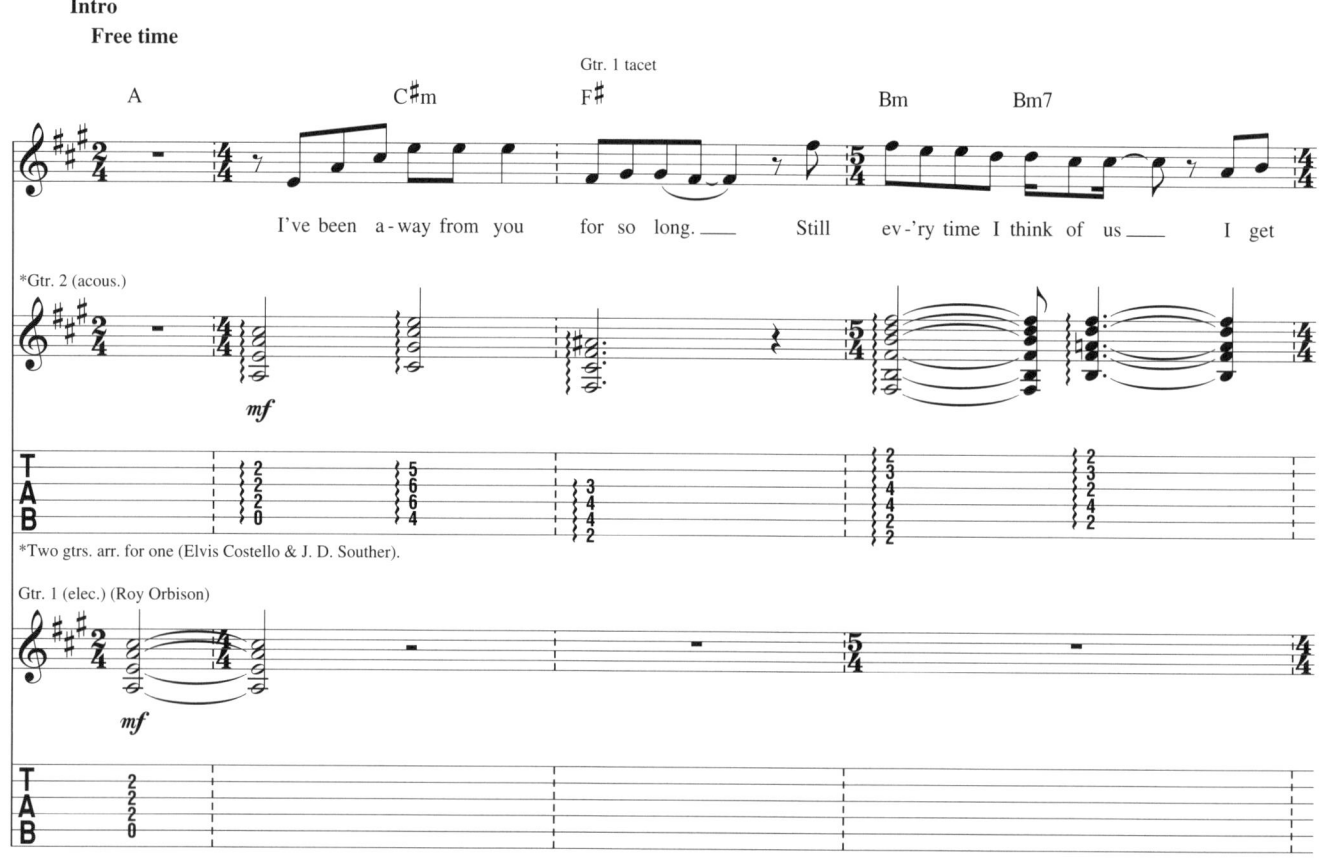

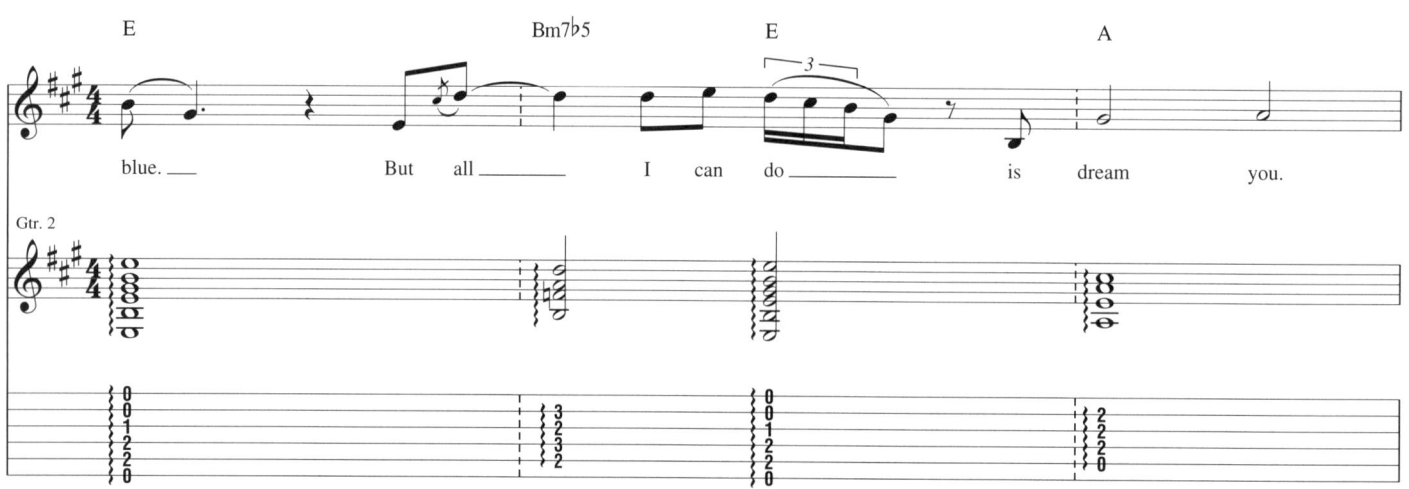

Copyright © 1987 Chrysalis Music, Billy Beau Music, Irving Music, Inc. and David Malloy Music Publishing
All Rights for Billy Beau Music Administered by Chrysalis Music
All Rights for David Malloy Music Publishing Controlled and Administered by Irving Music, Inc.
All Rights Reserved   Used by Permission

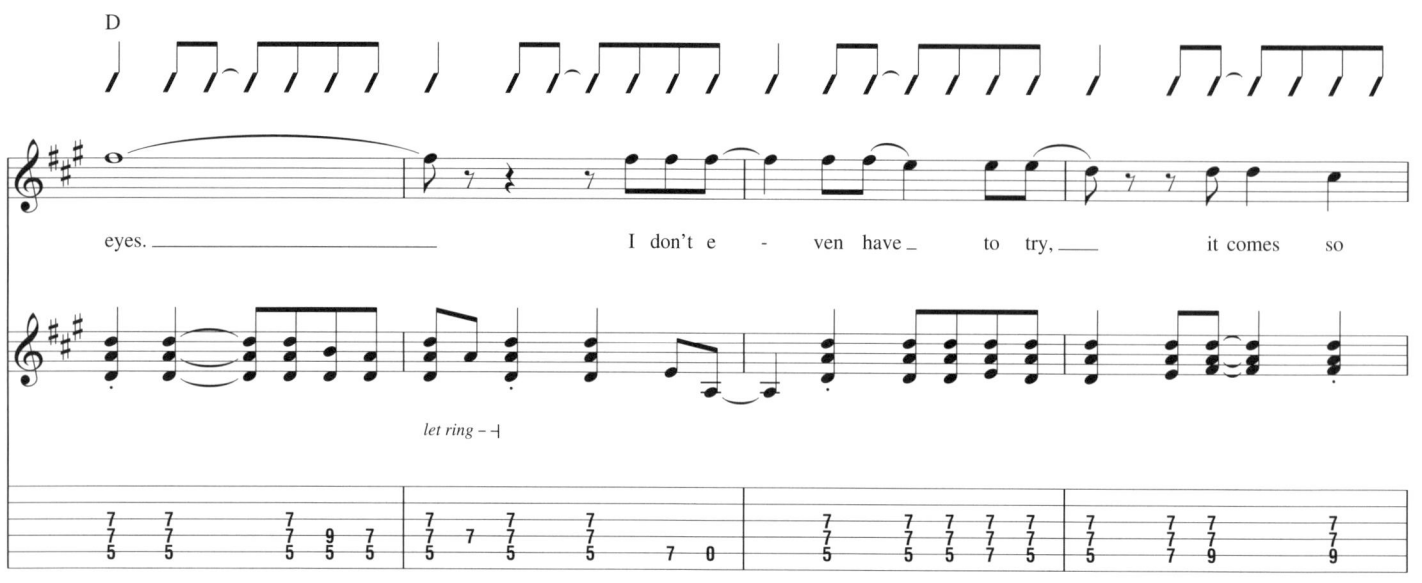

Verse

166

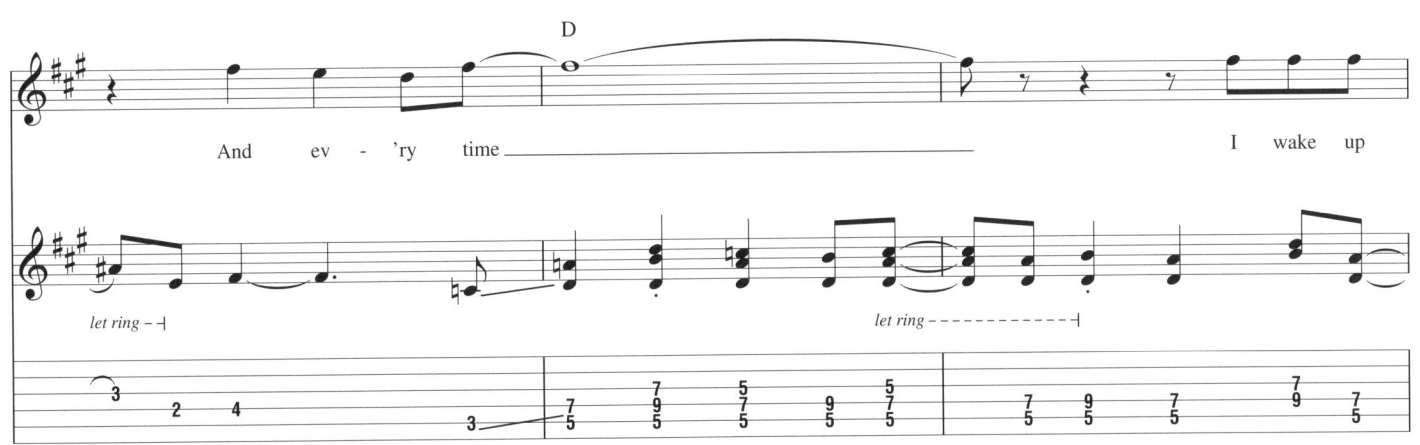
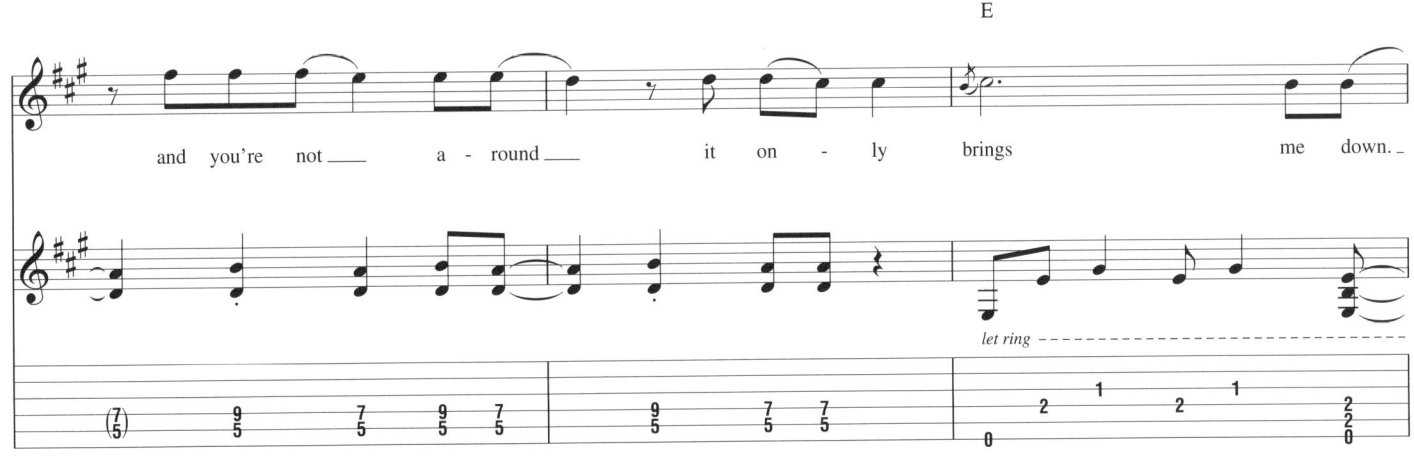

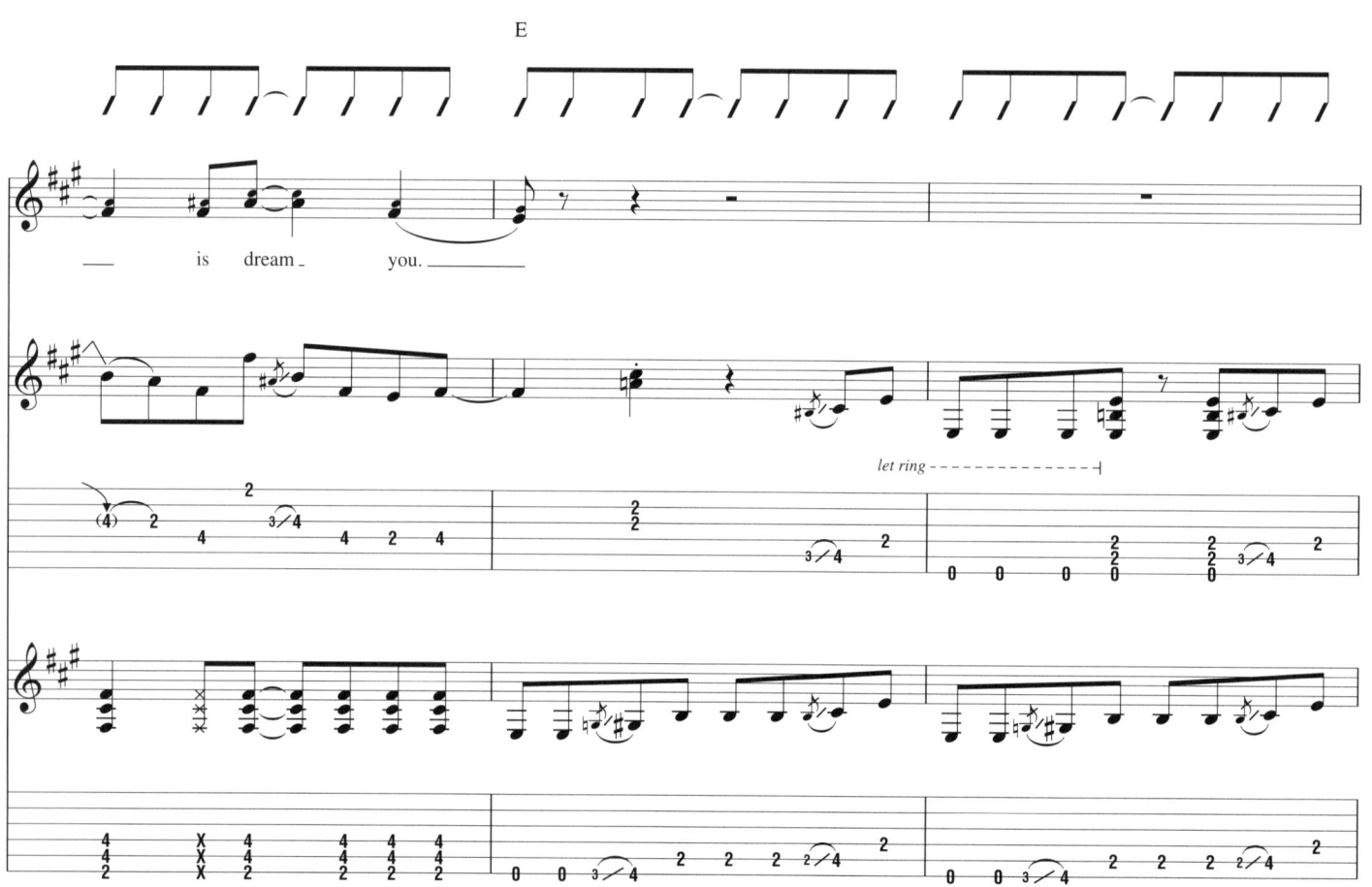

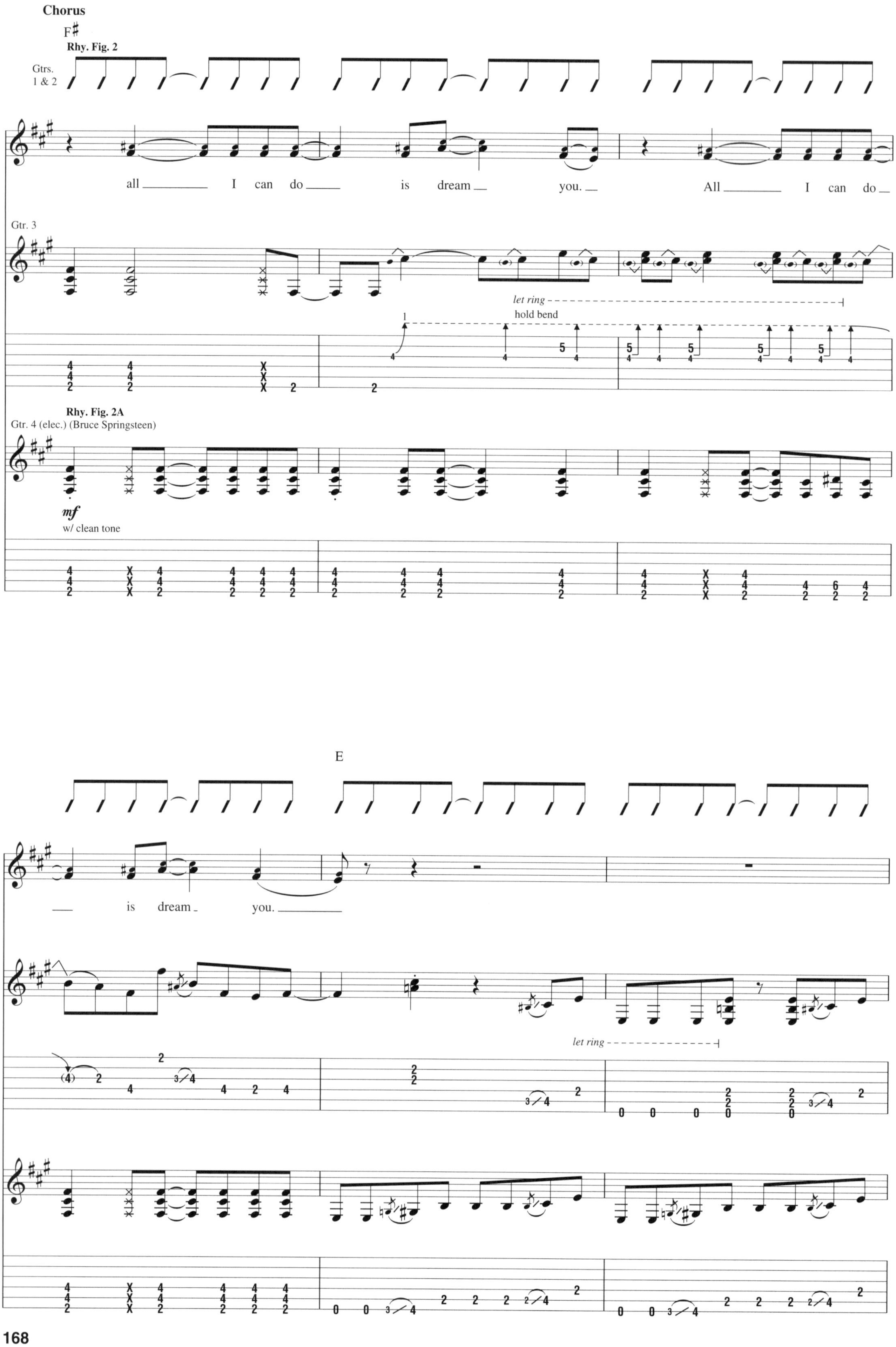
Chorus
F♯
Rhy. Fig. 2
Gtrs. 1 & 2
all ___ I can do ___ is dream ___ you. ___ All ___ I can do ___
Gtr. 3
let ring
hold bend
Rhy. Fig. 2A
Gtr. 4 (elec.) (Bruce Springsteen)
mf
w/ clean tone
E
___ is dream ___ you. ___
let ring

169

Guitar Solo

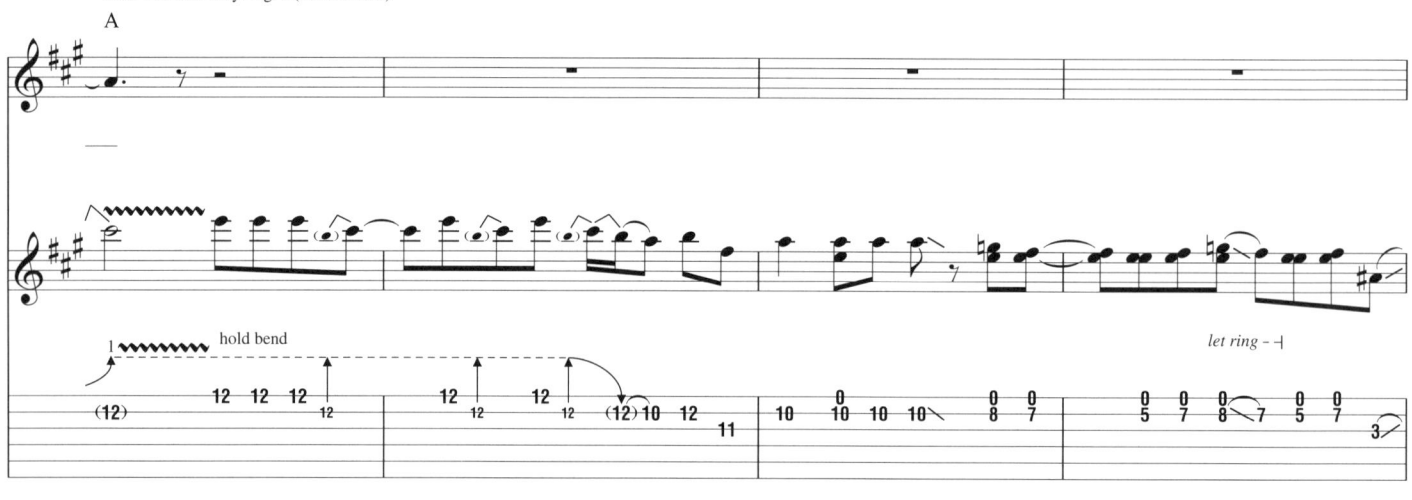

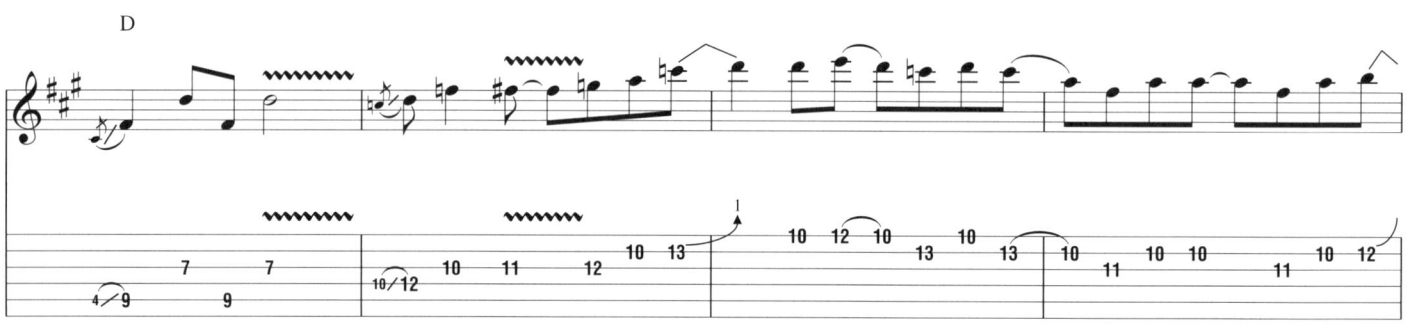

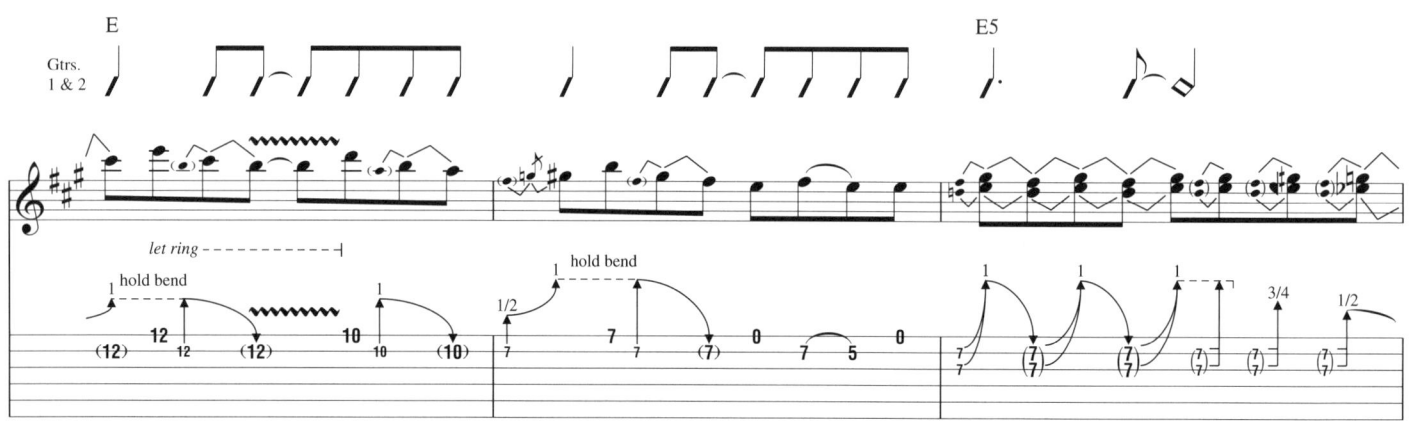

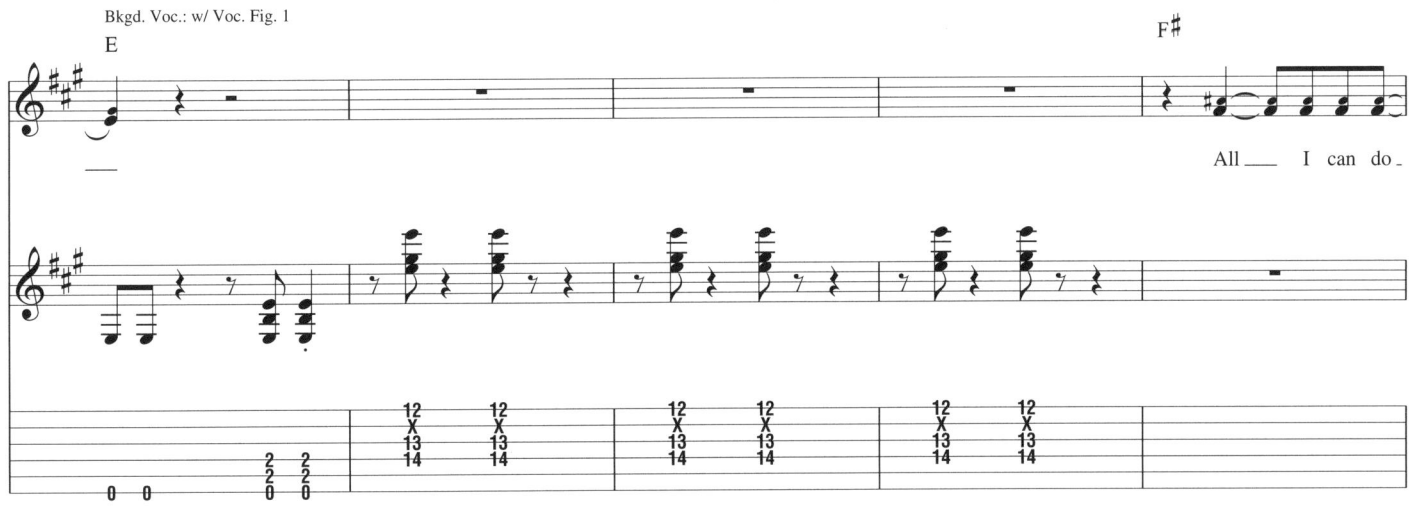
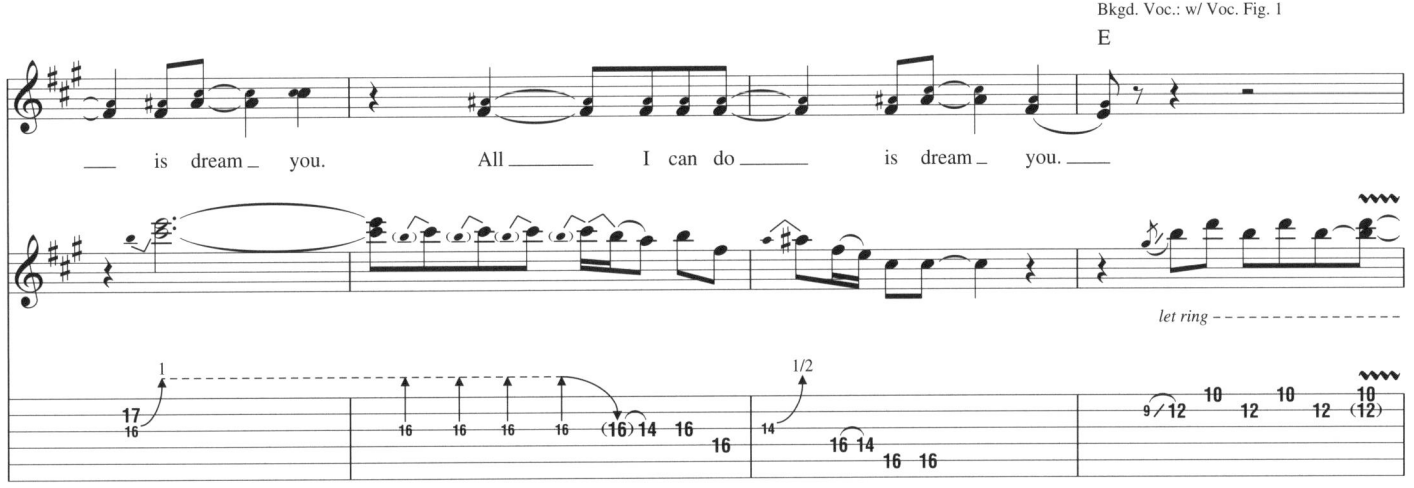
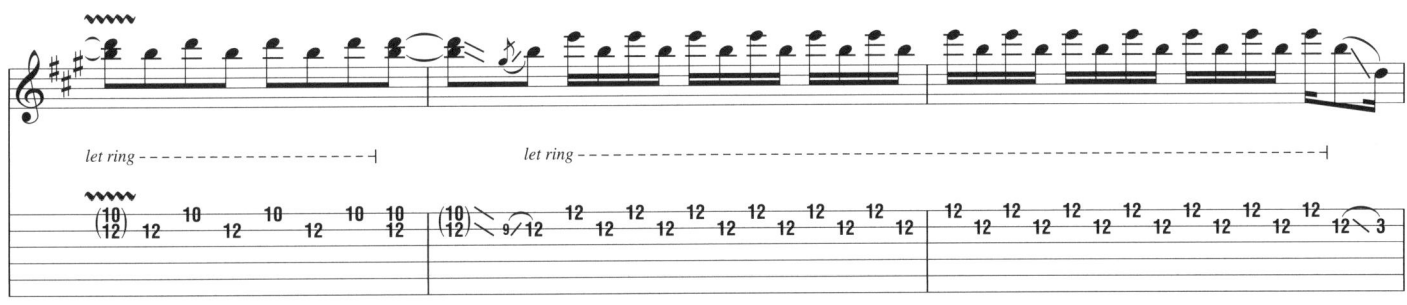

Outro

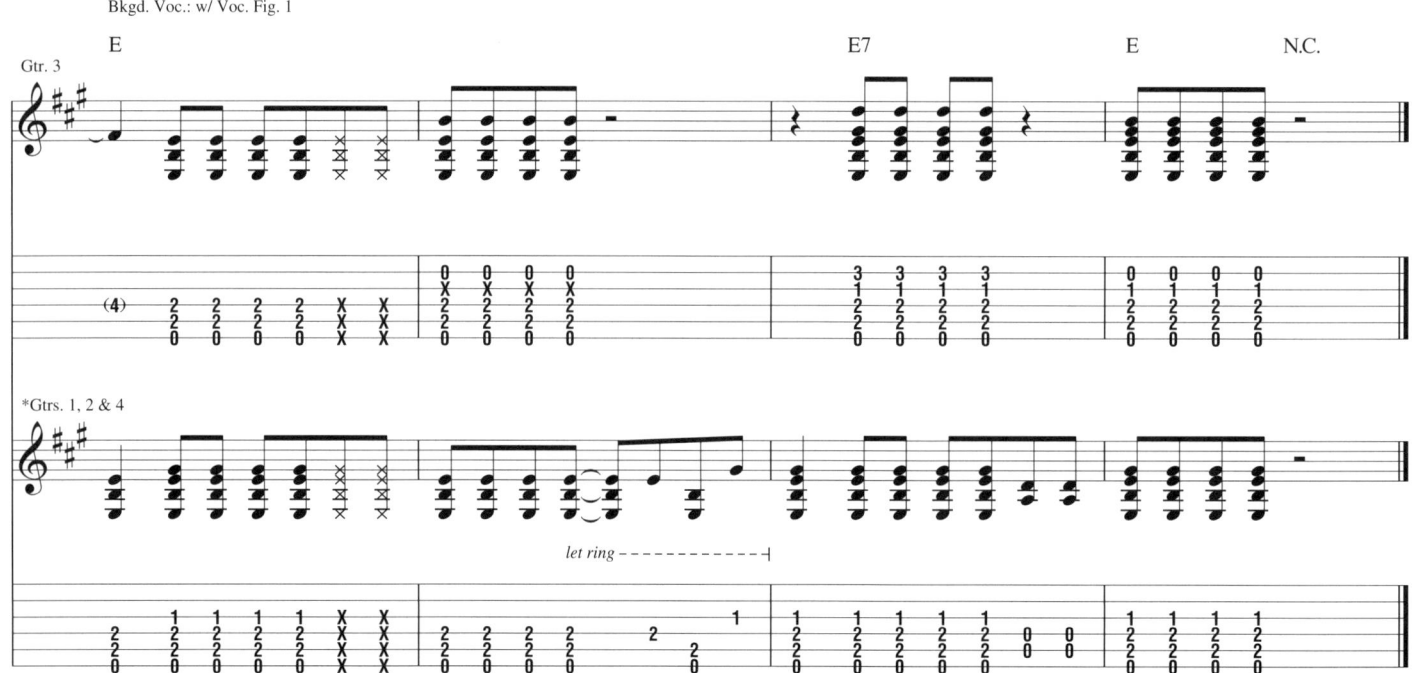

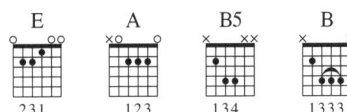

*Composite arrangement

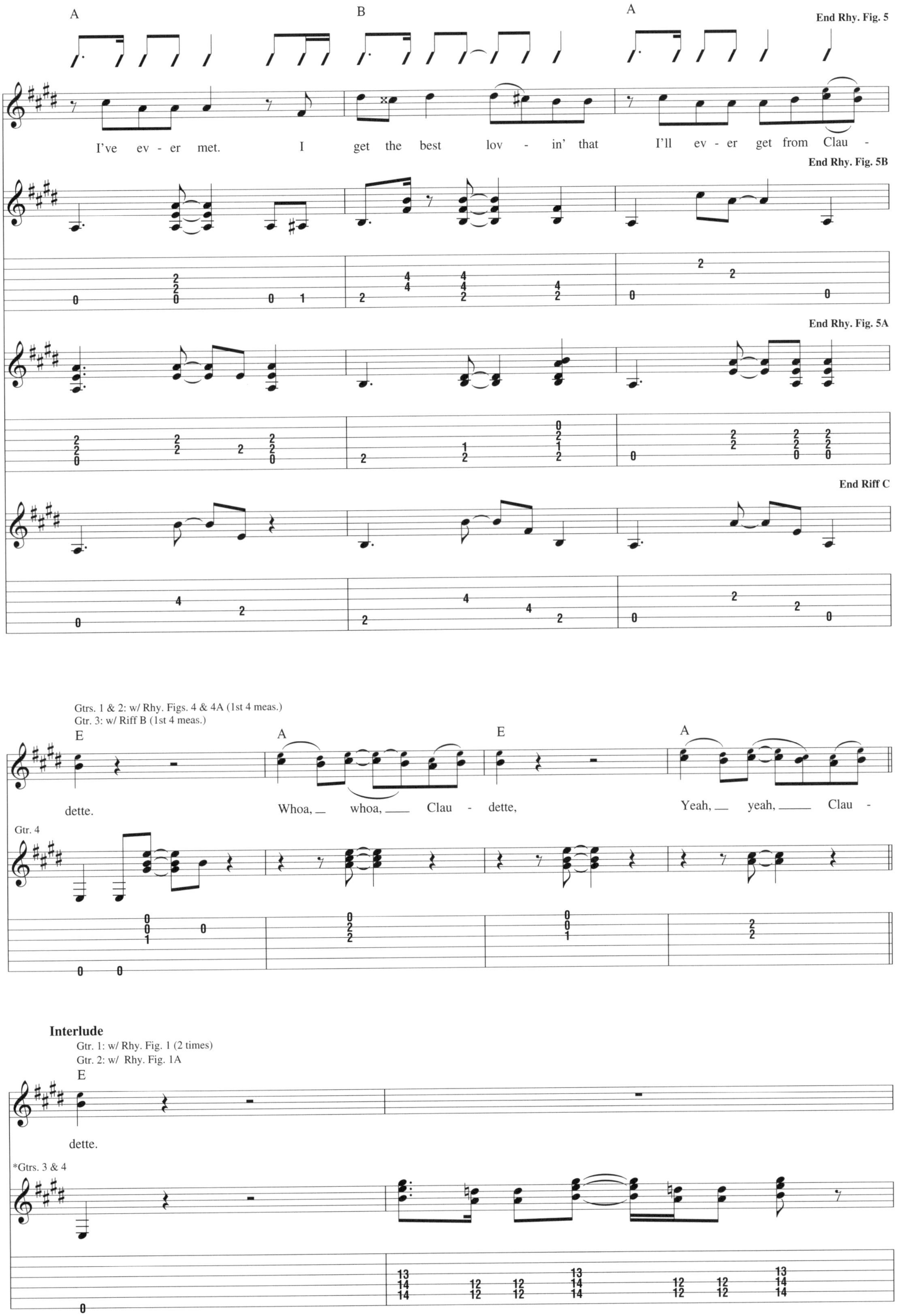

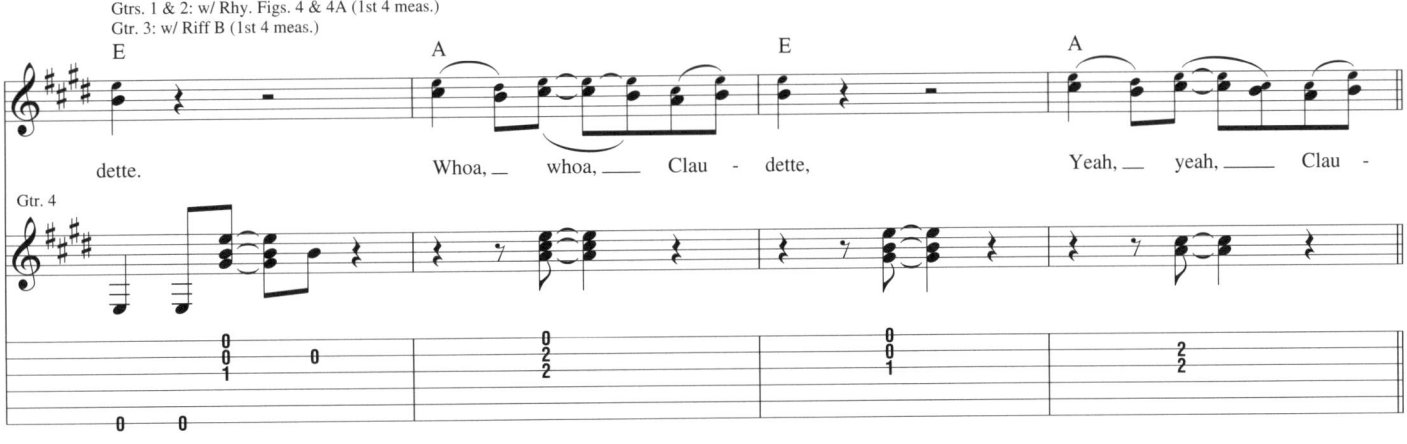

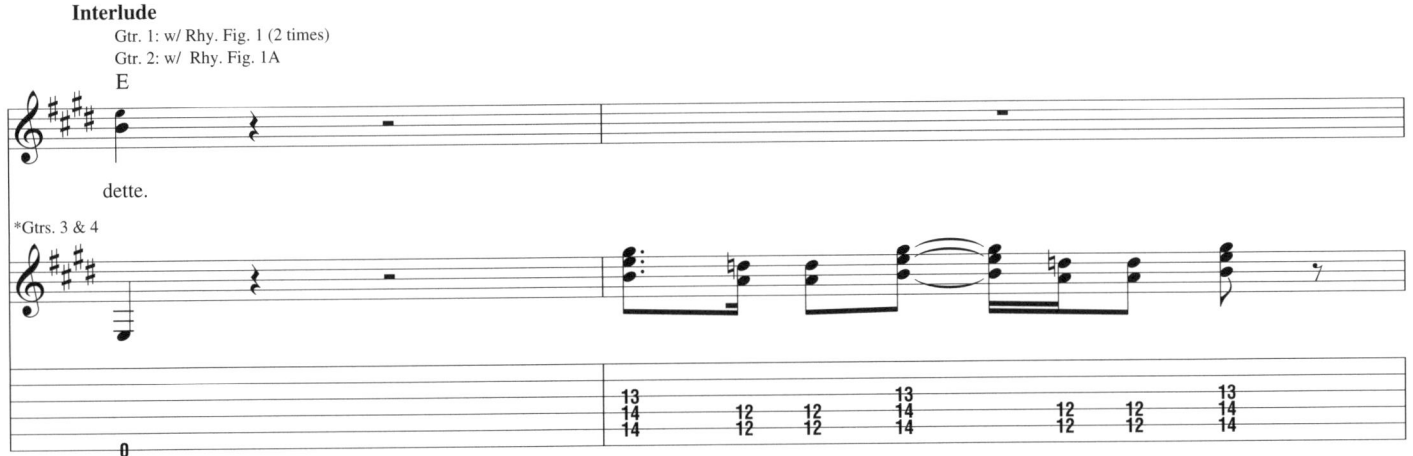

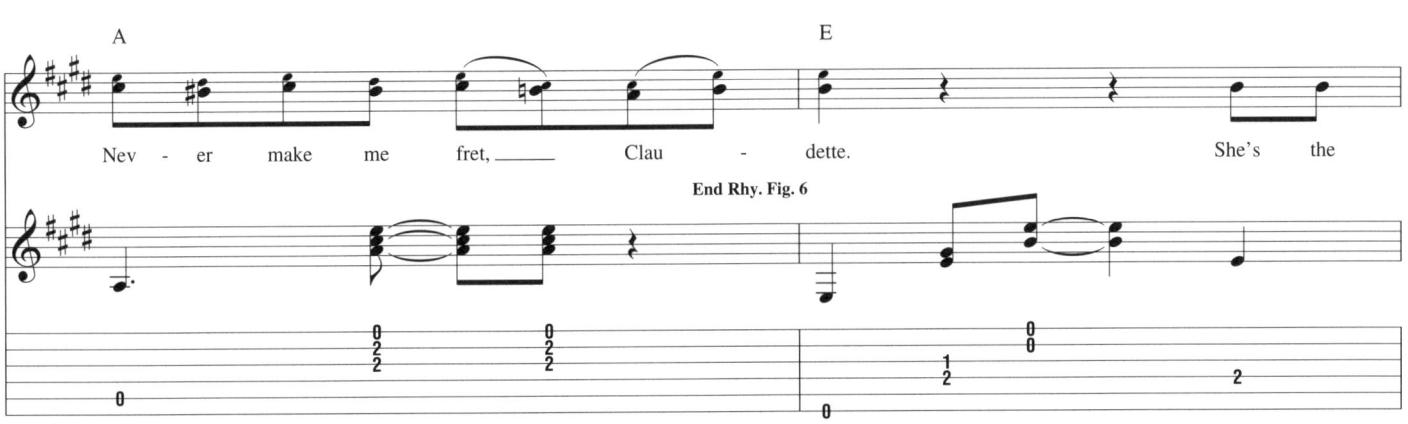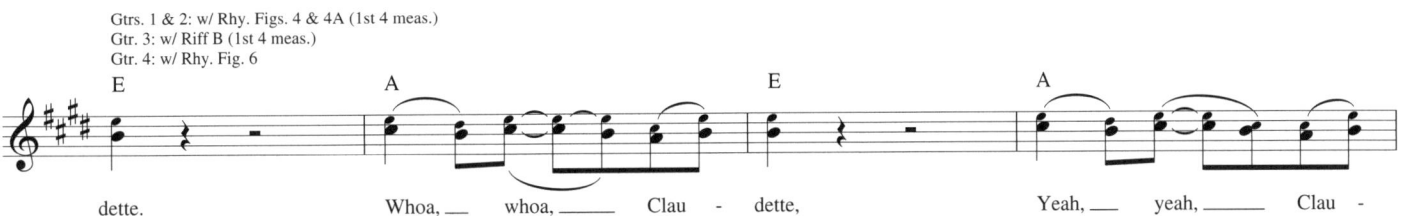

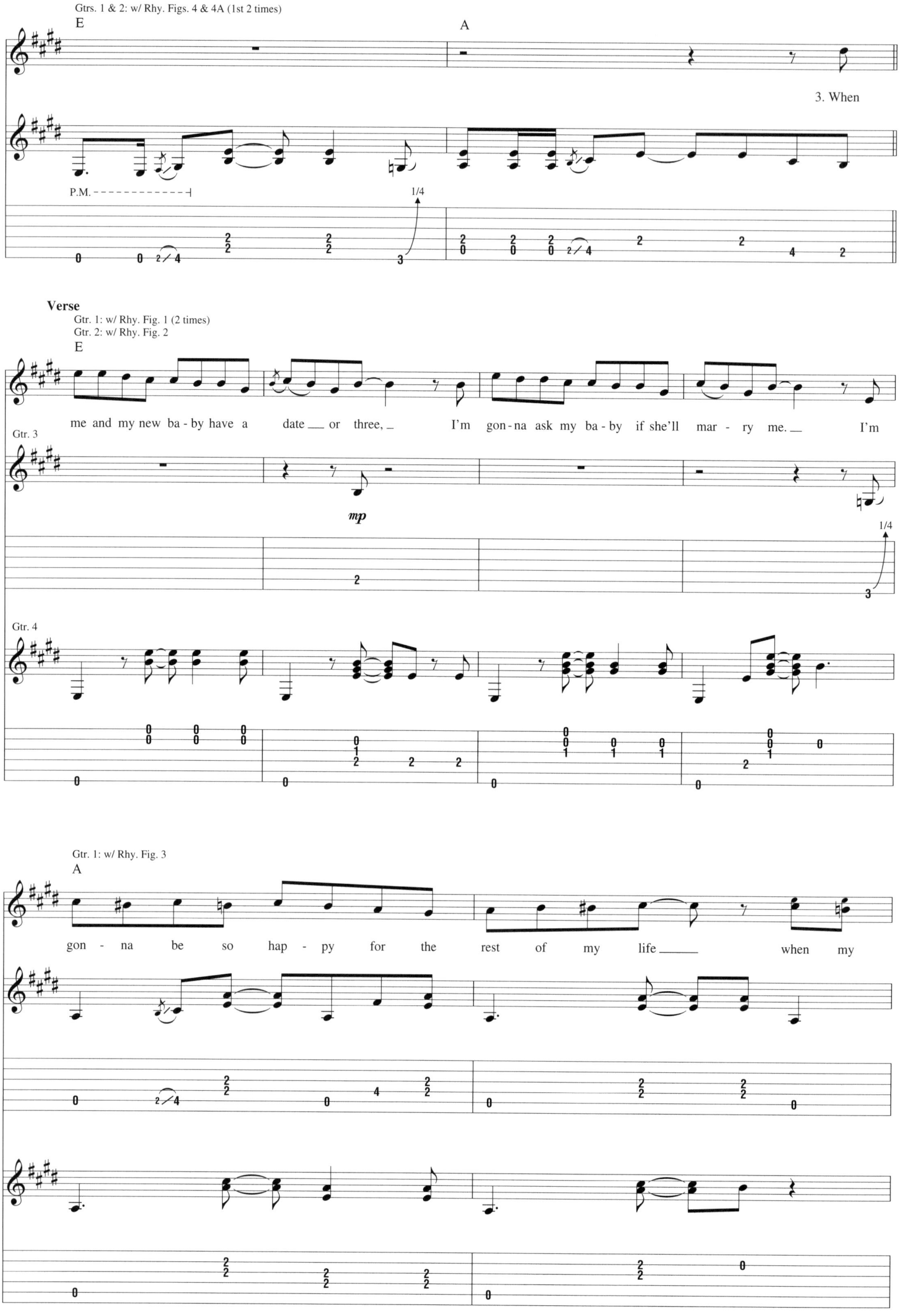
Gtrs. 1 & 2: w/ Rhy. Figs. 4 & 4A (1st 2 times)
E
A
3. When
P.M.
1/4
Verse
Gtr. 1: w/ Rhy. Fig. 1 (2 times)
Gtr. 2: w/ Rhy. Fig. 2
E
me and my new ba - by have a date or three, I'm gon - na ask my ba - by if she'll mar - ry me. I'm
Gtr. 3
mp
1/4
Gtr. 4
Gtr. 1: w/ Rhy. Fig. 3
A
gon - na be so hap - py for the rest of my life when my

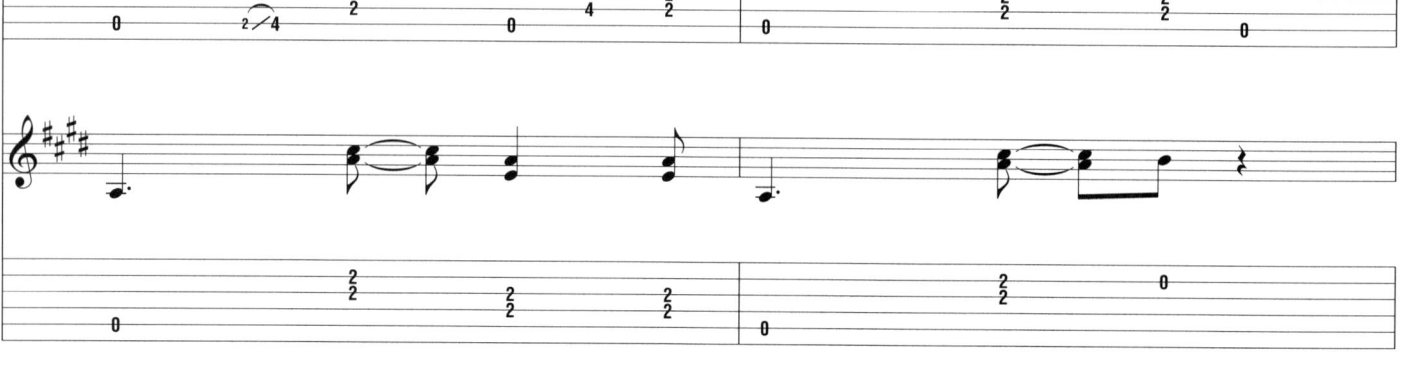

B
get the best lov - in' that
A
I'll ev - er get from Clau -
Gtrs. 1 & 2: w/ Rhy. Figs. 4 & 4A (1st 4 meas.)
Gtr. 3: w/ Riff B (1st 4 meas.)
Gtr. 4: w/ Riff C (1st 4 meas.)
E
dette.
A
Whoa, whoa, Clau -
E
dette.
A
Yeah, yeah, Clau -
Outro
E
Gtr. 1
dette.
Gtr. 3
14 14 12 12 14 14 0
13 14 14 12 12 12 12 13 14 14 12 12 12 12 13 14 14
Gtr. 2
1 2 2 0 13 14 14 12 12 14 14
13 14 14 12 12 12 12 13 14 14 12 12 12 12 13 14 14
Gtr. 4
0
13 14 14 12 12 12 12 13 14 14 12 12 12 12 13 14 14

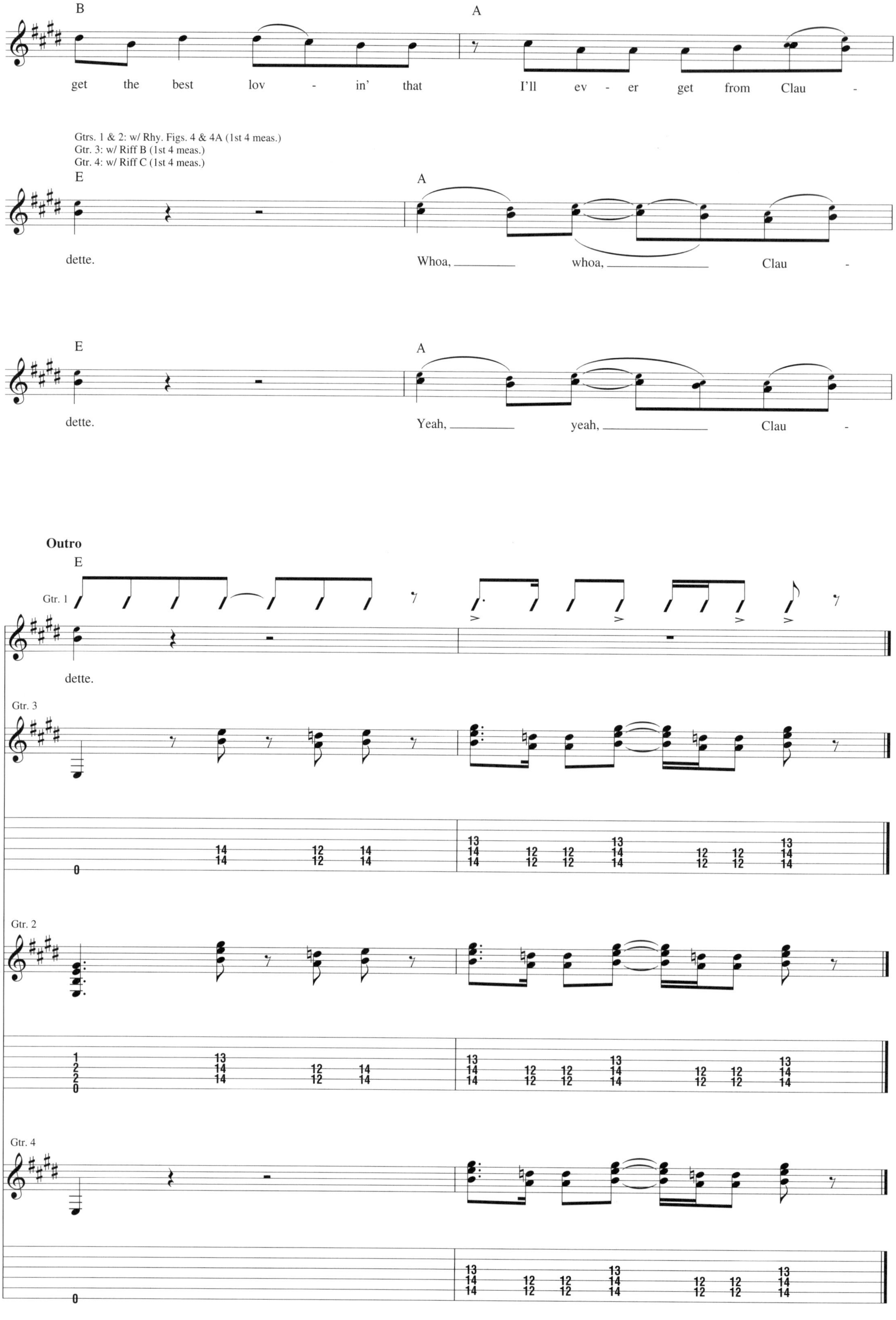

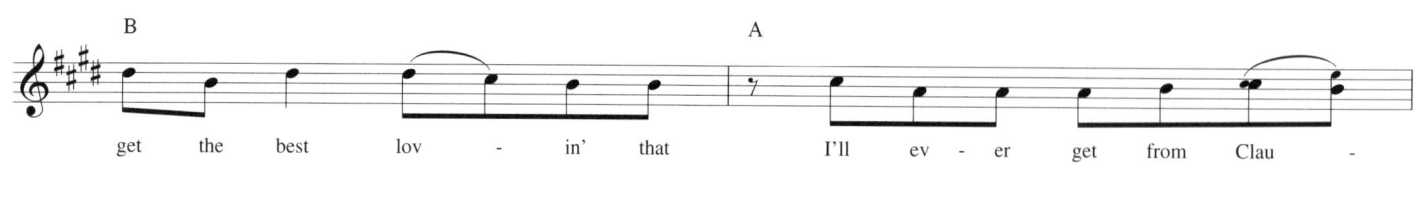

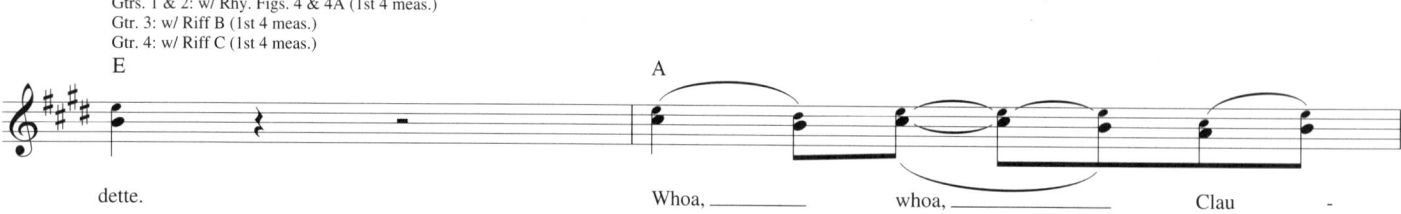

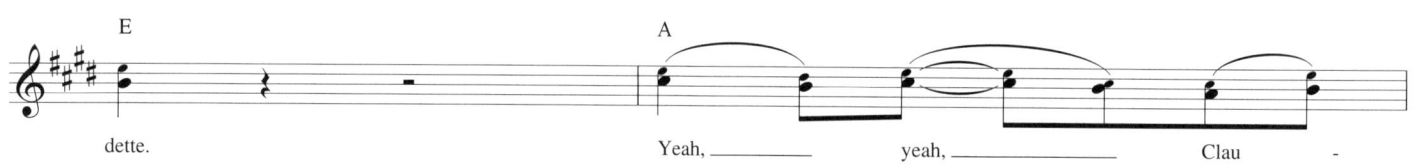

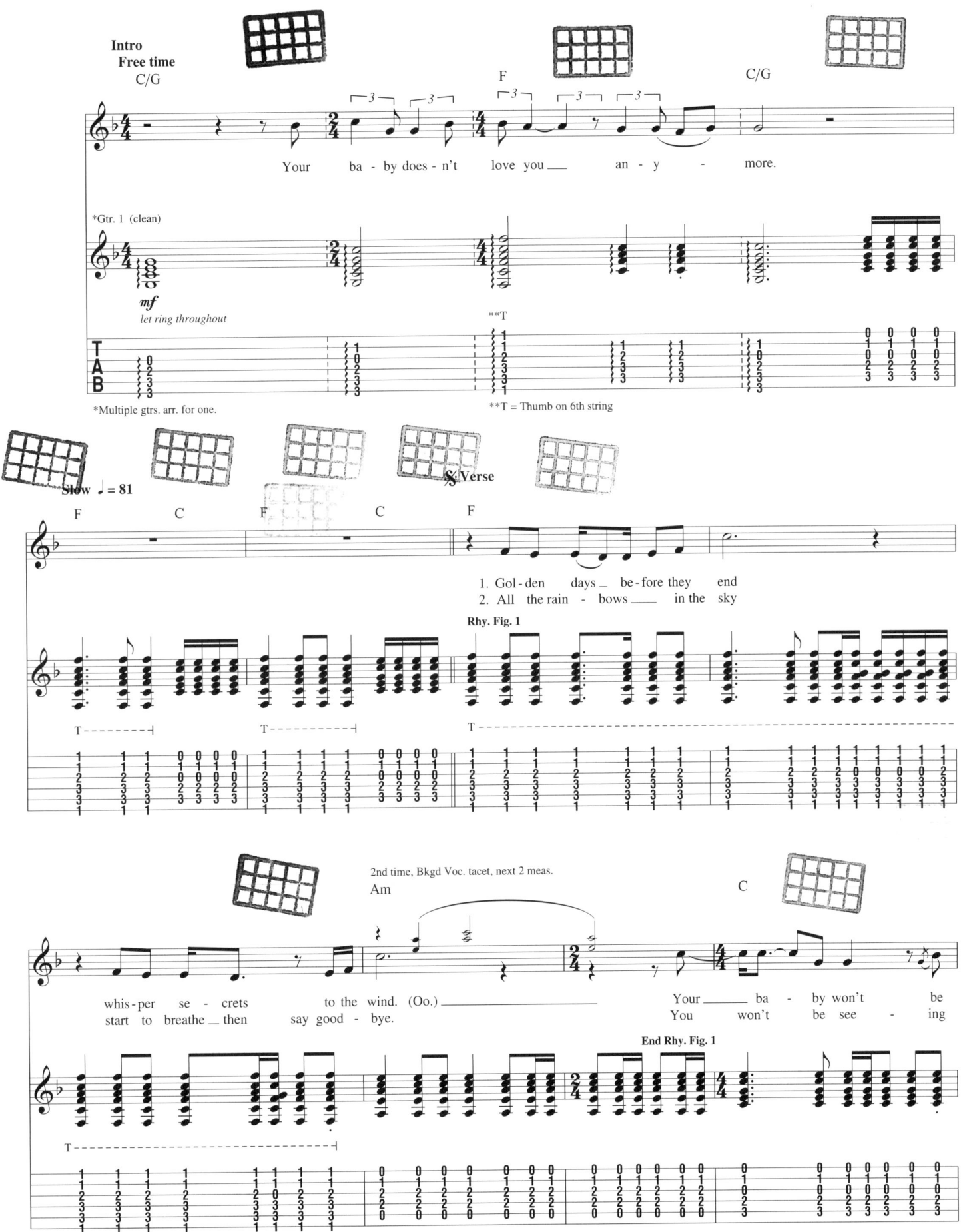

F
C
Verse
Gtr. 1: w/ Rhy. Fig. 1
F
near you ___ an - y - more.
rain - bows ___ an - y - more.
2. Ten - der nights be - fore they
4. Set - ting suns be - fore they
(Oo, ah.
Am
To Coda
fly send fall - ing stars that seem to cry. ___ Your ___
fall ech - o to you, "That's all, that's all." ___ But ___
Doo - bie wah, wah. Oo, ah. Doo - bie wah, doo bie wah.
Dm
B♭
G7
G
C
F
___ ba - by ___ does - n't want you ___ an - y - more. ___ It's o - ver.
Oo. ___ Oo.) ___
Gtr. 1

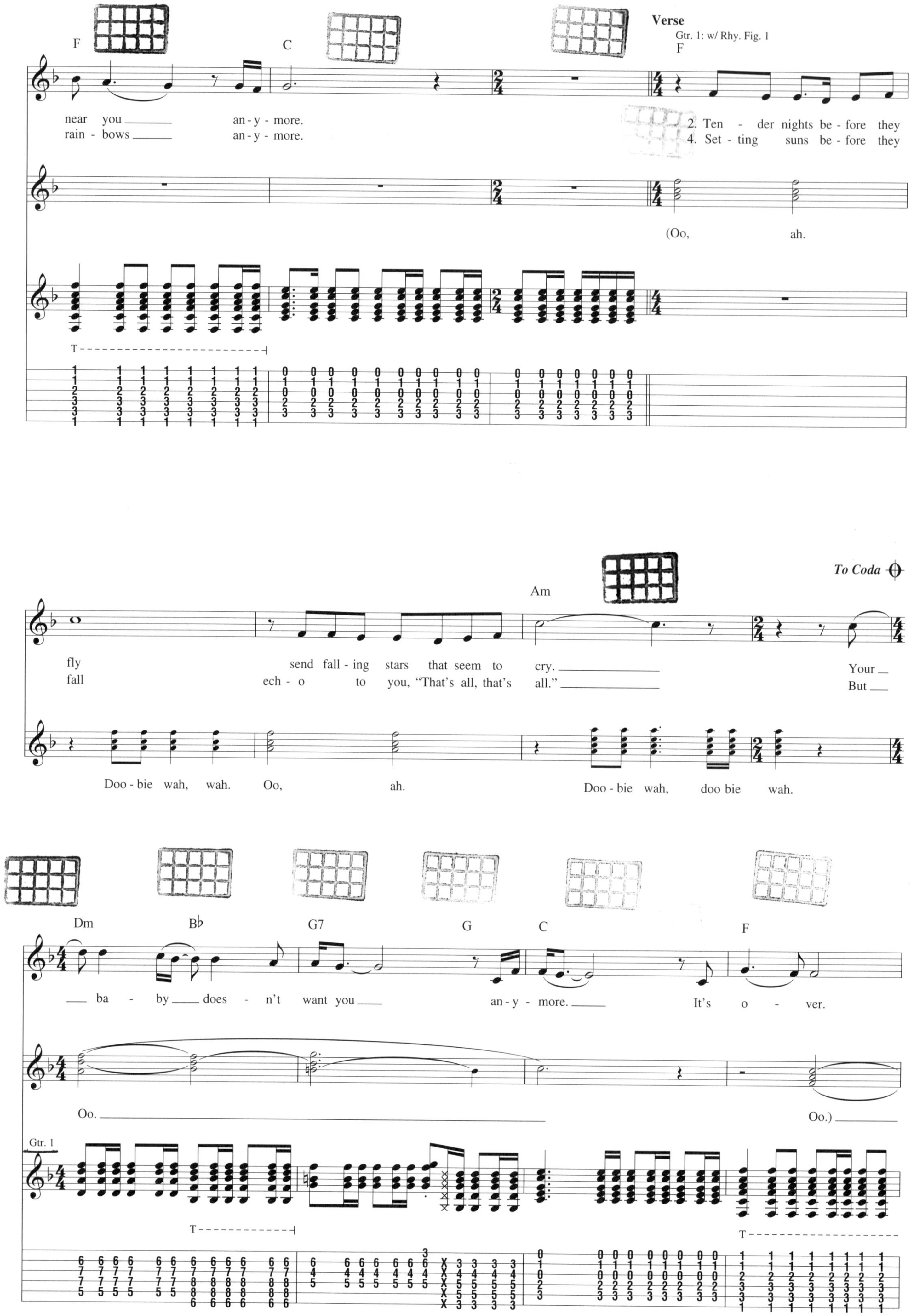

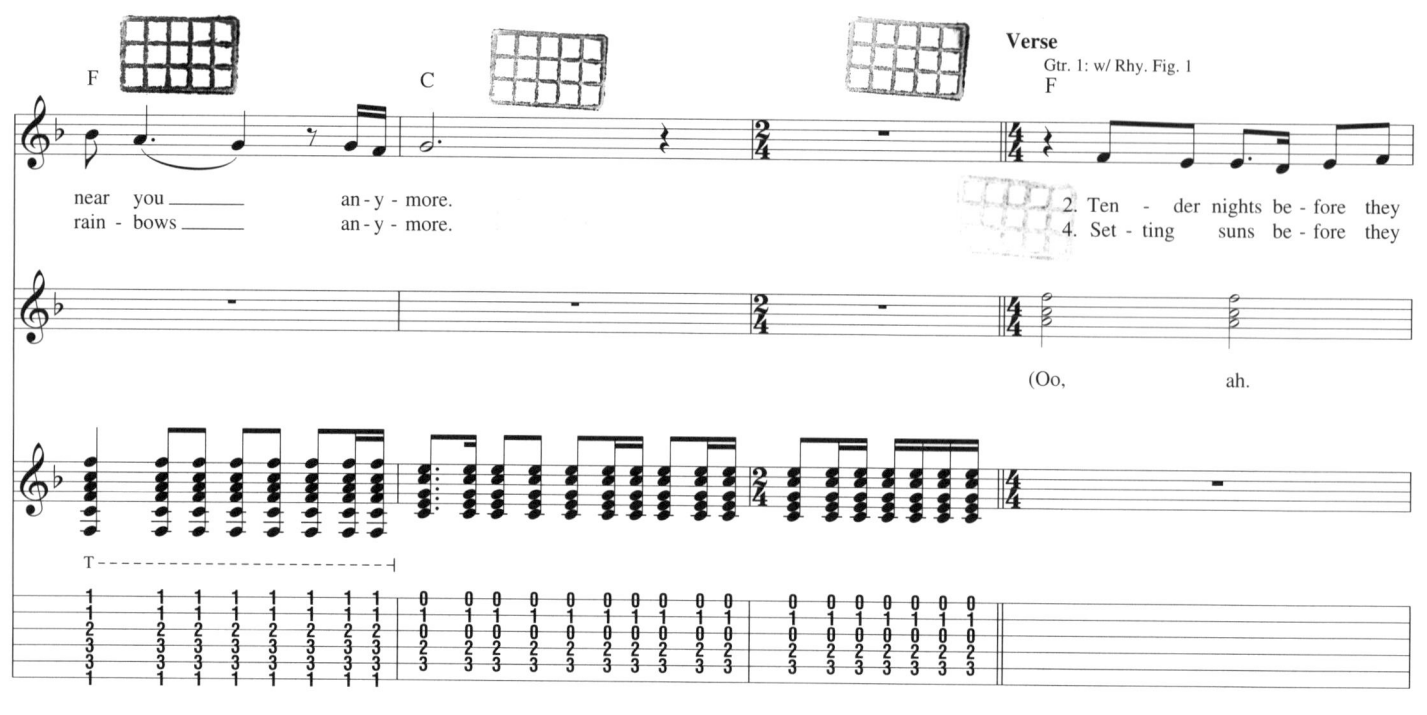

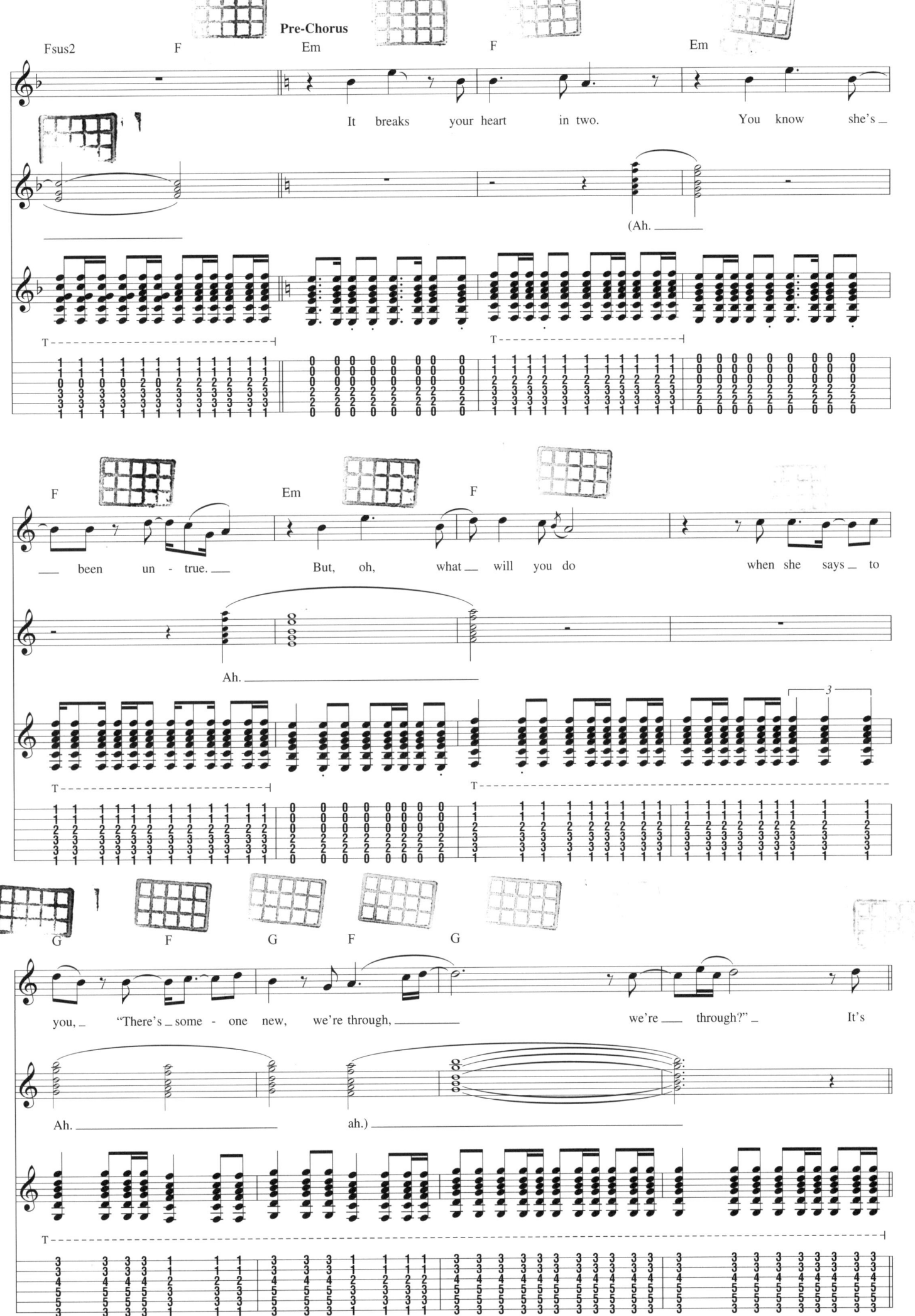

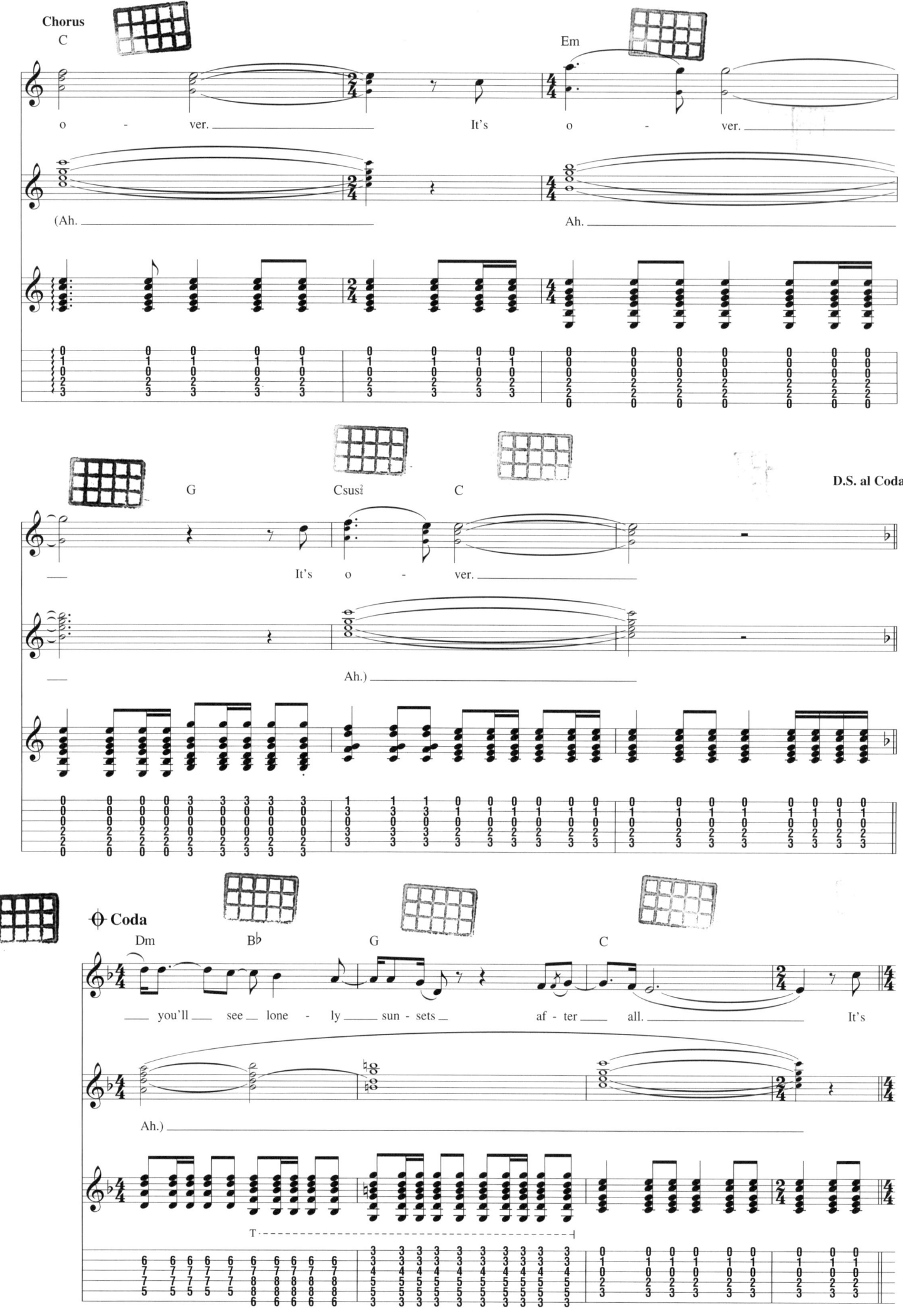

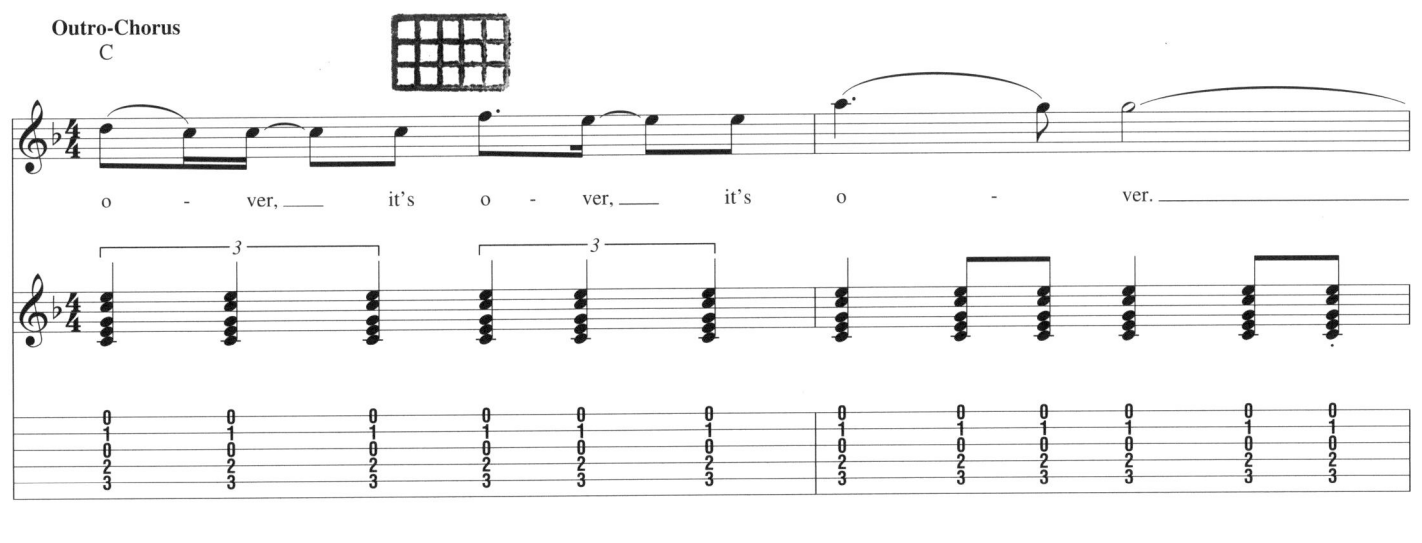
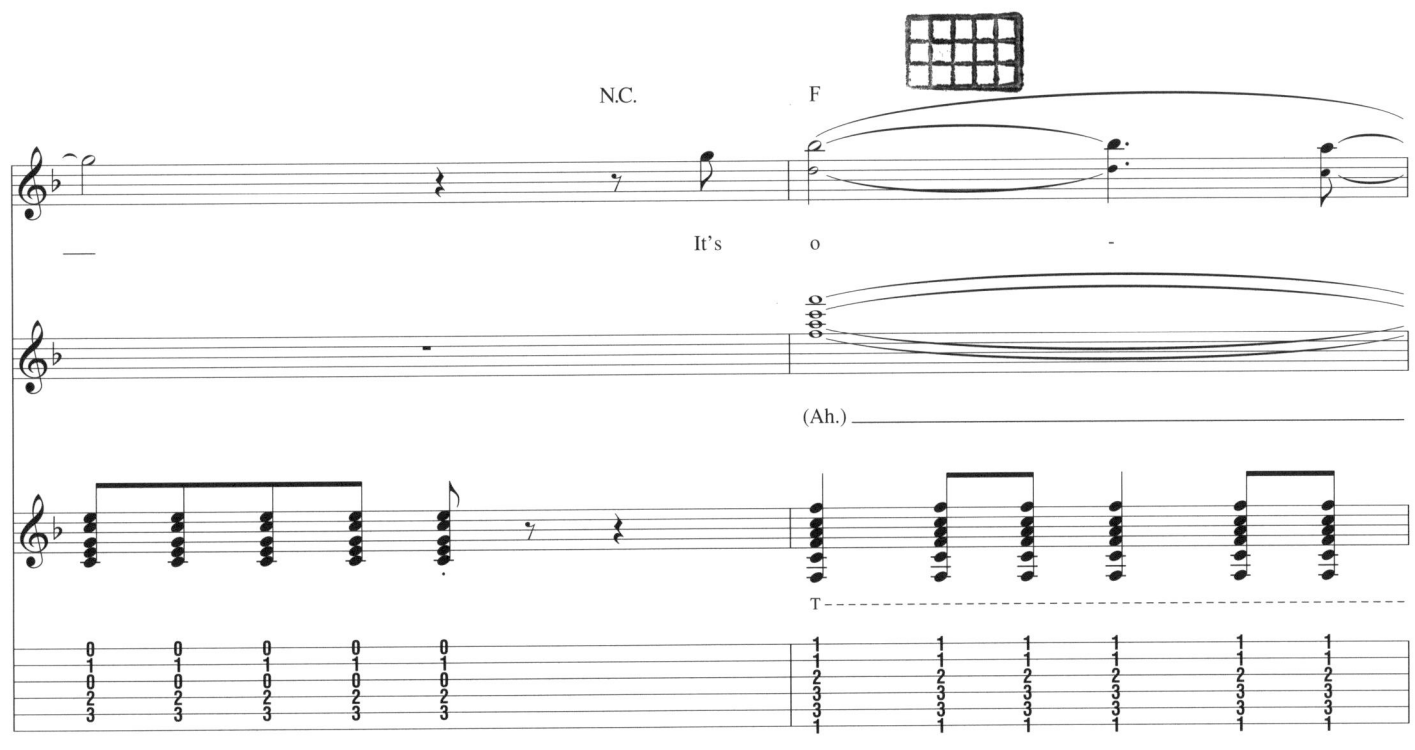
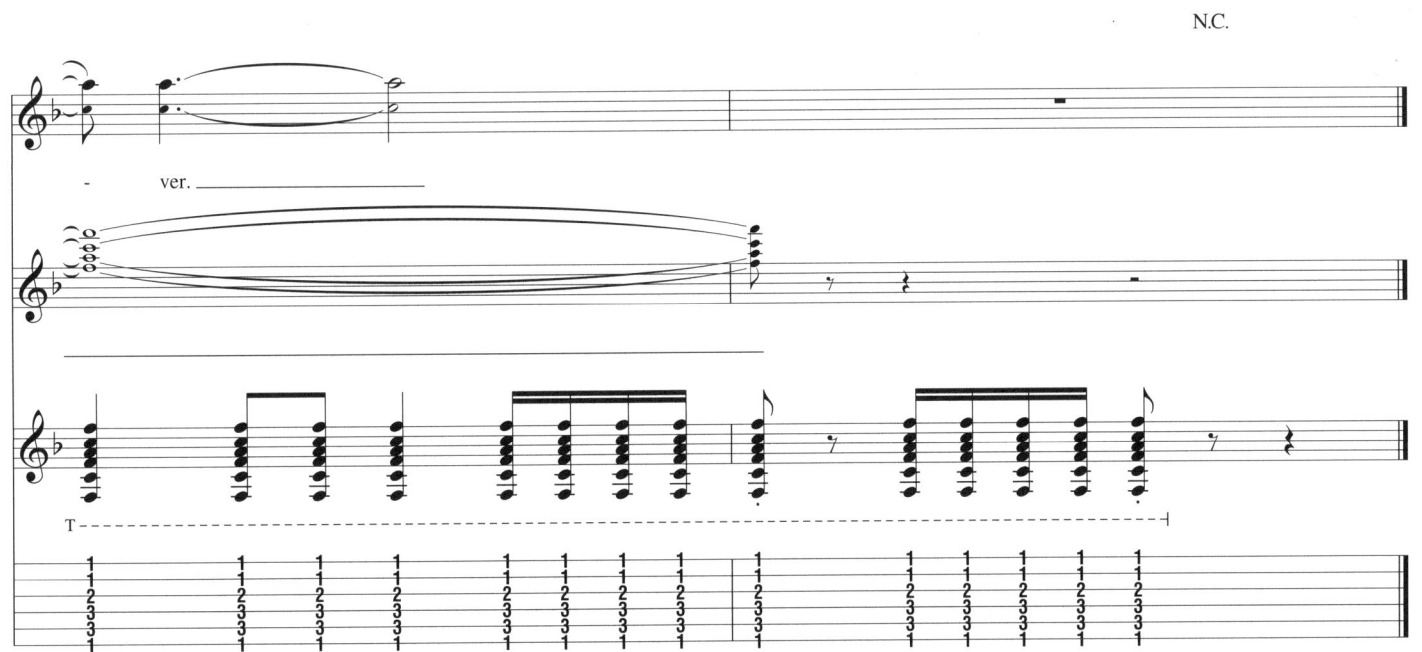

Oh, Pretty Woman

Words and Music by Roy Orbison and Bill Dees

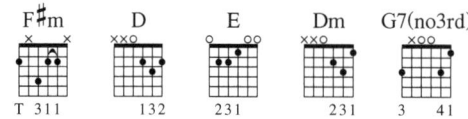

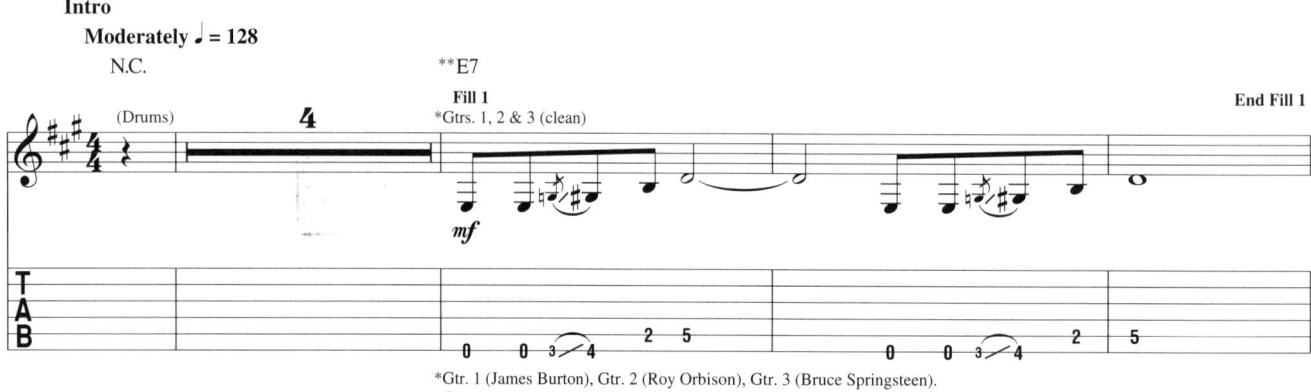

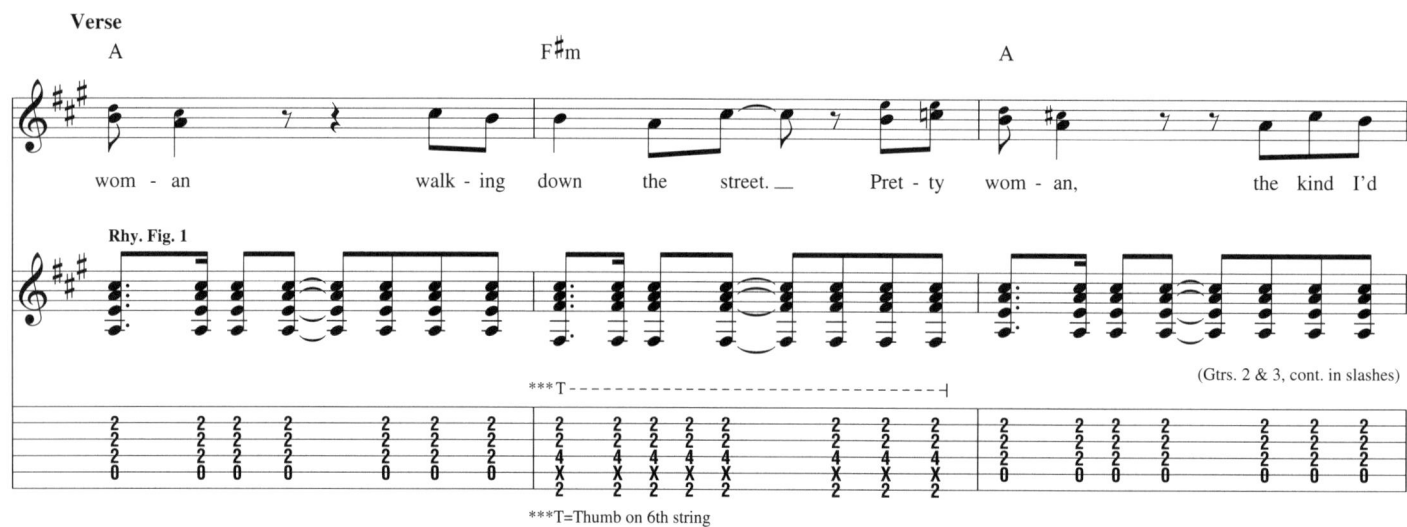

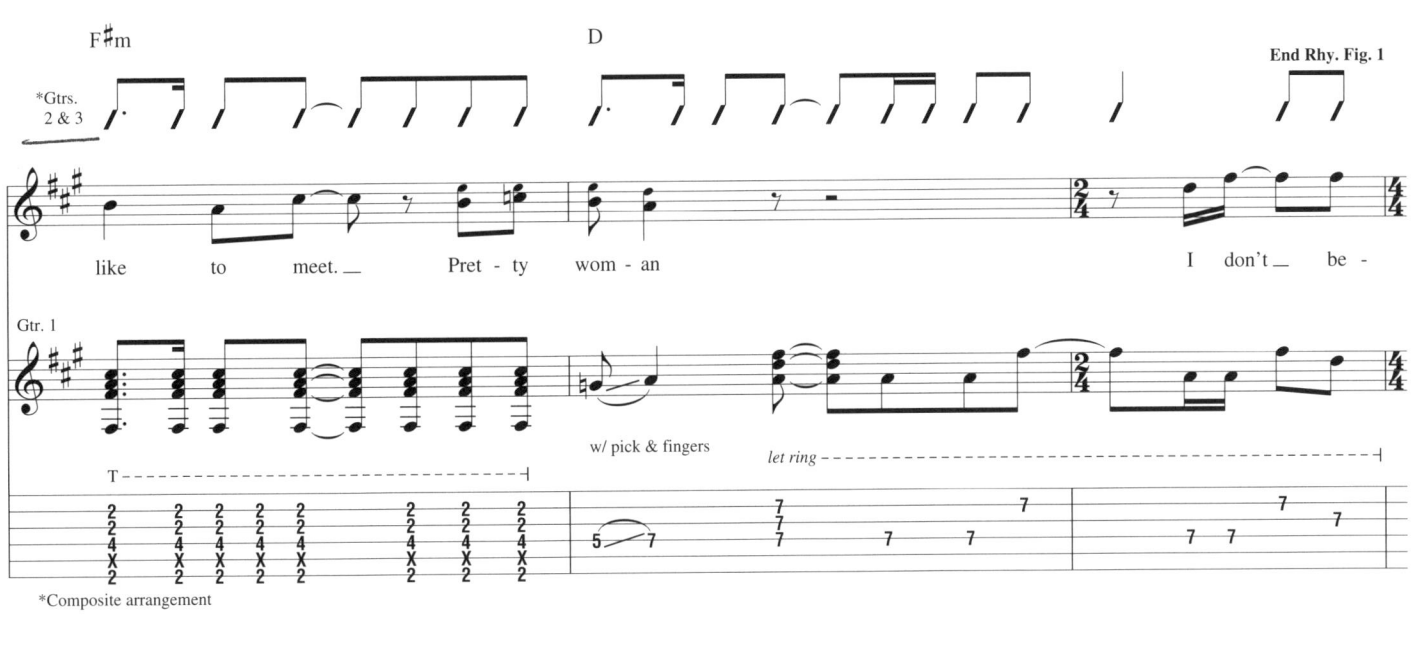

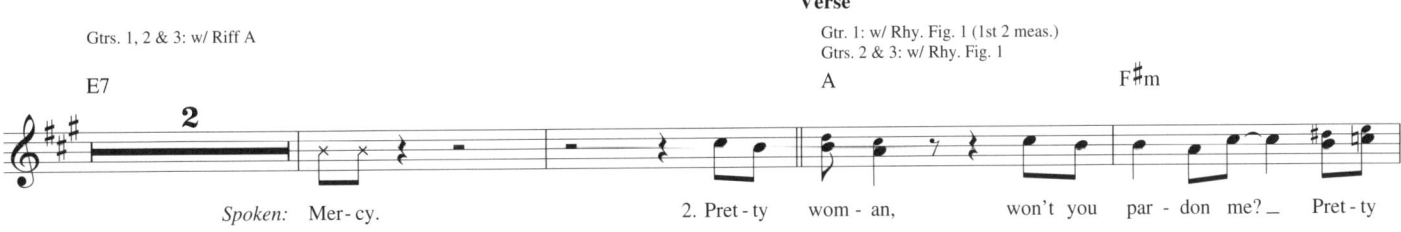
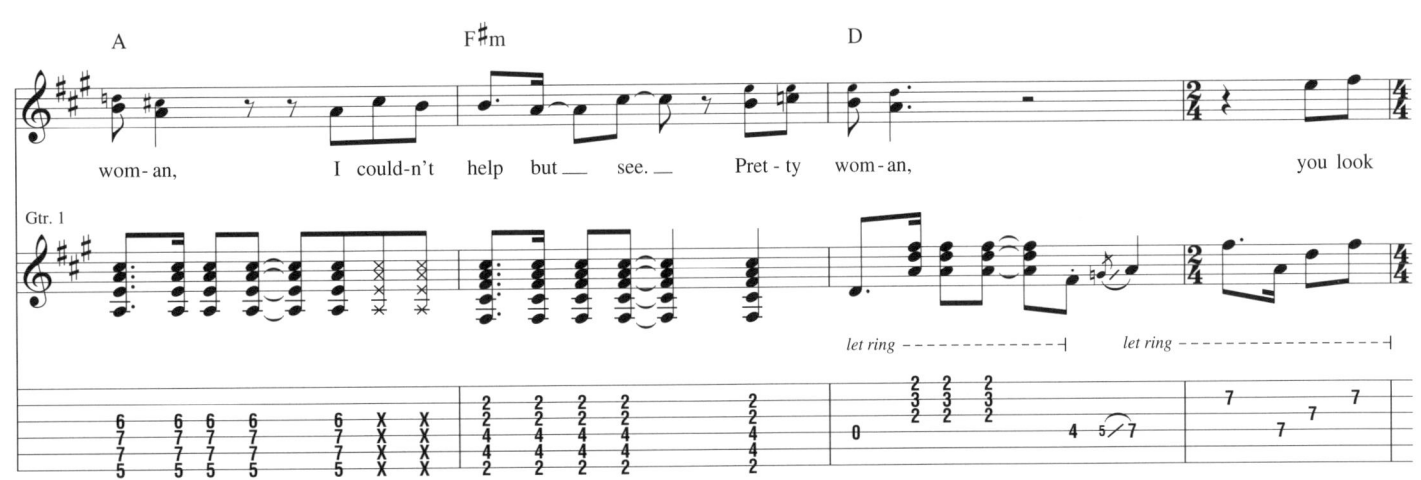

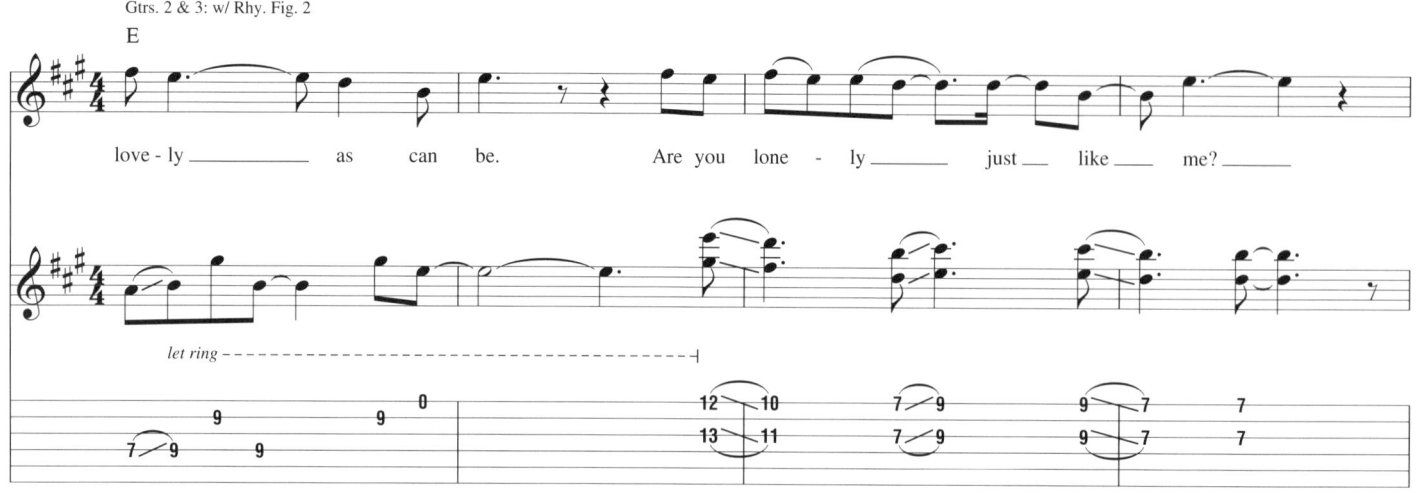

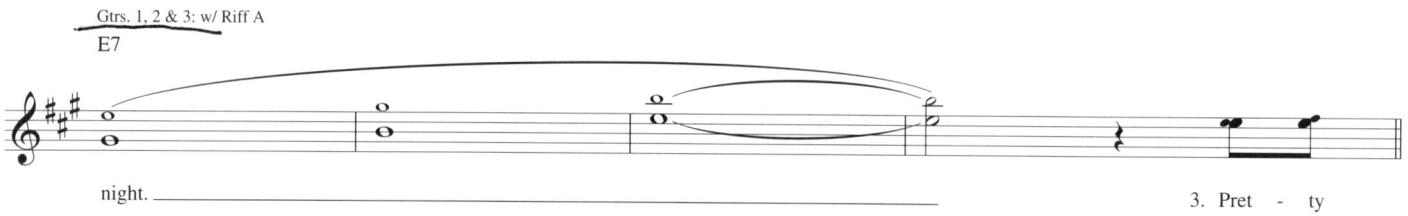

Verse

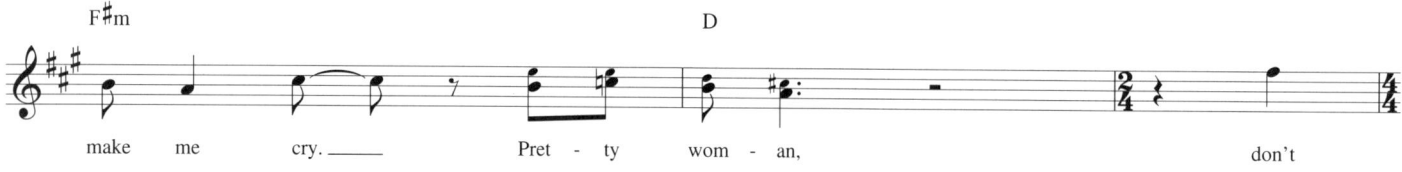

Guitar Solos

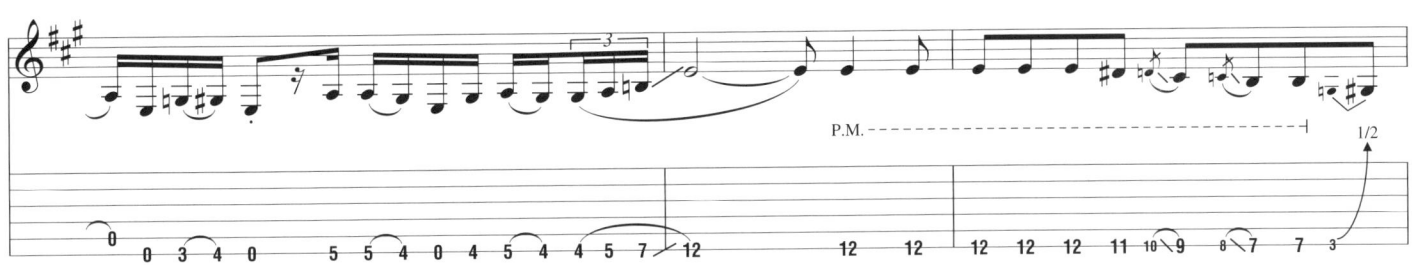

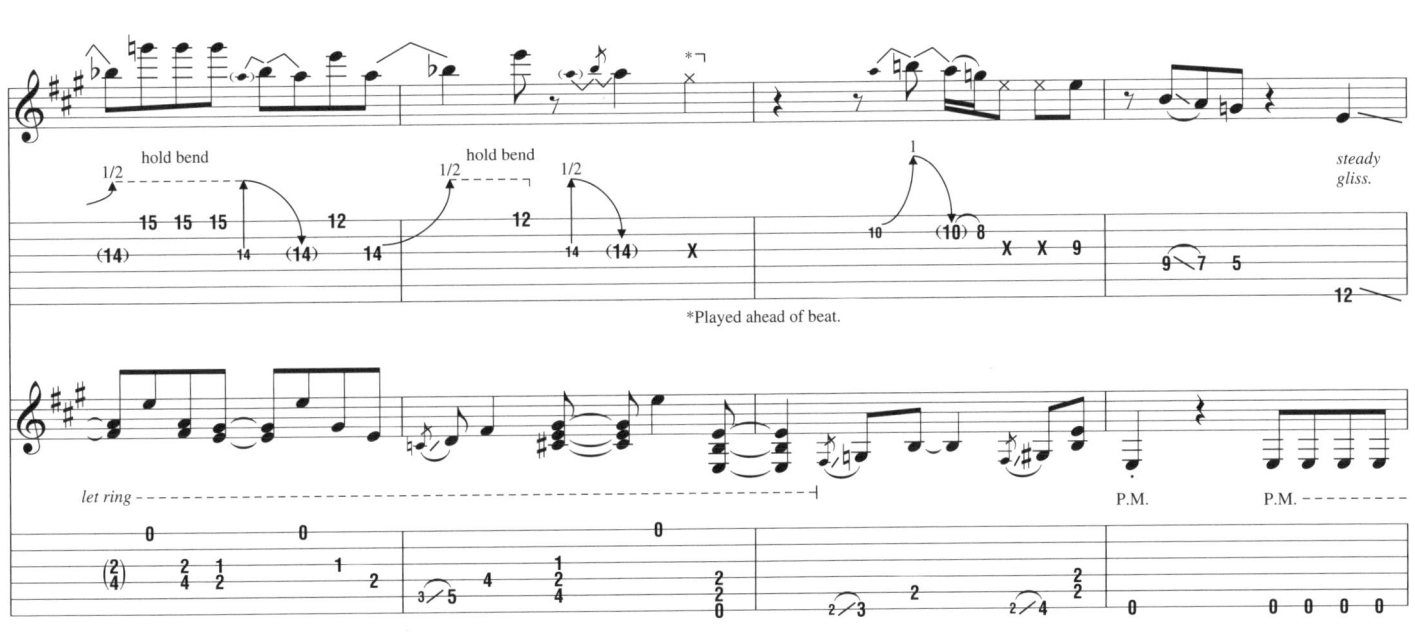

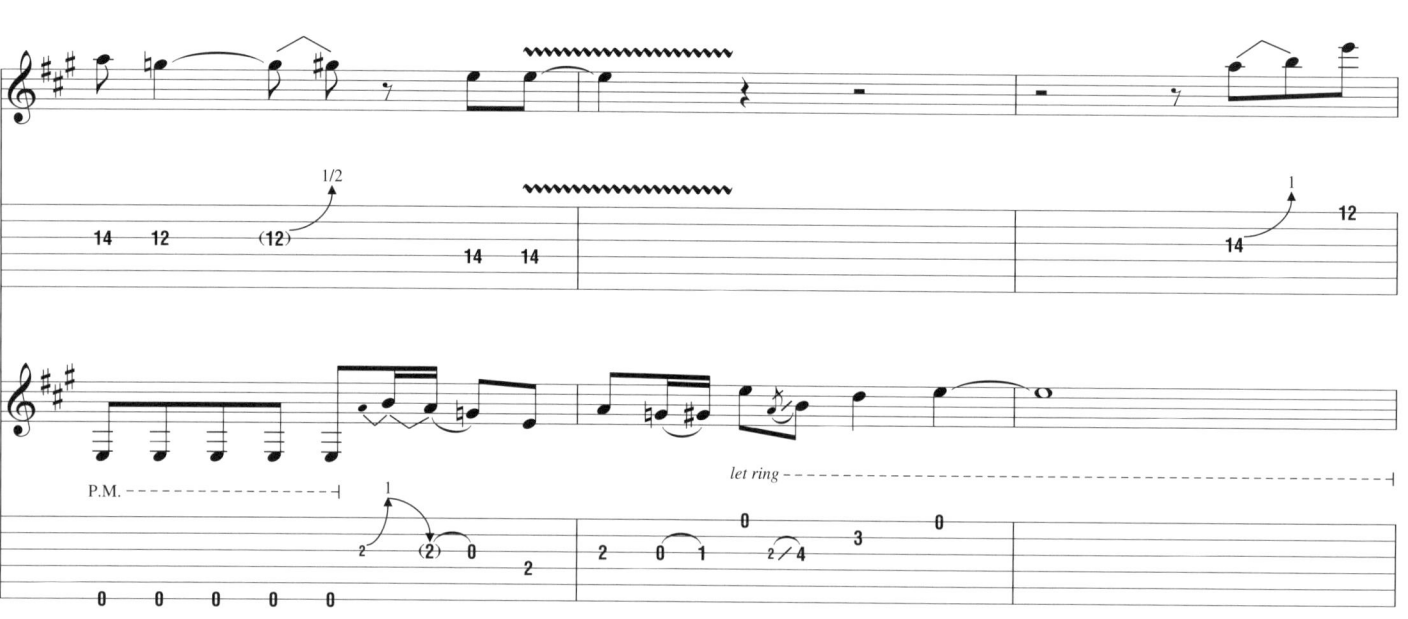
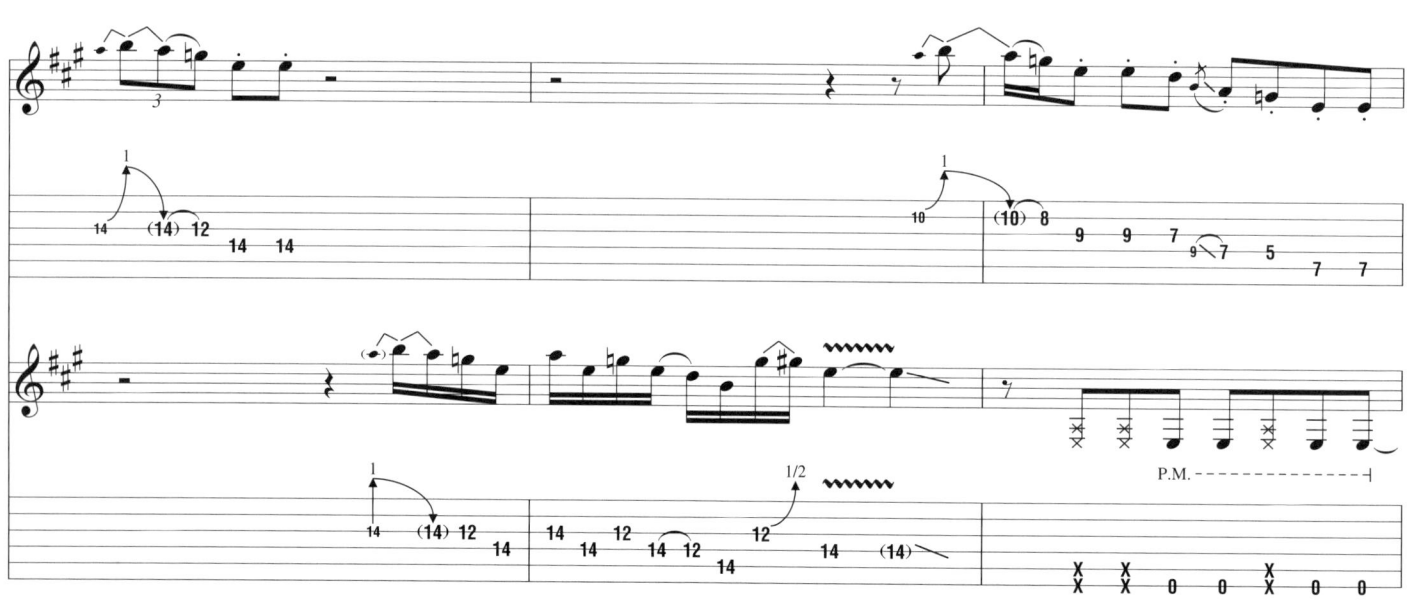

203

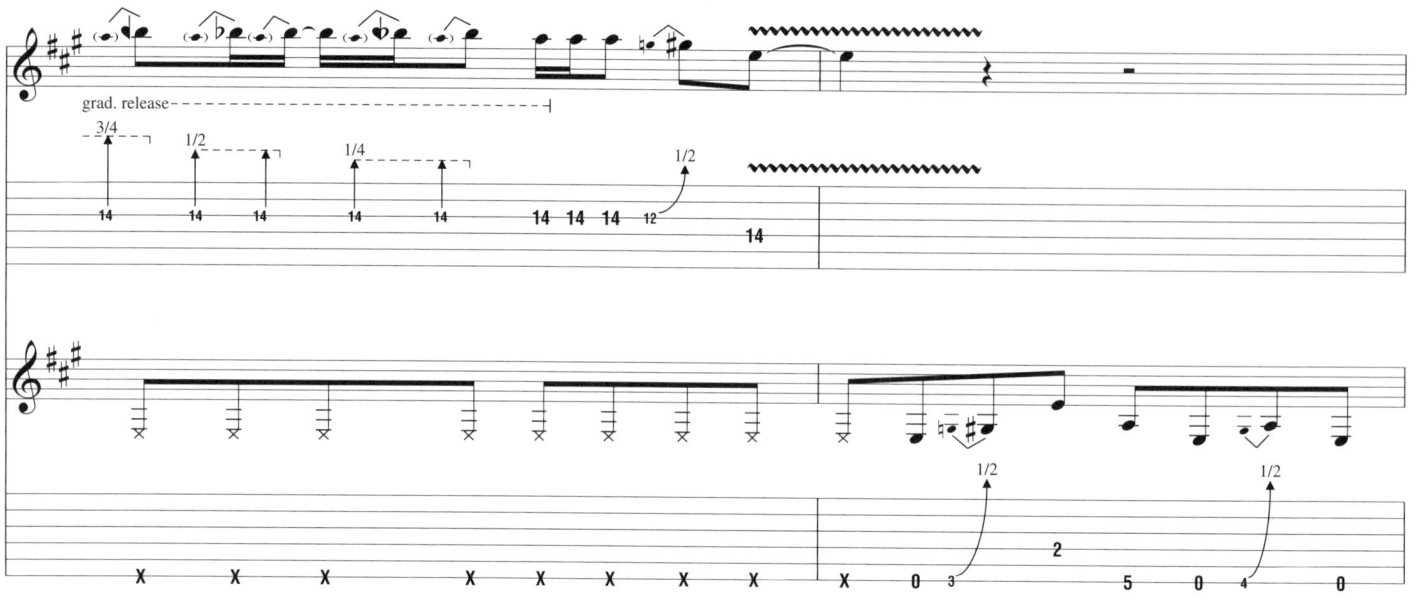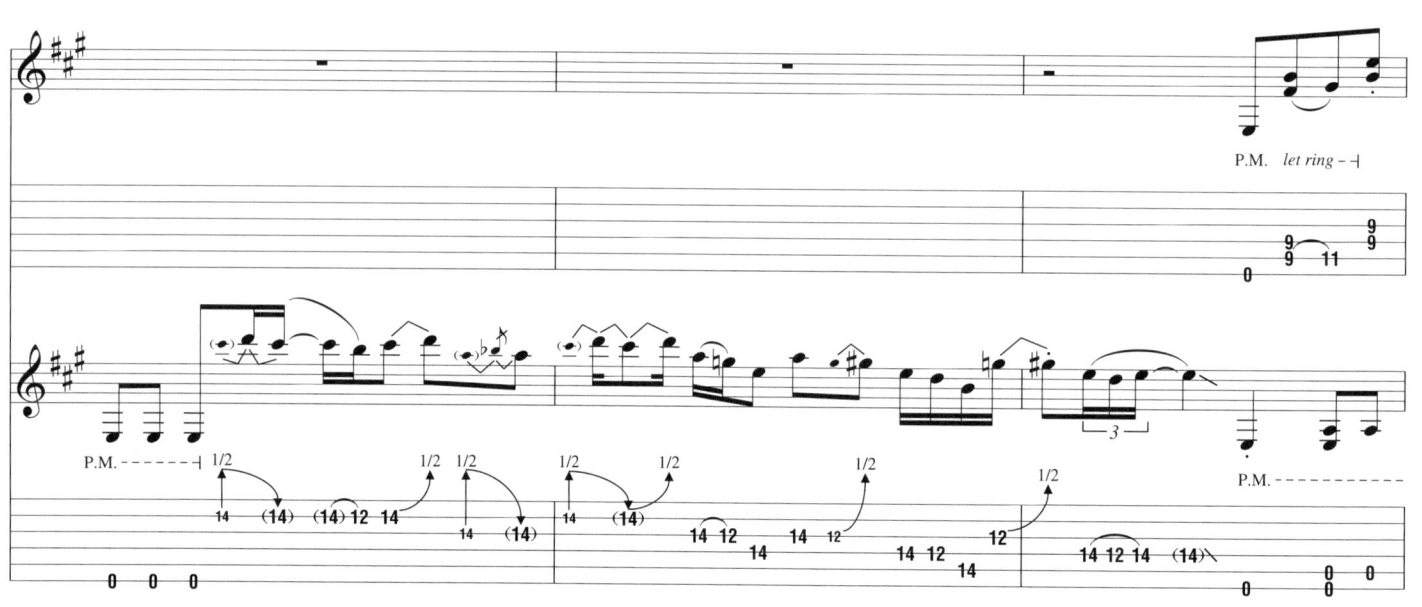

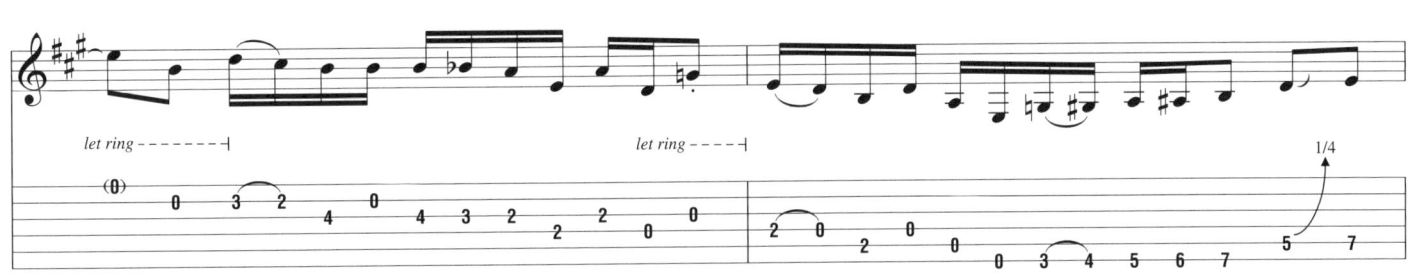

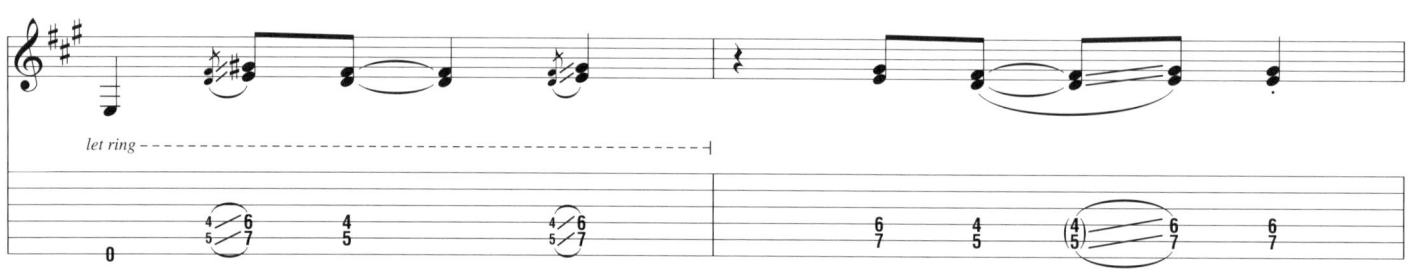

GUITAR NOTATION LEGEND

Guitar music can be notated three different ways: on a *musical staff*, in *tablature*, and in *rhythm slashes*.

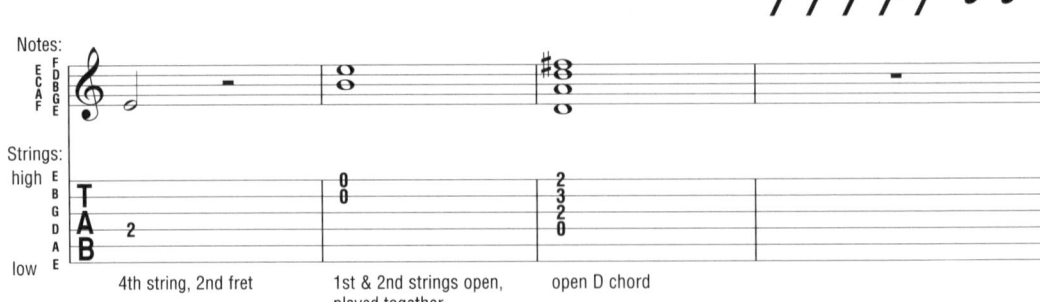

RHYTHM SLASHES are written above the staff. Strum chords in the rhythm indicated. Use the chord diagrams found at the top of the first page of the transcription for the appropriate chord voicings. Round noteheads indicate single notes.

THE MUSICAL STAFF shows pitches and rhythms and is divided by bar lines into measures. Pitches are named after the first seven letters of the alphabet.

TABLATURE graphically represents the guitar fingerboard. Each horizontal line represents a string, and each number represents a fret.

HALF-STEP BEND: Strike the note and bend up 1/2 step.

WHOLE-STEP BEND: Strike the note and bend up one step.

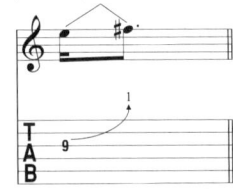

GRACE NOTE BEND: Strike the note and immediately bend up as indicated.

SLIGHT (MICROTONE) BEND: Strike the note and bend up 1/4 step.

BEND AND RELEASE: Strike the note and bend up as indicated, then release back to the original note. Only the first note is struck.

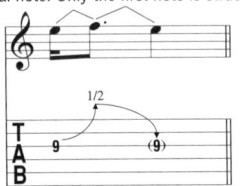

PRE-BEND: Bend the note as indicated, then strike it.

VIBRATO: The string is vibrated by rapidly bending and releasing the note with the fretting hand.

WIDE VIBRATO: The pitch is varied to a greater degree by vibrating with the fretting hand.

HAMMER-ON: Strike the first (lower) note with one finger, then sound the higher note (on the same string) with another finger by fretting it without picking.

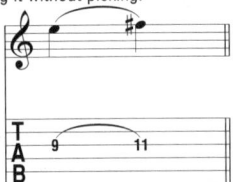

PULL-OFF: Place both fingers on the notes to be sounded. Strike the first note and without picking, pull the finger off to sound the second (lower) note.

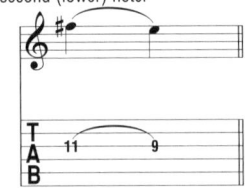

LEGATO SLIDE: Strike the first note and then slide the same fret-hand finger up or down to the second note. The second note is not struck.

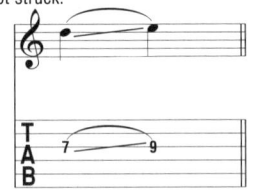

SHIFT SLIDE: Same as legato slide, except the second note is struck.

TRILL: Very rapidly alternate between the notes indicated by continuously hammering on and pulling off.

TAPPING: Hammer ("tap") the fret indicated with the pick-hand index or middle finger and pull off to the note fretted by the fret hand.

NATURAL HARMONIC: Strike the note while the fret-hand lightly touches the string directly over the fret indicated.

PINCH HARMONIC: The note is fretted normally and a harmonic is produced by adding the edge of the thumb or the tip of the index finger of the pick hand to the normal pick attack.

PICK SCRAPE: The edge of the pick is rubbed down (or up) the string, producing a scratchy sound.

MUFFLED STRINGS: A percussive sound is produced by laying the fret hand across the string(s) without depressing, and striking them with the pick hand.

PALM MUTING: The note is partially muted by the pick hand lightly touching the string(s) just before the bridge.

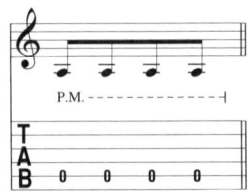

RAKE: Drag the pick across the strings indicated with a single motion.

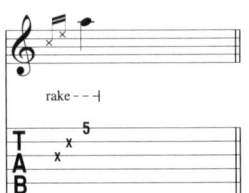

TREMOLO PICKING: The note is picked as rapidly and continuously as possible.

VIBRATO BAR DIVE AND RETURN: The pitch of the note or chord is dropped a specified number of steps (in rhythm), then returned to the original pitch.

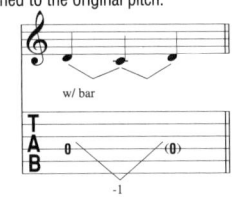

VIBRATO BAR SCOOP: Depress the bar just before striking the note, then quickly release the bar.

VIBRATO BAR DIP: Strike the note and then immediately drop a specified number of steps, then release back to the original pitch.